EU Principles on Jurisdiction and Recognition and Enforcement of Judgments in Civil and Commercial Matters

EU Principles on Jurisdiction and Recognition and Enforcement of Judgments in Civil and Commercial Matters

according to the case law of the
European Court of Justice

Jannet A. Pontier
Edwige Burg

T·M·C·Asser press
The Hague

Published by T.M.C.ASSER PRESS
P.O.Box 16163, 2500 BD The Hague, The Netherlands
www.asserpress.nl

T.M.C.ASSER PRESS English language books are distributed exclusively by:

Cambridge University Press, The Edinburgh Building, Shaftesbury Road,
Cambridge CB2 2RU, UK,
or
for customers in the USA, Canada and Mexico:
Cambridge University Press, 40 West 20th Street, New York, NY 10011-4211, USA

www.cambridge.org

ISBN 90-6704-173-4

PREFACE

The present book offers the reader insight into how the Court of Justice of the European Communities justifies its interpretations of the European legal rules on international jurisdiction and the recognition and enforcement of judgments in civil and commercial matters. Our examination of the more than one hundred decisions which the Court has delivered under the 1968 Brussels Convention shows that the Court uses the principles, which in its opinion underlie the explicit rules, as reasons to justify its decisions. These principles are described in the book and it is shown how they relate to each other.

The system of principles that has been identified in this study forms an important part of the Brussels Convention's legacy for the new Regulation No. 44/2001, which replaced the Convention on March 1, 2002. It constitutes a catalogue of arguments that will be employed by the Court to justify its interpretation of the provisions of the new regulation. As such, this book will be of great value to practitioners in international law as well as to academics and students alike.

JANNET A. PONTIER (PH.D.)
Professor of Law
Department of Private International Law
Senior Research Associate at the
Amsterdam Institute for Private Law
University of Amsterdam

EDWIGE BURG (PH.D.)
Lecturer and researcher
Department of Private International Law
Research Associate at the
Amsterdam Institute for Private Law
University of Amsterdam

Amsterdam, The Netherlands, January 2004

TABLE OF CONTENTS

INTRODUCTION

On 1 March 2002, the EC Regulation on jurisdiction and the recognition and enforcement of judgments in civil and commercial matters (Council Regulation No. 44/2001) entered into force. This Regulation is meant to promote judicial co-operation in civil matters among EC Member States as required by Article 65 in conjunction with Article 61(c) of the EC Treaty.[1] It essentially replaced the 1968 Brussels Convention on Jurisdiction and the Enforcement of Judgments in Civil and Commercial Matters.[2]

The 1968 Brussels Convention regulated the jurisdiction and the recognition and enforcement of judgments in civil and commercial matters among EC Member States for more than thirty years.[3] Over time, some of the Convention's provisions were amended when new EC Member States acceded to the Convention.[4] In 1988, a parallel convention to this Brussels Convention, the Lugano Convention, was concluded between the EC Member States and the EFTA States, thereby extending the territorial sphere of these rules on jurisdiction and the recognition and enforcement of judgments. Both treaties, and the work that was undertaken in the 1990s by the EC and the EFTA Member States for their revision, form the basis of Regulation No. 44/2001. As a result, the Regulation closely corresponds to the Brussels Convention: most provisions are similar, and the basic structure, the underlying principles and the objectives are the same.[5]

As is explicitly stated in the preliminary considerations of Regulation No. 44/2001, continuity between the Brussels Convention and the Regulation should be ensured.[6] This also applies to the interpretation of the Convention's provisions, which has been in the hands of the Court of Justice of the European

[1] OJ L 12/1, 16.1.2001.

[2] OJ L 299, 31.12.1972, p. 32. Denmark is the only EC Member State that has not participated in the adoption of Regulation No. 44/2001. The Brussels Convention remains in force in relations between Denmark and the Member States that are bound by this Regulation.

[3] In concluding the Brussels Convention, the EC Member States acted under Article 293, fourth indent (formerly: 220(4)), of the EC Treaty. The 1968 Convention entered into force on 1 February 1973, originally, between Belgium, Federal Republic of Germany, France, Italy, Luxembourg and the Netherlands.

[4] OJ L 304, 30.10.1978, p. 1; OJ L 388, 31.12.1982, p. 1; OJ L 285, 3.10.1989, p. 1; OJ C 15, 15.1.1997, p. 1; for the consolidated text of the Brussels Convention, see OJ C 27, 26.1.1998, p. 1.

[5] Compare Initial Proposal 14.7.1999, CE COM(1999)0348, OJ C 376 28.12.1999.

[6] See preliminary considerations Nos. 5 and 19. This wish for continuity also explains why the 1971 Protocol will remain applicable, also to cases already pending when the Regulation entered into force (OJ L 204, 2.8.1975, p. 28; OJ L 304, 30.10.1978, p. 1; OJ L 388, 31.12.1982, p. 1; OJ L 285, 3.10.1989, p. 1; OJ C 15, 15.1.1997, p. 1; for the consolidated text of the 1971 Protocol, see OJ

Communities. Hence, although there are certain differences between Regulation No. 44/2001 and the Brussels Convention, the body of case law of the EC Court of Justice under this Convention will, for a long period of time, remain of great importance for understanding the Regulation.[7]

The transition from the Brussels Convention to the EC Regulation appears to be an opportune moment to reflect on what the Court's legacy amounts to for this new Regulation. This study is based on an analysis of all of the 118 decisions that the Court has up to now taken under the Brussels Convention.[8] We have tried to uncover what, in our view, is an important aspect of this legacy. Our focus has not been on the ultimate outcomes of the Court's decisions, but rather on the argumentation on which they are based. An examination of the Court's case law from this perspective clearly shows that the Court uses what we will refer to as 'principle-based reasoning': in almost all of its decisions, the Court has used the principles underlying the Convention's provisions to justify its interpretations. A considerable part of the Court's legacy is to be found at this deeper level of the system of principles that apparently guides the Court's interpretations.

This study attempts to piece together the system of principles used by the Court. It contains a description of the main principles that underlie the Convention's rules on jurisdiction and the recognition and enforcement of judgments, as well as the more concrete principles and requirements that flow therefrom. In addition, it attempts to show, as far as possible, how the various principles are weighed in relation to each other when they conflict. An understanding of this system of principles not only sheds some light on how the Court reached its decisions in the past, but it also enables us to see the confines within which the Court's argumentation is likely to take place in future cases that will arise under the Regulation.

Chapter 1 of this study contains a theoretical description of the technique of reasoning used by the Court, the technique of 'principle-based reasoning' also referred to as 'reasoning according to the model of principles'. This interpretative method implies that a legal provision is interpreted not only in light of the rationale or principle immediately underlying the provision itself, but also in light of the principles underlying the legal system as a whole. Ideally, the explicit legal provisions can be seen to have their foundation in a coherent system of principles, which is used to resolve questions regarding the interpretation of these provisions.

C 27, 26.1.1998, p. 28; and compare 56/84 *Gallera v Maître* 4,5; C-220/95 *Boogaard v Laumen* 16; C-295/95 *Farrell v Long* 11; C-159/97 *Castelletti v Trumpy* 14; C-38/98 *Maxicar v Renault II* 23; C-111/01 *Gantner v Basch* 34,38; C-116/02 *Gasser v MISAT* 21-26).

[7] See Initial Proposal, note 5.

[8] Our investigations of the Court's case law were closed on January 1st, 2004.

Chapter 2 presents a bird's-eye view of the system of principles underlying the Convention as a whole. It identifies the four main principles underlying the Convention: the principle of free movement of judgments, the principle of the protection of the defence, the principle of legal certainty and the principle that disputes are to be decided by an appropriate court. These four principles can in turn be seen as contributing to one overarching principle: the principle of strengthening the legal protection of persons established within the Community.

In chapters 3 to 6, we fill in, in more detail, the system of principles that is used by the Court. In each of these chapters, one of the four main principles will be discussed. The more concrete sub-principles that flow therefrom are described, as well as the requirements that, in their turn, follow from these sub-principles. As will appear, in many cases the various principles and sub-principles conflict, pulling in opposite directions. Hence, throughout these chapters, attention will be devoted to the way in which the various principles and sub-principles are weighed in relation to each other. As is evident from the provisions of the Convention, its designers have already made choices as to how the different principles should be weighed in relation to each other. However, the Court is also confronted with the fact that in many cases presented before it, the principles underlying the Convention present themselves within a constellation of conflict. Hence, the Court has to continue this process of weighing and balancing the Convention's principles.

In the final conclusions we evaluate our findings as regards the Court's case law under the Brussels Convention, in particular with regard to how it has used the method of principle-based reasoning. We also consider the relevance of the outcome of this study for the new Regulation. The main point is that the system of principles underlying the Brussels Convention is (almost) identical to the system of principles underlying Regulation No. 44/2001, and it is this system of principles that the Court will use to argue for or against particular interpretations of this Regulation.

THE SYSTEM OF REFERENCE USED

- We refer to the Court's case law by stating the number of the case, the names of the parties to the case and the point of consideration. In the event that the Court refers to earlier cases, we will mention these cases between brackets directly after the consideration concerned. For example: C-7/98 *Krombach v Bamberski* 21 (re 145/86 *Hoffmann v Krieg* 2; C-78/95 *Hendrikman v Magenta* 23), 31-33. In appendix 3 the reader will find a list of cases, including references to their exact location in the European Court Reports.

- Highlighted throughout the text, we refer to the provisions of Regulation No. 44/2001 that correspond to the provisions of the Brussels Convention that are mentioned in the text. In appendix 2 the reader will find the text of most of the provisions of the Brussels Convention with, alongside, the text of the corresponding provisions of Regulation No. 44/2001.

- Notice also, that in appendix 1, the reader will find a scheme of the principles and sub-principles that are discussed in this study.

Chapter 1
THE METHOD OF INTERPRETATION USED BY THE COURT OF JUSTICE: THE MODEL OF PRINCIPLES

INTRODUCTION

An investigation of the Court's decisions under the Brussels Convention clearly shows that one method of legal interpretation is predominant in the Court's reasoning. As the Court has stated in many of its decisions, the Convention must be interpreted 'having regard to its principles and objectives'.[1] This technique of interpretation used by the Court has been described as 'a teleological style of interpretation'.[2] Though this characterisation is not incorrect in itself, the notion of 'teleological interpretation' is, in our view, too indeterminate for the purpose of analysing the technique of reasoning used by the Court. In this study we will refer to the Court's method of interpretation as *reasoning according to the model of principles* or *principle-based reasoning*. As will appear from the description of the model of principles below, this model is a more specific species of the general model of teleological interpretation. This chapter contains a brief presentation of the theory of the model of principles, thus providing the framework in terms of which the Court's case law will be analysed in more detail in the next chapters.

1. REASONING ACCORDING TO THE MODEL OF PRINCIPLES

When explaining the technique of reasoning implied by the model of principles, it is useful to first provide a brief exposition of the method of legal interpretation that can be seen as the small-scale predecessor of the model of principles. We will refer to this small-scale predecessor as the *model of purposive interpretation*. This model advocates that the meaning to be attributed to a legal rule must be found by reading the rule in the light of its underlying purpose. This purpose represents 'the good the rule aims to promote or the evil it seeks to avert'.[3] The pure version of the purpose theory holds that the rationale of a rule does and should always determine what it means, even if this implies deviating from the plain

[1] See for example 12/76 *Tessili v Dunlop* 9.

[2] See for example C.M.V. Clarkson, J. Hill, *Jaffey on the Conflict of Laws*, Butterworths, London, 1997, p. 61.

[3] Lon L. Fuller, *Positivism and the Fidelity to Law – A Reply to Professor Hart*, Harvard Law Review, Vol. 71, 1958, p. 665.

meaning of the words of the rule.[4] Lon Fuller, a major proponent of this model of purposes, pointed out that true fidelity to law demands that statutory provisions should be read in light of their underlying purposes, even if one would thereby at times deviate from the plain meaning of a statute. If a court, in implementing the purpose of the rule, needs to deviate from its plain meaning, the court is not supplanting the will of the legislator; instead, it is making that will fully effective.[5]

The model of principles has in common with the model of purposes the basic idea that legal rules should be read in light of their underlying rationale. Purposive interpretation is more limited, however, in that it adopts a *narrow and shallow* view of the law. In determining what the law has to say about a case, a judge is supposed to identify the most immediately relevant legal rule and to read it in light of the purpose or objective immediately underlying it. The model of principles, on the other hand, tells a judge to look at the law on a much grander scale. He is supposed to take a *broad and deep* look at the rules of the whole legal system: he has to have in mind at all times the principles underlying the body of legal rules as a whole and he should interpret legal provisions in the light of these principles. The American legal theorist Ronald Dworkin is the most well known proponent of this large-scale model of principles.[6]

Within the model of principles, two conceptions of law can be distinguished: the *positive law* and the *real law*. The positive law represents the law that is generally accepted within the legal community as being authoritative. Within a national context, the positive law consists of statutory provisions and court decisions. The positive law is the law as it presents itself at a first, rather superficial glance: as a multitude of largely disconnected legal provisions and judicial decisions whose words will present themselves in their plain meaning. Within the model of principles, this positive law is only the starting point in the process of uncovering the real law.

In order to uncover the real law, several operations need to be performed. First of all, the system of principles that underlies the legal provisions and court decisions needs to be identified. When doing so, one has to take a deep and broad look at the positive law as a whole. 'Deep' refers to the fact that one should not stop at the principles immediately underlying the concrete rules. Instead, these immediate principles should in turn be seen as expressions of more general prin-

---

[4] For a debate between proponents of the theory of plain meaning and of the theory of purposive interpretation, see H.L.A. Hart, *Positivism and the Separation of Law and Morals*, Harvard Law Review, Vol. 71, 1958, pp. 583-629, and Lon L. Fuller, *Positivism and the Fidelity to Law – A Reply to Professor Hart*, Harvard Law Review, Vol. 71, 1958, pp. 630-672.

[5] See Lon L. Fuller, *The Case of the Speluncean Explorers*, Harvard Law Review, Vol. 62, 1948, pp. 625-626.

[6] See Ronald Dworkin, *Taking Rights Seriously*, Harvard University Press, Cambridge, Massachusetts, 1986 and Ronald Dworkin, *Law's Empire*, Harvard University Press, Cambridge, Massachusetts, 1986. Dworkin actually did not refer to his model as 'the model of principles' but as 'law as integrity'.

ciples. 'Broad' refers to the fact that one should consider all of the rules and decisions contained in the positive law. The view should not be limited to one or a limited set of provisions and their underlying principles, or even to an area of the legal system. The object is to transform all of the positive law of the legal system, as far as possible, into one coherent whole, in the sense that the legal provisions and court decisions, and the principles immediately underlying them, are ultimately justifiable under one or a relatively small number of general principles. As long as the system of principles fits most of the positive law, one can maintain that one has found the 'principled system' presupposed by the positive law.

Next, having identified the principles underlying the law, the positive law should be read in the light thereof. The main idea guiding this process is that the principles that are part of a legal system should be applied in a consistent manner throughout the legal order as a whole, so that cases that are alike from the perspective of the law's principles, are treated alike. If a judge decides according to this method, he has, according to the supporters of the model of principles, merely identified what the law really was all along.

It is apparent from this sketch of the model of principles that it demands quite a lot from a judge. It requires a deep understanding and a total overview of the legal system, into all its nooks and corners, and the capacity to reconstruct the positive law into one principled whole. Not without reason, Dworkin introduced a judge with superhuman intellectual power and patience, appropriately named Hercules, who represents the ideal judge who can perform all the operations demanded by the model: identifying the system of principles presupposed by the positive law, and elaborating all of its implications.[7] As Dworkin acknowledged, ordinary judges may not be able to reach the level of knowledge and insight that Hercules can attain. However, this does not render the model useless in real life. Dworkin pointed out that the model consists of an approach, and the main point is that judges at least try to take a deep and broad look at the positive law when determining what the law really implies. The important thing is that they ask the right questions: which are the principles underlying the law and what do they imply for the case to be decided.[8]

It should be noted that Dworkin made an important distinction. He distinguishes the rationales underlying the legal rules into *policies* and *principles*. Both principles and policies are of the same kind in the general sense that they both refer to 'the good which legal rules intend to promote' or 'the evil they seek to avert'. However, they are different in that policies refer to collective goals (for instance, the protection of national defence or increasing economic growth) whereas principles refer to individual rights (such as 'protection of the weaker

---

[7] Hercules is introduced in Dworkin, *Taking Rights Seriously*, p. 105, and he reappears in *Law's Empire*, see especially p. 239.

[8] See Dworkin, *Law's Empire*, p. 239.

party', 'the right to a fair trial'). He argued that policies function differently in the process of legal reasoning than principles do. Policies do not and should not have any influence beyond the statutory rules that have been generated by them. In fact, policies function just like a legal rule's underlying rationale does in the theory of purposive interpretation: they are to be used only to determine what the statutory rule, which has been generated by it, implies. This is unlike the influence of principles in the legal system: they are to be applied in a consistent manner throughout the legal order as a whole, so that cases that are alike from the point of view of the law's principles are treated alike. The influence of policies is not extended in this way as it is not required that all that are alike in the light of policies, should be treated alike.[9]

As has been pointed out before, the Court of Justice has stated in many of its decisions that the provisions of the Brussels Convention need to be interpreted in light of the Convention's 'principles and objectives'. An analysis of the Court's case law clearly shows that the Court does not merely use the narrow and shallow type of reasoning typical of the model of purposive interpretation described above. The Court does not just identify the provision that is most relevant to the case at hand and then interpret it in light of the 'principle or objective' that immediately underlies this provision. As will become evident in the description of the Court's case law in the following chapters, the Court tries to take into account all the principles and objectives underlying the Convention as a whole to the extent that they are relevant to the case to be decided.

The Court of Justice refers in its case law to the Convention's 'principles and objectives'. At first sight, it would seem that the Court's 'objectives' are equivalent to what has earlier been referred to as 'policies'. However, on closer inspection it appears that, in fact, the Court's 'principles and objectives' are virtually all principles (individual rights) and not policies (collective goals). As will become clear in the following chapters, almost all of the various 'goods that the Convention's provisions intend to promote' or 'the evils that they seek to avert' can be transformed into principles in that they refer to rights of individuals and not to collective goals.[10] Affirmation of this thesis can also be found in the fact that the most general aim that, according to the Court, underlies (almost) all of the other more concrete aims of the Convention is a principle, namely the principle of the 'legal protection of persons established within the Community'. Hence, we will from now on replace the Court's notion of 'principles and objectives' by the notion of 'principles' only.

---

[9] See Dworkin, *Law's Empire* pp. 221-224 and *Taking Rights Seriously*, pp. 82-84 and pp. 113-114. Actually, Dworkin's position is somewhat more refined than this. He stated that there is some limit to the arbitrariness of the distinctions which the legislature may make in its pursuit of a collective goal, see *Taking Rights Seriously*, p. 114.

[10] One of these exceptions concerns the protection of the public policy interests of Contracting States, under Article 27, point 1. The notion of 'public policy' will be discussed in chapter 2, section 2.

In quite a number of cases the Court has stated that consideration should not only be given to the principles underlying the Convention, but also to a provision's place within the overall scheme of the Convention's provisions. One could be led to think that this indicates that, in addition to the model of principles, the Court employs another method: the method of systematic interpretation. On closer inspection, however, it appears that a provision's place in the scheme of the Convention can only be determined and understood by taking into account the principle directly underlying the provision, and this principle's relationship to the principles underlying other provisions or underlying the Convention as a whole. In other words, the Court's contention that provisions must be interpreted by reference to their systematic context is in fact an instruction to read the Convention's provisions in light of the system of principles underlying these provisions.

As has been described previously, the model of principles demands a great deal from a judge: only a Hercules would be able to operate the model of principles in a perfect way. Although this may be true in the context of an entire national legal system, the situation is different in the context of the Brussels Convention. Compared to a national legal order, the scope of the Brussels Convention is quite limited: the positive law consists of a mere 68 Articles and approximately 115 court decisions. Compared to the task that a national judge would face when applying the model of principles, the work of the Court looks relatively easy.

In identifying the principles underlying the Convention, the Court has in some cases referred to principles mentioned in the Preamble to the Convention and in the Expert Reports. As is evident from the Convention's provisions, the designers of the Convention have also taken decisions as to how the various principles are to be weighed in relation to each other in case they conflict. However, all this still leaves a considerable part of the work of identifying and constructing the system of principles to the Court. As will be seen in this study, the Court has taken an active role in filling in the system of principles. It has identified sub-principles that flow from the main principles that the Convention's designers had in mind, determined which concrete requirements in turn follow from these sub-principles and, last but not least, continued the process of weighing and balancing the principles in case of conflict. It is clear that in the first cases it decided, the Court did not yet have a complete view of the system of principles presupposed by the Convention. Over the years, however, the Court seems to have gained a better insight into which principles, in its view, underlie the Convention and how they relate to each other. Accordingly, the Court's later decisions are more complete than the earlier decisions in that they take more of the Convention's principles into account and pay more attention to how the various principles relate to each other.

2. The model of principles and judicial constraints

A question that needs to be considered is how far a judge may go in actually reforming the positive legal rule in the name of the principles underlying these rules. Clearly, supporters of a pure version of the model of principles would answer this question as follows: judges should in all cases read the positive rules in light of the principles underlying them and should feel free to bring the positive law into line with these principles. One could attribute a far more modest role to the model of principles. For example, one could adopt the position that only when the words of the positive rules are ambiguous, should the model of principles be used to determine what the law implies. In this position, principles are only given a role when the theory of plain meaning is found to be lacking. Obviously, in-between positions are possible as well: one could argue that a judge should be allowed to bring the positive law into line with the law's principles, as long as he does not venture too far away from the words of the positive rules. The latter position would imply that, within limits, the law's principles are allowed to trump the letter of the law.

Not surprisingly, the Court does not feel inhibited in applying the model of principles when 'the letter' of a provision is unable to suggest an answer to the legal question. Cases in which the words of the Convention are inconclusive and the system of principles provides a solution, are unproblematic from the point of view of judicial constraints: the words have run out and the principles are able to solve the legal question.

An examination of the Court's case law clearly shows that the Court does not only have recourse to the model of principles after it has established that the words of the Convention are not able to provide a clear answer. Also in cases in which the words of the Convention, considered by themselves, clearly point to a solution, the Court still feels obliged to consider what the Convention's principles have to say. In some of these cases, the words of the relevant provision points in the direction of one decision and the principles in the direction of another. In these cases, the question regarding the limits of the Court's power to reform the letter of the Convention's provisions arises. When considering this category of cases, it appears that the Court has at times adopted a 'principle-based' interpretation that has deviated from the literal meaning of the relevant provision. In other cases, the Court has not felt itself to be free to implement the solution that would be most in agreement with the substantive principles of the Convention. It is not possible to capture in a general formula where exactly the Court starts to feel constrained. Generally, it seems that the Court is rather cautious in venturing away from the literal wording of the provisions, as can be illustrated by the following examples.

C Art. 16(1) R 22(1)
C Art. 17 R 23

In the case *Meeth v Glacetal* the Court allowed principles to trump the letter of Article 17 of the Convention.[11] Article 17, which concerns forum selection clauses, states that if the parties have agreed that a court or the courts of a Contracting State are to have jurisdiction, that court or those courts have jurisdiction. A business contract concluded between Meeth, a German company, and Glacetal, a French company, contained the following clause: 'If Meeth sues Glacetal, the French courts alone shall have jurisdiction. If Glacetal sues Meeth, the German courts alone shall have jurisdiction'. The Court was asked whether this forum selection clause, which attributes jurisdiction to the courts of two Contracting States depending on which party is the defendant, was valid according to Article 17. The system of principles underlying the Convention, and in this case particularly the principle underlying Article 17 itself, the principle of party autonomy, indicated that this clause should be considered valid. The wording of Article 17, on the other hand, implies that only an agreement to submit a dispute to the court(s) of a single Contracting State should be allowed. The Court allowed the principle to trump the letter of the law, and decided that Article 17 implied that the parties' forum selection clause was valid.[12]

Although the Court is willing to deviate from the letter of the law in order to give effect to the law's underlying principles, it appears that the Court is not prepared to deviate too far from the wording of the Convention's provisions. The case *Rösler v Rottwinkel* offers a clear illustration.[13] At issue was Article 16, point 1, which (in its original version) stated that the courts of a Contracting State in which immovable property is situated have exclusive jurisdiction in proceedings which concern rights in rem or tenancies of such properties. The principle underlying this provision did not really apply to a situation of a short-term lease of property between two private parties for holiday use.[14] In other words, the wording of the provision was overinclusive from the point of view of the underlying principle. The Court decided, however, that it would be going too far by reading an exception into Article 16 for short-term leases between private parties for holiday purposes. Even though the Court seemed to (more or less implicitly) recognise that in light of the principle underlying Article 16, point 1, such an exception would be justified[15], the Court felt that such a reformulation of the positive law would be going too far.

The differences between *Rösler v Rottwinkel* and *Meeth v Glacetal* are evident. The interpretation in the latter case, even though it deviated from the strict

[11] 23/78 *Meeth v Glacetal.*
[12] 23/78 *Meeth v Glacetal* 5,6.
[13] 241/83 *Rösler v Rottwinkel.*
[14] For a description of the principle underlying Art. 16, see chapter 6, section 3.1.3.
[15] See *Rösler v Rottwinkel* 19-21 (and see 10).

letter of the law in the name of the underlying principle, stretched the wording of the provisions only to a limited degree. In the case *Rösler v Rottwinkel*, on the other hand, reforming the positive law in the name of the Convention's underlying principles would demand a more radical change into the positive law: a completely new exception would have to be added to Article 16, point 1. The Court appeared to imply that such reforms should be left to the legislator (that is, the Contracting States). In fact, as soon as an opportunity presented itself, when some changes were made to the Brussels Convention on the occasion of the accession of Denmark, Ireland and the United Kingdom in 1978, an exception was added to Article 16 for short-term agreements between private individuals for the use and occupation of immovable property.[16]

3. The problem of conflicting principles

Principles are pure statements of something good which one wants to achieve or an evil which one wants to avert. Even though principles are stated as being absolute – 'party autonomy', 'protection of the socio-economically weaker party', 'free movement of judgments' and 'protection of the rights of the defence' – they do not function as being absolute within a normative system: they are actually not always fully applied in cases where they are relevant. The reason for this is that it is quite common for principles belonging to a legal order to conflict – 'free movement of judgments' can come into conflict with 'the protection of the rights of the defence' and 'party autonomy' with 'the protection of the socio-economically weaker contract party'.[17] As will be seen in the next chapters, our examination of the Court's case law confirms the fact that the majority of legal questions, when analysed in terms of the legal order's principles, appear to involve conflicting principles.

The fact that principles quite often present themselves in a constellation of conflict raises the question of what use is it for the judge to analyse a legal question in terms of (conflicting) legal principles. In our view, knowing which conflicting legal principles are at stake is always helpful to the decision-maker in that they make visible what values are really at stake on a deeper level. The question remains, however, whether the conflicting principles can have any *guiding*

[16] See Schlosser Report, OJ 1979, C 59, No. 164, p. 120. The reason given in the Expert Report for this change was that the principle underlying Art. 16 quite clearly does not require its application to short-term agreements for use and occupation such as, for example, holiday accommodation.

[17] See also Joseph Raz who remarks that '[I]t is natural to find reflected in the law conflicting values, goals and aims', J. Raz, *Ethics in the Public Domain; Essays in the Morality of Law and Politics*, Clarendon Press, Oxford, 1994, p. 315. Dworkin also contends that the principles (and policies) of a given legal system will typically present themselves in constellations of conflict, which is why he describes a principle as stating 'a reason that argues in one direction' that does not necessitate a particular decision, see R. Dworkin, *Taking Rights Seriously*, p. 24.

capacity in the sense that they can lead the decision-maker towards a solution. In other words, can a conflict between principles be resolved on the basis of rational grounds, so that reasonable people would all agree, upon reflection, that there is one right solution, or is it a matter of subjective choice?

The most obvious direction in which to search for a rational resolution of situations in which conflicting principles pertain, is this: underlying the duelling principles is a common entity in terms of which they can be evaluated and which suggests how the conflict should be resolved. This entity consists of a single overarching principle, an ultimate 'good' that should be realised as much as possible. From the range of possible decisions, each representing a different weighing of the conflicting principles, that option should be chosen which contributes most to the realisation of this overarching principle.

From the Court's case law it appears that the Court considers one principle to be the single overarching principle under which all the more concrete principles of the system can be subsumed: the principle of the 'legal protection of persons established within the Community'. All of the more concrete mid-level principles, such as 'free movement of judgments', 'protection of the rights of the defence', 'legal certainty' and 'disputes should be decided by an appropriate court', are considered as more specific principles that are meant to strengthen the legal protection of persons established within the Community. However, our conclusion is that this most general principle does not have the capacity to provide guidance when the Court is faced with conflicting mid-level principles. It is not the case that reasonable people would all agree that a particular way of weighing the conflicting mid-level principles follows from the application of the principle of the 'legal protection of persons established within the Community'. This most general principle is too vague, and even though all of the mid-level principles are intended to increase the legal protection of persons within the Community, they are not commensurable in terms thereof. The principle of the 'legal protection of persons established within the Community' cannot provide a measure in terms of which the more concrete principles that are supposed to contribute thereto, can be weighed in relation to each other when they conflict.[18]

The fact that the single overarching principle cannot function as a device that can provide a rational ground for the attribution of weight to conflicting principles does not mean the end of rationality in the implementation of conflicting principles. There are several standards of rationality that can provide guidance

[18] Commensurability is defined as 'having a common measure or being reducible to one' (see *Webster's Dictionary of the English Language*, The World Publishing Company, New York, 1953); the following illustration is used: a yard and a foot are commensurable since they may both be measured in terms of inches. Entities are incommensurable when there is no common unit in terms of which they can be evaluated. This is the case with the Convention's more concrete principles: though they all contribute to improving the legal protection of persons established in the Community, this general protection principle is not able to provide a measure by means of which the relative weight of the more concrete principles can be determined in case they conflict.

when resolving a conflict between conflicting principles: *(a)* the requirement of consistency, *(b)* the requirement of optimisation, and *(c)* the prohibition of disproportionality. These standards provide compelling guidelines when resolving conflict between principles in a normative system, so that reasonable people, upon reflection, will agree to them.

The requirement of '*consistency* in the implementation of conflicting principles' demands that cases that are alike from the perspective of the principles of the legal system, are also treated alike, and that cases that are unalike should be decided in accordance with their unalikeness. This requirement of consistency in the application of conflicting principles is always comparative. It takes some situation(s) and the decision(s) taken in these situations as a reference point; this is then used to reason a decision (or to rule out some possible decisions) in another situation. Clearly, the more of these reference points one actually has within a system, the more guidance the requirement of principled consistency can give. This means that as more decisions are taken within a legal system on how to resolve conflicts between principles in various situations, the more footholds one generally has – given of course that the decisions taken have resolved the conflicts between principles in a consistent manner.[19] Our investigation of the case law of the Court under the Brussels Convention shows that the Court attempts to act consistently in the way it weighs the various principles. This is apparent from the fact that the Court in its decisions often refers back to the way it has reasoned in terms of the Convention's principles in earlier decisions, and tries to relate this to the way it resolves the conflict between principles in the case at hand.

A second requirement of rationality applicable to situations of conflicting principles is the requirement of optimisation.[20] A principle has been defined as 'something good to be promoted'. Given this definition of a principle, it is clear that more of it is better than less. In contexts in which only one principle pertains (or several principles that all pull in the same direction) the requirement of maximisation applies: that decision should be chosen which maximises the realisation of the applicable principle(s). The requirement of *optimisation* embodies this same idea for contexts in which conflicting principles pertain. It prescribes that when choosing between alternative decisions that are possible in a given situation, each representing a different weighing of the principles involved, an optimal alternative needs to be chosen as opposed to a non-optimal alternative. A decision is non-optimal whenever it is possible to choose, in the situation at hand, another alternative that realises more of at least one principle without realising less of another. A decision is optimal if it is impossible to improve the

[19] The notion of 'principled consistency' forms the basis of Ronald Dworkin's theory of 'law as integrity'; see Ronald Dworkin, *Taking Rights Seriously*, Harvard University Press, Cambridge, Massachusetts, 1986 and *Law's Empire*, Harvard University Press, Cambridge, Massachusetts, 1986.

[20] Unlike the requirement of consistency which only applies to principles (individual rights) and not to policies (collective goals), the requirement of optimisation also applies to the implementation of policies.

decision in this way.[21] In the decisions taken by the Court under the Brussels Convention, the optimisation requirement does not appear. This by no means implies that the Court does not consider this requirement to be relevant when dealing with opposing principles, it just means, in our view, that it remains implicit.

The third standard which may provide guidance in the application of conflicting principles is the prohibition of *disproportionality*. It implies that in any situation, the sacrifice of some principle(s) to be made in order to realise a gain in the realisation of one or more conflicting principles, should not be out of reasonable proportion. We assume that the Court uses arguments that are based on this requirement when it rejects certain interpretations, representing a particular way of weighing conflicting principles, because they would lead 'to the very existence of one of the principles being called into question'.[22]

CONCLUDING REMARKS

In this chapter we have provided an exposition of the *method of interpretation* the Court has used to solve legal questions regarding the Brussels Convention. This method, which we have referred to as 'principle-based reasoning' or 'reasoning according the model of principles', uses the system of principles underlying the legal system as a whole (in this case: the Convention as a whole) to interpret the system's provisions. In the next chapters, we will try to uncover, as far as possible, *the content of the system of principles* that the Court has used to solve legal questions and demonstrate its role in the Court's actual decisions.

---

[21] This optimality requirement refers to what is also known as 'Pareto optimality'. For a discussion of the notion of Pareto optimality, see for instance Rawls, *A Theory of Justice*, Oxford University Press, Oxford, 1992 (12th edn.), on pp. 66-69. Dworkin paid no attention to this requirement of optimisation in his theory of law. The German legal theorist Robert Alexy did mention the fact that principles are entities that should be optimised. He referred to principles as 'commands to optimise', which implies that principles are norms that command that something should be realised to the highest degree possible given the legal and actual possibilities; what is legally possible is mainly dependent on conflicting legal principles. See Robert Alexy, *Theorie der Grundrechte*, Nomos Verlaggesellschaft, Baden-Baden, 1985, pp. 75-77, and Alexy, *Zum Begriff des Rechtsprinzips*, in: Rechtstheorie, Beiheft 1, 1979, p. 80

[22] See for example 189/87 *Kalfelis v Schröder* 8.

Chapter 2
A BIRD'S-EYE VIEW OF THE SYSTEM OF PRINCIPLES

INTRODUCTION

In this chapter we introduce what we consider to be the main principles that underlie the Convention's provisions and the most general principle from which, in our view, these main principles are derived. The most general principle underlying the Convention is:

The Principle of Strengthening the Legal Protection of Persons established in the Community

and the four main principles that follow from this most general principle in the context of the Convention, are:

(1) The Principle of Free Movement of Judgments
(2) The Principle of the Protection of the Rights of the Defence
(3) The Principle of Legal Certainty, and
(4) The Principle that Disputes should be Decided by an Appropriate Court

In section 1 of this chapter we will present the view that these principles are the four main principles underlying the Convention, and that they all contribute to a common, most general principle, namely the principle that the legal protection of persons established in the Community needs to be strengthened. In section 2, we will consider the significance of this most general principle.

1. THE FOUR MAIN PRINCIPLES AND THEIR RELATION TO THE MOST GENERAL PRINCIPLE UNDERLYING THE CONVENTION

C Art. 19	R 25	C Art. 27(2)	R 34(2)
C Art. 20	R 26	C Art. 27(3)	R 34(3)

The principles that underlie a specific area of positive law (in this study, the principles underlying the rules on jurisdiction and the recognition and enforcement of judgments in civil and commercial matters, as contained in the 1968 Brussels Convention) are mostly not directly laid down in the rules themselves. This means that they must be derived from other legal sources. In the case of the Convention, we consider the judgments of the Court of Justice, which frequently refer to the principles underlying the Convention, and the Preamble of the Convention to be the primary sources from which the Convention's principles can be derived.[1] We also refer to the Expert Reports to the Convention and the Accession Conventions, but only as far as the Court itself has done so.[2] Our research did not include an examination of the Opinions of the Advocates-General of the EC Court, as their views with respect to the Convention's principles, however interesting, are in the end not authoritative; in this respect, only the decisions adopted by the Court matter.

It should be recalled here that the Court only occasionally uses the term 'principles'. It often uses words such as 'objectives', 'purposes' or 'aims' when it justifies its interpretation of the provisions of the Convention.[3] As was seen in the previous chapter, virtually all of these justifying reasons, representing 'a good that the Convention aims to promote', can be qualified as 'principles': they aim to strengthen the rights of individuals (and not collective goals).[4] Hence we mostly refer to these justifying reasons, as far as appropriate, as 'principles'.[5]

In its case law, the Court has frequently referred to the Convention's Preamble when establishing what the most important principles of the Convention are.[6] In this respect the Preamble states that:

> 'The High Contracting Parties to the Treaty establishing the European Economic Community, desiring to implement the provision of Article 220 of that Treaty by virtue of which they undertook to secure the simplification of formalities governing the reciprocal recognition and enforcement of judgments of courts or tribunals,
>
> Anxious to strengthen in the Community the legal protection of persons therein established,

---

[1] See section 1 of chapter 1; see also, Malcolm N. Shaw, International law, 4th edn., Cambridge, 1997, p. 54 ff; compare Art. 31, point 2, sub. b, of the Vienna Convention on the Law of Treaties 1969.

[2] Among others 145/86 *Hoffmann v Krieg* 10 (re Jenard Report, OJ 1979 C 59, pp. 42 and 43); C-351/89 *OUI v NHIC* 22 (re Jenard Report, p. 1); C-26/91 *Handte v TMCS* 12 (re Jenard Report, p. 1); and C-129/92 *Owens v Bracco* 21 (re Jenard Report, p. 15).

[3] Among others 33/78 *Somafer v Saar-Ferngas* 4; 125/79 *Denilauler v Couchet Frères* 12; 38/81 *Effer v Kantner* 6; 288/82 *Duijnstee v Goderbauer* 10; C-26/91 *Handte v TMCS* 11; C-172/91 *Sonntag v Waidmann* 18 (re 29/76 *LTU v Eurocontrol* 3,4; 133/78 *Gourdain v Nadler* 3; 814/79 *Netherlands v Rüffer* 7,8); C-474/93 *Hengst v Campese* 24; C-80/00 *Leather v Polstermöbel* 51 (re *Effer v Kantner* 6; C-440/97 *Concorde v Panjan* 23; C-256/00 *Besix v Kretzschmar* 24).

[4] Compare chapter 1, section 1, text following note 9.

[5] Compare also the Preamble of the 1989 Accession Convention, in which reference was made to the 'principles' of the Brussels Convention, OJ 10.3.1989 L 285, p. 1.

[6] Among others 14/76 *De Bloos v Bouyer* 8; 38/81 *Effer v Kantner* 6; 288/82 *Duijnstee v Goderbauer* 11; 144/86 *Gubisch v Palumbo* 8; C-26/91 *Handte v TMCS* 11; C-129/92 *Owens v Bracco* 20; C-406/92 *Tatry v Maciej Rataj* 24; C-256/00 *Besix v Kretzschmar* 25 (re C-288/92 *Custom Made* 15).

> Considering that it is necessary for this purpose to determine the international jurisdiction of their courts, to facilitate recognition and to introduce an expeditious procedure for securing the enforcement of judgments, authentic instruments and court settlements,
>
> Have decided to conclude this Convention ...'[7]

The most general principle, the principle of 'strengthening the legal protection of persons established in the Community' can easily be recognised in this Preamble. One of the four main principles, the free movement of judgments, can also be detected in this quotation: it is expressed in the idea 'to facilitate recognition and to introduce an expeditious procedure for securing the enforcement of judgments, authentic instruments and court settlements'. As will be seen below, the purpose 'to determine the international jurisdiction of their courts' refers indirectly to the principle that disputes should be decided by appropriate courts as well as to a particular aspect of one of the other main principles, the principle of legal certainty.

In the early judgments in which the Court referred to the Convention's objectives as stated in the Preamble, it was not clear how, in the view of the Court, the principles expressed in the Preamble relate to each other. In these judgments, the Court simply referred to the objectives 'to strengthen in the Community the legal protection of persons therein established', 'to determine the international jurisdiction of the courts of the Contracting States', 'simplification of formalities governing the reciprocal recognition and enforcement of judgments', 'to facilitate the recognition' and 'to introduce an expeditious procedure for securing the enforcement of judgments'. It was not until the Court's decision in *Duijnstee v Goderbauer*, that it became clear that the Court considered the principle of 'strengthening in the Community the legal protection of persons therein established', to be the most general principle underlying the Convention, and that the other principles referred to in the Preamble were subordinate to it. In this judgment, in which the Court had to answer a question regarding the interpretation of Article 19, the Court stated:

> 'In order to reply to that question, it is necessary to consider the aims of the Convention. According to the Preamble to the Convention, the Contracting States, anxious to "strengthen in the Community the legal protection of persons therein established", considered that it was necessary for that purpose "to determine the international jurisdiction of their courts, to facilitate recognition and to introduce an expeditious procedure for securing the enforcement of judgments, authentic instruments and court settlements". Both the provisions on jurisdiction and those on the recognition and enforcement of judgments are therefore aimed at strengthening the legal protection of persons established in the Community.'[8]

---

[7] See Consolidated version, OJ 26.1.1998, C 27, p. 1.

[8] 288/82 *Duijnstee v Goderbauer* 10,11,12.

In *Gubisch v Palumbo* the Court confirmed that the principle 'free movement of judgments' is closely related to the principle of 'strengthening in the Community the legal protection of persons therein established'. In this judgment, the Court stated:

> 'According to its Preamble ... the Convention seeks in particular to facilitate the recognition and enforcement of judgments of courts or tribunals and to strengthen in the Community the legal protection of persons therein established. Article 21, together with Article 22 on related actions ... are ... designed to preclude, in so far as possible and from the outset, the possibility of a situation arising such as that referred to in Article 27(3), that is to say the non-recognition of a judgment on account of its irreconcilability with a judgment given in a dispute between the same parties in the state in which recognition is sought.'[9]

In emphasizing the importance of both objectives of the Convention in this way, the Court confirms that they are closely connected and that the principle of 'strengthening the legal protection of persons' requires 'free movement of judgments'.

In *Handte v TMCS*, the Court confirmed that also 'the establishment of common rules of jurisdiction', another objective of the Convention mentioned in the Preamble, is meant to contribute to the general principle of 'strengthening the legal protection of persons in the Community'. In this judgment, it also becomes clear which ideas have inspired these common rules of jurisdiction: the principle that 'disputes should be decided by an appropriate court' and the principle of 'legal certainty'. In *Handte v TMCS*, the Court had to answer a question on the interpretation of Article 5, point 1. In its decision, the Court referred to the Jenard Report – the Expert Report prepared at the time when the Convention was drawn up – and stated:

> 'Secondly, it should be noted that, according to the Preamble to the Convention, one of its objectives is to "strengthen in the Community the legal protection of persons therein established". In that connection, the Expert Report prepared at the time when the Convention was drawn up (OJ 1979 C 59, p. 1) states that: "... the purpose of the Convention is ... by establishing common rules of jurisdiction, to achieve, ... in the field which it was required to cover, a genuine legal systematization which will ensure the greatest possible degree of legal certainty. To this end, the rules of jurisdiction codified in Title II determine which State's courts are most appropriate to assume jurisdiction ...".'[10]

Other judgments in which the Court has confirmed the relationship between the principle of strengthening the legal protection of persons in the Community, the

---

[9] 144/86 *Gubisch v Palumbo* 8.
[10] C-26/91 *Handte v TMCS* 11,12.

principle that disputes should be decided by an appropriate court and the principle of legal certainty, are, among others, *Effer v Kantner, Owens v Bracco, Benincasa v Dentalkit, Farrell v Long* and *Rutten v Cross Medical.*[11]

From *Duijnstee v Goderbauer*, it appears that the principle of legal certainty does not only play a role in the context of the rules of jurisdiction, but, that it has a much wider, general significance in the context of the Convention.[12] The principle of legal certainty is not to be found in the Preamble, but as appears from the following quotation, the Court takes account of this principle because it is part of the Community legal order in general:

> 'The principle of legal certainty in the Community legal order and the aims pursued by the Convention in accordance with Article 220 of the Treaty, on which it is based, require that the equality and uniformity of rights and obligations arising from the Convention ... must be ensured.'[13]

Although the Court in *Duijnstee v Goderbauer* did not explicitly mention that there is a relation between the principle of legal certainty and the most general principle of 'strengthening the legal protection of persons established in the Community', it becomes clear from other judgments of the Court that it considers the principle of legal certainty to contribute to this most general principle.[14]

Several of the Court's judgments make it clear that the principle of legal certainty, which flows from the most general principle of strengthening the legal protection of persons in the Community, not only affects the interpretation of the rules of jurisdiction, as laid down in Title II of the Convention, but also the interpretation of the rules of recognition and enforcement of judgments, as laid down in Title III of the Convention. The Court expressly referred to legal certainty when it justified its interpretation of Article 27, point 3, in *Leather v Polstermöbel*:

> 'Finally, it would be contrary to the principle of legal certainty, which the Court has repeatedly held to be one of the objectives of the Brussels Convention ... to interpret

[11] 38/81 *Effer v Kantner* 6; C-129/92 *Owens v Bracco* 20,21 (re Jenard Report); C-269/95 *Benincasa v Dentalkit* 26 (re *Effer v Kantner* 6; C-125/92 *Mulox v Geels* 11),27,28 (re C-106/95 *Mainschiffahrts* 34); C-295/95 *Farrell v Long* 13 (re *Mulox* 11; *Rutten* 13); and C-383/95 *Rutten v Cross Medical* 13 (re *Mulox* 11).

[12] 288/82 *Duijnstee v Goderbauer* 13; compare 38/81 *Effer v Kantner* 6; C-26/91 *Handte v TMCS* 12; C-129/92 *Owens v Bracco* 32 (re *Effer* 6); C-288/92 *Custom Made v Metallbau* 15; C-80/00 *Leather v Polstermöbel* 51 (re *Effer* 6; C-440/97 *Concorde v Panjan* 23; C-256/00 *Besix* 24); C-256/00 *Besix v Kretzschmar* 24 (re *Effer* 6; *Handte* 11,12,18,19; *Owens* 32; *Custom Made* 18; *Concorde* 23).

[13] 288/82 *Duijnstee v Goderbauer* 13.

[14] See in particular C-256/00 *Besix v Kretzschmar* 24 (re *Effer v Kantner* 6; *Handte* 11,12,18,19; *Owens Bank* 32; *Custom Made* 18; *Concorde* 23), 25 (re *Custom Made* 15) and compare 38/81 *Effer v Kantner* 6.

> Article 27(3) as conferring on the court of the State in which recognition is sought the power to authorise recognition of a foreign judgment when it is irreconcilable with a judgment given in that Contracting State.'[15]

The fourth main principle underlying the Convention is the principle of the 'protection of the rights of the defence'. Although this principle is not referred to in the Preamble of the Convention, it does underlie the provisions of the Convention, as is already evident from some of the specific provisions of the Convention, particularly Article 27, point 2, and Article 20. Moreover, starting with *Denilauler v Couchet Frères*, followed by *Klomps v Michel*, *Pendy v Pluspunkt*, *Debaecker v Bouwman*, *Lancray v Peters*, *Minalmet v Brandeis*, *Hengst v Campese* and, more recently, in *Krombach v Bamberski*, the Court has clarified that the principle of the 'protection of the rights of the defence' must be considered as an overall interest of the Convention as a whole.[16] For example, in *Pendy v Pluspunkt*, the Court states:

> 'the provisions of the Brussels Convention are designed to ensure that the defendant's rights are effectively protected.'[17]

We consider this principle to be equally important to the understanding of the Convention as the other three main principles. It needs no argument that the principle of the 'protection of the rights of the defendant' contributes to the principle of 'strengthening the legal protection of persons in the Community'.

In this section we have shown that the four main principles underlying the Convention – the principle of free movement of judgments, the principle that disputes should be decided by an appropriate court, legal certainty, and the principle of the protection of the rights of the defence – are indeed part of the system of principles underlying the Convention. Even though these four principles, as will be seen in the next chapters, will often conflict, they are closely related and all flow from the most general principle of 'strengthening the legal protection of persons established in the Community'.

---

[15] 80/00 *Leather v Polstermöbel* 51 (re 38/81 *Effer v Kantner* 6; C-440/97 *Concorde v Panjan* 23; C-256/00 *Besix v Kretzschmar* 24-27).

[16] 125/79 *Denilauler v Couchet Frères* 12,13: 166/80 *Klomps v Michel* 7; 228/81 *Pendy v Pluspunkt* 13; 49/84 *Debaecker v Bouwman* 10,11; C-305/88 *Lancray v Peters* 21 (re *Debaecker*); C-123/91 *Minalmet v Brandeis* 18 (re *Klomps* 9); C-474/93 *Hengst v Campese* 16 (re *Denilauler* 13); C-7/98 *Krombach v Bamberski* 38.

[17] 228/81 *Pendy v Pluspunkt* 13.

2. The significance of the most general principle of 'strengthening the legal protection of persons established in the Community'

C Arts. 3,4	R 3, 4
C Art. 27(1)	R 34(1)

We have just established that the principle of 'strengthening in the Community the legal protection of persons therein established' has significance in the context of the Convention: it is the most general principle underlying the Convention and, within the context of the Convention, four main principles can be derived from it. For a good understanding of the role which this principle has in the context of the Convention, some further issues need to be considered.

We will see that the four main principles that flow from the principle 'strengthening of the legal protection of persons in the Community' in many cases pull in different directions. The question arises whether this most general principle actually has any significance of its own in that it can actually provide guidance when determining how the conflict between the more concrete principles needs to be resolved. As was seen in the previous chapter, this overarching principle cannot provide guidance as to *how* the main principles that contribute to its realization are to be weighed when they conflict. It can, however, be seen to indicate *that* these main principles need to be weighed and balanced in relation to each other.[18] The significance of the principle of 'strengthening the legal protection of persons in the Community' lies in guaranteeing the pursuit of all of the four main principles, as far as possible, together and at the same time. In this sense, the principle of strengthening the legal protection of persons in the Community, contributes, more or less, to a coherent application and interpretation of the provisions of the Convention.

Another aspect of the role of this most general principle, aiming at the legal protection of persons in the Community, can be seen by contrasting this principle with objectives that aim to protect the interests of the Contracting States and their legal orders or the interests of the European Community itself.[19] In the Convention, some room has been left for the interests of the Contracting States. First of all, Article 27, point 1, provides that a Contracting State can invoke its public policy interests in order to prevent the recognition and enforcement of a foreign judgment. The Court has made it clear, though, that the protection of the public policy of a Contracting State should only be taken into account in exceptional cases. As will be seen later in this study, in most of those rare cases in which the Court has allowed a Contracting State to invoke the exception of public policy, the public policy interest of the Contracting State was actually primarily concerned with the protection of the (fundamental) interests of persons.[20]

[18] Compare chapter 1, section 3.

[19] Compare in this respect also, Takis Tridimas, *The General Principles of EC Law*, Oxford, Oxford University Press, 1999, pp. 1-4.

[20] See hereafter chapter 4, section 4, text following note 65.

Another exception to the overall idea that the Convention's most general objective is to strengthen the legal position of persons established in the Community, is laid down in Article 27, point 3. This provision is based on the general idea that the interests of a Contracting State must be protected if it is confronted with irreconcilable judgments. In such a case the protection of the interests of states is assumed to be legitimate from the perspective of the Rule of Law. In *Solo v Boch*, it was held by the Court, while referring to the Jenard Report, that:

> 'the rule of law in a State would be disturbed if it were possible to take advantage of two conflicting judgments.'[21]

The foregoing illustrates that the principle of strengthening the legal protection of persons, though being the most general principle in the context of the Convention, is not absolute: the protection of the interests of states may override this principle, albeit only in very exceptional cases.

It is also clear that the principle of strengthening the legal protection of persons primarily focuses on those persons established in the Community. This restriction is not only expressed in the Preamble and in Articles 3 and 4 of Title II of the Convention, but also in the Court's case law, as for example in *Réunion européenne v Spliethoff's*.[22]

Conclusions and outlook

Having established the significance of the most general principle underlying the Convention, we will take a closer look in the next chapters at the four main principles. The order in which these four main principles are discussed is not determined by their relative weight or hierarchy, but rather by their increasing complexity. When taking a closer look at these four main principles, it appears that a number of more concrete principles and requirements are implied by them. In the next chapters, we will describe in detail these four main principles as well as the more concrete principles and requirements that flow from them.

As will be seen as we go along, these main principles and sub-principles often come into conflict with each other. This implies that these principles have to be weighed in relation to each other. It should be noted that the designers of the Convention have already taken decisions as to how various conflicting principles underlying the Convention are to be weighed. This weighing, which is evident from the provisions of the Convention, represents a starting point for the Court

---

[21] C-414/92 *Solo v Boch* 21 (re Jenard Report, OJ 1979 C 59, p. 45). Compare also chapter 6, section 3.1.3, on Art. 16, text following note 359; and see, for example, 266/85 *Shenavai v Kreischer* 10.

[22] C-51/97 *Réunion européenne v Spliethoff's* 46.

which is to be taken as given. From the Court's case law it appears, though, that the process of weighing and balancing is to be continued when the provisions of the Convention are applied and interpreted. In the following chapters, we will attempt to uncover this process. In the course of this study, a more complete picture of the complex nature of the Court's principle-based reasoning will be exposed.

We conclude this chapter with a schematic presentation of the most general principle and the four main principles underlying the Convention:

The Legal Protection of Persons established in the Community
entails:

(1) Free movement of Judgments

(2) Protection of the Rights of the Defence

(3) Legal Certainty

(4) Disputes should be Decided by an Appropriate Court

Chapter 3
THE FIRST MAIN PRINCIPLE: FREE MOVEMENT OF JUDGMENTS

Introduction

The Preamble to the Convention states that one of the objectives of the Convention is the simplification of formalities governing the reciprocal recognition and enforcement of judgments of courts or tribunals.[1] This objective can be restated in a more concise, pure form: the described simplification is ultimately aimed at promoting the 'free movement of judgments' among Contracting States. The Court has on various occasions referred to this notion of free movement of judgments and has made it clear that it will interpret the Convention in the light of this objective.[2] For example, in *Unibank v Christensen*, the Court stated:

> 'one of the fundamental objectives of the Brussels Convention, which is to facilitate, to the greatest possible extent, the free movement of judgments ...'[3]

As was seen in the previous chapter, the Court sees the free movement of judgments as contributing to the most general principle which underlies the Convention, namely the principle of the 'legal protection of persons established in the Community'.[4]

Within the context of the principle of the free movement of judgments, the person whose legal protection is at stake is the party seeking recognition and enforcement of the foreign judgment in another Contracting State; it is the judgment creditor, being the party who has obtained a foreign judgment awarding him some relief, who benefits from the principle of 'free movement of judgments'.

---

[1] Compare chapter 2, section 1, text following note 7.

[2] Compare 145/86 *Hoffmann v Krieg* 10 (re Jenard Report, OJ 1979 C 59, pp. 42, 43); C-183/90 *Dalfsen v Van Loon* 21; C-414/92 *Solo v Boch* 20; C-260/97 *Unibank v Christensen* 14 (re 148/84 *Deutsche Genossenschaftsbank* 16; C-414/92 *Solo v Boch* 20); C-267/97 *Coursier v Fortis* 25 (re *Deutsche Genossenschaftsbank* 17; C-172/91 *Sonntag v Waidmann* 32,33); C-7/98 *Krombach v Bamberski* 19 (re C-414/92 *Solo v Boch* 20; *Coursier v Fortis* 25); C-38/98 *Maxicar v Renault II* 20 (re C-7/98 *Krombach* 19).

[3] C-260/97 *Unibank v Christensen* 14 (re *Deutsche Genossenschaftsbank* 16; C-414/92 *Solo v Boch* 20). Conditional for this liberal attitude of the Convention towards the recognition and enforcement of other Contracting States' judgments is complete confidence in the jurisdictional functioning of the court of the Contracting State in which the judgment was delivered; compare Jenard Report, OJ 1979 C 59, p. 46.

[4] See chapter 2, section 1, text following note 8.

A full implementation of 'free movement of judgments' would require the absence of two types of obstacles. First of all, Contracting States should not be able to refuse the recognition and enforcement of judgments delivered in other Contracting States. In other words, judgments should be fully respected and grounds for refusing them should not be allowed. Secondly, free movement of judgments requires the absence of procedural obstacles. One could be giving full effect to judgments of other Contracting States by allowing them to be recognized, while raising a significant threshold to the free movement of judgments by maintaining long and complex procedures for obtaining the full recognition and enforceability of foreign judgments.[5] Corresponding to these different aspects, the principle of free movement of judgments can be subdivided into two separate sub-principles. These sub-principles are:

(1) the principle of *full* respect for another Contracting State's judgments
(2) the principle of a *swift and simple procedure* for recognition and enforcement of another Contracting State's judgments.

The two sub-principles appear to correspond to the two objectives distinguished in the Preamble to the Convention, namely, the objective of facilitating the recognition and enforcement of judgments and the objective of an expeditious enforcement procedure. As will be seen below, these principles can also be recognized in various provisions laid down in Title III of the Convention and in the case law of the Court. These principles guide the Court's interpretation of the Convention's provisions.

C Art. 25	R 32	C Art. 51	R 58
C Art. 50	R 57		

Before subjecting these principles to a closer investigation, the concept of 'judgment' as used in the Convention needs to be clarified. In order to fall within the scope of Title III of the Convention, which contains the rules regarding the free movement of judgments, a judgment first of all needs to fall within the substantive scope of the Convention, as defined in Article 1 ('civil and commercial matters').[6] Next, a definition of the term 'judgment' is given in Article 25. It refers to 'any judgment given by a court or tribunal of a Contracting State, whatever the judgment may be called, including a decree, order, decision or writ of execution,

[5] The costs of a procedure can form another obstacle to the free movement of judgments. That obstacle has been a concern for the Court, as becomes evident from *De Wolf v Cox*. The Court stated in that judgment, 'it must be observed that the Convention, which, in the words of the Preamble thereto, is intended "to secure the simplification of formalities governing the reciprocal recognition and enforcement of judgments of courts or tribunals", ought to induce the Contracting States to ensure that the costs of the procedure described in the Convention are fixed so as to accord with that concern for simplification.' (42/76 *De Wolf v Cox* 15).

[6] As regards Art. 1 of the Convention, see chapter 5, section 3, text following note 74.

as well as the determination of costs or expenses by an officer of the court'. Although Article 25 gives a broad definition of judgments, the Court has set certain limits to that definition.[7]

The Convention does not only regulate the recognition and enforcement of judgments. Title IV of the Convention contains special rules pertaining to the free movement of authentic instruments and court settlements (Articles 50 and 51). Hence, the principle of 'free movement of judgments' is not restricted to judgments, within the meaning of Article 25, but applies also to authentic instruments and court settlements, within the meaning of Articles 50 and 51 of the Convention.[8]

[7] The rather broad definition of judgments in Art. 25 has been confirmed by the Court in *Leather v Polstermöbel.* In that judgment it was established that this provision refers to judgments without further precision, and therefore also applies to decisions on interim measures (C-80/00 *Leather v Polstermöbel* 41). In *Denilauler v Couchet Frères,* the Court however decided that, notwithstanding the broad formulation of 'judgment' in Art. 25, the provisions of Title III do not apply to provisional measures which, in accordance with national law, are ordered by a court without the party against whom they are directed having been summoned to appear and which are intended to be enforced without prior service on that party (C-125/79 *Denilauler v Couchet Frères* 13). As will be seen hereafter, the Court based its decision on the principle of the protection of the rights of the defence (see chapter 4, section 3, text following note 47. And, in *Owens v Bracco*, the Court confirmed that the procedures envisaged by Title III of the Convention apply only in the case of judgments delivered by the courts of a Contracting State. When justifying that decision, the Court referred to the wording of Arts. 25, 26 and 31, in accordance with the principle of legal certainty (C-129/92 *Owens v Bracco* 17,18,24; compare C-414/92 *Solo v Boch* 15,16; and see hereafter chapter 5, sections 2 and 3).

[8] As regards the concept of 'authentic instruments' under Art. 50, the Court has stated in *Unibank v Christensen* that their authentic nature must be established beyond dispute so that the court in the state in which enforcement is sought, can rely on their authenticity. Consequently, since instruments drawn up between private parties (for example, an acknowledgement of indebtedness) are not inherently authentic, the involvement of a public authority or any other authority empowered for that purpose by the state of origin is needed in order to endow them with the character of authentic instruments within the meaning of Art. 50 (C-260/97 *Unibank v Christensen* 15,21). The Court referred to the principle of 'free movement of judgments' (point 14) and the Expert's Report (points 16,17) and to the wording of the Convention (point 20) when it justified its interpretation of Art. 50.

The concept 'court settlements' under Art. 51 refers to settlements between parties approved by a court in the course of proceedings. Though approved by a court, a court settlement is not to be treated as a 'judgment', as the Court stated in *Solo v Boch.* The Court pointed out that in order to be a 'judgment' for the purposes of the Convention the decision must emanate from a judicial body of a Contracting State deciding on its own authority on the issues between the parties. That condition is not fulfilled in the case of a court settlement, even if it was reached in a court of a Contracting State and brings proceedings to an end. Settlements in court are essentially contractual in that their terms depend first and foremost on the parties' intention (C-414/92 *Solo v Boch* 15-20). Consequently, the obstacle 'irreconcilable' which applies to judgments only, does not apply to court settlements. As will be discussed hereafter (see this chapter, text following note 32, the Court justified its restrictive interpretation of Art. 25 not only by referring to its wording (point 15) but also with reference to the principle of 'free movement of judgments' (point 20).

1. THE PRINCIPLE OF *FULL* RESPECT FOR ANOTHER CONTRACTING STATE'S JUDGMENTS

C Art. 26	R 33	C Art. 31	R 38	C Art. 50	R 57
C Art. 29	R 36	C Art. 34	R 41	C Art. 51	R 58

The principle of 'full respect for another Contracting State's judgments' implies that these judgments should be fully recognized and enforceable. This principle has found expression in the Convention, especially in Articles 26, 29, 31 and 34, first and third paragraph (for authentic instruments and court settlements in Articles 50 and 51). In the Court's case law the principle of full respect for another Contracting State's judgments can be recognized as well. It has been interpreted as meaning that a judgment should be attributed the authority and effectiveness which it has in the state in which it was given. This interpretation, already to be found in the Jenard Report, has been confirmed by the Court in the case *Hoffmann v Krieg*. In that judgment the Court had to answer the question whether a foreign judgment, which has been recognized pursuant to Article 26, must in principle have the same effects in the state in which enforcement is sought as it does in the state in which judgment was given. The Court states:

> 'In that regard it should be recalled that the Convention "seeks to facilitate as far as possible the free movement of judgments, and should be interpreted in this spirit". Recognition must therefore "have the result of conferring on judgments the authority and effectiveness accorded to them in the state in which they were given" ... It follows that ... a foreign judgment which has been recognized by virtue of Article 26 of the Convention must in principle have the same effects in the state in which enforcement is sought as it does in the state in which judgment was given.'[9]

The principle 'full respect for another Contracting State's judgments' weighed in relation to other principles and the interests of Contracting States

C Art. 27	R 34	C Art. 29	R 36
C Art. 28	R 35	C Art. 34	R 41

Although the promotion of the free movement of judgments (as well as of court settlements and authentic instruments) has clearly been one of the most important principles that has inspired the Convention, the principle does not function as an absolute. With regard to the notion 'full respect for judgments given in other Contracting States' this is already evident from the fact that the Convention provides for several grounds for refusing the recognition and enforcement of foreign judgments. And, although Articles 29 and 34, third paragraph, prohibit any review of foreign judgments as to their substance, Articles 27 and 28 (in conjunction with Article 34, second paragraph) list several grounds that can be used to bar the recognition and enforcement of foreign judgments.

---

[9] 145/86 *Hoffmann v Krieg* 10 (re Jenard Report, OJ 1979, C 59, pp. 42 and 43),11.

The reasons for the refusal of foreign judgments mentioned in Articles 27 and 28 have been generated by several principles or interests that, according to the designers of the Convention, should outweigh the principle of 'full respect for foreign judgments': Article 27, point 1, which states that judgments can be refused if they are contrary to the public policy of the state in which recognition or enforcement is sought, intends to protect the interests of the Contracting States and their legal orders as far as these interests are essential or fundamental.[10] Article 27, point 2, aims to protect the party who was a defendant in the original proceedings by allowing a foreign judgment to be refused, where it was given in default of appearance and the defendant was not properly serviced with the document instituting the proceedings. Here, the principle of the protection of the rights of the defence outweighs the principle of the free movement of judgments.[11] Article 27, points 3 and 5, allows the refusal of a foreign judgment if it is irreconcilable with an earlier judgment. This provision aims at the protection of the interests of the Contracting States in complying with the Rule of Law.[12] And Article 27, point 4, confirms that under the Convention the principle of the protection of a person's interest in a judgment that is fully respected in other Contracting States, applies only to those judgments that fall within the substantive scope of the Convention.[13]

Article 28, first paragraph, is concerned with two other principles that underlie the Convention, in particular the principle of 'the protection of the socio-economically weaker party' and the principle of 'sound administration of justice' as far as it underlies Article 16; these two principles will be discussed later.[14] If these principles have been violated in the state of origin, the principle of free movement of judgments will be overruled.

For authentic instruments and court settlements, a more liberal regime of grounds of refusal applies: Articles 50 and 51 state that the enforcement of authentic instruments and court settlements may only be refused if they are contrary to public policy in the state addressed.[15]

Clearly, Articles 27 and 28, which provide for several grounds for refusing the recognition and enforcement of judgments, generated by several principles and interests, come into conflict with the principle of 'free movement of judgments'. These provisions are taken as given as far as the Court is concerned. The Court's case law shows, though, that the process of weighing opposing principles, within

---

[10] See also this section, text following note 19; and compare section 2 of chapter 2, text following note 20.

[11] See also this section, text following note 25; and chapter 4, section 1.

[12] See section 2 of chapter 2, text following note 21. See, as regards Art. 27, point 3, also section 5 of chapter 5, text following note 163.

[13] Compare 145/86 *Hoffmann v Krieg* 15,16; and see section 3 of chapter 5.

[14] Both principles flow from the fourth main principle that disputes should be decided before an appropriate court, and will be discussed in further detail in chapter 6, sections 1.2 and 3.1.3.

[15] See this section, text following note 33.

the constraints provided by the provisions of the Convention, is to be continued, when interpreting the provisions of the Convention. As appears from the Court's case law, the principle 'free movement of judgments', particularly the sub-principle 'full respect for another Contracting State's judgments', is reinforced by the Court, in the sense that it follows two guidelines for the interpretation of the Convention's provisions: *(a)* provisions containing grounds for the refusal of judgments should in principle be interpreted as restrictively as possible, and *(b)* provisions of the Convention regarding the original procedure should be interpreted, as far as possible, so as to prevent situations that could lead to the refusal of the recognition and enforcement of judgments.

It has become settled case law that a strict interpretation of the provisions in which the grounds for the refusal of a foreign judgment are enlisted, Articles 27 and 28, is required.[16] For example, in *Solo v Boch*, the Court held with respect to the interpretation of Article 27:

> 'Article 27 constitutes an obstacle to the achievement of one of the fundamental objectives of the Convention, which is to facilitate, to the greatest extent possible, the free movement of judgments ... Article 27 must therefore be interpreted strictly, which precludes treating a court settlement as a judgment given by a court or tribunal.'[17]

In *Krombach v Bamberski*, the Court made clear that the grounds for refusing the recognition and enforcement of judgments laid down in Article 28, also need to be interpreted strictly. The Court indicated in that judgment that, under the system of the Convention, these grounds cannot be extended, for example, by recourse to the public policy clause as in point 1 of Article 27 (compare, Article 28, third paragraph). The Court held that the public policy of the State in which enforcement is sought cannot be raised as a barrier to the recognition or enforcement of a judgment delivered in another Contracting State solely on the ground that the court of origin failed to comply with the rules of the Convention which relate to jurisdiction, with the exception of the cases exhaustively listed in the first paragraph of Article 28. Having regard to the generality of the wording of the third paragraph of Article 28, the Court argued, that this is the case even where the court of the state of origin wrongly founded its jurisdiction, in regard to a defendant domiciled in the territory of the state in which enforcement is sought, on a rule based on a criterion of nationality, in violation of the rules of jurisdiction of the Convention.[18]

---

[16] C-414/92 *Solo v Boch* 20; and, C-7/98 *Krombach v Bamberski* 21 (re 145/86 *Hoffmann v Krieg* 21; C-78/95 *Hendrikman v Magenta* 23),31-33.

[17] C-414/92 *Solo v Boch* 20; compare C-38/98 *Maxicar v Renault II* 26 (re C-414/92 *Solo v Boch* 20, 145/86 *Hoffmann v Krieg* 21, C-78/95 *Hendrikman v Magenta* 23).

[18] C-7/98 *Krombach v Bamberski* 21 (re 145/86 *Hoffmann v Krieg* 21; C-78/95 *Hendrikman v Magenta* 23),31-33.

A strict interpretation is particularly required as regards Article 27, point 1. The Court has stated repeatedly that recourse to the public-policy clause in Article 27, point 1, is only to be had in exceptional cases.[19] In *Hoffmann v Krieg* for example, the Court stated:

> 'it should be noted that, according to the scheme of the Convention, use of the public-policy clause, which "ought to operate only in exceptional cases" (Jenard Report ... p. 44) is in any event precluded when, as here, the issue is whether a foreign judgment is compatible with a national judgment; the issue must be resolved on the basis of the specific provision under Article 27(3)...'[20]

More specifically, it has stated, in *Krombach v Bamberski* as well as in *Maxicar v Renault II*, that the public-policy clause of Article 27, point 1, can be invoked only where recognition or enforcement of the judgment delivered in another Contracting State would be at variance to an unacceptable degree with the legal order of the state in which enforcement is sought inasmuch as it infringes upon a fundamental principle. This infringement would have to constitute a manifest breach of a rule of law regarded as essential in the legal order of the state in which enforcement is sought or of a right recognized as being fundamental within that legal order.[21] The requirement that such a breach has to be 'manifest' is intended to accommodate the prohibition (laid down in Articles 29 and 34, third paragraph) of any review of the foreign judgment as to its substance, as the Court indicated in both judgments.[22] Applying this criterion, the Court has established that Article 27, point 1, does not allow the refusal of recognition or enforcement of a judgment solely on the ground that there is a discrepancy between the legal rule applied by the court of the state of origin and that which would have been applied by the court of the state in which enforcement is sought had it been seised of the dispute.[23] Neither can it refuse recognition or enforcement on the ground that it considers that national or Community law was misapplied in that decision.[24]

The interpretation of Article 27, point 2, needs special attention, because two of the main principles underlying the Convention are pulling in different directions

[19] 145/86 *Hoffmann v Krieg* 21 (re Jenard Report, OJ 1979 C 59, p. 44); C-78/95 *Hendrikman v Magenta* 23 (re Jenard Report, p. 44); C-7/98 *Krombach v Bamberski* 21 (re 145/86 *Hoffmann v Krieg* 21; C-78/95 *Hendrikman v Magenta* 23), compare chapter 4, section 4, text following note 66; and C-38/98 *Maxicar v Renault II* 26 (re C-414/92 *Solo v Boch* 20, 145/86 *Hoffmann v Krieg* 21, C-78/95 *Hendrikman v Magenta* 23).

[20] 145/86 *Hoffmann v Krieg* 21 (re Jenard Report OJ 1979 C 59, p. 44).

[21] C-38/98 *Maxicar v Renault II* 30 (re C-7/98 *Krombach v Bamberski* 37).

[22] C-7/98 *Krombach v Bamberski* 36,37; and C-38/98 *Maxicar v Renault II* 29 (re C-7/98 *Krombach v Bamberski* 36).

[23] C-7/98 *Krombach v Bamberski* 36; C-38/98 *Maxicar v Renault II* 29 (re *Krombach v Bamberski* 36).

[24] C-38/98 *Maxicar v Renault II* 33.

here. Article 27, point 2, ensures that the defendant has an opportunity of arranging for his defence before the court in which judgment is to be delivered.[25] Safeguarding the rights of the defence, Article 27, point 2, is a reflection of what may be seen as one of the most fundamental of the four main principles underlying the Convention: the principle of the protection of the rights of the defence. While the principle of the free movement of judgments, in particular the principle that judgments are to be fully respected in other Contracting States, requires a reduction of the number of grounds of refusal in order to facilitate the recognition and enforcement of judgments and therefore pulls in the direction of a strict interpretation of this provision, the principle of the protection of the rights of the defence may pull in the opposite direction. As will be seen hereafter in chapter 4, the principle of the protection of the rights of the defence requires Article 27, point 2, to be construed sufficiently broadly, so as to ensure the protection of the rights of the defence, as far as possible. The Court has held that view among others in *Klomps v Michel*.[26]

C Art. 22	R 28	C Arts. 50, 51	R 57, 58
C Art. 27 (3 and 5)	R 34 (3 and 4)		

Article 27, point 3, provides for another obstacle to the recognition and enforcement of judgments, in case the foreign judgment is irreconcilable with a judgment delivered in a dispute between the same parties in the state in which recognition is sought (see also, Article 27, point 5). An investigation of the Court's case law shows that the Court favours a restrictive interpretation of this provision with the aim of realizing the principle that full effect should be given to another Contracting State's judgments as much as possible.[27]

This implies, first, as the Court held in *Hoffmann v Krieg*, that in order to ascertain whether two judgments are irreconcilable within the meaning of Article 27, point 3, it should be examined only whether they entail legal consequences that are mutually exclusive.[28] For example, as the Court observed in that judgment, a foreign judgment ordering a person to make maintenance payments to his

[25] 166/80 *Klomps v Michel* 7.

[26] See chapter 4, in particular, section 1.

[27] Compare C-414/92 *Solo v Boch* 20.

[28] 145/86 *Hoffmann v Krieg* 22. 145/86 *Hoffmann v Krieg* 12-20. When answering the questions of the national court with regard to the recognition and enforcement of the foreign judgment, the Court stated, first, 'that a foreign judgment which has been recognized by virtue of Art. 26 of the Convention must in principle have the same effects in the state in which enforcement is sought as it does in the state in which judgment was given' (11). The Court then decided, however, that a foreign judgment whose enforcement has been ordered in a Contracting State pursuant to Art. 31 and which remains enforceable in the state of origin must not continue to be enforced in the state where enforcement is sought when, under the law of the latter state, that judgment ceases to be enforceable for reasons which lie outside the scope of the Convention (18). In a case such as in this judgment, a national court may draw the necessary inferences from a national decree of divorce when considering the enforcement of a foreign maintenance order (12-17).

spouse by virtue of his conjugal obligation to support her, is irreconcilable within the meaning of Article 27, point 3, with a national judgment pronouncing the divorce of the spouses.[29] The irreconcilability of judgments does however not concern the requirements governing admissibility and procedure which determine whether judgment can be given and which may vary from one Contracting State to another. 'Irreconcilability' lies in the effect of the judgments involved, as the Court indicated in *Leather v Polstermöbel*.[30] It should be noted, though, that the term irreconcilability in Article 27, point 3, must, as the Court stated in *Tatry v Maciej Rataj*, be distinguished from the same term in Article 22, since the objectives or underlying principles are different. Article 27, point 3, enables a court, by way of derogation from the principles and objectives of the Convention, particularly the principle of the free movement of judgments, to refuse to recognize a foreign judgment. The objective of the third paragraph of Article 22 is to improve co-ordination of the exercise of judicial functions within the Community as well as to avoid conflicting and contradictory decisions, even where the separate enforcement of each of them is not precluded. Hence, the latter concept, as laid down in Article 22, is broader.[31]

Secondly, a strict interpretation of Article 27, point 3, implies that irreconcilability, within the meaning of Article 27, point 3, is only an obstacle for recognition and enforcement as far as it concerns court judgments. A strict interpretation of Article 27, point 3, implies that a court settlement cannot be treated as a judgment delivered by a court or tribunal, as the Court pointed out in *Solo v Boch*.[32] Irreconcilability is not an obstacle when it concerns the recognition or enforcement of an authentic instrument (Article 50) or a court settlement (Article 51, point 1). As the Court expressly held in *Solo v Boch*, Article 50, point 1, contains only one obstacle: enforcement of an authentic instrument or court settlement in another Contracting State may be refused only if enforcement is contrary to public policy in the State in which enforcement is sought. [33]

Although the principle of 'free movement of judgments', in particular the principle of full respect for another Contracting State's judgments, requires that Articles 27 and 28 be interpreted strictly, it can be assumed that, in the light of the interests and principles underlying these provisions, they should not be construed

---

[29] 145/86 *Hoffmann v Krieg* 25.

[30] C-80/00 *Leather v Polstermöbel* 44 (re 145/86 *Hoffmann v Krieg* 22).

[31] C-406/92 *Tatry v Maciej Rataj* 54; see hereafter also chapter 6, section 3.2.2, text following note 446.

[32] C-414/92 *Solo v Boch* 20, compare note 8 of this section.

[33] C-414/92 *Solo v Boch* 24. From this judgment it does not follow, however, that the term 'authentic instrument' should be construed extensively. As we have seen before (note 8), an acknowledgment of indebtedness which is enforceable under the law of the State of origin whose authenticity has not been established by a public authority does not constitute an authentic instrument within the meaning of Art. 50 (C-260/97 *Unibank v Christensen* 15,21).

in such a way as to make them fully redundant. An interpretation that would deprive these provisions of their legal effect, cannot be accepted.[34]

C Art. 21 to 23	R 27 to 30	C Art. 5	R 5	C Art. 27	R 34
C Art. 6	R 6	C Art. 17	R 23		

The principle of the free movement of judgments, in the form of the sub-principle that full effect should be given to foreign judgments, also has an influence on the interpretation of the Convention's provisions regarding the original procedure that are contained in Title II. The principle that full effect should be given to foreign judgments prescribes that these provisions should be interpreted in a way that minimizes the chances of a situation arising that could lead to a reason for refusing the recognition or enforcement of judgments in other Contracting States. In the Court's case law, particularly the ground for the refusal of judgments contained in Article 27, point 3, plays a role in this respect. The guideline that irreconcilable judgments should be avoided, thereby minimizing the possibility of Article 27, point 3, having to be invoked, figures in a number of decisions pertaining to provisions laid down in Title II.

The influence of the sub-principle that full effect should be given to foreign judgments is particularly evident in the Court's case law regarding Article 21 on *lis pendens*, and Article 22 on related actions (compare also Article 23). The Court implicitly refers to that principle in *Gubisch v Palumbo*. In that judgment, the Court stated that:

> 'Article 21, together with Article 22 on related actions, is contained in Section 8 of Title II of the Convention; that section is intended ... to prevent parallel proceedings before the courts of different Contracting States and to avoid conflicts between decisions which might result therefrom. Those rules are therefore designed to preclude, in so far as is possible and from the outset, the possibility of a situation arising such as that referred to in Article 27, point 3, that is to say the non-recognition of a judgment on account of its irreconcilability with a judgment given in a dispute between the same parties in the state in which recognition is sought.'[35]

In order to meet the sub-principle that full effect should be given to foreign judgments, the Court has indicated that Articles 21 and 22 should be interpreted sufficiently widely so as to avoid a situation of irreconcilability of judgments. For example, the Court has stated in *OUI v NHIC*, that Article 21 must be interpreted broadly so as to cover, in principle, all situations of *lis pendens* before courts in Contracting States, irrespective of the parties' domicile.[36] There is, however, a

[34] Compare chapter 6, section 3.1, text following note 196.

[35] 144/86 *Gubisch v Palumbo* 8,18; compare C-406/92 *Tatry v Maciej Rataj* 31,51 (re Jenard Report, OJ 1979 C 59, p. 41),52; and C-351/96 *Drouot v CMI* 17 (re *Tatry* 31).

[36] C-351/89 *OUI v NHIC* 15 (re C-220/88 *Dumez France v Hessische Landesbank*),16 (re 144/86 *Gubisch v Palumbo*),17 (re *Gubisch v Palumbo* and *Dumez France v Hessische Landesbank*),18.

limit to the extent to which Articles 21 to 23 can be applied. This limit lies, in accordance with the principle of legal certainty, at any rate in the wording of these provisions. Since, other principles also have an influence on the interpretation of these provisions, we will discuss these interpretations in further detail later in this study.[37]

The principle that judgments are to be fully respected in other Contracting States also has an influence on the interpretation of other rules laid down in Title II of the Convention, particularly those conferring jurisdiction on the national courts: these provisions are therefore also to be interpreted so as to limit the risk of irreconcilable judgments.[38]

The Court has made clear, for example in *Kalfelis v Schröder*, that it is aware of the Convention's concern with the principle that judgments are to be fully respected in other Contracting States, particularly in relation to the obstacle 'irreconcilable judgments'. In that judgment the Court had to answer questions on the interpretation of Article 6, point 1, which provides that a person domiciled in a Contracting State may also be sued, where he is one of a number of defendants, in the courts of the place where any one of them is domiciled. Referring to the Jenard Report, the Court, argued its (apparently broad) interpretation of Article 6, point 1, as regards the connection which must exist between the claims made by the plaintiff against the defendants involved. The Court stated in this respect:

> 'The rule laid down in Article 6(1) therefore applies where the actions brought against the various defendants are related when the proceedings are instituted, that is to say where it is expedient to hear and determine them together in order to avoid the risk of irreconcilable judgments resulting from separate proceedings. It is for the national court to verify in each individual case whether that condition is satisfied.'[39]

The principle that judgments are to be fully respected in other Contracting States has also influenced the interpretation of Article 5. It requires, as regards the special jurisdictions provided for in Article 5, that the creation of a situation in which a number of courts have jurisdiction in respect of one and the same legal relationship should be avoided. As the Court put it recently in *Besix v Kretzschmar*, this is required 'in order to preclude the risk of irreconcilable decisions and to facilitate the recognition and enforcement of judgments in States other than those in which they were delivered'.[40] The requirement to interpret

---

[37] Compare C-406/92 *Tatry v Maciej Rataj* 32; and see chapter 5, section 2, and chapter 6, in particular section 3.2.2.

[38] 189/87 *Kalfelis v Schröder* 11 (re Jenard Report, OJ 1979 C. 59, p. 27); C-51/97 *Réunion européenne v Spliethoff's* 48.

[39] 189/87 *Kalfelis v Schröder* 12.

[40] C-256/00 *Besix v Kretzschmar* 27 (re 14/76 *De Bloos* 9; 266/85 *Shenavai* 8; C-125/92 *Mulox* 21; C-383/95 *Rutten* 18; C-420/97 *Leathertex* 31),28.

rules of jurisdiction in such a manner so as to avoid irreconcilable decisions also has, for example, an influence on the interpretation of Article 17.[41]

Since other principles underlying the Convention, such as the main principle of legal certainty and the main principle that disputes should be decided by an appropriate court, also apply to these provisions laid down in Title II of the Convention and have an influence on how these provisions are to be construed, we will elaborate on these issues in further detail hereafter.[42]

2. THE PRINCIPLE OF A *SWIFT* AND *SIMPLE* PROCEDURE FOR THE RECOGNITION AND ENFORCEMENT OF ANOTHER CONTRACTING STATE'S JUDGMENTS

C Art. 31 to 49 R 38 to 56

The second sub-principle implied by 'free movement of judgments' concerns the requirement that the party seeking recognition and enforcement of a foreign judgment delivered in his favour should not be impeded by procedural obstacles. From the point of view of the free movement of judgments, the ideal would be that a foreign judgment's recognition and enforcement would be automatic, without any special procedure for recognition or enforcement in other Contracting States being required. However, if some procedure would be required, the principle of free movement of judgments implies that it should not constitute a real obstacle: the procedure would have to be simple and swift.

The following quotation, taken from *Coursier v Fortis*, illustrates the Court's willingness to interpret the rules regarding the enforcement procedure in a way that keeps the procedure as simple and as expeditious as possible. When answering questions from the national court on the interpretation of provisions concerning the enforcement procedure, the Court stated:

> 'The Brussels Convention is intended to facilitate the free movement of judgments by establishing a simple and rapid procedure in the Contracting State where enforcement of a foreign decision is applied for ... Thus, under Article 34 of the Brussels Convention, the procedure for obtaining authorisation for enforcement is carried out with the utmost speed ...'[43]

---

[41] Compare 23/78 *Meeth v Glacetal* 7-9; C-269/95 *Benincasa v Dentalkit* 31 (re C-214/89 *Duffryn v Petereit* 33),32; and see chapter 5, section 4.2.2, text following note 143.

[42] See, in particular, chapter 5, section 4.2, text following note 116 and section 5, text following note 159, and chapter 6.

[43] C-267/97 *Coursier v Fortis* 25 (re 148/84 *Deutsche Genossenschaftsbank v Brasserie du Pêcheur* 17; C-172/91 *Sonntag v Waidmann* 32,33); C-183/90 *Dalfsen v Van Loon* 21; and compare C-414/92 *Solo v Boch* 20; C-7/98 *Krombach v Bamberski* 19 (re C-414/92 *Solo v Boch* 20; C-267/97 *Coursier v Fortis* 25); and C-38/98 *Maxicar v Renault II* 20 (re *Krombach* 19),21 (re 178/83 *P v K* 11).

The principle is expressed in the Convention's provisions, laid down in Title III of the Convention, Articles 31 to 49, particularly, in Article 31, the first and third paragraph of Article 34 and Article 35. These provisions provide for a simple procedure for securing the enforcement of judgments. They constitute an autonomous and complete system, to which, as the Court stated in *Coursier v Fortis*, no further complicating factors may be added.[44] The procedure for obtaining authorisation for enforcement is to be carried out with the utmost speed. The national court shall give its decision without delay and under no circumstances may the foreign judgment be reviewed as to its substance.[45]

The principle of a swift and simple enforcement of another Contracting State's judgments weighed in relation to other principles

C Art. 31	R 38	C Art. 35	R 42(1)
C Art. 32	R 39	C Art. 36 (1st and 2nd para.)	R 43 (1 and 5)
C Art. 33 (2nd para.)	R 40(2)	C Art. 37	R 44
C Art. 34	R 41	C Art. 38 (1st para.)	R 46(1)

The principle of a swift and simple enforcement procedure would require the Court to interpret the rules pertaining to the enforcement procedure in a way that keeps the procedure as simple and as quick as possible. As is apparent from the following description of the Court's case law, *(a)* the Court tends to consistently restrict the procedural requirements that are laid down in the Convention as far as possible, thereby attributing a great deal of weight to the principle of the free movement of judgments. However, as will be seen as we go along, it is evident from certain provisions of Title III of the Convention and from the Court's case law on the interpretation of these provisions that, *(b)* the principle of a swift and simple enforcement procedure finds its limitations in the guarantees that are needed to secure the rights of the defence.

Especially with respect to the initial *ex parte* phase of the enforcement procedure (Articles 31 to 35), the Court has held that this is intended to enable the applicant seeking enforcement of a judgment in another Contracting State to obtain satisfaction swiftly.[46] In this respect, the Court states for example in *Carron v Federal Republic of Germany*:

> 'It must be pointed out that in Articles 31 to 49 the Convention establishes an enforcement procedure common to all Member States. At the initial ex parte stage, that procedure enables the applicant seeking enforcement of a judgment in another Member State to obtain satisfaction swiftly.'[47]

[44] Compare C-267/97 *Coursier v Fortis* 25 (re 148/84 *Deutsche Genossenschaftsbank v Brasserie du Pêcheur* 16,17; and, C-172/91 *Sonntag v Waidmann* 32, 33).

[45] Compare C-183/90 *Dalfsen v Van Loon* 31; C-267/97 *Coursier v Fortis* 26.

[46] 125/79 *Denilauler v Couchet Frères* 14; 178/83 *P v K* 11 (re *Denilauler*); 119/84 *Capelloni v Pelkmans* 15 (re 258/83 *Brennero)*; 198/85 *Carron v Federal Republic Germany* 8,14.

[47] 198/85 *Carron v Federal Republic of Germany* 8.

The purpose of a rapid enforcement procedure, particularly at the initial stage (Articles 31 to 35), is to produce the necessary surprise effect and to prevent a defendant from having the opportunity to protect his assets against enforcement measures. The Court has established this in several cases, among others in *Denilauler v Couchet Frères*: the unilateral character of the first phase of the enforcement procedure under Article 34, first paragraph, is intended to fully safeguard that surprise effect.[48]

The principle of a simple and rapid enforcement procedure has guided the Court in a number of decisions, of which the following judgments are illustrative.

In *Coursier v Fortis*, for example, the Court had to answer a question on the interpretation of the term 'enforceable' in Article 31. This Article provides that a judgment given in a Contracting State and 'enforceable' in that State shall be enforced in another Contracting State, when on the application of any interested party, it has been declared enforceable there. The Court held that the term 'enforceable' has to be interpreted narrowly, in that it solely refers to the enforceability, in formal terms, of foreign decisions and not to the circumstances in which such decisions may be executed in the state of origin.[49] The Court referred expressly to the principle of a swift and simple enforcement of another Contracting State's judgments.[50]

In *Brennero v Wendel*, the Court stated that the second paragraph of Article 37, providing that the judgment delivered on appeal against the decision authorizing enforcement may be contested by an appeal in cassation, cannot be extended so as to enable an appeal in cassation to be lodged against a judgment other than that given on appeal, as for instance, against a preliminary or interlocutory order requiring preliminary inquiries to be made. The Court justified its decision by referring to the specific objective of the Convention of simplifying and speeding up procedures in the state in which enforcement is sought and to the general scheme of Title III of the Convention.[51]

In *Dalfsen v Van Loon*, the Court recalled its judgment in *Brennero v Wendel*, when it argued that the concept of 'judgment given on the appeal (against the decision authorizing enforcement)' must indeed be interpreted strictly, in order to prevent that an excessive number of avenues of appeal might be used by the los-

---

[48] 125/79 *Denilauler v Couchet Frères* 14; 178/83 *P v K* 11 (re *Denilauler*); 258/83 *Brennero v Wendel* 10; 198/85 *Carron v Federal Republic of Germany* 8; C-267/97 *Coursier v Fortis* 26; C-38/98 *Maxicar v Renault II* 21 (re 178/83 *P v K* 11).

[49] C-267/97 *Coursier v Fortis* 29. The case was concerned with a judgment closing a court-supervised liquidation for lack of assets, which has the effect in the state of origin of preventing creditors individually from bringing action against the debtor.

[50] C-267/97 *Coursier v Fortis* 25 (re 148/84 *Deutsche Genossenschaftsbank* 17; C-172/91 *Sonntag v Waidmann* 32,33).

[51] 258/83 *Brennero v Wendel* 15.

ing party purely as delaying tactics.[52] The Court, referring to the Jenard Report, held that:

> 'The committee of experts set up on the occasion of the drafting of the Convention ... also emphasized the need for a strict interpretation of the second paragraph of Article 37 of the Convention. According to that report, "an excessive number of avenues of appeal might be used by the losing party purely as delaying tactics, and this would constitute an obstacle to the free movement of judgments which is the object of the Convention".'[53]

Hence, the Court decided that 'judgment given on the appeal' lodged against an enforcement order, in the second paragraph of Article 37, must be interpreted as denoting only judgments deciding on the substance of the appeal, to the exclusion of judgments given under Article 38.[54]

In *SISRO v Ampersand*, the Court continued this line of reasoning. It stated that a decision taken under Article 38 by which a national court has refused to stay the proceedings or by which it has lifted a stay previously ordered, does not constitute a 'judgment given on the appeal' within the meaning of Article 37, second paragraph.[55]

From the perspective of a simple and rapid enforcement procedure, it furthermore follows, as the Court observed in *Deutsche Genossenschaftsbank v Brasserie du Pêcheur*, that Article 36 excludes any procedure whereby interested third parties may challenge an enforcement order, even where such a procedure is available to third parties under the domestic law of the state in which the enforcement order is granted.[56] This principle applies as well to a subsequent appeal brought under Article 37, second paragraph, as the Court argued in *Sonntag v Waidmann*:

> 'To preclude an interested third party from bringing an appeal under Article 36, whilst allowing that party to intervene at a later stage in the proceedings by means of an appeal under Article 37, would be contrary to the abovementioned system [of the enforcement procedure, *ebjp*] and also to one of the principal objectives of the Convention, which is to simplify the procedure in the State in which enforcement is sought.'[57]

---

[52] C-183/90 *Dalfsen v Van Loon* 19 (re 258/83 *Brennero v Wendel* 15),20 (re Jenard Report, OJ 1979 C 59, p. 1).

[53] C-183/90 *Dalfsen v Van Loon* 20 (re Jenard Report, OJ 1979 C 59, p. 1); compare, C-172/91 *Sonntag v Waidmann* 32 (re 258/83 *Brennero v Wendel* 15; C-183/90 *Dalfsen v Van Loon* 19); C-432/93 *SISRO v Ampersand* 28(re Jenard Report, OJ 1979 C 59, p. 52; Schlosser Report, OJ 1979 C 59, p. 133)30 (re 258/83 *Brennero v Wendel* 15),31(re C-183/90 *Dalfsen v Van Loon* 21).

[54] C-183/90 *Dalfsen v Van Loon* 21.

[55] C-432/93 *SISRO v Ampersand* 31 (re C-183/90 *Dalfsen v Van Loon* 21),32-33. In this judgment the Court also referred to the wording and the general scheme of the Convention (34).

[56] 148/84 *Deutsche Genossenschaftsbank v Brasserie du Pêcheur* 16 (re 258/83 *Brennero v Wendel*),17-19; and, C-172/91 *Sonntag v Waidmann* 33 (re *Deutsche Genossenschaftsbank* 17).

[57] C-172/91 *Sonntag v Waidmann* 34.

The Convention only regulates the procedure for obtaining an order for the enforcement of foreign judgments and does not deal with the execution itself. The execution continues to be governed by the domestic law of the state in which execution is sought. The Court has however held that those domestic rules regarding the execution, including those on legal remedies, may not impair the effectiveness of the Convention, of which the principal objective is 'to simplify procedures in the state in which enforcement is sought'.[58] In the light of this requirement, the Court stated in *Hoffmann v Krieg* that the legal remedies available under national law must be precluded when an appeal against the execution of a foreign judgment for which an enforcement order has been issued, is lodged by the same person who could have appealed against the enforcement order and is based on an argument which could have been raised in such an appeal. In those circumstances, to challenge the execution would be tantamount to again calling into question the enforcement order after the expiry of the strict time-limit laid down by the second paragraph of Article 36, and would thereby render that provision ineffective. In view of the mandatory nature of the time-limit laid down in Article 36, the national court must ensure that it is observed. It should therefore of its own motion dismiss as inadmissible an appeal lodged pursuant to national law when that appeal has the effect of circumventing that time-limit. According to the Court, Article 36 must therefore be interpreted, meaning that:

> 'a party who has not appealed against the enforcement order referred to in that provision is thereafter precluded, at the stage of execution of the judgment, from relying on a valid ground which he could have pleaded in such an appeal against the enforcement order, and that that rule must be applied of their own motion by the courts of the state in which enforcement is sought.'[59]

The same argument, that a valid ground which could be pleaded at an earlier stage of the proceedings must be precluded at a later stage, applies when interpreting Article 38, first paragraph. This provision stipulates that the court with which the appeal under Article 37, first paragraph, is lodged may, on the application of the appellant, stay the proceedings if an ordinary appeal has been lodged against the judgment in the state of origin; if the time for such an appeal has not yet expired in the latter case, the court may specify the time within which such an appeal is to be lodged. Since the first paragraph of Article 38 constitutes a derogation from the principle of free movement of judgments, particularly from the principle of a swift and simple enforcement procedure, it must be interpreted strictly.[60] Thereby, the Court held in *Dalfsen v Van Loon*:

---

[58] Compare 148/84 *Deutsche Genossenschaftsbank v Brasserie du Pêcheur* 16 (re 258/83 *Brennero v Wendel)*-19; compare chapter 5, section 1.2, text following note 47.

[59] 145/86 *Hoffmann v Krieg* 34, and 27 (re 148/84 *Deutsche Genossenschaftsbank v Brasserie du Pêcheur*),28-30.

[60] C-183/90 *Dalfsen v Van Loon* 30.

> 'The scheme of the Convention and in particular the principle of the free movement of judgments, which is one of the Convention's essential objects, prevents a party from invoking before the court called upon to decide, under the first paragraph of Article 38, upon an application for a stay of the proceedings in the appeal lodged against the enforcement order, grounds which he could have pleaded before the foreign court.'[61]

The principle of free movement of judgments, including the principle of a swift and simple procedure for the recognition and enforcement of another Contracting State's judgment, does not work as an absolute though. In this respect, the Court has consistently held that the requirement of speeding up enforcement procedures finds its limitations in the guarantees needed to secure the rights of the defendant. For example, under the Convention, the person against whom enforcement is sought will not be heard in the initial stage of the enforcement procedure, in order to produce the necessary surprise effect. In the second stage of the enforcement procedure, the rights of the defendant are respected, however. As is evident from the provisions of the Convention, in particular Articles 36 to 41, the enforcement procedure loses its unilateral character in the second stage of the enforcement procedure. At that stage, the person against whom enforcement is sought is entitled to be heard by virtue of Article 36. The Court has confirmed this in quite a number of cases in which it referred to the principle of the protection of the rights of the defence and used it to arrive at its interpretation.[62] Since the principle of the protection of the rights of the defence will be discussed in more detail in the next chapter, we will elaborate on this and other issues in that chapter.[63]

In *Carron v Federal Republic of Germany,* when answering questions on the interpretation of Article 33, the Court balanced the interests of both parties: the party seeking enforcement and the defendant, being the party against whom enforcement is sought. Article 33, second paragraph, requires that the applicant for the enforcement order must give an address for service of process within the area of jurisdiction of the court applied to. Article 35 provides that the decision given on the application should be brought to the notice of the applicant without delay. Since the Convention provides no sanction for failure to comply with Article 33, that sanction must, like the other procedural rules, be determined by the law of the state in which enforcement is sought. Such a sanction must, however, conform to the aims of the Convention. In this respect, the Court stated that the sanction provided for in the domestic law 'may neither cast doubt on the validity of the enforcement order nor in any way prejudice the rights of the party against whom enforcement is sought'.[64]

---

[61] C-183/90 *Dalfsen v Van Loon* 35.

[62] 125/79 *Denilauler v Couchet Frères* 13,14; 178/83 *P v K* 11 (re *Denilauler*); 258/83 *Brennero v Wendel* 10; 198/85 *Carron v Federal Republic of Germany* 8; C-38/98 *Maxicar v Renault II* 21 (re 178/83 *P v K* 11); and see chapter 4, section 3, text following note 53.

[63] See chapter 4, in particular, sections 1,3,5 and 6.

[64] 198/85 *Carron v Federal Republic of Germany* 14, and 13,15.

CONCLUSIONS AND SUMMARY

We may conclude from the foregoing that it follows from the Preamble of the Convention, from the provisions laid down in Title III of the Convention (in particular Articles 31 to 49) and from the Court's case law, that the principle of the free movement of judgments is firmly established. This principle, that flows from the most general principle of strengthening the legal protection of a person established within the Community, has a major impact on the interpretation of the provisions which have directly been generated by that principle as well as on the interpretation of other provisions of the Convention. The principle of free movement of judgments contains two more concrete principles which guide the Court's interpretation of the Convention. The following scheme of the first main principle can be presented:

(1) The Principle of Free Movement of Judgments
entails:

(1.1) Full respect for another Contracting State's judgments

(1.2) A swift and simple procedure for recognition and enforcement

Each of these sub-principles in turn contains more specific requirements. The main requirements flowing from these sub-principles are:

(1.1) Full respect for another Contracting State's judgments, *requires*:
- a restrictive interpretation of the exception of public policy and other obstacles to the recognition and enforcement of judgments provided for by the Convention, and
- an interpretation of the provisions on jurisdiction of Title II of the Convention so as to avoid irreconcilable decisions

(1.2) Swift and simple recognition and enforcement proceedings, *requires*:
- the unilateral character of enforcement proceedings, at least in the initial phase of the procedure so as to safeguard the surprise effect of execution proceedings
- an interpretation of the provisions concerning the enforcement proceedings, in such a way as to safeguard a swift satisfaction, implying among other things: restriction of the number of avenues of appeal; a prohibition on invoking a ground which could have been pleaded previously; no intervention by a third party, and a swift satisfaction of judgments not to be frustrated by national procedural law.

Chapter 4
THE SECOND MAIN PRINCIPLE: THE PROTECTION OF THE RIGHTS OF THE DEFENCE

INTRODUCTION

Unlike the principle of the free movement of judgments, the principle of legal certainty and the principle that disputes should be decided by an appropriate court, the principle of the protection of the rights of the defence has not been a motivating force for the creation of the Convention in the sense that it has been a primary aim. Hence, the principle of the protection of the rights of the defence is not to be found in the Preamble to the Convention. Nevertheless, this principle has played a significant role in the design of the Convention's rules on jurisdiction and on the recognition and enforcement of judgments: an important consideration of the designers of the Convention was that it should be constructed in such a way that sufficient regard would be paid to the protection of the rights of the defendant. The Court also takes account of this principle when interpreting the Convention's provisions. In *Denilauler v Couchet Frères*, the Court captured the significance of the principle of the protection of the rights of the defence in the context of the Convention as follows:

> 'All the provisions of the Convention, both those contained in Title II on jurisdiction and those contained in Title III on recognition and enforcement, express the intention to ensure that, within the scope of the objectives of the Convention, proceedings leading to the delivery of judicial decisions take place in such a way that the rights of the defence are observed.'[1]

Clearly, the principle of the protection of the rights of the defence can be subsumed under the most general principle that underlies the Convention as a whole, namely, the principle of (strengthening) the legal protection of persons established in the Community.[2]

In the context of the Convention, there are two proceedings leading to the delivery of judicial decisions in which, as the Court states in the above quotation, the rights of the defence need to be observed: the original proceedings and the proceedings that may take place in the phase of the recognition and enforcement of the original judgment. It should be noted that observing the rights of the de-

---

[1] 125/79 *Denilauler v Couchet Frères* 13. The Court confirmed this in C-474/93 *Hengst v Campese* 16 (re 125/79 *Denilauler v Couchet Frères* 13); see also 166/80 *Klomps v Michel* 7.

[2] Compare chapter 2, section 1, text following note 17.

fence in the original proceedings is considered to be of particular importance. The idea is that the more the defendant is protected in the original proceedings, the more justified it is to be very liberal with regard to the recognition and enforcement of the resulting judgment. As the Court formulated this in *Denilauler v Couchet Frères*:

> 'It is because of the guarantees given to the defendant in the original proceedings that the Convention, in Title III, is very liberal in regard to recognition and enforcement.'[3]

Within the context of the Convention, more concrete principles give further substance to the rather indeterminate notion that the rights of the defence are to be observed. These more concrete principles all relate to current procedural principles, such as those requiring fair notice, fair hearing and, more generally, a fair legal process.

Protection of the rights of the defence implies, first of all, a proper service of the documents instituting the proceedings: the defendant should be informed of the fact that proceedings are instituted against him; he should have the opportunity to appear in court and to prepare his defence before court proceedings commence. Within the context of the Convention, protection of the defendant implies, secondly, that the defendant should be heard before an appropriate court, ideally in the court of the state of his domicile.

In addition, the principle of protecting the rights of the defence implies the defendant's right to legal proceedings with an *inter partes* character, the defendant's right to have a fair opportunity to state the substance of his case, the defendant's right to be defended by a lawyer and the defendant's interest as to the stay of the execution proceedings when an appeal has been lodged in the state of origin. Finally, within the context of the Convention, protection of the rights of the defence also refers to the right to be properly served with the decision delivered.

Summarising, the manifold aspects of the second main principle, the principle of the protection of the rights of the defence, can be encapsulated by the following sub-principles:

(1) the defendant's right to a proper service of the document instituting the proceedings
(2) the defendant's right to be heard in an appropriate court, ideally in the court of the state of his domicile
(3) the defendant's right to an *inter partes* hearing
(4) the right to be defended by a lawyer
(5) the right to submit a defence on the substance of the case

---

[3] 125/79 *Denilauler v Couchet Frères* 13.

(6) the defendant's interest as to the stay of execution proceedings when an appeal has been lodged in the state of origin
(7) the defendant's right to be properly served with the decision delivered

As will be seen below, each of these issues illustrates different aspects of the principle of the protection of the rights of the defence. Each of them contributes to a fair opportunity for the defendant to defend his case or, once a judgment based on fair proceedings is delivered against him, to comply with that judgment. In the following sections, we will examine what these sub-principles require in particular and how they are weighed in relation to other principles that underlie the Convention.

1. THE DEFENDANT'S RIGHT TO A PROPER SERVICE OF THE DOCUMENT INSTITUTING THE PROCEEDINGS

C Art. 20	R 26	C Art. 34 (2nd para.)	R 41,45
C Art. 27(2)	R 34(2)	C Art. 34 (3rd para.)	R 45(2)
C Art. 29	R 36	C Art. 46(2)	R 53(2)

The defendant's right to a proper service of the document instituting the proceedings is an important aspect of the more general principle of the protection of the rights of the defence. It requires fair notice of the institution of proceedings and is one of the fundamental principles of civil procedure. Several Articles in the Convention are an expression of the right of the defendant to be properly informed of the fact that proceedings will be instituted against him. Article 20, second paragraph, laid down in Title II of the Convention, provides that, where a defendant domiciled in one Contracting State is sued in a court of another Contracting State and does not enter an appearance, the national court shall stay the proceedings so long as it is not shown that the defendant has been able to receive the document instituting the proceedings or an equivalent document in sufficient time to enable him to arrange for his defence, or that all necessary steps have been taken to this end. Judgments given in default of the defendant's appearance are allowed, but only after the national court has established that the conditions of Article 20 have been complied with. The importance attached to this right to a proper service of the document instituting the proceedings is stressed by the fact that it reappears in the context of the recognition and enforcement of judgments in Title III of the Convention. Article 27, point 2, in conjunction with Article 34, second paragraph, provides that a judgment shall not be recognized and enforced, where it was given in default of appearance, if the defendant was not duly served with the document which instituted the proceedings or with an equivalent document in sufficient time to enable him to arrange for his defence. In light of this ground for refusing recognition and enforcement, Article 46, point 2, requires that a party seeking recognition or applying for enforcement in one Contracting State of a judgment given in default in another Contracting State, should produce the original or a certified true copy of the document which establishes that the party in default was served with the document instituting the proceedings.[4]

The defendant's right to a proper service of the document instituting the proceedings weighed in relation to other principles

The way in which the defendant's right to be properly informed of the fact that proceedings have been instituted against him has been incorporated in the provisions of the Convention, illustrates the great weight that the designers of the Convention attached to this principle. The Convention not only requires that the court in the original proceedings establishes that this right is observed, but it even allows for a second check as to whether this right has been observed when recognition and enforcement is sought in another Contracting State of a judgment given in default. Non-observance is a reason for refusing the recognition and enforcement of such a judgment. The principle of the free movement of judgments which, as was seen in the previous chapter, requires that no ground for refusing a foreign judgment be allowed, is in the case of judgments given in default (almost) completely outweighed by the defendant's right to be properly served with the document instituting the proceedings.[5] However, when examining the Court's case law with respect to the latter principle, it becomes evident that, under the Convention, there are limits to the extent to which that principle applies.

The importance that the Court attaches to the right to a proper service of the document instituting the proceedings appears in particular from its case law on the interpretation of Article 27, point 2. In *Klomps v Michel*, for example, the Court referred to the significance of that right in light of the Convention as a whole. In that judgment, the Court first recalled that Title II of the Convention contains provisions regulating directly and in detail the jurisdiction of the courts of the state in which a judgment was delivered, and also provisions concerning the verification of that jurisdiction and of admissibility, and that these provisions are of such a nature as to protect the interests of defendants.[6] Next, the Court stated that because of these provisions laid down in Title II of the Convention, it is possible at the stage of recognition and enforcement, which is governed by

---

[4] Compare 228/81 *Pendy v Pluspunkt* 10.

[5] See chapter 3, section 1, text following note 25; compare 49/84 *Debaecker v Bouwman* 10; C-305/88 *Lancray v Peters* 21 (re 49/84 *Debaecker v Bouwman*); C-78/95 *Hendrikman v Magenta* 15 (re 166/80 *Klomps v Michel* 9; C-172/91 *Sonntag v Waidmann* 38). The principle is weakened, though, under Regulation 44/2001. Under that regulation (see Arts. 41 and 45) the party against whom enforcement it sought has to invoke that right himself. The Court is no longer allowed to examine of its own motion whether that right has been complied with, but only when an appeal has been lodged.

[6] 166/80 *Klomps v Michel* 7; compare note 1 of the introduction of this chapter.

Title III of the Convention, to facilitate the free movement of judgments within the Community by simplifying the procedure for recognition and enforcement of judgments and by reducing the number of grounds which may operate to prevent the recognition and enforcement thereof. Nonetheless, as the Court pointed out then, one of these grounds for refusal was intended for the sole purpose of safeguarding the rights of the defendant and was laid down in Article 27, point 2.[7] That ground for refusing recognition cannot be easily ignored. As the Court put it, Article 27, point 2, provides for a ground for refusing the recognition and, read together with Article 34, for refusing to enforce foreign judgments, for those cases where the guarantees contained in the law of the state in which the judgment was delivered and in the Convention itself (Article 20 second and third paragraph) are insufficient.[8]

In *Minalmet v Brandeis* and *Sonntag v Waidman*, the Court again expressed its concern with the right to a proper service of the document instituting the proceedings. It consistently held in these judgments that Article 27, point 2, is intended to uphold the rights of the defence and to ensure that a judgment is not recognized or enforced, if the defendant has not had an opportunity to defend himself before the Court first seised.[9] Moreover, and in accordance with a series of earlier decisions, the Court stated in this respect, that although the Convention is intended to 'secure the simplification of formalities governing the reciprocal recognition and enforcement of judgments of courts or tribunals', that aim cannot be attained by undermining in any way the right to a fair hearing.[10]

To ensure the right to a proper service of the document instituting the proceedings, the Court has sought, first of all, a proper understanding of the terms constituting the scope of Article 27, point 2, which usually implies that the provision should be interpreted independently, in the light of the underlying principle(s).

For instance, the Court has concluded that a 'Vollstreckungsbefehl' (an enforcement order, which is issued following the service of an order for payment) in German law is (naturally) not covered by the words 'document which instituted the proceedings' in Article 27, point 2, whereas a 'Zahlungsbefehl' (order for payment) in German law and the 'decreto ingiuntivo' (together with the application instituting the proceedings) in Italian law, must be regarded as the document which instituted the proceedings or an equivalent document within the meaning of Article 27, point 2.[11]

---

[7] 166/80 *Klomps v Michel* 7; compare 49/84 *Debaecker v Bouwman* 10; C-305/88 *Lancray v Peters* 21 (re 49/84 *Debaecker v Bouwman* 10).

[8] 166/80 *Klomps v Michel* 7.

[9] C-123/91 *Minalmet v Brandeis* 18 (re 166/80 *Klomps v Michel*); and C-172/91 *Sonntag v Waidmann* 38 (re 166/80 *Klomps v Michel* 9, C-123/91 *Minalmet v Brandeis* 18).

[10] In particular, 49/84 *Debaecker v Bouwman* 10; and 305/88 *Lancray v Peters* 21 (re 49/84 *Debaecker*).

[11] 166/80 *Klomps v Michel* 9. Notice that the Court in particular respects the linguistic boundaries of Art. 27, point 2, in accordance with the principle of legal certainty; see hereafter chapter 5, section 2, text following note 56; see also C-474/93 *Hengst v Campese* 26.

Not only has the Court sought a proper understanding of the words 'document which instituted the proceedings', but it has also clarified the words 'judgment given in default of appearance' in Article 27, point 2.[12] As follows from that provision, the ground for refusing recognition and enforcement under Article 27, point 2, can only be invoked successfully, if the judgment is given in default. In this respect, the Court has held, in *Klomps v Michel*, that in a case in which the defendant has lodged an objection against the decision given in default by the court first seised and that court has held that objection to be inadmissible on the ground that the time for lodging an objection has expired, such a decision remains in principle a decision in default. Therefore, Article 27, point 2, remains applicable. In a case in which the defendant did not submit a defence as to the substance of the case, it is required that the court in the state in which enforcement is sought should carry out the examination prescribed by that provision.[13]

Thus, the non-recognition of a judgment for the reasons set out in Article 27, point 2, is possible only where the defendant was in default of appearance in the original proceedings. Consequently, as the Court pointed out in *Sonntag v Waidmann*, that provision may not be relied upon where the defendant entered an appearance.[14] The Court stated in that judgment, that a defendant is even deemed to have entered an appearance for the purposes of Article 27, point 2, where, in connection with a claim for compensation joined to criminal proceedings, he answered at the trial, through a counsel of his own choice, to the criminal charges but did not express a view on the civil claim, on which oral argument was also submitted in the presence of his counsel.[15] However, as the Court held in *Hendrikman v Magenta*, a judgment delivered in a situation in which someone purporting to represent the defendant appeared before the court first seised, but without the knowledge and authority of the defendant, is a 'judgment given in default of appearance' in the sense of Article 27, point 2. That provision is applicable to such judgments, because the defendant was not duly served with, or notified of, the document instituting proceedings in sufficient time and was not validly represented during the proceedings.[16]

---

[12] 166/80 *Klomps v Michel* 12,13; C-172/91 *Sonntag v Waidmann* 39,43; C-78/95 *Hendrikman v Magenta* 21.

[13] 166/80 *Klomps v Michel* 12,13. Compare in this respect Art. 34, point 2, of Regulation 44/2001.

[14] C-172/91 *Sonntag v Waidmann* 39.

[15] C-172/91 *Sonntag v Waidmann* 40-44; see also this chapter, section 4, text following note 60.

[16] C-78/95 *Hendrikman v Magenta* 18-20 (re C-123/91 *Minalmet v Brandeis* 19),21. The judgments *Hendrikman v Magenta* and *Klomps v Michel,* which have just been discussed here in the context of the right to a proper service of the document instituting the proceedings, are also relevant in the context of the defendant's right to be defended by a lawyer and the defendant's right to submit a defence on the substance of the case. These aspects of the principle of the protection of the rights of the defence will be discussed in sections 4 and 5 of this chapter, in which we will again refer to the implications of these judgments; see hereafter, section 4 and section 5 of this chapter.

The Court has also emphasized the right to a proper service of the document instituting the proceedings, when it expressed its vision on the role of the court of the state in which enforcement is sought of a judgment delivered in another Contracting State. In *Pendy v Pluspunkt*, the Court indicated that Article 27, point 2, should be interpreted as offering a real second 'check' as to whether the defendant's right to be properly served with the document instituting the proceedings has been respected in the original proceedings. The Court stated in this respect that the court of the state in which enforcement is sought, must, by virtue of Article 27, point 2, examine the question whether the document introducing the proceedings was properly served, notwithstanding the decision delivered by the court of the original state on the basis of the second and third paragraphs of Article 20.[17] As the Court pointed out in this judgment, both courts, the court of the original state as well as the court of the state in which enforcement is sought, should determine whether the document introducing the proceedings was properly served. The Court stated:

> 'Although they do not seek to harmonize the different systems of service abroad of legal documents which are in force in the Member States, the provisions of the Brussels Convention are designed to ensure that the defendant's rights are effectively protected. For that reason, jurisdiction to determine whether the document introducing the proceedings was properly served was conferred both on the court of the original state and on the court of the state in which enforcement is sought. Thus, in accordance with the objective of Article 27 of the Convention, the court of the state in which enforcement is sought must examine the question posed by paragraph (2) of that Article, notwithstanding the decision given by the court of the original state on the basis of the second and third paragraphs of Article 20. That examination is subject only to the limitation set by the third paragraph of Article 34 of the Convention to the effect that the foreign judgment may under no circumstances be reviewed as to its substance.'[18]

Further proof of the fact that the Court attaches considerable importance to the defendant's right to be properly informed of the fact that proceedings will be instituted against him is to be found in the way the Court has interpreted the requirements that have to be fulfilled for a service of documents instituting the proceedings to be 'proper'. As the Court observed in *Klomps v Michel*, Article 27, point 2, contains two important requirements, namely *the requirement of due service* of the document instituting the proceedings and *service in sufficient time*. As the Court stated, the first requirement entails a decision based on the legislation of the State in which judgment was given and on the Conventions (or other inter-

[17] 228/81 *Pendy v Pluspunkt* 13,14; compare 166/80 *Klomps v Michel* 12.

[18] 228/81 *Pendy v Pluspunkt* 13; compare C-305/88 *Lancray v Peters* 24-31, in which the Court held that 'questions concerning the curing of defective service are governed by the law of the state in which judgment was given, including any relevant international agreements'.

national legal instruments) which are binding on that State with regard to service, whilst the second implies appraisals of a factual nature.[19]

In *Lancray v Peters*, the Court confirmed that the requirements of 'due service' and 'service in sufficient time' constitute, in accordance with the wording of the different language versions, two separate and concurrent safeguards for a defendant who fails to appear.[20] The absence of one of those safeguards is therefore a sufficient ground for refusing to recognise a foreign judgment.[21] This implies that a judgment given in default of appearance may not be recognized where the document instituting the proceedings was not served on the defendant in due form, even though it was served in sufficient time to enable him to arrange for his defence.[22] The Court stated that the interpretation was supported both by the wording of Article 27, point 2, in accordance with the principle of legal certainty, and by the principle directly underlying that provision.[23] As the Court pointed out, if the sole issue was whether the document came to the defendant's attention in sufficient time, then the plaintiffs would be tempted to ignore the prescribed form of due service. As a result the defendant could not know with certainty whether proceedings which might lead to a finding against him have been properly instituted and whether it was therefore necessary to arrange for a defence. Such a situation would be inconsistent with the aims of the Convention.[24]

Obviously, in the reverse case in which the document instituting the proceedings was duly served, but not in sufficient time, a judgment may not be recognized either according to the Court's interpretation of Article 27, point 2.[25]

In the cases *Klomps v Michel*, *Debaecker v Bouwman* and *Hendrikman v Magenta*, the Court determined what the requirement of *service in sufficient time* for the defendant to arrange for his defence implies. It is apparent from the Court's interpretation of this concept that it takes the protection of the defendant very seriously. First of all, the Court has held that the court in which enforcement is sought, has the duty to examine, under Article 27, point 2, whether service was effected in sufficient time to enable the defendant to arrange for his defence, even where service was effected within a period prescribed by the court of the state in which the judgment was delivered or by the law of the state where the defendant

[19] 166/80 *Klomps v Michel* 15; 228/81 *Pendy v Pluspunkt* 14; C-305/88 *Lancray v Peters* 14 (re 166/80 *Klomps v Michel*),29. Notice that Art. 26, point 3, of EC Regulation 44/2001, refers to EC Regulation 1348/2000 on the service in the Member States of judicial and extrajudicial documents in civil and commercial matters, which regulation provides for a uniform system for the service abroad of legal documents within the Community.

[20] C-305/88 *Lancray v Peters* 16,17 (re Jenard Report, OJ 1979 C 59, p. 44),18,23.

[21] 166/80 *Klomps v Michel* 15; 228/81 *Pendy v Pluspunkt* 14; C-305/88 *Lancray v Peters* 14 (re 166/80 *Klomps v Michel*),29.

[22] C-305/88 *Lancray v Peters* 23.

[23] As regards the principle of legal certainty, see hereafter chapter 5, particularly section 2.

[24] C-305/88 *Lancray v Peters* 20.

[25] Compare 228/81 *Pendy v Pluspunkt* 14.

resided.[26] In this respect, the Court has pointed out that the national court that examines whether service was effected in sufficient time, must take account only of the time available to the defendant for the purpose of preventing the issue of a judgment in default, being the period from the date on which service was duly effected up to the time at which proceedings are commenced.[27] On examining this issue, that court has the duty to take into account even exceptional circumstances which warrant the conclusion that the defendant was not able to take the necessary steps to arrange for his defence and, accordingly, could not cause the time stipulated by Article 27, point 2, to begin to run.[28] Not only must that court take into account the circumstances which existed at the time of service and which the plaintiff could take into consideration at that time but also circumstances which arose after service was effected.[29] The defendant's behaviour cannot automatically rule out the possibility of taking such circumstances into account.[30] As the Court established in *Debaecker v Bouwman*, the fact that the plaintiff was apprised of the defendant's new address, after service was effected, and the fact that the defendant was responsible for the failure of the duly served document to reach him, are matters which the court in which enforcement is sought may take into account in assessing whether service was effected in sufficient time.[31]

As regards the requirement of *due service* of the document instituting the proceedings, the Court has held in *Minalmet v Brandeis* that a decision given in default of appearance in a Contracting State must not be recognized or enforced in another Contracting State, where the defendant was not duly served with the document which instituted the proceedings, even if he subsequently became

---

[26] 49/84 *Debaecker v Bouwman* 13; 166/80 *Klomps v Michel* 8-11,14-21; C-78/95 *Hendrikman v Magenta* 20 (re C-123/91 *Minalmet v Brandeis* 19) .

[27] 166/80 *Klomps v Michel* 10,11; C-78/95 *Hendrikman v Magenta* 20 (re C-123/91 *Minalmet v Brandeis* 19).

[28] 166/80 *Klomps v Michel* 20,21. The Court indicated in that judgment: 'In considering whether it is confronted with such a case the court in which enforcement is sought may take account of all the circumstances of the case in point, including the means employed for effecting service, the relations between the plaintiff and the defendant or the nature of the steps which had to be taken in order to prevent judgment from being given in default. If, for example, the dispute concerns commercial relations and if the document which instituted the proceedings was served at an address at which the defendant carries on his business activities the mere fact that the defendant was absent at the time of service should not normally prevent him from arranging his defence, above all if the action necessary to avoid a judgment in default may be taken informally and even by a representative.' (point 20). In that same judgment, the Court held that, in this respect, Art. 52 implies that, where the habitual residence of the defendant may be a decisive factor for the purpose of considering whether service has been duly effected, the question where the defendant has its habitual residence must in any case be resolved by applying the internal law of the state in which the judgment was given and of the relevant conventions (compare points 24 and 25).

[29] 49/84 *Debaecker v Bouwman* 15,22.

[30] 49/84 *Debaecker v Bouwman* 32.

[31] 49/84 *Debaecker v Bouwman* 33.

aware of the judgment which was given in default and did not avail himself of the remedies provided for under the procedure of the state where it was delivered.[32]

Where the case law discussed in the foregoing paragraphs is illustrative of the Court's concern with the right of a proper service of the document instituting the proceedings, the following cases demonstrate that there are limits to the extent to which this right applies. Since a violation of that right is one of the grounds for refusing the recognition and enforcement of judgments and for that reason may come into conflict with the principle of the free movement of judgments, it must be assumed that in the end the Court takes account of the exceptional nature of that ground for refusing enforcement. In this respect, we refer here to the Court's general viewpoint in *Klomps v Michel* that the exceptional nature of the grounds for refusing enforcement is to be observed.[33]

Also, the Court has set some limitations as to how far the notion of 'due service' can be stretched in order to serve the protection of the defendant. As the Court indicated in *Klomps v Michel*, Article 27, point 2, does not require proof that the document which instituted the proceedings was actually brought to the knowledge of the defendant. The court in which enforcement is sought is ordinarily justified in considering that following due service, the defendant is able to take steps to defend his interests as soon as the document has been served on him at his habitual residence or elsewhere.[34]

Next, and as is already clear from the Convention itself, the interpretation of Article 20 and Article 27, point 2 (in conjunction with Article 34, second paragraph) and Article 46, point 2, cannot be too broad, taking into account the limitation set by Article 29 and by the third paragraph of Article 34. The prohibition of a 'révision au fond' of the judgment, as laid down in these provisions, is particularly essential to the free movement of judgments.[35] In *Hengst v Campese*, for example, the Court referred to such limitations, when it held:

> 'the sole aim of Article 27(2) is to ensure that a document which instituted the proceedings or an equivalent document was duly served on the defendant in sufficient time to enable him to arrange for his defence. It does not entitle the court of the state in which recognition is sought to refuse recognition and enforcement of a judgment because of a possible breach of provisions of the law of the state in which it was given other than those governing proper service.'[36]

Furthermore, we may recall here what was observed by the Court in *Debaecker v Bouwman* and what was already implied upon the drafting of the Convention,

[32] C-123/91 *Minalmet v Brandeis* 14-18 (re 166/80 *Klomps v Michel* 9)-21.

[33] Compare 166/80 *Klomps v Michel* 19.

[34] 166/80 *Klomps v Michel* 19.

[35] Compare also Jenard Report, OJ 1979 C 59, p. 46.

[36] C-474/93 *Hengst v Campese* 24; compare 228/81 *Pendy v Pluspunkt* 13, and see also note 18.

namely, that although Art. 27, point 2, is to ensure the adequate protection of the rights of a defendant against whom judgment is given in default of appearance, that provision at the same time leaves unimpeded the possibility that certain Contracting States make provision for the fictitious service of process where the defendant has no known place of residence.[37]

An interpretation that would render Article 27, point 2, completely inoperative, can of course not be accepted either. An indication of this viewpoint is to be found in the following quotation drawn from *Lancray v Peters*. As was seen before, the Court did not accept the view that it is not necessary to insist on a proper service if the defendant has, in any event, had sufficient time to arrange for his defence. The Court stated:

> 'That reasoning cannot be accepted. First, it is difficult to reconcile that interpretation with the wording of the relevant provision or with the Court's ruling cited above. Secondly, it would render completely inoperative the requirement of a due service.'[38]

2. THE DEFENDANT'S RIGHT TO BE HEARD IN AN APPROPRIATE COURT

C Art. 2	R 2
C Art. 28	R 35

On several occasions, the Court has stated that the rules of jurisdiction laid down in Title II of the Convention are of such a nature as to protect the interests of defendants.[39] The Court referred to that viewpoint in *Klomps v Michel*, when it held:

> 'it must be recalled that Title II of the Brussels Convention contains provisions regulating directly and in detail the jurisdiction of the courts of the state in which judgment was given, and also provisions concerning the verification of that jurisdiction and of admissibility. These provisions, which are binding on the court in which judgment was given, are of such a nature as to protect the interests of defendants.'[40]

A further examination of the rules of jurisdiction and of the Court's case law on the interpretation of these rules shows that, within the context of the Convention, the principle of the protection of the rights of the defence does not only require a proper service of the document instituting the proceedings but also certain safeguards on behalf of the defendant as regards the jurisdiction of the courts in which the defendant can be sued.

---

[37] 49/84 *Debaecker v Bouwman* 11.

[38] 305/88 *Lancray v Peters* 20; compare text following note 21 of this section.

[39] Compare text following note 1 of the introduction of this chapter; 125/79 *Denilauler v Couchet Frères* 13 and C-474/93 *Hengst v Campese* 16 (re *Denilauler*).

[40] 166/80 *Klomps v Michel* 7.

The defendant's right to be heard in an appropriate court weighed in relation to other principles

The right of the defendant to be heard in an appropriate court ideally implies the right to be heard in one's own state. That right is laid down in Article 2 of the Convention. That provision is particularly intended to protect the rights of the defendant, as becomes evident from the following quotation, taken from *Autoteile v Malhé*:

> 'According to Article 2, persons domiciled in a Contracting State are to be sued in the courts of that state. That provision is intended to protect the rights of the defendant; it serves as a counterpoise to the facilities provided by the Convention with regard to the recognition and enforcement of foreign judgments.'[41]

As is clear from the system of rules of jurisdiction laid down in Title II of the Convention, Article 2 is the cornerstone of these provisions. It requires that persons domiciled in a Contracting State are to be sued in the courts of that State, irrespective of their nationality. As will be seen later, it also requires that the rules of jurisdiction that derogate from Article 2 should be interpreted restrictively.[42]

The right of the defendant to be heard in an appropriate court is not only sustained by the principle of the protection of the rights of the defence, it is also implied by the fourth main principle underlying the Convention, the principle that disputes should be decided by an appropriate court. The latter principle will be discussed in chapter 6. As will be seen in that chapter, this fourth main principle particularly underlies the rules conferring jurisdiction on the national courts, as contained in Title II of the Convention. It entails more specific sub-principles, such as the principle of the protection of the party who is weaker due to his procedural or socio-economic position, the principle of party autonomy and the principle of a sound administration of justice. The principle of the protection of the party who is weaker due to his procedural position clearly relates to the right of the defendant to be heard in one's own state.[43]

In view of the perspective that the defendant should be heard in an appropriate court, the Court has advanced several other considerations. We will discuss these considerations later in this study. One of them is that a defendant should not be removed by the plaintiff from the court(s) that would otherwise be competent, without proper justification.[44] Another consideration concerns an interpretation of

---

[41] 220/84 *Autoteile v Malhé* 15; compare C-26/91 *Handte v TMCS* 14; compare C-295/95 *Farrell v Long* 19; and see C-412/98 *Josi Reinsurance v UGIC* 35 (re C-26/91 *Handte v TMCS* 14; Jenard Report, OJ 1979 C 59, p. 18)

[42] See hereafter, chapter 6, section 1.1, text following notes 25 and 26.

[43] See section 1.1 of chapter 6, text following note 12.

[44] Among others 189/87 *Kalfelis v Schröder* 8,9; 73/77 *Sanders v Van der Putte* 17; C-115/88 *Reichert v Dresdner Bank I* 9 (re *Sanders v Van der Putte*); 25/76 *Segoura v Bonakdarian* 8. This viewpoint relates to the overall ideal that an entire dispute should be decided as far as possible by a

the rules of jurisdiction that would result in a (further) multiplication of the bases of jurisdiction.[45] Such an interpretation should be avoided, particularly, where it would make it difficult for the defendant to predict before which court he will be sued, other than that of the state in which he is domiciled.[46] We therefore assume that the right of the defendant to be heard in an appropriate court includes the right to be heard before a court that is predictable for the defendant.[47]

The right of the defendant to be heard in an appropriate court, particularly the right to be heard in one's own state, is not absolute though. This already follows from the general scheme of the Convention, from the system of rules of jurisdiction as laid down in Title II of the Convention, and from the main principles underlying the Convention as a whole. For example, Article 2 does not constitute an obstacle to the free movement of judgments (compare Article 28). Also, the right to be heard in one's own state, as laid down in Article 2 of the Convention, is weighed in relation to the other sub-principles that flow from the principle that disputes should be decided by an appropriate court, such as the principle of the protection of the party who is weaker due to his socio-economic position, the principle of party autonomy and the principle of a sound administration of justice. Since these principles will be discussed in chapter 6, we will elaborate on these issues in that chapter.

3. THE DEFENDANT'S RIGHT TO AN *INTER PARTES* HEARING

The right to an *inter partes* hearing is not directly laid down in the Convention. This aspect of the principe of a fair hearing is however implied by the Convention, as the Court has stated in its case law.

The right to an inter partes hearing weighed in relation to other principles

Although the right of an *inter partes* hearing is to be respected *(a)* in the context of the original proceedings as well as *(b)* in the enforcement procedure, it does not work as an absolute. This is particularly true as regards the enforcement procedure, where the right of an *inter partes* hearing would come into conflict with the principle of the free movement of judgments.

---

single *and* appropriate court – that ideal emerges from the Court's case law on the interpretation of the rules of jurisdiction as a whole. We will elaborate on this issue in chapter 6, in which that overall ideal will be discussed; compare section 4.1 of chapter 6, text following note 468.

[45] Compare 33/78 *Somafer v Saar-Ferngas* 7; 34/82 *Peters v ZNAV* 17; C-214/89 *Duffryn v Petereit* 20; C-125/92 *Mulox v Geels* 11; C-269/95 *Benincasa v Dentalkit* 26.

[46] Compare in particular C-256/00 *Besix v Kretzschmar* 26,27,34,35.

[47] As the right of the defendant to be heard before a court that is predictable relates in particular to certain aspects of the principle of legal certainty, we will elaborate on this issue in the next chapter which is dedicated to that principle; see chapter 5, in particular, sections 4.1 and 4.2.

C Arts. 2, 5 to 18,24 R 2,5 to 24,31

On several occasions, the Court has made it clear that it attaches great importance to the fact that in the original phase, proceedings should have an *inter partes,* adversary character. In *Denilauler v Couchet Frères*, the Court has held that only judicial decisions that have been, or have been capable of being the subject in the state of origin of *inter partes* proceedings can be recognized or enforced under Title III of the Convention. That is, judicial decisions that are the result of legal proceedings that do not allow a defendant to be heard, are not judgments that can be recognized or enforced under the rules of Title III of the Convention. Although that requirement is not explicitly stated in any of the Convention's provisions, the Court reasoned that this requirement follows very clearly from the system of principles underlying the Convention:

> 'All the provisions of the Convention, both those contained in Title II on jurisdiction and those contained in Title III on recognition and enforcement, express the intention to ensure that, within the scope of the objectives of the Convention, proceedings leading to the delivery of judicial decisions take place in such a way that the rights of the defence are observed. It is because of the guarantees given to the defendant in the original proceedings that the Convention, in Title III, is very liberal in regard to recognition and enforcement. In the light of these considerations, it is clear that the Convention is fundamentally concerned with judicial decisions which, before the recognition and enforcement of them are sought in a state other than the state of origin, have been, or have been capable of being, the subject in that state of origin ... of an inquiry in adversary proceedings.'[48]

Applying this interpretation to Article 24 of the Convention, the Court concluded that the simplified procedure for the recognition and enforcement, provided for by the Convention, does not apply to cases in which provisional or protective measures are ordered or authorized by a court, without the party against whom they are directed having been summoned to appear and which are intended to be enforced without prior notice on that party. The Court stated that Article 24 does not preclude provisional and protective measures ordered in the state of origin pursuant to adversary proceedings – even though by default – from being the subject of recognition and enforcement in other Contracting States. However, recognition and enforcement of a decision by which provisional and protective measures are ordered is precluded when the legal procedure leading to these measures does not provide for a hearing of the person against whom these measures are directed.[49] In the case *Hengst v Campese*, the Court repeated this position by stating that a judgment is capable of recognition and enforcement under Title III

---

[48] 125/79 *Denilauler v Couchet Frères* 13; The Court has confirmed this in C-474/93 *Hengst v Campese* 16 (re 125/79 *Denilauler v Couchet Frères* 13); see also 166/80 *Klomps v Michel* 7.

[49] 125/79 *Denilauler v Couchet Frères* 17.

of the Convention only if there could have been an *inter partes* hearing in the state of origin.[50]

C Art. 34	R 41	C Art. 38	R 46	C Art. 40(2)	R 42(4)
C Art. 36, 37(1)	R 43(1)	C Art. 39	R 47		

Although the main emphasis in the context of the Convention is on the protection of the rights of the defence in the original proceedings, the defendant (or rather, the party against whom recognition or enforcement is sought) is also protected in the phase of recognition and enforcement, but only to a certain degree. Within the rather narrow scope of possibilities for resisting the recognition and enforcement of the original judgment, the Convention creates some room for the principle of a fair hearing: the defendant is given the opportunity to state his case against recognition and enforcement within the context of the enforcement procedure.[51]

As regards the procedure for recognition and enforcement, the Court held in *Denilauler v Couchet Frères* that the guarantee that in the state of origin both parties have either stated their case or had the opportunity to do so, justifies the unilateral character of the first stage of the enforcement procedure under Article 34.[52] The *ex parte* character of the proceedings in this stage is intended, as was seen in the previous chapter, to enable the applicant seeking enforcement of a judgment in another Contracting State to obtain satisfaction swiftly and to prevent a defendant from having the opportunity to protect his assets against any enforcement measures.[53] However, in the second stage of the enforcement procedure, the Convention allows for the defendant's right to a fair hearing: Article 36 and Article 37, first paragraph, provide the defendant with the possibility to appeal against the recognition and enforcement of a foreign decision and Article 40, second paragraph, requires that the party against whom enforcement is sought shall be summoned to appear before the court before which the applicant has lodged an appeal against the refusal of its application for enforcement. In *P v K*, *Brennero v Wendel* and *Carron v Federal Republic of Germany*, the Court confirmed that the interests of the applicant and the defendant (or rather the party against whom enforcement is sought) are balanced: The Convention reconciles the necessary surprise effect in the initial *ex parte* stage of the enforcement procedure with the necessary respect for the defendant's right to a fair hearing in the second stage of the enforcement proceedings.[54]

In *P v K*, the Court established that no exceptions are to be made to the adversary character of the appeal procedure in this second stage of the enforcement

[50] C-474/93 *Hengst v Campese* 14.

[51] Compare chapter 3, sections 1 and 2.

[52] 125/79 *Denilauler v Couchet Frères* 13,14.

[53] 125/79 *Denilauler v Couchet Frères* 14; and 198/85 *Carron v Federal Republic of Germany* 8; see section 2 of chapter 3, text following note 47.

[54] 178/83 *P v K* 11,12; 258/83 *Brennero v Wendel* 10; 198/85 *Carron v Federal Republic of Germany* 8-14; and see also C-38/98 *Maxicar v Renault II* 22.

proceedings. The Court was asked whether Article 40, second paragraph, implies that the party against whom enforcement is sought must be summoned to appear before the court hearing an appeal by a party seeking enforcement, even in a case in which the application for the enforcement order was dismissed simply because documents were not produced at the appropriate time and the enforcement order was applied for in a state which is not the state of residence of the party against whom enforcement is sought.[55] The Court answered this question in the affirmative.

The right to an *inter partes* hearing in the second stage of the enforcement proceedings also implies that Article 39 only admits protective measures against the property of the party against whom enforcement is sought when an appeal has been lodged against the decision authorizing enforcement; enforcement measures may not be taken until the court with which this appeal has been lodged, delivers a final judgment on the appeal. This was held by the Court in *Brennero v Wendel*.[56] In that same judgment, the Court also interpreted the second paragraph of Article 38, which applies to a situation in which an ordinary appeal has been lodged in the state of origin. The Court stated, first of all, that Article 38 clearly allows the court with which an appeal has been lodged against the decision authorizing enforcement, to take a final decision ruling that enforcement is allowed, even though no decision has yet been taken on the ordinary appeal in the state of origin. Next, the Court established that it is naturally only when the court takes a final decision on the enforcement of the foreign judgment, in that it allows the enforcement, that the interests of the judgment debtor need protection by making the enforcement conditional upon the provision of security.[57]

It is evident that in the context of the enforcement proceedings, the right of an *inter partes* hearing is weighed and balanced against the principle of the free movement of judgments. As was seen, the right to an *inter partes* hearing is absent in the initial stage of the enforcement proceedings, in which the defendant is not entitled to be heard. However, in order to reconcile the necessary surprise effect in the initial stage with the necessary respect for the rights of the defence, the party against whom enforcement is sought is to be heard in the second stage of the enforcement proceedings. The protection of the rights of the defence in this second phase of the enforcement proceedings is limited, though, to the narrow scope of possibilities for resisting the recognition and enforcement of the original judgment.[58]

---

[55] 178/83 *P v K* 12.

[56] 258/83 *Brennero v Wendel* 11.

[57] 258/83 *Brennero v Wendel* 11-13.

[58] Compare this section, note 51 and chapter 3, section 1, text following note 9 and section 2, text following note 47.

4. The right to be defended by a lawyer

C Art. 5(4)	R 5(4)	C Art. 27(2)	R 34(2)
C Art. 27(1)	R 34(1)		

The principle of the protection of the rights of the defence includes the right to be defended by a lawyer during court proceedings. As was seen in *Hendrikman v Magenta*, the Court established that only a lawyer who is chosen by the defendant and who has his authority to act, may be supposed to validly represent the defendant.[59] The Court held in this case that if proceedings are initiated against a person without his knowledge, and a lawyer appears before the court first seised on his behalf but without his authority, this person must be regarded as 'a defendant in default of appearance' within the meaning of Article 27, point 2.[60]

A specific aspect of the right to be defended by a lawyer relates to civil claims brought before a criminal court. Such a claim must be considered as a 'civil matter' and falls within the substantive scope of the Convention, laid down in Article 1. Article 5, point 4, which provides that a claim for damages or restitution which is based on an act giving rise to criminal proceedings, can be brought in the court seised of those proceedings (provided that that court has jurisdiction under its own law to entertain civil proceedings), and is based upon this concept of 'civil matters'.[61] Under the Convention, the principle of the protection of the rights of the defence implies, as the Court observed in *Rinkau*, the right of a person domiciled in a Contracting State to be defended by persons qualified to do so *without appearing in person* in criminal proceedings for an offence which was *not intentionally committed.* This right is explicitly granted by Article II of the Protocol annexed to the 1968 Convention.[62] As the Court recalled in *Rinkau*, the extension of the scope of the Convention to the criminal field is justified in the light of the consequences which a judgment given in the course of such proceedings may entail in civil and commercial matters. However, this right of the defendant only applies during criminal proceedings in which the liability of the defendant under civil law is in question or on which such liability might subsequently be based.[63] The Court decided, as regards the right of a person charged with an offence in cases relating to criminal proceedings to be defended by a lawyer without appear-

[59] Compare section 1 of this chapter, text following note 16.

[60] C-78/95 *Hendrikman v Magenta* 18; and compare C-172/91 *Sonntag v Waidmann* 44.

[61] C-172/91 *Sonntag v Waidmann* 16,19. *Sonntag v Waidmann* was a case in which an action for damages was brought before a criminal court. That action was against a teacher in a state school who, during a school trip, caused injury to a pupil through a culpable and unlawful breach of his duties of supervision and where cover was provided under a social insurance scheme governed by public law. The Court held that even such an action falls within the ambit of the Convention; see C-172/91 *Sonntag v Waidmann* 29; see also hereafter chapter 5, section 3 and before this chapter, section 1, text following note 14.

[62] See OJ 26.1.1998, C 27, p. 1; and 157/80 *Rinkau* 6.

[63] 157/80 *Rinkau* 6,20.

ing in person, that the expression 'an offence which was not intentionally committed' in Article II of the Protocol, must be interpreted as 'any offence the legal definition of which does not require, either expressly or as appears from the nature of the offence defined, the existence of intent on the part of the accused to commit the punishable act or omission.'[64]

As regards the right of a person charged with an offence in cases relating to criminal proceedings to be effectively defended by a lawyer, we also refer to the Court's decision in *Krombach v Bamberski*. The question submitted to the Court concerned the interpretation of the term 'public policy' in Article 27, point 1, in a case in which enforcement was sought of a foreign judgment delivered in the course of criminal proceedings. The Court recalled that the right to be effectively defended by a lawyer occupies a prominent position in the organisation and conduct of a fair trial and is one of the fundamental rights deriving from the constitutional traditions common to the Member States.[65] Therefore, although recourse to the public policy clause in Article 27, point 1, by the court of a state in which enforcement is sought is to be had only in exceptional cases, it can however be justified in a case where the guarantees laid down in the legislation of the state of origin and in the Convention itself have been insufficient to protect the defendant from a manifest breach of his right to defend himself before the court of origin.[66] The court of the State in which enforcement is sought of a judgment related to criminal proceedings and with respect to a defendant domiciled in its territory and charged with an *intentional offence*, can take account of the fact that the court of the state of origin refused to allow that person to have his defence presented unless he appeared in person.[67]

Under the Convention, the right to be defended by a lawyer in proceedings related to civil and commercial matters is firmly established. It can be limited, though, in cases related to criminal proceedings with regard to a defendant prosecuted for an intentional offence and who does not appear in person.

5. The right to submit a defence on the substance of the case

C Art. 18	R 24
C Art. 27(2)	R 34(2)

Obviously, the principle of the protection of the rights of the defence would be violated if the legal proceedings formally had an *inter partes* character, but the defendant would actually be barred from making his submissions as to the sub-

[64] 157/80 *Rinkau* 16.
[65] C-7/98 *Krombach v Bamberski* 38.
[66] C-7/98 *Krombach v Bamberski* 44.
[67] C-7/98 *Krombach v Bamberski* 45.

stance of the case. The requirement that a defendant should actually be able to state the substance of his case has determined some of the Court's interpretations. The Court made this clear in *Elefanten Schuh v Jacqmain*, *C.H.W. v G.J.H.* and *Rohr v Ossberger*: an interpretation of Article 18, which would have the result that a defendant who raises the sole issue of jurisdiction might be barred from making his submissions as to the substance if the court rejects his plea that it has no jurisdiction, is contrary to the right of the defendant to defend himself in the original proceedings. Consequently, the Court held that Article 18 allows a defendant to contest jurisdiction and at the same time to submit, in the alternative, a defence on the substance of the case.[68] It is obvious that an interpretation of Article 18 that safeguards the right of the defendant to submit a defence on the substance of the case is in accordance with the principle of the protection of the rights of the defence.

The view that the principle of the protection of the rights of the defence includes the right to submit a defence as to the substance of the case, has also influenced the Court's interpretation of the term 'judgment given in default' in Article 27, point 2. As was seen before, the Court stated in *Klomps v Michel* that if the defendant did not submit a defence as to the substance of the case before the court first seised, the judgment of that court must be considered to have been given in default by the court before which proceedings have been brought for the recognition or enforcement of that judgment.[69] That is even so where the defendant has lodged an objection against the decision given in default and the court of the state in which the judgment was given has held that objection to be inadmissible on the ground that the time for lodging an objection has expired. In such a case Article 27, point 2, remains applicable.[70] The proper time to submit a defence as to the substance of the case, as we learned from *Minalmet v Brandeis*, is at the time at which proceedings are commenced. The possibility of having recourse, at a later stage, to a legal remedy against a judgment given in default of appearance, which has already become enforceable, cannot constitute an equally effective alternative to a defence in proceedings before judgment is given.[71]

As appears from the Court's case law, the defendant's right to submit a defence on the substance of the case in the original proceedings is considered to be of the utmost importance. In fact, this right is given full weight in any situation where it is applicable – other considerations which might run counter to it are in the end not considered to be sufficient to outweigh it.

Of course, arguments as to the substance of the case in the original proceedings must be pleaded at the proper moment. And, at the stage of the recognition and

[68] 150/80 *Elefanten Schuh v Jacqmain* 14-17; 25/81 *C.H.W. v G.J.H.* 13; 27/81 *Rohr v Ossberger* 7; and, 201/82 *Gerling v Tesoro dello Stato* 21.

[69] This chapter, section 1, text following note 13.

[70] 166/80 *Klomps v Michel* 12; compare though Art. 34, point 2, of Regulation 44/2001.

[71] C-123/91 *Minalmet v Brandeis* 18 (re 166/80 *Klomps v Michel* 9),19-21.

enforcement procedures, there are, in order to promote free movement of judgments, limitations to the case that a defendant can present.[72] The case that the defendant is allowed to state in the phase of recognition and enforcement is, as was seen in the previous chapter, essentially limited to stating that one or more of the grounds for refusing the recognition and enforcement, as laid down in Articles 27 and 28, are applicable.[73] There is no need to recall here that a review of the substance of the original case is prohibited at this phase, by virtue of Article 29 and 34, third paragraph.[74]

6. The defendant's interest in staying the execution proceedings when an appeal has been or will be lodged in the state of origin

C Art. 30	R 37
C Art. 38	R 46

Another aspect of the principle of the protection of the rights of the defence is to be found in Articles 30 and 38 of the Convention. These Articles provide that the court before which recognition or enforcement is sought may stay the proceedings if an ordinary appeal has been lodged against the judgment in the state of origin or may be lodged within a specific period. We understand these provisions as rules that aim to protect the defendant (in the form of the party against whom recognition or enforcement is sought). We thereby refer, in particular, to the Court's judgment in *Diamond v Riva*, in which it answered questions on the interpretation of Articles 30 and 38. The Court stated:

> 'Although, as a whole, the Convention is intended to ensure the rapid enforcement of judgments with a minimum of formalities when those judgments are enforceable in the state in which they were given, the specific purpose of Article 30 and 38 is to prevent the compulsory recognition or enforcement of judgments in other Contracting States when the possibility that they might be annulled or amended in the state in which they were given still exists.'[75]

Moreover, the Court stated that a sufficiently broad interpretation of the concept of 'ordinary appeal' in Articles 30 and 38 is required, in order to enable the court to stay the proceedings whenever reasonable doubt arises with regard to the fate

---

[72] See 145/86 *Hoffmann v Krieg* 34; and 183/90 *Dalfsen v Van Loon* 30,35; compare C-38/98 *Maxicar v Renault II* 31,33.

[73] See section 1 of chapter 3, text following note 10; compare in particular C-38/98 *Maxicar v Renault II* 29 (re C-7/98 *Krombach* 36),31-33.

[74] Compare this chapter, section 1, text following note 35.

[75] 43/77 *Diamond v Riva* 30.

of the decision in the state in which it was given.[76] On the other hand, though, the term 'ordinary appeal' within the meaning of Articles 30 and 38, does not include appeals 'which are dependent either upon events which were unforeseeable at the date of the original judgment or upon the action taken by persons who are extraneous to the case, and who are not bound by the period for entering an appeal which starts to run from the date of the original judgment.'[77]

The interest of the defendant in being protected against the recognition and enforcement of a foreign decision when an appeal has been lodged in the state of origin is, in the context of the Convention, clearly not absolute. As the Court points out in *Diamond v Riva*, the court before which the appeal under Article 37, first paragraph, is lodged, is not under a duty to stay the proceedings but merely has the power to do so.[78] Apparently, the court is given the power to weigh the interests of the party against whom enforcement is sought in relation to the interests of the applicant for the enforcement order.

7. The defendant's right to be properly served with a decision delivered in a Contracting State

C Art. 36 (1st and 2nd paras.)	R 43(5)
C Art. 47	R 53

Finally, we mention here the right to be properly served with the decision delivered in a Contracting State, which is expressed in Article 36, first and second paragraphs, and in Article 47, point 1 of the Convention.

Article 36, first and second paragraphs, implies that the party against whom enforcement is sought, is served with the decision of the court of a Contracting State authorizing the enforcement of a judgment given in another Contracting State. Article 47 determines that proof is provided of the service of the judgment of a Contracting State given in default on the defendant. The purpose of serving the original judgment on the defendant is to inform him of the judgment given against him and to give him the opportunity to satisfy it voluntarily before enforcement can be applied for.[79] In the light of this perspective, the Court held in *Van der Linden v Berufsgenossenschaft*, that Article 47 is to be interpreted as meaning that, where the domestic procedural rules so permit, proof of service of the judgment may be produced after the application for enforcement has been made, in particular during the course of appeal proceedings subsequently brought

[76] 43/77 *Diamond v Riva* 30-33.
[77] 43/77 *Diamond v Riva* 39, and see: 33.
[78] 43/77 *Diamond v Riva* 30,31.
[79] C-275/94 *Van der Linden v Berufsgenossenschaft* 15 (re Jenard Report OJ 1979 C 59, p. 1, at 55, 19).

by the party against whom enforcement is sought, provided that that party is given a reasonable period of time in which to satisfy the judgment voluntarily and that the party seeking enforcement bears all the costs unnecessarily incurred.[80] From this judgment, it also appears that the interests of the party against whom enforcement is sought and the interests of the applicant for the enforcement order, are weighed and balanced against each other.

Conclusions and summary

From the foregoing, we may conclude that the principle of the protection of the rights of the defence, being an overall interest of the Convention as a whole, is one of the main principles underlying the Convention and is firmly established under the Convention. The principle has a strong influence on the interpretation of the provisions of the Convention. The principle is not absolute though, and is weighed in relation to other principles. However, as far as the principle of fair notice is concerned, which lies at the core of this principle of the protection of the rights of the defence, it may at the end of the day often outweigh the principle of the free movement of judgments. As has become clear from this section, the principle of the protection of the rights of the defence consists of several, more concrete sub-principles. We present the following scheme for the principle of the protection of the rights of the defence:

(2) The Principle of the Protection of the Rights of the Defence
entails:

(2.1) The defendant's right to a proper service of the document instituting the proceedings

(2.2) The defendant's right to be heard in an appropriate court

(2.3) The defendant's right to an inter partes hearing

(2.4) The right to be defended by a lawyer

(2.5) The right to submit a defence on the substance of the case

(2.6) The defendant's interest in staying the execution proceedings when an appeal has been or will be lodged in the state of origin

---

[80] C-275/94 *Van der Linden v Berufsgenossenschaft* 19.

(2.7) The defendant's right to be properly served with the decision delivered in a Contracting State

The main requirements that flow from these sub-principles, are:

2.1 the defendant's right to a proper service of the document instituting the proceedings, *requires*:
- an interpretation of Article 27, point 2, in light of the principle of the protection of the rights of the defence
- an examination by both courts, the court of origin and the court in which recognition or enforcement is sought, of the requirement of a proper service
- a proper service entailing two requirements; 'due service' and 'service within sufficient time'

2.2 the defendant's right to be heard in an appropriate court, *requires*:
- ideally, the right of the defendant to be heard before the court of his own state

2.3 the defendant's right to an *inter partes* hearing, *requires*:
- an *inter partes* hearing in the state of origin, or at least the possibility thereof, even in a case in which provisional or protective measures are ordered or authorized
- an *inter partes* hearing in the second stage of the execution proceedings

2.4 the right to be defended by a lawyer, *requires*:
- the right of the defendant to be defended by a lawyer of his own choice and having his authority to act
- the right of the defendant to be defended by a lawyer without appearing in person in criminal proceedings for an offence which was not intentionally committed, and
- the right of the defendant to be defended by a lawyer without appearing in person in criminal proceedings for an offence which was intentionally committed, but only in exceptional cases

2.5 the right to submit a defence on the substance of the case, *requires*:
- the right to submit a defence on the substance of the case, when raising at the same time the issue of jurisdiction, under Article 18
- a sufficiently broad interpretation of the phrase 'a judgment given in default of appearance' in Article 27, point 2, in view of the underlying principle

2.6 the protection of the interest of the defendant in staying the enforcement proceedings when an appeal has been or will be lodged in the state of the original proceedings, *requires*:
– a sufficiently broad interpretation of the words 'ordinary appeal'

2.7 the right to be properly served with the decision delivered by a court, *requires*:
– certain guarantees in that such decisions are properly served.

Chapter 5
THE THIRD MAIN PRINCIPLE: LEGAL CERTAINTY

INTRODUCTION

The third main principle underlying the Convention is the principle of legal certainty. This principle is not directly expressed in the Convention. However, as was seen in chapter 2, the Court considers the principle of legal certainty as part of the Community legal order and as one of the objectives of the Convention.[1] As the Court stated in *Besix v Kretzschmar*, one of its most recent cases:

> 'the Court has repeatedly held that the principle of legal certainty is one of the objectives of the Brussels Convention ...'[2]

Naturally, this principle contributes to the most general principle underlying the Convention, the principle of legal protection of persons established in the Community.[3]

In a general sense, legal certainty within the context of the Convention requires that with respect to the topics that the Convention aims to regulate, certainty exists as to what the Convention implies. This means, in particular, that it should be clear which matters fall within the scope of the Convention, which court(s) have jurisdiction to decide cases concerning these matters and under what conditions and according to which procedures judgments regarding these issues obtained in one of the Contracting States should be recognized and enforced in other Contracting States.

When taking a closer look at the Court's case law, it appears that, within the context of the Convention, the general idea of legal certainty encompasses various distinctly different aspects, each of which can be subsumed under the heading of a separate sub-principle.

There are two general sub-principles that apply to all provisions of the Convention. The first sub-principle, 'equality and uniformity of rights and obligations

---

[1] See section 1 chapter 2, text following notes 10 and 13; and below, note 2 of this chapter.

[2] C-256/00 *Besix v Kretzschmar* 24. In establishing this, the Court refers back to the following line of cases: 38/81 *Effer v Kantner* 6; C-26/91 *Handte v TMCS* 11,12,18,19; C-129/92 *Owens Bank v Bracco* 32; C-288/92 *Custom Made v Stawa* 15,18; and C-440/97 *Concorde v Panjan* 23. See also C-80/00 *Leather v Polstermöbel* 51 (re *Effer v Kantner* 6; *Concorde v Panjan* 23; *Besix v Kretzschmar* 24).

[3] Compare among others 38/81 *Effer v Kantner* 6; 288/82 *Duijnstee v Goderbauer* 10,11,13; C-26/91 *Handte v TMCS* 11,12 (re Jenard Report, OJ 1979 C 59, p. 1).

arising from the Convention', figures explicitly in the Court's case law.[4] It implies that the Convention should be considered as a set of provisions that forms an autonomous system, independent from the national law of one or the other of the Contracting States concerned.[5] This requires that the provisions of the Convention should, as far as possible, be interpreted in an autonomous way and that the Convention overrules national legal provisions that are incompatible with it. The second general sub-principle, which we have called 'respect for the wording of the Convention's provisions', clearly figures in the Court's reasoning as well.[6] It manifests itself in the fact that in many decisions the Court takes great care to establish that its interpretation does not go beyond the 'linguistic boundaries' of the Convention's provisions. It is evident that persons established within the Community generally benefit from the applicability of these sub-principles and that the parties directly concerned do so in particular.

In addition to these two sub-principles which are relevant for the Convention as a whole, there are aspects of legal certainty that only pertain to specific topics: legal certainty with regard to the scope of the Convention, legal certainty with regard to the allocation of jurisdiction and legal certainty with regard to the recognition and enforcement of judgments within the Community area. The Court has referred to these aspects of legal certainty in its case law.[7]

Naturally, legal certainty as to the scope of the Convention is in the interest of all persons established within the Community, and equally in the interest of the parties directly concerned. With respect to legal certainty regarding the allocation of jurisdiction, the interests of the parties directly concerned, the plaintiff and the defendant, may diverge. As becomes clear from the Court's case law, the Court takes account of these diverging interests.[8] In this respect, two more concrete sub-principles guide the Court's interpretation of the rules of jurisdiction. In short, these principles are: the principle of the ease of identification of the competent court for the plaintiff and foreseeability and predictability for the defendant. With respect to legal certainty regarding the recognition and enforcement of judgments, it is the judgment-creditor who is to benefit most from the application of this principle.

---

[4] Among others 29/76 *LTU v Eurocontrol* 3; 9/77 *Bavaria v Eurocontrol* 4 (re *LTU v Eurocontrol* 3); 43/77 *Diamond v Riva* 25-27; 33/78 *Somafer v Saar-Ferngas* 8; C-51/97 *Réunion européenne v Spliethoff's* 15 (re 34/82 *Peters v ZNAV* 9,10; 9/87 *Arcado v Haviland* 10,11; C-26/91 *Handte v TMCS* 10).

[5] Compare, for example, 148/84 *Deutsche Genossenschaftsbank v Brasserie du Pêcheur* 17; and C-7/98 *Krombach v Bamberski* 20 (re C-432/93 *SISRO v Ampersand* 39).

[6] Among others 14/76 *De Bloos v Bouyer* 11,12 ;119/84 *Capelloni v Pelkmans* 28; C-305/88 *Lancray v Peters* 16; C-96/00 *Gabriel* 38; C-256/00 *Besix v Kretzschmar* 29; and hereafter note 56 of this chapter.

[7] Among others C-190/89 *Rich v Impianti* 26,27 (re 38/81 *Effer v Kantner* 6); C-26/91 *Handte v TMCS* 12; C-80/00 *Leather v Polstermöbel* 51 (re 38/81 *Effer v Kantner* 6; C-440/97 *Concorde v Panjan* 23; C-256/00 *Besix v Kretzschmar* 24).

[8] Among others C-269/95 *Benincasa v Dentalkit* 26 (re 38/81 *Effer v Kantner* 6; C-125/92 *Mulox v Geels* 11).

From the above, it follows that within the context of the Convention, we can distinguish the following aspects as regards legal certainty:

Two general aspects of legal certainty:

(1) Equality and uniformity of rights and obligations arising from the Convention

(2) Respect for the wording (the linguistic boundaries) of the Convention's provisions

Three aspects of legal certainty that concern specific topics:

(3) Legal certainty with regard to the scope of the Convention

(4) Legal certainty with regard to the allocation of jurisdiction

(5) Legal certainty with regard to judgments

In the following sections we will discuss these different aspects of the main principle of legal certainty. We will examine what these sub-principles require in particular.

In quite a number of cases the Court has used arguments based on these general and specific aspects of legal certainty when justifying its interpretation of terms and concepts of the Convention. An interpretation based on such arguments may result in a broad or restrictive interpretation. In a number of cases the principle of legal certainty is used as the only argument to justify the Court's interpretation. In most cases, though, the Court uses arguments based on other (sub-)principles as well. In such cases both types of arguments may point in different directions, but usually they do not. Where these other arguments also relate to the sub-principles which flow from the fourth main principle, the principle that disputes should be decided by an appropriate court, most of the cases involved will be picked up again in the next chapter, chapter 6, and will be discussed there in further detail.

1. Equality and uniformity of rights and obligations arising from the Convention

In order to strengthen the legal protection of persons established within the Community, the Convention aims to determine the international jurisdiction of their courts, to facilitate the recognition and to introduce an expeditious procedure for securing the enforcement of judgments. With regard to these topics which the Convention aims to regulate, legal certainty implies equality and uniformity of rights and obligations arising from the Convention, in particular, for the parties concerned.[9] Although 'equality and uniformity of rights and obligations' figures

[9] Compare note 13 chapter 2, section 1.

explicitly in the Court's case law, the relationship between the principle of legal certainty and this more concrete principle is only incidentally expressed within it. A connection must be assumed, though, as becomes clear from the following quotation, taken from *Krombach v Bamberski*:

> 'It follows from the Court's case law that ... the principle of legal certainty in the Community legal system and the objectives of the Convention in accordance with Article 220 of the EC Treaty (now Article 293 EC), on which it is founded, require a uniform application in all Contracting States of the Convention rules and the relevant case-law of the Court ...'[10]

The principle of equality and uniformity of rights and obligations arising from the Convention requires a uniform application in all Contracting States of the Convention. This in turn implies, first of all, that concepts and classifications used in the Convention's rules should receive an autonomous interpretation. Secondly, the principle of equality and uniformity of rights and obligations implies that the Convention overrides national rules that are incompatible with them.

1.1 **Autonomous interpretation of concepts used in the Convention**

C Art. 1 R 1

The Convention frequently uses terms and legal concepts that are drawn from civil, commercial and procedural law, such as 'matters relating to a contract', 'obligation', 'consumer' or 'ordinary appeal'. Many of these concepts have a different meaning in the various Contracting States. The question has arisen how these words and concepts must, within the context of the Convention, be interpreted: should they be regarded as having their own independent meaning, common to all Contracting States, or as referring to the national law of one or the other of the states concerned?[11]

As becomes evident from the Court's case law, the principle of equality and uniformity of rights and obligations requires that legal concepts used in the Convention should receive an autonomous, independent interpretation, rather than an interpretation that simply refers to the national law of one or other of the States concerned.[12] That requirement does not only apply to concepts constituting the substantive scope of the Convention, but also to concepts used in the rules of jurisdiction as well as in those concerning the recognition and enforcement of jurisdiction. A number of cases illustrate this.

---

[10] C-7/98 *Krombach v Bamberski* 20 (re C-432/93 *SISRO v Ampersand* 39); compare 33/78 *Somafer v Saar-Ferngas* 8.

[11] 12/76 *Tessili v Dunlop* 10.

[12] For example 157/80 *Rinkau* 11; see also note 15 of this chapter and compare: A-G Darmon's opinion, paragraph 6, in C-68/93 *Shevill v Presse Alliance*.

The following quotation from *Bavaria v Eurocontrol* shows that the Court considers an independent interpretation as a requirement that flows from the principle of equality and uniformity of rights and obligations and that that sub-principle, in turn, can be derived from the principle of legal certainty. In that judgment, the Court made it particularly clear that the term 'civil and commercial matters' mentioned in Article 1 of the Convention and determining its substantive scope, requires an independent interpretation:

> 'The Court .... has determined the scope of the Brussels Convention ... by interpreting 'civil and commercial matters' as an independent concept and not as a reference to the internal law of one or other of the states concerned. This interpretation is based on the desire to ensure ... that the Contracting States and parties concerned have equal and uniform rights and duties under the Brussels Convention. The principle of legal certainty in the Community legal system and the objectives of the Brussels Convention ... require in all Member States a uniform application of the legal concepts and legal classifications developed by the Court in the context of the Brussels Convention.'[13]

Other judgments confirm that the requirement of an autonomous interpretation applies as well to the rules on jurisdiction and the rules on recognition and enforcement of judgments.[14]

The idea that concepts used in the Convention should be given, as far as possible, an autonomous interpretation seems to be firmly established.[15] After quite a number of cases in which the Court concluded that various concepts used in the Convention had to be seen as having an independent, autonomous meaning, the Court, in *Shearson v TVB*, referred to a:

> 'principle, established by case-law ... according to which the concepts used in the Convention, which may have a different content depending on the national law of the Contracting States, must be interpreted independently ... in order to ensure that the Convention is uniformly applied in all the Contracting States.'[16]

---

[13] 9/77*Bavaria v Eurocontrol* 4 (re 29/76 *LTU v Eurocontrol* 4). Most recently: C-167/00 *Konsumenteninformation v Henkel* 26 (re 29/76 *LTU v Eurocontrol* 4; 814/79 *Netherlands v Rüffer* 8; C-172/91 *Sonntag v Waidmann* 20)-30; see also section 3 of this chapter, text following note 74.

[14] Compare 33/78 *Somafer v Saar-Ferngas* 8; and 43/77 *Diamond v Riva* 25-27.

[15] Compare 29/76 *LTU v Eurocontrol* 3; 133/78 *Gourdain v Nadler* 3; 814/79 *Netherlands v Rüffer* 7,14; 34/82 *Peters v ZNAV* 9,10; 288/82 *Duijnstee v Goderbauer* (13)17,18; 144/86 *Gubisch v Palumbo* 6-11; 9/87 *Arcado v Haviland* 10,11; 189/87 *Kalfelis v Schröder* 10,15,16; C-214/89 *Duffryn v Petereit* 13,14; C-261/90 *Reichert v Dresdner Bank II* 15,16; C-89/91 *Shearson v TVB* 13; C-269/95 *Benincasa v Dentalkit* 12; C-51/97 *Réunion européenne v Spliethoff's* 15; see also 43/77 *Diamond v Riva* 26; 33/78 *Somafer v Saar-Ferngas* 8; 7/98 *Krombach v Bamberski* 20,23.

Exceptions are to be found in 12/76 *Tessili v Dunlop*; C-420/97 *Leathertex v Bodetex* 33; C-440/97 *Concorde v Panjan* 11-14,19,32 and compare C-125/92 *Mulox v Geels* 12-14; C-37/00 *Weber v Universal Ogden* 38; 129/83 *Zelger v Salinitri II* 15; 144/86 *Gübisch v Palumbo* 6-11.

[16] C-89/91 *Shearson v TVB* 13 (re 150/77 *Bertrand v Ott* 14-16,19; C-26/91 *Handte v TMCS* 10).; and compare C-125/92 *Mulox v Geels* 10; and C-7/98 *Krombach v Bamberski* 20.

The technique used by the Court in attributing the required autonomous meaning to the Convention's provisions has been described by the Court in quite a number of judgments, such as, for example, in *Sonntag v Waidmann.*[17] In most of its case law, the Court has consistently held that an independent concept is to be interpreted by reference, first, to the objectives and scheme of the Convention and, secondly, to the general principles which stem from the corpus of the national legal systems.[18] As far as the second element of this technique is concerned, it cannot always be applied successfully. It fails when a common concept cannot be arrived at by a rapprochement of the various relevant national provisions.[19] And although it may appear, by a comparison of the legislation of the various Contracting States, that concepts used in the provisions of the Convention generally can be recognized in the legal systems of the Contracting States and have a common core, their precise scope will differ in the majority of the cases. In these cases the interpretation of such concepts can only be usefully sought within the framework of the Convention itself, as the Court put it in *Diamond v Riva.*[20] Hence, it does not come as a surprise that, in more recent cases, such as, for example, in *Konsumenteninformation v Henkel*, the Court's general description of this technique of interpreting concepts independently, is restricted as follows: 'concepts ... of the Brussels Convention are to be interpreted independently, having regard primarily to the objectives and general scheme of that Convention.'[21] The latter technique has been described earlier in this study as 'principle-based' reasoning.[22] However, when attributing an autonomous meaning to the Convention's provisions, the Court nowadays also refers more and more to the substance of concepts used in other European legal instruments, such as conventions, regulations and directives, as also becomes evident from its more recent case law.[23] It can be assumed that the Court will do this more regularly, in particular with a view to the increasing number of EC regulations and directives in the field of private (international) law.

---

[17] C-172/91 *Sonntag v Waidmann* 18, in which the Court refers back to the following line of cases: 29/76 *LTU v Eurocontrol* 3,4; 133/78 *Gourdain v Nadler* 3; and 814/79 *Netherlands v Rüffer* 7,8. Compare also 157/80 *Rinkau* 11.

[18] Idem.

[19] Compare 129/83 *Zelger v Salinitri II* 13.

[20] 43/77 *Diamond v Riva* 22-27.

[21] C-167/00 *Konsumenteninformation v Henkel* 35 (re 34/82 *Peters v ZNAV* 9,10; 189/87 *Kalfelis v Schröder* 15,16; C-261/90 *Reichert v Dresdner Bank II* 15); and compare C-96/00 *Gabriel* 37 (re 150/77 *Bertrand v Ott* 14,15,16; C-89/91 *Shearson v TVB* 13; C-269/95 *Benincasa v Dentalkit* 12; C-99/96 *Mietz v Intership* 26). Exceptions to this trend are seen in C-271/00 *Gem. Steenbergen v Luc Baten*, in which the Court mentioned 'the general principles which stem from national legal systems as a whole' (point 28, re 29/76 *LTU* 3; 133/78 *Gourdain* 3; 814/79 *Rüffer* 7; C-172/91 *Sonntag* 18) and C-266/01 *TIARD v Staat der Nederlanden* 20.

[22] See chapter 1, section 1.

[23] Compare C-96/00 *Gabriel* 42; C-167/00 *Konsumenteninformation v Henkel* 43,49; and C-271/00 *Gem. Steenbergen v Luc Baten* 43 (re C-398/92 *Mund & Fester* 12; C-7/98 *Krombach* 24).

Limits with respect to the requirement of an autonomous interpretation

As was seen above, the principle of equality and uniformity of rights and obligations arising from the Convention, as far as it requires an autonomous interpretation, is firmly established in the Court's case law. However, there are a number of cases in which the Court has ruled that it is either *(a)* impossible or *(b)* inappropriate to impose equality and uniformity on the Contracting States, and that in this context a distinction is to be made between issues that belong to the Convention's core business and those that are not at the core of the Convention.

C Art. 5(1) R 5(1)

The most well-known exception to the principle of equality and uniformity, as far as it requires an autonomous interpretation of the concepts and expressions used in the Convention, was made in the first case that the Court had to decide under the 1968 Brussels Convention: the case of *Tessili v Dunlop*.[24]

This case concerned the interpretation of the words 'place of performance' of the obligation in question, which is one of the key elements of the jurisdictional rule laid down in Article 5, point 1, providing that in matters relating to a contract, a person domiciled in a Contracting State may be sued in the courts of the place of performance of the obligation in question. Since the concept 'place of performance' is part of the connecting factor which attributes cases concerning matters relating to a contract to a particular court, we would expect the Court to give an autonomous, uniform interpretation to this concept. However, the Court decided differently. It stated that it is for the national court before which the matter is brought to establish whether the place of performance of the obligation in question is situated within its territorial jurisdiction. In doing so, the national court must determine, in accordance with its own rules of conflict of laws, which law is applicable to the case at hand and determine in accordance with that law the place of performance of the obligation in question.[25] The reason for this decision not to provide an autonomous interpretation is that the Court considered this to be impossible, mainly due to the fact that determining the place of performance depends on the contractual context of the obligation and the existence of differences between national laws of contract in this respect, as well as the absence of any development towards unification in this area.[26] The Court's decision in *Tessili v Dunlop* was confirmed years later in *Leathertex v Bodetex* and *Concorde v Panjan*, and most recently in *Besix v Kretzschmar*, when it had become established case law that the Court generally interprets concepts and terms used in the Convention in an autonomous, independent manner.[27] An exception

[24] 12/76 *Tessili v Dunlop*.

[25] 12/76 *Tessili v Dunlop* 13.

[26] 12/76 *Tessili v Dunlop* 14.

[27] C-420/97 *Leathertex v Bodetex* 33 (12/76 *Tessili v Dunlop* 13; C-288/92 *Custom Made v Stawa* 26; C-440/97 *Concorde v Panjan* 32); C-440/ 97 *Concorde v Panjan* 11(re C-125/92 *Mulox v*

to this viewpoint that the concept 'place of performance' ought to be interpreted with reference to national law was made for contracts of employment.[28]

C Art. 27(1) R 34(1)

A second exception to the idea that, in order to meet the principle of equality and uniformity of rights and obligations, an autonomous interpretation of concepts of the Convention is necessary, concerns the 'public policy' clause laid down in Article 27, point 1. Naturally, it would be inappropriate to construe a concept such as 'public policy' completely independently from what national states consider to be their public policy. In fact, such an interpretation would be incompatible with the core of that concept.

With regard to the notion of 'public policy' as used in Article 27, point 1, of the Convention, the Court has confirmed this viewpoint in *Krombach v Bamberski,* when it held that Contracting States remain, in principle, free to determine according to their own conceptions what public policy requires and that it is not for the Court to define the content of the public policy of a Contracting State.[29] On the other hand, the concept of 'public policy' clearly effects the core issues that the Convention aims to regulate. It has a direct relation to one of the main objectives of the Convention, namely the free movement of judgments: after all, public policy is a ground for refusing the recognition and enforcement of judgments originating from other Contracting States. In *Krombach v Bamberski*, the Court stated that while it is not for the Court to define the content of the public policy of a Contracting State, it is nonetheless required to review the limits within which the courts of a Contracting State may have recourse to that concept for the purpose of refusing the recognition and enforcement of a judgment emanating from another Contracting State.[30] Hence, the Court is, by assuming the

Geels 10), 13 (re *Tessili* 13; *Custom Made* 26),14 (re *Mulox* 20),17,18 (re 133/81 *Ivenel v Schwab* 20; *Mulox* 14),19 (re 266/85 *Shenavai v Kreischer* 17),20,29 (*Shenavai* 18; *Custom Made v Stawa* 12,13),32; and see C-288/92 *Custom Made v Stawa* 26 (re *Tessili* 13; *Shenavai* 7); and C-256/00 *Besix v Kretzschmar* 33 (re *Tessili* 13,15; *Custom Made* 26; *Concorde* 32; *Leathertex* 33).

[28] The Court has given different reasons when justifying this exception. It referred to the principle of a sound administration of justice as well as to the principle of the protection of the employee as the weaker party from the social point of view; compare chapter 6, section 1.2, text following note 45 and section 3.1.1, text following note 179; see also section 4.2.1 of this chapter, text following note 130. The twofold manner of interpretating Art. 5(1), namely the general rule applicable to all contracts and the special rule laid down for contracts of employment as was established by the Court, was corroborated by means of the 1989 Accession Convention, in which a specific connecting factor was introduced for contracts of employment, in conformity with previous decisions of the Court; compare in this respect also Regulation 44/2001, Arts. 18 to 21. Notice furthermore that this Regulation gives an autonomous definition of place of performance in two categories of situation in Art. 5(1) sub. b. However, that provision does not fully resolve the problem, since under this Regulation, depending on the circumstances of the case, reference to national law may still be required in order to establish what the place of performance of the obligation in question actually is.

[29] C-7/98 *Krombach v Bamberski* 22.

[30] C-7/98 *Krombach v Bamberski* 23.

prerogative of a 'right of veto' regarding the acceptability of a state's public policy defence, in effect capable of imposing uniform standards on the notion of public policy in the context of the Convention.[31] In this case the principle of the free movement of judgments reinforces the requirement of an autonomous interpretation of the concepts of the Convention.

C Art. 21 R 27

An answer to the question of whether the Court should impose uniformity on the Contracting States may also depend on the distinction between legal issues that do and those that do not belong to the core of the Convention. If the interpretation concerns an issue that does not belong to the core of the Convention, the Court does not think it appropriate to interpret the concepts involved independently.

An examination of *Zelger v Salinitri* and *Gübisch v Palumbo* with regard to the interpretation of Article 21, shows how the Court, incidentally, has drawn the borderline between legal questions that should and those that should not be given a uniform answer independent from the national laws of the states involved in the case at hand.[32]

In *Zelger v Salinitri*, the Court had to answer a question from the national court with regard to the words 'first seised' in Article 21 of the Convention. In that judgment, the Court first of all pointed out that the rules of procedure of the various Contracting States are far from identical as regards determining the date at which the courts are seised, and that from a comparison of the legislation of the Contracting States a common concept of *lis pendens* could not be arrived at.[33] Next, the Court held that Article 21 gives no indication of the nature of the procedural formalities which must be taken into account for the purposes of considering whether a situation of *lis pendens* is established. In particular, it gives no indication as to whether *lis pendens* comes into being upon the receipt by a court of an application or upon service or notification of that application on or to the party concerned.[34] Apparently, the Court could not decide on an autonomous interpretation of these words, when it held:

> 'Since the object of the Convention is not to unify those formalities, which are closely linked to the organization of judicial procedure in the various states, the question as to the moment at which the conditions for definitive seisin for the purposes of Article 21 are met must be appraised and resolved, in the case of each court, according to the rules of its own national law. That method allows each court to establish with a sufficient degree of certainty, by reference to its own national law, as regards itself, and by

[31] For a more elaborate discussion of the concept 'public policy' in Art. 27, point 1, see section 2 of chapter 2, text following note 20 and section 1 of chapter 3, text following note 19.

[32] 129/83 *Zelger v Salinitri II*; 144/86 *Gubisch v Palumbo*.

[33] 129/83 *Zelger v Salinitri II* 10,13.

[34] 129/83 *Zelger v Salinitri II* 14.

> reference to the national law of any other court which has been seised, as regards that court, the order or priority in time of several actions brought within the conditions laid down by the Convention.'[35]

When justifying its negative answer to the question of the autonomous interpretation of the words 'first seised', the Court did not hold that it was impossible to argue for an autonomous interpretation, but rather that it would be inappropriate, since the Convention's core objective is not to unify procedural rules.

Contrary to the Court's viewpoint on the interpretation of the words 'first seised' in Article 21, the Court in *Gübisch v Palumbo* held that as far as the substantive conditions of *lis pendens* are concerned, namely 'same cause of action' and 'between the same parties', the terms used in Article 21 must be regarded as independent. The Court held that such a result is not in conflict with the Court's stance in *Zelger v Salinitri*, since its reasoning in that judgment was based on the absence of any indication in Article 21 as to the nature of the relevant procedural formalities and on the fact that the Convention does not have the aim of unifying those formalities, which are closely connected with the procedural systems of the different Contracting States.[36] Moreover, leaving the interpretation of such formalities to the national law of the courts concerned, would, in principle, not undermine the objectives of the Convention.[37] Such an interpretation guarantees a sufficient degree of certainty, according to the Court.[38]

1.2 The Convention prevails over national provisions that are incompatible with it

C Art. 5(3)	R 5(3)	C Art. 17	R 23	C Art. 36(1st para.)	R 43(5)
C Art. 6(2)	R 6(2)	C Art. 19	R 25		
C Art. 16	R 22	C Art. 31	R 38		

The sub-principle 'equality and uniformity of rights and obligations' which flows from the principle of legal certainty, also requires that the Convention must prevail over national provisions that are incompatible with it.

The case *Duijnstee v Goderbauer* illustrates this. This case was concerned with national procedural rules directly conflicting with Article 19 of the Convention. That provision stipulates that where a court of a Contracting State is seised of a claim which is principally concerned with a matter over which the courts of another Contracting State have exclusive jurisdiction by virtue of Article 16, it shall declare of its own motion that it has no jurisdiction. Contrary to that provi-

---

[35] 129/83 *Zelger v Salinitri II* 15.

[36] 144/86 *Gubisch v Palumbo* 6,10 (re 129/83 *Zelger v Salinitri II*)-12 (re *Zelger v Salinitri II*).

[37] Compare 144/86 *Gubisch v Palumbo* 18.

[38] 129/83 *Zelger v Salinitri II* 15. Notice that Art. 30 of Regulation No. 44/2001 determines in detail when a court shall be deemed to be seised, for the purposes of that Regulation.

sion, the Dutch Code of Civil Procedure provides that the 'Hoge Raad' (the Supreme Court) of the Netherlands is to confine its consideration of a case to the grounds on which the appeal is based. The Court ruled, though, that Article 19 of the Convention overrides the provision of the Dutch Civil Code, which means that the national court would have to declare of its own motion that it has no jurisdiction whenever it finds that the court of another Contracting State has exclusive jurisdiction under Article 16 of the Convention, even though the national rules of procedure limit the national court's review to the grounds raised by the parties.[39]

The Court's reasoning in *Duijnstee v Goderbauer* clearly shows that the Court uses the principle of 'equality and uniformity of rights and obligations'. It also shows that the Court considers that principle to be based on the principle of legal certainty, which in turn flows from, or is related to, the principle of strengthening the legal protection of persons established within the European Community. And it shows that in matters which belong to those issues which the Convention aims to regulate, the principle 'equality and uniformity of rights and obligations' requires that the Convention prevails over national rules that are incompatible with it. Here, we recall the Court's reasoning:

> 'In order to reply to that question, it is necessary to consider the aims of the Convention.
> According to the preamble of the Convention, the Contracting States, anxious to "strengthen in the Community the legal protection of persons therein established", considered that it was necessary for that purpose "to determine the international jurisdiction of their courts, to facilitate recognition and to introduce an expeditious procedure for securing the enforcement of judgments". Both the provisions on jurisdiction and those on the recognition and enforcement of judgments are therefore aimed at strengthening the legal protection of persons established in the Community.The principle of legal certainty in the Community legal order and the aims pursued by the Convention ... require that equality and uniformity of rights and obligations arising from the Convention for the Contracting States and the persons concerned must be ensured, regardless of the rules laid down in that regard in the laws of those states. It must be concluded that the Convention ... must override national provisions which are incompatible with it.'[40]

In the case of *Elefanten Schuh v Jacqmain*, which is of an earlier date than *Duijnstee v Goderbauer*, the Court was faced with a similar situation, in that national rules appear to be at odds with a provision of the Convention.[41] The question concerned the validity of an agreement conferring jurisdiction on the court(s) of (a) Contracting State(s). According to Article 17, first paragraph, sub a, such

[39] 288/82 *Duijnstee v Goderbauer* 9,14,15.
[40] 288/82 *Duijnstee v Goderbauer* 10,11,13,14.
[41] 150/80 *Elefanten Schuh v Jacqmain.*

agreements must take the form of an agreement in writing or an oral agreement evidenced in writing. Belgian national law contained the rule that in employment contracts, agreements conferring jurisdiction had to be written in Dutch. Belgian law would imply that the choice of forum clause in the employment contract at hand, which had been written in German, would be invalid. The Court ruled, however, that Contracting States are not free to lay down formal requirements other than those contained in the Convention. Consequently, the legislation of a Contracting State may not allow the validity of an agreement conferring jurisdiction to be called into question solely on the grounds that the language used is not that prescribed by that legislation.[42] Although the Court did not explicitly refer to the need for 'equality and uniformity of the rights and obligations arising from the Convention', its remark that a choice of forum made in accordance with the formal requirements of Article 17 'must ... be respected by the courts of all the Contracting States' seems to refer to this principle.[43]

Deutsche Genossenschaftsbank v Brasserie du Pêcheur is another case concerned with a conflict between the Convention's provisions and a Contracting State's national law.[44] The conflict concerned Article 36 of the Convention, providing that if enforcement of a judgment is authorized according to the Convention's rules, the party against whom enforcement is sought may appeal against the decision. The question was, as was seen before, whether interested third parties, who under a Contracting State's domestic law are allowed to challenge an enforcement order, may do so or whether Article 36 excludes this.[45] The Court first established that limiting the opportunities of an appeal against the decision of a court authorizing enforcement contributes to one of the main objectives of the Convention, namely to simplify and speed up procedures in the state in which enforcement is sought (in accordance with the principle of free movement of judgments).[46] Having established this, the Court goes on to argue that the autonomous nature of the Convention's enforcement procedure requires its core provisions regarding enforcement to override national legal provisions that are incompatible with it. Thereto, the Court considered as follows:

> 'It is appropriate to recall first that in its judgement ... the Court stated that the Convention 'provides for a very simple enforcement procedure whilst giving the party against whom enforcement is sought an opportunity to lodge an appeal'. It also stated that the principal objective of the Convention 'is to simplify procedures in the state in which enforcement is sought'. In order to attain that objective the Convention established an enforcement procedure which constitutes an autonomous and complete system, including the matter of appeals. It follows that Article 36 of the Convention ex-

---

[42] 150/80 *Elefanten Schuh v Jacqmain* 26-29.
[43] 150/80 *Elefanten Schuh v Jacqmain* 28.
[44] 148/84 *Deutsche Genossenschaftsbank v Brasserie du Pêcheur*.
[45] Compare section 2 of chapter 3, text following note 56.
[46] Idem.

cludes procedures whereby interested third parties may challenge an enforcement order under domestic law.'[47]

Hagen v Zeehaghe also illustrates the Court's stance that the Convention overrides national law that is incompatible with it.[48] The Court had to answer several questions on the interpretation of Article 6, point 2. These questions sought to establish whether that provision requires a national court to grant leave to bring an action on a warranty or guarantee, or whether, on the contrary, the court may assess the admissibility of the application for leave in the light of the rules of the national procedural law.[49] In answering these questions the Court stressed that it was not the object of the Convention to unify procedural rules, that a clear distinction is to be made between jurisdiction and the conditions governing the admissibility of an action, and that, as regards procedural rules, reference must be made by the national court to the national rules applicable.[50] The Court then pointed out, though, that the application of national procedural rules may not impair the effectiveness of the Convention, and that 'a court may not apply conditions of admissibility laid down by national law which would have the effect of restricting the application of the rules of jurisdiction laid down in the Convention.'[51]

A similar line of reasoning was followed by the Court in *Shevill v Presse Alliance*, when it answered questions on the interpretation of Article 5, point 3, which provides that in matters relating to tort, delict or quasi-delict, the courts for the place where the harmful event occurred have jurisdiction. One of these questions was essentially whether the national court should follow independent (autonomous) criteria or criteria laid down by national law for assessing whether the harmful event in question is harmful and as regards the evidence required of the existence and extent of the harm alleged by the plaintiff. When answering that question, the Court first observed that the object of the Convention is not to unify the rules of substantive law and of procedures of the different Contracting States, but to determine which court has jurisdiction in disputes relating to civil and commercial matters and to facilitate the enforcement of judgments.[52]After having repeated what was by that time settled case law in case reference must be made to the national rules of procedural law, namely that the application of these rules must not impair the effectiveness of the Convention, the Court followed a similar line of argument in case reference must be made to national rules of substantive law. It stated:

[47] 148/84 *Deutsche Genossenschaftsbank v Brasserie du Pêcheur* 16 (re 258/83 *Brennero v Wendel*),17.

[48] C-365/88 *Hagen v Zeehaghe.*

[49] C-365/88 *Hagen v Zeehaghe* 13.

[50] C-365/88 *Hagen v Zeehaghe* 17-19 (re 129/83 *Zelger v Salinitri II*; 148/84 *Deutsche Genossenschaftsbank v Brasserie du Pêcheur*, and 145/86 *Hoffmann v Krieg*).

[51] C-365/88 *Hagen v Zeehaghe* 20 (re 288/82 *Duijnstee v Goderbauer*).

[52] C-68/93 *Shevill v Presse Alliance* 35 (re C-365/88 *Hagen v Zeehaghe* 17).

> 'the criteria for assessing whether the event in question is harmful and the evidence required of the existence and extent of the harm alleged by the victim of the defamation are not governed by the Convention but by the substantive law determined by the national conflict of laws rules of the court seised, provided that the effectiveness of the Convention is not thereby impaired.'[53]

The relationship between national (substantive or procedural) law and the provisions of the Convention has been an issue in quite a number of cases.[54] From all these cases, the Court's stance is evident. National substantive or procedural rules, although not at the core of the Convention, must not impair its effectiveness.

Weighing and determining the principle of equality and uniformity of rights and obligations arising from the Convention

The principle of equality and uniformity of rights and obligations is firmly established by the Court's case law. The principle requires an autonomous interpretation of the provisions of the Convention, unless such an interpretation is impossible or inappropriate, and it requires the Convention to prevail over any national law that is incompatible with it. From the cases that have been discussed in this section, it appears that if one of the following conditions is fulfilled, the Court will in principle impose a uniform, autonomous interpretation and/or put aside national law that is incompatible with it:

- the legal issue concerned belongs to the core issues which the Convention aims to regulate (that is the determination of jurisdiction, the facilitation of the recognition and enforcement of judgments and the scope of the Convention), or
- the legal issue concerned does not in itself belong to the core issues which the Convention aims to regulate, but the answer given by the applicable national (substantive or procedural) law would undermine the objectives of the Convention.

If neither of these two conditions is fulfilled, the Court does not consider it to be its task to impose its views, and leaves the answer to the applicable national law. If one of these conditions is fulfilled, though, the Court will not leave matters to national law but will impose, as far as it is possible, its own interpretation and/or overrule any national law that is incompatible with it.[55]

---

[53] C-68/93 *Shevill v Presse Alliance* 41.

[54] C-267/97 *Coursier v Fortis Bank* 28 (re *Deutsche Genossenschaftsbank* 18; 145/86 *Hoffman v Krieg* 27); C-37/00 *Weber v Universal Ogden Services* 59 (re 25/79 *Sanicentral* 5). See also C-43/95 *Delecta v Aktiebolag*; C-323/95 *Hayes v Kronenberger*; C-122/96 *Saldanha v Hiross Holding*.

[55] Compare 145/86 *Hoffman v Krieg* 31; C-365/88 *Hagen v Zeehaghe* 20 (re 288/82 *Duijnstee v Goderbauer)*.

2. Respect for the wording of the Convention's provisions

C Art. 27(2)	R 34(2)
C Art. 39(1st para.)	R 47(1)

When considering how to interpret the provisions of the Convention, the Court invariably also takes account of the words of the different language versions of the relevant provision(s).[56]

Capelloni v Pelkmans is one of a number of cases that illustrates the Court's stance on the linguistic boundaries of the Convention's provisions. The Court had to answer the question whether the protective measures referred to in Article 39, first paragraph, are subject to the rule embodied in the national law of the forum whereby a protective measure must be taken within a limited period of time. The Court answered that question as follows:

> 'the reply to that question is to be inferred from the very wording of the first paragraph of Article 39. Since the Convention provides that 'during the time specified for an appeal pursuant to Article 36 and until any such appeal has been determined, no measures of enforcement may be taken other than protective measures', the right to proceed with the measures in question cannot be restricted in time by the application of national measures prescribing a shorter period.'[57]

In quite a number of cases, the Court has explicitly taken account of the fact that there are different language versions of the Convention.[58] For example, in *Lancray v Peters*, the Court referred to the wording of the different language versions of Article 27, point 2, when it answered the question whether the conditions of due service and sufficient time laid down in that provision must both be met concurrently for a foreign judgment to be recognized. The Court answered that question in the affirmative by reference, first, to the wording of the different language versions of the provision and, secondly, to the Jenard Report.[59]

---

[56] Cases in which reference is made to the wording or language versions of the (Accession versions of the) Convention are among others 14/76 *De Bloos v Bouyer* 11,12; 23/78 *Meeth v Glacetal* 5; 150/80 *Elefanten Schuh v Jacqmain* 14; 166/80 *Klomps v Michel* 9; 119/84 *Capelloni v Pelkmans* 28; C-305/88 *Lancray v Peters*; C-365/88 *Hagen v Zeehaghe*; C-351/89 *OUI v NHIC* 13-15; C-89/91 *Shearson v TVB* 20,22; C-172/91 *Sonntag v Waidmann* 16; C-129/92 *Owens v Bracco* 17; C-406/92 *Tatry v Maciej Rataj* 32,37; C-414/92 *Solo v Boch* 15; C-269/95 *Benincasa v Dentalkit* 15; C-295/95 *Farrel v Long* 23; C-351/96 *Drouot v CMI* 18; C-51/97 *Réunion européenne v Spliethoff's* 44; C-260/97 *Unibank v Christensen* 19-21; C-8/98 *Dansommer v Götz* 18; C-387/98 *Coreck v Handelsveem* 15, 17; C-412/98 *Josi Reinsurance v UGIC* 54; C-96/00 *Gabriel* 38; C-256/00 *Besix v Kretzschmar* 29.

[57] 119/84 *Capelloni v Pelkmans* 28.

[58] Among others in 14/76 *De Bloos v Bouyer* 11,12 ; 150/80 *Elefanten Schuh v Jacqmain* 14; C-406/92 *Tatry v Maciej Rataj* 37; C-341/93 *Danvaern v Schuhfabriken* 14; C-163/95 *Von Horn v Cinnamond* 12; C-99/96 *Mietz v Intership* 31.

[59] C-305/88 *Lancray v Peters* 15-17 (re Experts' Report, OJ 1979, C 59, p.1).

Thus, as appears from the Court's case law, the Court is very careful to establish that its interpretations remain within the linguistic boundaries of the Convention's provisions. Although in most cases the Court does not explicitly state that its concern for the wording of the provisions follows from the principle of legal certainty, the constraint that the Court apparently feels, implying that it should keep its interpretations within the linguistic boundaries of the provisions, can be seen as an implication of the principle of legal certainty.[60] It needs no further argument than that the principle works, in general, to the benefit of all persons established within the Community, and of the parties directly concerned in particular, since by applying that principle the (legitimate) expectations of the parties as regards the wording of the Convention are respected. The Court's stance on judicial constraint, as discussed in chapter 1, can be considered as related to this issue.[61]

The principle of respect for the wording of the Convention weighed in relation to other principles

In those cases in which the Court takes account of the wording (of the different language versions) of the Convention, it may occur that the wording of the relevant provision cannot bear the interpretation suggested by some other principle underlying the Convention, such as the principle of free movement of judgments, the principle of the protection of the rights of the defence, the principle that disputes should be decided by an appropriate court or other aspects of the principle of legal certainty as described in section 1 and sections 3 to 5 of this chapter. This can be seen in several decisions in which the Court considers interpretations that would be in line with some of the Convention's principles, but that would clearly go against the wording of the relevant provisions.[62] At this point we need a clearer view on what the Court's position with regard to this issue is. In order to analyse the Court's position on this issue, it is useful to distinguish between three types of cases:

1. cases in which the interpretation suggested by other principles underlying the Convention (or other aspects of legal certainty) is quite clearly also supported by the words of the relevant rule(s),
2. cases in which the interpretation suggested by other (sub-)principles is not clearly supported by the words of the relevant rule(s), but the words can be seen as 'not prohibiting' the interpretation, and

---

[60] Compare, among others, 241/83 *Rösler v Rottwinkel* 21-23; C-256/00 *Besix v Kretzschmar* 24-28,29.

[61] See previously section 2 of chapter 1.

[62] See the discussion on the case *Rösler v Rottwinkel* later in this section, text following note 68.

3. cases in which the interpretation suggested by other (sub-)principles is very clearly at odds with the wording of the relevant rule(s).

C Art. 13	R 15	C Art. 17(1st para.)	R 23(1)
C Art. 16(1)	R 22(1)		

In cases belonging to the *first* category, the other (sub-)principles are clearly in line with the words of the provision concerned: the 'principled' interpretation clearly stays within the linguistic boundaries of the rule. That was the case, for example, in *Gabriel.*[63] In that judgment, the Court had to answer the question whether an action having certain characteristics, as in the case at hand, could be classified as being based on a consumer contract and would therefore fall within the scope of Article 13, laid down in section 4 of Title II of the Convention.[64] The Court first recalled that concepts of the Convention must in principle be interpreted independently.[65] The Court then established that from the wording of Article 13 and from the purpose of the regime introduced in that section (which is the idea that the party who is weaker due to his socio-economic position should be protected), it follows that those provisions cover only a private final consumer, not engaged in trade or professional activities, who is bound by one of the three types of contract listed in Article 13 and who is also personally a party to the action, in accordance with Article 14.[66] Therefore, the application of these rules should not be extended to a plaintiff who is acting in pursuance of his trade or professional activity and who is not himself a consumer party.[67] Here, the 'principled' interpretation of the provision in question is clearly in line with its wording.

In cases belonging to the *third* category, an interpretation suggested by one or more of the other (sub-)principles is clearly incompatible with the wording of the rules: in such a case the 'principled' interpretation would clearly go beyond the linguistic boundaries of the rules. The Court took the position that in these cases 'words trump principles'. That position became clear in *Rösler v Rottwinkel.*[68] In this case, both the government of the Federal Republic of Germany and the Court held the opinion that a 'principled' interpretation of Article 16, point 1,[69] would

[63] C-96/00 *Gabriel*; see also C-288/92 *Custom Made v Stawa* 18-20 (re 34/82 *Peters v ZNAV* 17); C-406/92 *Tatry v Maciej Rataj* 32; and C-295/95 *Farrel v Long* 17- 24 (re Jenard Report OJ 1979 C 59, p. 25)-27.

[64] C-96/00 *Gabriel* 36.

[65] C-96/00 *Gabriel* 37 (re 150/77 *Bertrand* 14,15,16), C-89/91 *Shearson v TVB* 13, C-269/95 *Benincasa* 12, C-99/96 *Mietz v Intership* 26).

[66] C-96/00 *Gabriel* 38,39 (re C-89/91 *Shearson v TVB* 19,20,22,24).

[67] C-89/91 *Shearson v TVB* 24.

[68] 241/83 *Rösler v Rottwinkel*; see also chapter 1, section 2, text following note 13.

[69] As it occurred in the 1968 Brussels Convention, i.e., before the entry into force of the 1989 Accession Convention, in which Art. 16(1) was amended. See Art. 6 of the 1989 Accession Convention.

require an interpretation in light of the principle of sound administration of justice, which underlies that provision. This principle implies that a court that has certain practical advantages, such as first-hand knowledge of the facts, ease of taking evidence and proximity of law, should be competent to hear the case.[70] The German government held that an interpretation of Article 16, point 1, in light of this principle would imply that that provision does not apply to agreements which relate only to the short-term letting of holiday homes. Article 16, point 1, should only apply to tenancies of immovable property, especially of dwellings, because such cases are generally governed by complex legislation which is strongly influenced by social considerations and which is best applied by the courts of the country in which it is in force and in which the property is situated. As regards agreements which relate only to the short-term letting of holiday homes, the court of the place in which the property is situated would not necessarily have that practical advantage, since complex social legislation as in the matter of tenancies of immovable property in force in the state in which that property is situated do not apply to these agreements. This viewpoint of the German government was at the basis of the question by the national court as to whether exceptions may be made to the general rule laid down in Article 16, with regard to the short-term letting of holiday homes, even where the wording of that Article gives no indication in that respect. The Court decided that such an exception, in violation of the wording of Article 16, point 1, could not be accepted in view of the principle of legal certainty.[71]

The *second* category appears to be crucial for a good understanding of the Court's position as regards the linguistic boundaries of a rule. This category shows how far the Court is willing to stretch the notion of the linguistic boundaries of a rule. The Court takes the position that whenever an interpretation supported by the substantive principles is not completely in line with the plain meaning of the words of a rule, but the words can be seen 'not to prohibit' the interpretation, the interpretation is allowed: it does not fall outside of the linguistic boundaries of the rule. *Meeth v Glacetal* sufficiently clarifies this notion of the linguistic boundaries of the Convention's provisions.[72] The Court had to answer a question on the interpretation of Article 17, first paragraph. That Article states: 'If the parties ... have agreed that a court or the courts of a Contracting State are to have jurisdiction ... that court or those courts shall have ... jurisdiction.' The question was whether that provision permits an agreement under which the two parties to a contract for sale, who are domiciled in different states, can be sued

---

[70] The principle of a sound administration will be discussed hereafter, in chapter 6, section 3; see in particular, section 3.1.3, text following note 353.

[71] 241/83 *Rösler v Rottwinkel* 10,19,20-24. The (third) Accession Convention, by which Art. 16(1) was amended, made it clear that the viewpoint of the German government was very plausible.

[72] 23/78 *Meeth v Glacetal* 4-6; compare section 2 of chapter 1, text following note 11.

only in the courts of their respective states, despite the fact that the wording of Article 17 only refers to a court or the courts of a *single* state. When answering that question the court referred to the principle directly underlying Article 17, the principle of party autonomy, and decided that Article 17 cannot be interpreted as prohibiting such an agreement.

Finally, from *Elefanten Schuh v Jacqmain* we may learn that if an indeterminacy arises from differences between different language versions – in such a case a solution derived from the wording of the Convention cannot be arrived at – the Court chooses the interpretation that is more in keeping with the objectives and spirit of the Convention, as opposed to any another.[73]

3. Legal certainty with regard to the scope of the Convention

C Art. 1	R 1	C Art. 4	R 4	C Art. 25	R 32
C Art. 3	R 3	C Art. 6(1)	R 6(1)		

In addition to these general observations of the Court as regards the principle of legal certainty which are relevant to the Convention as a whole, the Court has occasionally clarified that legal certainty also implies specific requirements with regard to the specific topics of the Convention, such as its scope, jurisdiction, and recognition and enforcement of judgments.

With respect to the scope of the Convention, which encompasses substantive and formal aspects, the Court has incidentally referred to the principle of legal certainty when it had to decide on the interpretation of the provisions involved. Several cases will be discussed in this context.

As regards the *substantive* scope of the Convention, as determined in Article 1, the Court has stated that it is settled case law that this provision must be interpreted independently. As was seen earlier, this means: an interpretation 'by reference, first, to the objectives and the scheme of the Convention and, secondly, to the general principles which stem from the corpus of the national legal systems'.[74] The Court's usual technique of attributing an autonomous meaning to the Convention's provisions, the part that implies the application of 'principled-based reasoning', cannot be fully pursued here. The principles 'free movement of judgments', 'protection of the rights of the defence' and 'sound administration of

---

[73] 150/80 *Elefanten Schuh v Jacqmain* 14.

[74] C-271/00 *Gem. Steenbergen v Luc Baten* 28 (re 29/76 *LTU v Eurocontrol* 3; 133/78 *Gourdain v Nadler* 3; 814/79 *Netherlands State v Rüffer* 7; C-172/91 *Sonntag v Waidmann* 18); 29/76 *LTU v Eurocontrol* 3; 9 & 10/77 *Bavaria v Eurocontrol* 4 (re 29/76 *LTU v Eurocontrol* 3); 133/78 *Gourdain v Nadler* 3; 814/79 *Netherlands State v Rüffer* 7 (re 29/76 *LTU v Eurocontrol* , 9 & 10/77 *Bavaria v Eurocontrol*; 133/78 *Gourdain v Nadler*); and compare section 1.1 of this chapter, text following note 17.

justice' and the sub-principles that flow from these main principles, are not of any significance as far as the substantive scope of the Convention is concerned. Therefore, it must be assumed that the principle of legal certainty is the only principle that could play a role when interpreting Article 1 of the Convention. The question arises, however, what the principle of legal certainty actually could require in addition to what is already required by the general observations of the Court as regards legal certainty.

In the cases concerning the interpretation of Article 1, the Court has consistently held that the field of application of the Convention, as laid down in Article 1, is essentially determined either by reason of the legal relationship between the parties to the action or of the subject-matter of the action.[75] The applicability of the Convention cannot for example be determined in the light of the division of jurisdiction between the various types of courts existing in certain Contracting States, as is already evident from the wording of Article 1.[76] Neither can the application of the Convention depend on the question whether a claim is ancillary to proceedings which do not fall within the scope of the Convention.[77] Also, it is settled case law that actions between a public authority and a person governed by private law may fall within the scope of the Brussels Convention, in so far as that authority is not acting in the exercise of public powers.[78]

In most of the cases which are concerned with the interpretation of Article 1, the Court neither referred to the principle of legal certainty nor to any other principle when it justified its interpretation of that provision. In *Rich v Impianti*, however, the Court expressly referred to the principle of legal certainty. The Court had to answer a question on the interpretation of Article 1, point 4, of the Convention, which provision excludes arbitration from the substantive scope of the Convention. In answering that question, the Court held that, in order to meet the principle of legal certainty, a national court must, when determining whether a dispute falls within the scope of the Convention, solely take account of the subject matter of the dispute (or the legal relationship between the parties to the action).[79] If a dispute falls outside the scope of the Convention by virtue of its subject-matter, such as the appointment of an arbitrator, the existence of a preliminary issue which the court must resolve in order to determine the dispute cannot,

---

[75] Among others 29/76 *LTU v Eurocontrol* 4; 133/78 *Gourdain v Nadler* 3; 143/78 *Cavel v Cavel I* 7; 120/79 *Cavel v Cavel II* 4; 814/79 *Netherlands State v Rüffer* 14.

[76] 133/78 *Gourdain v Nadler* 3; 814/79 *Netherlands State v Rüffer* 14; and C-172/91 *Sonntag v Waidmann* 16.

[77] 120/79 *Cavel v Cavel II* 9.

[78] Among others C-167/00 *Konsumenteninformation v Henkel* 26 (re 29/76 *LTU v Eurocontrol* 4; 814/79 *Netherlands State v Rüffer* 8; and C-172/91 *Sonntag v Waidmann* 20); C-271/00 *Gem. Steenbergen v Luc Baten* 30 (re *LTU* 4; *Rüffer* 8).

[79] C-190/89 *Rich v Impianti* 26; and compare 814/79 *Netherlands State v Rüffer* 14; see also C-391/95 *Van Uden v Deco-Line* 31.

whatever that issue may be, justify the application of the Convention. The Court stated:

> 'It would also be contrary to the principle of legal certainty, which is one of the objectives pursued by the Convention ... for the applicability of the exclusion laid down in Article 1(4) of the Convention to vary according to the existence or otherwise of a preliminary issue, which might be raised at any time by the parties.'[80]

From the foregoing, it follows that the substantive scope of the Convention, within the meaning of Article 1, requires that the applicability of the Convention is to be determined only by virtue of the subject-matter of the action or the legal relationship between the parties to the action. However, in our view, mere reference to these issues in a case at hand cannot provide content to the concept of 'civil and commercial matters'. We therefore assume that the Court (explicitly or implicitly) makes reference to the scheme of the Convention, the general principles which stem from the corpus of the national legal systems, to the Experts' Report or, as is seen more recently, the substance of such concepts in Community law or other relevant sources.[81] Mere reference to the internal law of one or other of the States concerned cannot constitute an autonomous interpretation.

---

[80] C-190/89 *Rich v Impianti* 27 (re 38/81 *Effer v Kantner* 6).

[81] For example, in *Cavel v Cavel II*, the Court decided that the Convention applies to 'the enforcement of an interlocutory order made by a French judge in divorce proceedings, whereby one of the parties to the proceedings is awarded maintenance payable monthly'. Such an order falls within the scope of the concept 'civil matter', even if that order is ancillary to proceedings which, because of their subject-matter, do not come within the Convention's sphere of application. The Court referred to the general scheme of the Convention, that, according to the Court unequivocally demonstrates that the treatment of an ancillary claim is not necessarily linked to that of a principal claim; 120/79 *Cavel v Cavel II* 7,8,9 (re 143/78 *Cavel v Cavel I*)-12. In *Sonntag v Waidmann*, the Court held that 'civil matters' cover a claim for damages made before a criminal court against a teacher in a State school who, during a school trip, caused injury to a pupil through a culpable and unlawful breach of his duties of supervision, even in a case where cover is provided under a social insurance scheme governed by public law. The Court referred to the wording of Article 1, first paragraph: 'shall apply in civil and commercial matters whatever the nature of the court or tribunal', and to the general principles which stem from the corpus of the national legal systems. The Court then held that in the legal systems of the Contracting States the right to obtain compensation for injury suffered as a result of conduct regarded as culpable in criminal law is generally recognized as being a civil law right and that that concept also underlies Art. 5, point 4; C-172/91 *Sonntag v Waidmann* 16,17,18 (re 29/76 *LTU v Eurocontrol* 3,4; 133/78 *Gourdain v Nadler* 3; 814/79 *Netherlands State v Rüffer* 7,8),19. As regards the question whether an action against a teacher in a State school falls within the scope of the Convention, the Court referred to *LTU* and *Rüffer*, in which it was decided that such an action falls outside the scope of the Convention only where the author of the damage against whom it is brought must be regarded as a public authority which acted in the exercise of public powers. The Court decided that the action in the present case falls within the Convention's scope (20 re *LTU* and *Rüffer*)-24 (re 66/85 *Lawrie v Land Baden-Württemberg* 28)-29; see also section 1.1 of chapter 5, text following note 17. Most recently, in *Gem. Steenbergen v Luc Baten*, the Court decided that an action by which a public body seeks from a person governed by private law recovery of sums paid by it by way of social assistance to the former spouse and the child of that

In quite a number of judgments, the Court had to decide on the substantive scope of the Convention, not by determining concepts used in Article 1 of the Convention, such as 'civil and commercial matters', or the exclusions laid down in that provision, but by determining the *core issues* of the Convention: jurisdiction, and recognition and enforcement of judgments.[82] As was seen in section 1.1 of this chapter, an autonomous interpretation of concepts which are closely linked to issues not concerned with jurisdiction or recognition and enforcement, but rather with the organization of judicial procedures, with the execution of judgments itself or with substantive law, is not appropriate according to the Court.[83] Such concepts must be left to the national law, unless the application of these national rules impairs the effectiveness of the Convention. Obviously, the principle of legal certainty, as far as it requires equality and uniformity of rights and obligations, cannot be met as regards issues that do not lie at the core of the Convention. The Court has emphasized, though, that a clear distinction between the issues that fall within the scope of the Convention and issues concerned with, in particular, the organization of judicial procedures and the execution of judgments, must be drawn.[84] Such a distinction would contribute to legal certainty as to the substantive scope of the Convention. However, the court has only incidentally clarified how to draw the borderline between legal questions that do and those that do not belong to the core issues of the Convention.[85]

The *formal scope* of the Convention is determined by means of Articles 3 and 4 of the Convention and Article 25. In *Réunion européenne v Spliethoff's*, the Court held that the principle of legal certainty requires an interpretation of the relevant provisions, in particular of Articles 3 and 4, such as to ensure that persons domiciled in the territory of the Community benefit from the rules laid down in

person, does not fall within the scope of the Convention. Such an action cannot be regarded as a 'civil matter'. The Court argued that the action was founded on provisions by which the legislature conferred on the public body a prerogative of its own (32-37). It did not and probably could not justify that decision in terms of the objectives or scheme of the Convention, or the general principles which stem from the national legal systems as a whole (28). A second question in this case was whether such an action could be regarded as 'social security' as in point 3 of the second paragraph of Article 1. The Court held that in view of the link between the Convention and Community law, regard must be had to the substance of that concept in Community law. The Court referred to the concept 'social security' in Regulation No. 1408/71 and to the Jenard and Schlosser Reports (43-48), and decided that this concept did not cover such an action (49); C-271/00 *Gem. Steenbergen v Luc Baten* 28 (re 29/76 *LTU* 3; 133/78 *Gourdain* 3; 814/79 *Rüffer* 7; C-172/91 *Sonntag* 18), 31-37, 43 (re C-398/92 *Mund & Fester* 12; C-7/98 *Krombach* 24),44-48 (re Jenard Report, OJ 1979 C 59, p. 12,13; Schlosser Report, OJ 1979 C 59, p. 71, para. 60),49; similar lines of argumentation were followed in C-266/01 *TIARD v Staat der Nederlanden.*

[82] Compare C-365/88 *Hagen v Zeehaghe* 19 (re 129/83 *Zelger v Salinitri II* 15, C-148/84 *Deutsche Genossenschaftsbank v Brasserie du Pêcheur* 18, 145/86 *Hoffmann v Krieg* 27).

[83] See this chapter, section 1.1, text following note 32.

[84] C-365/88 *Hagen v Zeehaghe* 17.

[85] Compare section 1.1 of this chapter, text following note 32.

the Convention. Another interpretation would constitute a violation of the principle of legal certainty. In that judgment the Court had to answer the question whether a defendant domiciled in the territory of a Contracting State may be brought before the court of another Contracting State, hearing an action against a co-defendant not domiciled in the territory of any Contracting State, on the ground that the dispute is indivisible, rather than merely displaying a connection. When answering that question, the Court referred in particular to Article 3, which provides that persons domiciled in a Contracting State may be sued in the courts of another Contracting State only by virtue of the rules set out in Sections 2 to 6 of Title II. Next, the Court stated that the only provision that comes close to the issue involved, Article 6, point 1, only applies if the proceedings in question are brought before the courts of the Contracting States where one of the defendants is domiciled. The Court then continued:

> 'It must be observed that the objective of legal certainty pursued by the Convention would not be attained if the fact that a court in a Contracting State had accepted jurisdiction as regards one of the defendants not domiciled in a Contracting State made it possible to bring another defendant, domiciled in a Contracting State, before that same court in cases other than those envisaged by the Convention, thereby depriving him of the benefit of the protective rules laid down by it.'[86]

Weighing and determining legal certainty as to the scope of the Convention

To conclude, the principle of legal certainty as regards the scope of the Convention is incidentally referred to in the Court's case law. It appears from that case law that it is the only principle that has an influence on the interpretation of the provisions on the Convention's scope. The principle requires:

- as regards the substantive scope of the Convention, that the applicability of the Convention is to be determined only by reason of the subject-matter of the action or the legal relationship between the parties to the action, and by a clear distinction between issues that do (jurisdiction, recognition and enforcement) and do not belong to the Convention's core business (organization of proceedings and execution, and substantive law)
- as far as the formal scope is concerned, an interpretation of the provisions of the Convention so as to ensure that persons domiciled in the territory of the Convention benefit from the protective rules of the Convention.

---

[86] C-51/97 *Réunion européenne v Spliethoff's* 46; compare also C-129/92 *Owens v Bracco* 17-21 (re Jenard Report OJ 1979 C 59, p. 15)-25; Notice though, that Title III, by virtue of Art. 25, applies to any judgment delivered by a court of a Contracting State in those civil and commercial matters which fall within the substantive scope of the Convention, whether or not the parties are domiciled within the Community (see Jenard Report OJ 1979 C 59, p. 43).

4. Legal certainty with regard to the allocation of jurisdiction

Legal certainty as to which court has jurisdiction to decide a dispute which concerns a civil or commercial matter has been a major consideration in the design of the Convention. The Jenard Report clearly stated that:

> 'the purpose of the Convention is ... by establishing common rules of jurisdiction, to achieve ... in the field which it was required to cover, a genuine legal systematization which will ensure the greatest possible degree of legal certainty.'[87]

Accordingly, the Convention was intended to create a set of clear rules allocating jurisdiction, without a *forum non conveniens* exception.[88] The actual content of the Convention's rules of jurisdiction is dictated, though, by the fourth main principle that disputes should be decided by an appropriate court. The notion that disputes should be decided by an appropriate court, as will be discussed in the next chapter, encompasses various sub-principles which are weighed in relation to each other, such as the principles 'protection of the weaker party', 'party autonomy' and 'sound administration of justice'.[89] However, as regards the interpretation of the rules of jurisdiction, legal certainty has a role to play as well.

In the Court's case law, legal certainty with respect to jurisdiction is clearly recognized. The Court has referred to 'the general aim of the Convention, which is to establish rules guaranteeing certainty as to the allocation of jurisdiction to the various national courts.'[90] Legal certainty with respect to the allocation of jurisdiction is quite often used by the Court to argue for or against certain interpretations of the Convention's rules of jurisdiction. Obviously, the general aspects of legal certainty discussed before – the sub-principles 'equality and uniformity of rights and obligations flowing from the Convention' and 'respect for the linguistic boundaries of the Convention's provisions' – also contribute to 'legal certainty as to the allocation of jurisdiction'. In analysing the Court's case law, it appears that the general principle 'legal certainty as to the allocation of jurisdiction' encompasses more than just these two general aspects of legal certainty.[91] In addition to these general aspects of legal certainty, the Court generally employs two different sub-principles, that focus on the subjects that are supposed to benefit from legal certainty as regards the rules of jurisdiction, namely the parties to

---

[87] Jenard Report, OJ 1979 C 59, p. 1, p. 15; compare, among others, C-26/91 *Handte v TMCS* 12 (re Jenard Report, p. 15); C-129/92 *Owens v Bracco* 21 (re Jenard Report, p. 15)

[88] Schlosser Report, OJ 1979 C 59, No. 76,77 at p. 97.

[89] See sections 1 to 4 of chapter 6.

[90] 241/83 *Rösler v Rottwinkel* 23; C-26/91 *Handte v TMCS* 12 (re Jenard Report),19; C-129/92 *Owens v Bracco* 212 (re Jenard Report); C-288/92 *Custom Made v Stawa* 15; C-364/93 *Marinari v Lloyd's Bank* 19 (re 241/83 *Rösler v Rottwinkel* 23; C-26/91 *Handte v TMCS* 19).

[91] Sections 1 and 2.

the dispute: the *plaintiff* and the *defendant*. Legal certainty should be to the benefit of both the plaintiff and the defendant. This implies that (the interpretation of) the rules of jurisdiction should be such that it is easy for the plaintiff to identify the court in which he can sue the defendant and that the defendant can reasonably foresee and predict in which court he will be sued by the plaintiff. These sub-principles contribute, as the Court has explicitly stated in its case law, to the most general principle underlying the Convention, namely the legal protection of persons established in the Community.[92]

The Court's case law shows the Court's concern with these aspects of legal certainty with regard to the allocation of jurisdiction.[93] *Mulox v Geels* is illustrative of that case law. The Court held in that judgment, that the objectives of the Convention include:

> 'unification of the rules on jurisdiction of the Contracting States, so as ... to reinforce the legal protection available to persons established in the Community by, at the same time, allowing the plaintiff easily to identify the court before which he may bring an action and the defendant reasonably to foresee the court before which he may be sued.'[94]

In *Benincasa v Dentalkit*, the Court confirmed the relationship between these aspects of legal certainty as to the allocation of jurisdiction and the most general principle underlying the Convention, namely the principle of strengthening the legal protection of persons established in the Community. In that judgment the Court stated:

> 'Next, as the Court has consistently held, the objectives of the Convention include unification of the rules on jurisdiction of the Contracting States's courts, so as ... to reinforce the legal protection available to persons established in the Community by, at the same time, allowing the plaintiff easily to identify the court before which he may bring an action and the defendant reasonably to foresee the court before which he may be sued ...'[95]

---

[92] See this section, text following note 95.

[93] 34/82 *Peters v ZNAV* 17; C-26/91 *Handte v TMCS* 12 (re Jenard Report),18; C-288/92 *Custom Made v Stawa* 18; C-125/92 *Mulox v Geels* 11; C-295/95 *Farrell v Long* 13 (re *Mulox*); C-383/95 *Rutten v Cross Medical* 13 (re *Mulox*); C-51/97 *Réunion européenne v Spliethoff's* 36; C-159/97 *Castelletti v Trumpy* 48 (re *Peters; Custom Made;* C-269/95 *Benincasa v Dentalkit* 27); C-440/97 *Concorde v Panjan* 24 (re C-26/91 *Handte v TMCS* 19); C-256/00 *Besix v Kretzschmar* 26 (re *Handte*; *Concorde*).

[94] C-125/92 *Mulox v Geels* 11.

[95] C-269/95 *Benincasa v Dentalkit* 26 (re 38/81 *Effer v Kantner* 6; C-125/92 *Mulox v Geels* 11); compare C-334/00 *Tacconi v Sinto Maschinenfabrik* 20 (re C-295/95 *Farrell v Long* 13, C-256/00 *Besix v Kretzschmar* 25,26).

From the foregoing, we conclude that two sub-principles flow from the principle of legal certainty with respect to the allocation of jurisdiction:

(a) the principle that a plaintiff should be able *easily* to identify the court before which he may bring an action, and
(b) the principle that a defendant should be able *reasonably* to foresee the court before which he may be sued.

As will be seen in the next sections (4.1 to 4.3) these two different sub-principles overlap to some extent. This becomes evident from the more concrete sub-principles, mentioned below, which guide the Court's interpretations of the rules of jurisdiction in a more precise manner. These more concrete principles contribute to legal certainty for both the plaintiff and the defendant, in the sense that an interpretation based on these principles should make it easy for the plaintiff to identify the court before which he may bring an action against a defendant and reasonable for the defendant to foresee the court before which he may be sued. However, as will be seen below, legal certainty for the defendant contains more than legal certainty for the plaintiff.[96]

Since these more concrete sub-principles contribute to legal certainty as to jurisdiction in a more precise manner than principles (a) and (b) mentioned above, in that they play a more decisive role in the Court's case law, it will be these principles which will be discussed in further detail in the next sections. They are:

(1) clarity as to the rules of jurisdiction (section 4.1),
(2) avoiding multiplication of jurisdiction as regards one and the same legal relationship (section 4.2), and
(3) national courts should be able readily to decide whether they are competent to hear a case (section 4.3).

4.1 **Clarity as to the rules of jurisdiction**

Clarity as to the rules of jurisdiction undoubtedly contributes to legal certainty as regards jurisdiction and is, naturally, to the advantage of both the plaintiff and the defendant. Clarity as to the rules of jurisdiction can be accomplished in different ways, as is shown by the Court's case law.

C Art. 2	R 2	C Art. 5(5)	R 5(5)	C Art. 17	R 23
C Art. 5(1)	R 5(1)	C Art. 16(1)	R 22(1)		

First of all, the Court has made it clear that making exceptions to a general rule of jurisdiction laid down in the Convention, does not contribute to legal certainty. As was seen before, in *Rösler v Rottwinkel* the Court had to answer the question

[96] See section 4.2, text following note 153.

whether Article 16, point 1, also applies to the letting of immovable property where the letting was for a short term and related only to the use and occupation of a holiday home.[97] In addition to other considerations, the Court also pointed out that it would create uncertainty as to jurisdiction and, therefore, it would be contrary to the purpose of the Convention to assign jurisdiction in a certain and predictable way, to allow exceptions to that rule of jurisdiction. As the Court put it:

> 'Account must also be taken of the uncertainty which would be created if the courts allowed exceptions to be made to the general rule laid down in Article 16 (1), which has the advantage of providing for a clear and certain attribution of jurisdiction covering all circumstances, thus fulfilling the purpose of the Convention, which is to assign jurisdiction in a certain and predictable way.'[98]

It must also be assumed, therefore, that drawing distinctions with regard to concepts that serve as criteria to define the substantive scope of a rule of jurisdiction which are not evident from the wording of these concepts should be avoided as it is at odds with legal certainty. For example, the Court held in *Farrell v Long* that a concept such as 'maintenance creditor' in Article 5, point 2, should not be construed as drawing distinctions between those already recognized and those not yet recognized as entitled to maintenance.[99] When justifying that decision, the Court referred to the principle of legal certainty, and in addition to the wording of that rule of jurisdiction as well as to the intentions of the drafters of the Convention.[100]

The Court's case law shows that the Court considers a certain and reliable criterion for the allocation of jurisdiction to contribute to legal certainty.[101] In *Besix v Kretzschmar*, for example, the Court held that Article 2 of the Convention provides for such a certain and reliable criterion of jurisdiction.[102] The Court's observations in *Somafer v Saar-Ferngas* also mirrors the Court's viewpoint that a certain and reliable criterion for jurisdiction contributes to legal certainty as to jurisdiction.[103] The Court held in that judgment that the interpretation of the concepts of provisions that derogate from the general principle of jurisdiction of Article 2 of the Convention, such as the concept 'branch, agency or other establishment' in Article 5, point 5, 'must show without difficulty the special link justifying such derogation.'[104] Although the Court did not establish a direct link between the principle of legal certainty and the need for a certain and reliable criterion of ju-

[97] See section 2 of this chapter, text following note 68.
[98] 241/83 *Rösler v Rottwinkel* 23.
[99] C-295/95 *Farrell v Long* 27.
[100] C-295/95 *Farrell v Long* 13,23,24; compare section 1.2 of chapter 6, text following note 89.
[101] C-288/92 *Custom Made v Stawa* 15.
[102] C-256/00 *Besix v Kretzschmar* 50 (re 32/88 *Six Constructions v Humbert* 20).
[103] 33/78 *Somafer v Saar-Ferngas*.
[104] 33/78 *Somafer v Saar-Ferngas* 11.

risdiction, the relationship to legal certainty must be assumed, though, in light of the Court's explicit reference to that principle in the foregoing paragraphs in its judgment in *Somafer v Saar-Ferngas*.[105] Obviously, an interpretation that shows, without difficulty, the special link justifying a derogation from the general principle underlying Article 2 contributes to the requirement of clarity as to the rules of jurisdiction and therefore to legal certainty as to jurisdiction for both the plaintiff and the defendant.

The issue of clarity as to rules of jurisdiction furthermore surfaced in the cases concerning the interpretation of Article 17. In the case *Elefanten Schuh v Jacqmain*, which was discussed earlier in this chapter, the Court pointed out, with regard to the interpretation of that provision, that in order to ensure legal certainty as to jurisdiction, 'the formal requirements applicable to agreements conferring jurisdiction should be expressly prescribed' in the Convention.[106] Therefore, the enumeration of formal requirements in Article 17 is to be considered as limited and Contracting States are not free to lay down other requirements than those contained in the Convention.[107] In *Benincasa v Dentalkit*, the Court followed a similar line of argument. It stated in this respect:

> 'The aim of securing legal certainty by making it possible reliably to foresee which court will have jurisdiction has been interpreted in connection with Article 17 of the Convention ... Article 17 ... sets out to designate, clearly and precisely, a court in a Contracting State which is to have exclusive jurisdiction in accordance with the consensus formed between the parties, which is to be expressed in accordance with the strict requirements as to form laid down therein.'[108]

In *Castelletti v Trumpy*, the Court repeated its considerations on this purpose of Article 17, namely that it is intended to lay down itself the conditions as to form which jurisdiction clauses must meet, so as to ensure legal certainty.[109] Since the formal requirements laid down in Article 17 also have other purposes, namely to ensure that the parties have given their consent, which purpose lies at the core of the principle of party autonomy, and to protect the party who might be unaware of a jurisdiction clause incorporated in a contract by one party alone, we will elaborate on this issue in sections 1.3 and 2 of chapter 6. Chapter 6 discusses the fourth main principle, implying that disputes should be decided by an appropriate court, from which these sub-principles flow.

---

[105] 33/78 *Somafer v Saar-Ferngas* 7,8.

[106] 150/80 *Elefanten Schuh v Jacqmain* 24; see also section 1.2 of this chapter, text following note 43.

[107] 150/80 *Elefanten Schuh v Jacqmain* 25.

[108] C-269/95 *Benincasa v Dentalkit* 28 (re C-106/95 *Mainschiffahrts v Les Gravières Rhénanes* 34),29.

[109] C-159/97 *Castelletti v Trumpy* 34 (re 150/80 *Elefanten Schuh v Jacqmain* 25),35,37; and compare section 2.1 of chapter 6, text following note 3.

Although in general, as is shown for example by *Benincasa v Dentalkit*, the Court has held that clarity as to the rules of jurisdiction is to the advantage of both the plaintiff and the defendant, occasionally the Court has expressed its specific concern with 'foreseeability for the defendant' as regards the jurisdiction of a court other than that of the state in which he is domiciled.[110] It did so, among others, in *Handte v TMCS*.[111] This would imply that the rules of jurisdiction that derogate from Article 2, which by itself provides for a certain and reliable criterion of jurisdiction, should be given an interpretation that enables the defendant to foresee before which courts he may be sued.[112]

In *Handte v TMCS*, the Court had to answer the question whether the expression 'matters relating to a contract' in Article 5, point 1, applied to an action by the plaintiff, a sub-buyer, who sued the manufacturer for defects in the goods. The Court used several arguments to come to the conclusion that the term 'matters relating to a contract' does not cover a situation in which the manufacturer had not undertaken a contractual obligation towards the sub-buyer.[113] One of the arguments used to support this conclusion is that a rule of jurisdiction which derogates from Article 2 should not be given an interpretation that a normally well-informed defendant could not reasonably have foreseen. The Court established that the manufacturer/defendant could not reasonably have foreseen that an action by the sub-buyer brought against him would be considered as 'a matter relating to a contract' and thus could not have foreseen that the rule of jurisdiction contained in Article 5, point 1, would apply. As the Court put it:

> 'the application of the special jurisdictional rule laid down by Article 5(1) of the Convention to an action brought by a sub-buyer of goods against the manufacturer is not foreseeable by the latter and is therefore incompatible with the principle of legal certainty.'[114]

To conclude this paragraph, the Court's case law shows that clarity as to the rules of jurisdiction has an influence on the interpretation of the rules of jurisdiction and contributes to legal certainty for both the plaintiff and the defendant. It requires, in particular, an interpretation of the concepts of the rules of jurisdiction which ensures a certain and reliable criterion for jurisdiction, implying no exceptions or distinctions, which are not evident from the wording of the rules of jurisdiction.

---

[110] See text following note 102 of section 4 of this chapter.

[111] C-26/91 *Handte v TMCS*.

[112] C-26/91 *Handte v TMCS* 18,19; C-256/00 *Besix v Kretzschmar* 50 (re 32/88 *Six Constructions v Humbert* 20).

[113] C-26/91 *Handte v TMCS* 12 (re Jenard Report),13-19.

[114] C-26/91 *Handte v TMCS* 19.

4.2 Avoiding (further) multiplication of jurisdiction as regards one and the same legal relationship

C Art. 5(1) R 5(1)

In quite a number of judgments, the Court has made it clear that legal certainty with regard to the allocation of jurisdiction also implies that a multiplicity of courts having jurisdiction with regard to one and the same legal relationship (contract or tort, etc.) or 'one and the same type of case',[115] should be avoided.[116] The idea that a multiplicity of courts having jurisdiction with regard to one and the same legal relationship or type of case should be avoided, is not only related to the principle of legal certainty, but also to the most general principle of 'legal protection of persons established within the Community'. The following observation of the Court in *Peters v ZNAV*, in which it had to answer a question on the interpretation of Article 5, point 1, is illustrative in this respect:

> 'It should be noted that multiplication of the bases of jurisdiction in one and the same type of case is not likely to encourage legal certainty and effective legal protection throughout the territory of the Community.' [117]

As was seen before, the protection of persons established in the Community takes on the more specific form of protection of the plaintiff and the defendant. The

[115] In the Court's case law, in which the principle 'avoiding multiplication of jurisdiction' plays a role, the Court has used different expressions, namely 'same type of case', 'same legal relationship' or 'same dispute'. Where the Convention aims to avoid a multiplicity of courts having jurisdiction as regards one and the same legal relationship (contract, tort, etc.), generally, or in a specific type of case (for example, contractual or non-contractual relationships resulting from operations of a branch, as in Art. 5, point 5), the focus in this section is in principle on cases related to a controversy between one plaintiff and one defendant, and as regards one and the same legal relationship. A dispute can, however, cover different cases. It may for example include controversies (based on contract or tort etc.) between one plaintiff and different defendants or between one plaintiff and one defendant, and a third party, or between the same parties playing a different role in the proceedings (counterclaim). Exceptionally, a dispute can also encompass different, but closely connected legal relationships between the same parties. As will be seen in section 3.2 of chapter 6, a more complex dispute may encompass more than one action which can be brought before different courts.

[116] As was seen in chapter 3, section 1, text following note 40, the idea that a multiplicity of courts for one and the same type of legal relationship should be avoided, is also related to the principle of 'free movement of judgments', particularly to the sub-principle 'full respect for another Contracting State's judgments'. The avoidance of multiple courts having jurisdiction precludes the risk of irreconcilable decisions and facilitates the recognition and enforcement of judgments in states other than those in which they are delivered. Compare, for example, C-125/92 *Mulox v Geels* 21 (re C-220/88 *Dumez France v Hessische Landesbank* 18); C-256/00 *Besix v Kretzschmar* 27 (re C-37/00 *Weber v Universal Ogden* 42),28 and see hereafter section 5 of this chapter, text following note 160. Clearly, this effect of the principle of 'avoiding multiplication of jurisdiction' increases the relative weight of that principle.

[117] 34/82 *Peters v ZNAV* 17; compare 33/78 *Somafer v Saar-Ferngas* 7; and C-214/89 *Duffryn v Petereit* 20.

realisation of the principle of 'avoiding multiplication of jurisdiction' would allow the plaintiff easily to identify the court before which he may bring an action and the defendant reasonably to foresee the court before which he may be sued.[118] In *Benincasa v Dentalkit*, the Court stated in this respect:

> 'Next, as the Court has consistently held, the objectives of the Convention include unification of the rules on jurisdiction of the Contracting States's courts, so as to avoid as far as possible the multiplication of the bases of jurisdiction in relation to one and the same legal relationship and to reinforce the legal protection available to persons established in the Community by, at the same time, allowing the plaintiff easily to identify the court before which he may bring an action and the defendant reasonably to foresee the court before which he may be sued ...'[119]

A close investigation of the Court's case law on these issues teaches us that two different ideas are subsumed under this general principle of 'avoiding multiplication of jurisdiction with regard to one and the same legal relationship':

(1) avoiding a situation in which *alternative* courts have jurisdiction
(2) avoiding *different* courts having jurisdiction with regard to various aspects of one and the same legal relationship, in short: avoiding *fragmentation of proceedings*

The Court does not always make a clear distinction between these two aspects of the principle of avoiding multiplication of jurisdiction in relation to one and the same legal relationship.[120] However, in our view, the distinction is analytically sound and helps to improve the understanding of the Court's case law. As these two aspects are distinctly different in important respects, we attribute to each of them the status of a separate sub-principle. Although the Court has referred to these principles in quite a number of cases,[121] it is not always clear what the role of these principles is with regard to the decision given. In the following sections we will discuss some of those judgments in which in our opinion these principles have or should have had an influence.

---

[118] See this section, text following note 95.

[119] C-269/95 *Benincasa v Dentalkit* 26 (re 38/81 *Effer v Kantner* 6; C-125/92 *Mulox v Geels* 11).

[120] Compare, for example, 34/82 *Peters v ZNAV* 17; C-269/95 *Benincasa v Dentalkit* 27; 38/81 *Effer v Kantner* 6, on the one hand, with, for example, C-220/88 *Dumez France v Hessische Landesbank* 18, on the other.

[121] 14/76 *De Bloos v Bouyer* 9; 23/78 *Meeth v Glacetal* 8; 33/78 *Somafer v Saar-Ferngas* 7; 266/85 *Shenavai v Kreischer* 8; C-220/88 *Dumez France v Hessische Landesbank* 18; 38/81 *Effer v Kantner* 6; 34/82 *Peters v ZNAV* 17; C-125/92 *Mulox v Geels* 11,21; C-269/95 *Benincasa v Dentalkit* 26; C-295/95 *Farrell v Long* 13; C-383/95 *Rutten v Cross Medical* 18; C-37/00 *Weber v Universal Ogden* 42; C-96/00 *Gabriel* 57; C-420/97 *Leathertex v Bodetex* 31;C-256/00 *Besix v Kretzschmar* 27,34.

4.2.1 *Avoiding alternative courts having jurisdiction as regards one and the same legal relationship*

The principle of 'avoiding alternative courts having jurisdiction with regard to one and the same legal relationship' weighed in relation to other principles

C Art. 2	R 2	C Art. 8	R 9
C Art. 5 (1 and 3)	R 5(1 and 3)	C Art. 14(1st para.)	R 16(1)

As appears from the design of the Convention's provisions, the principle of 'avoiding alternative courts having jurisdiction with regard to one and the same legal relationship' is not absolute. The Convention's jurisdictional rules give the plaintiff in certain circumstances an option to bring a case in alternative courts. The plaintiff can for instance choose to commence proceedings according to Article 2 in the courts of the state of the defendant's domicile or in the courts that have jurisdiction according to the rules of special jurisdiction provided for in Article 5 of the Convention. Article 8 and Article 14, first paragraph, applying to matters of insurance and consumer contracts, respectively, also illustrate that alternative courts are allowed in some situations. These provisions are taken as given as far as the Court is concerned. For the Court, therefore, the principle of 'avoiding alternative courts having jurisdiction with regard to one and the same legal relationship' implies that the Court's interpretations of the Convention should prevent any further multiplication of jurisdiction beyond the cases allowed on the basis of the provisions of the Convention. The Court's case law confirms that the Court follows this interpretative guideline.

The principle of 'avoiding alternative courts having jurisdiction with regard to one and the same legal relationship' particularly plays a role when the Court interprets the *connecting link* of the Convention's jurisdictional rules. [122] This can be illustrated by the Court's case law on Article 5, point 3. As becomes evident from that case law a multifarious and broad interpretation of concepts and terms constituting the connecting link, which should exist between the case and the court that would be competent to hear the case, can only be exceptional and must be avoided as far as possible.[123] This implies that these concepts and terms should be interpreted in such a way that one type of case cannot be brought in various alternative courts. In *Bier v Mines de potasse*, one of the first cases to be decided by the Court under the Convention, the Court did not follow this interpretative guideline. The Court's interpretation of the concept 'place where the damage occurred' constituting the connecting link contained in Article 5, point 3, resulted in a multiplication of the bases of jurisdiction. The Court decided that this concept

---

[122] Compare 14/76 *De Bloos v Bouyer* 9,10,15; and 33/78 *Somafer v Saar-Ferngaz* 7.

[123] 21/76 *Bier v Mines de potasse*; C-220/88 *Dumez France v Hessische Landesbank*; and C-364/93 *Marinari v Lloyd's*.

covers both the 'place where the damage occurred' and the 'place of the event giving rise to it' and that the plaintiff can choose to bring the case in the courts of either one of these places.[124] In this case, the principle of 'avoiding multiplication of jurisdiction' was outweighed by the principle of 'a sound administration of justice', the principle which inspired Article 5, point 3. From the point of view of the principle of a sound administration of justice, no choice could be made for one of these two places as the one that would generally have the strongest connection with this type of case. Hence the Court reasoned that both places should be offered as alternatives to the plaintiff.[125] In *Shevill v Presse Alliance*, as will be seen later, the Court argued for an even broader interpretation of the term 'place where the damage occurred'. That interpretation, however, does not result in alternative courts having jurisdiction, but rather in the fragmentation of proceedings.[126]

In *Dumez France v Hessische Landesbank* and *Marinari v Lloyd's*, on the other hand, the Court avoided a further multiplication of the heads of jurisdiction by rejecting broad interpretations of the concept 'place where the damage occurred'.[127] In these judgments, the Court rejected the idea that this concept could be interpreted so extensively as to include the place where the indirect victim of the damage ascertains the repercussions on its own assets or where the direct victim claims to have suffered financial damage following upon initial damage arising and suffered in another Contracting State.[128] In these cases, the principle of 'avoiding multiplication of jurisdiction' and the principle of 'a sound administration of justice' apparently pulled in the same direction (unlike the case of *Bier v Mines de potasse*, in which they each pulled in opposite directions): both principles argued against an extensive interpretation of the expression 'place where the damage occurred'.[129]

In a number of cases the Court has stated that, when interpreting Article 5, point 1, in case the dispute concerns an individual contract of employment and the employee performs the obligations arising from his contract in several Contracting States, a multiplication of jurisdiction in relation to such a legal relationship is also to be avoided.[130] In these cases, the Court also referred to other principles, in particular the principle of a sound administration of justice and the prin-

---

[124] 21/76 *Bier v Mines de potasse* 19.

[125] 21/76 *Bier v Mines de potasse* 11,17. See for a more detailed discussion of this judgment, chapter 6, section 3.1, text following note 285.

[126] See hereafter, section 4.2.2, text following note 148.

[127] C-220/88 *Dumez France v Hessische Landesbank*; and C-364/93 *Marinari v Lloyd's*.

[128] C-220/88 *Dumez France v Hessische Landesbank* 22; and C-364/93 *Marinari v Lloyd's* 21.

[129] For a more detailed discussion of these judgments, see the next chapter, section 3.1, text following notes 125 and 129.

[130] Compare C-125/92 *Mulox v Geels* 11; C-383/95 *Rutten v Cross Medical* 13; C-37/00 *Weber v Universal Ogden Services* 42; and most recently in C-437/00 *Pugliese v Finmeccanica* 16 (re *Mulox* 10,11,16; *Rutten* 12,13; *Weber* 38).

ciple of the protection of the party who is weaker due to his socio-economic position.[131] As regards individual contracts of employment, Article 5, point 1, as amended by the 1989 Accession Convention, provides that the place of performance of the obligation in matters relating to individual contracts of employment is the place where the employee habitually carries out his work. The Court has held that in case the employee performs the obligations arising from his contract in several Contracting States, the place where he habitually carries out his work is the place where or from which he in fact performs the essential part of his duties *vis-à-vis* his employer.[132] In arriving at this interpretation, the Court referred, amongst other things, to the principle that a multiplicity of courts having jurisdiction in one and the same legal relationship should be avoided as far as possible.[133] The Court has reiterated that case law, most recently in *Weber v Universal Ogden* and *Pugliese v Finmeccanica*.[134]

One of the Court's most recent decisions, *Besix v Kretzschmar*, contains quite an interesting case in which the principle that a multiplicity of courts with respect to one and the same legal relationship should be avoided, plays a role.[135] The judgment was also concerned with the interpretation of the connecting link used in Article 5, point 1, being the 'place of performance of the obligation in question'. In the case at hand, the obligation in question was an obligation not to do something, consisting of the parties' undertaking not to commit themselves to other partners in connection with a procedure for the award of a public contract. The parties to the contract had neither designated the place of performance or the courts having jurisdiction to hear the case, or, for that matter, the law governing the contract. The question arose whether Article 5, point 1, must be interpreted as meaning that a defendant domiciled in a Contracting State may be sued in the courts of any of the places of performance of the obligation in question, in case that obligation is to be performed anywhere in the world. Clearly, an affirmative answer would have led to an extreme case of multiple alternative courts having jurisdiction. The Court's answer was, however, that in a case such as this, Article 5, point 1, does not apply. The main argument for this conclusion was found in the fact that the principle which had inspired this provision, the principle of a sound administration of justice, did not apply to this type of case in which the

---

[131] See section 1.2 of chapter 6, text following note 44 and section 3.1.1 of that chapter, text following note 184 and compare C-437/00 *Pugliese v Finmeccanica* 17 (re *Mulox* 17; *Rutten* 16; *Weber* 39),18 (re *Mulox* 18,19; *Rutten* 17; *Weber* 40).

[132] Compare C-437/00 *Pugliese v Finmeccanica* (re *Mulox* 20,26; *Rutten* 15, 23; *Weber* 41,58).

[133] C-125/92 *Mulox v Geels* 21 (re C-220/88 *Dumez France* 18); C-383/95 *Rutten v Cross Medical* 18 (re 125/92 *Mulox v Geels* 21, 23; C-220/88 *Dumez France* 18).

[134] C-37/00 *Weber v Universal Ogden Services* 42 (re *Mulox* 21,23; *Rutten* 18),43 (re *Mulox* 25,26), 44 (*Rutten*),49 (re *Rutten* 22-24)-58; C-437/00 *Pugliese v Finmeccanica* 16 (re *Mulox* 10,11,16; *Rutten* 12,13; *Weber* 38),19 (re *Mulox* 20,26; *Rutten* 15; *Weber* 41),20-26; see hereafter also chapter 6, section 1.2, text following notes 36, 40 and 84. However, the case law referred to in *Weber* and *Pugliese* could not be fully transposed to the present cases.

[135] C-256/00 *Besix v Kretzschmar*; see also chapter 6, section 3.1.1, text following note 249.

obligation in question is to be performed in any place in the world. An important additional consideration was, though, that an interpretation of the connecting factor of Article 5, point 1, that would imply that the courts of all the Contracting States would be competent, would greatly reduce the predictability of the competent court, in particular for the defendant; this would be incompatible with the principle of legal certainty.[136]

4.2.2 *Avoiding different courts having jurisdiction as regards different aspects of one and the same legal relationship: avoiding fragmentation of proceedings*

C Art. 5(1)	R 5(1)	C Art. 13 to 15	R 15 to 17
C Art. 5(3)	R 5(3)	C Art. 17	R 23

The sub-principle implying that a situation should be avoided where different courts have jurisdiction with regard to different aspects of one and the same legal relationship leads to different interpretative guidelines. It implies, first of all, that the *substantive scope* of the rules of jurisdiction should be interpreted sufficiently widely so as to preclude a fragmentation of proceedings as regards one and the same legal relationship. This can be illustrated by *Peters v ZNAV*.[137] In that judgment, the Court had to answer a question on the interpretation of the expression 'matters relating to a contract' in Article 5, point 1. The Court established, first, that obligations which have their basis in the legal relationship between an association and its members by virtue of membership must be regarded as 'matters relating to a contract'.[138] The Court then decided that a national court, in order to determine whether or not an obligation of a member towards an association falls within 'matters relating to a contract', should not draw a distinction according to whether the obligation in question arises simply from the act of becoming a member or results from that act in conjunction with a decision made by an organ of the association.[139] The Court justified that decision, as follows:

> 'It should be noted that multiplication of the bases of jurisdiction in one and the same type of case is not likely to encourage legal certainty and effective legal protection throughout the territory of the Community. The provisions of the Convention should therefore be interpreted in such a way that the court seised is not required to declare that it has jurisdiction to adjudicate upon certain applications but has no jurisdiction to hear certain other applications, even though they are closely related.'[140]

---

[136] C-256/00 *Besix v Kretzschmar* 26,35,54,55.

[137] 34/82 *Peters v ZNAV* 16-18.

[138] 34/82 *Peters v ZNAV* 13.

[139] 34/82 *Peters v ZNAV* 16-18. Compare also text following note 99 in section 4.1 of this chapter, and note 117 of this section.

[140] 34/82 *Peters v ZNAV* 17. Notice that another interpretation would not necessarily multiply the existing bases of jurisdiction, but may lead to the fragmentation of proceedings. See for a more detailed discussion of this judgment, section 3.1.1 of chapter 6, text following notes 206 and 241.

As is clear from this quotation, the Court used the principle of 'avoiding fragmentation of proceedings' so as to arrive at its decision.

The risk of a fragmentation of proceedings also played a role in *Effer v Kantner*. In that judgment, the Court established that in the cases provided for in Article 5, point 1, the national court's jurisdiction to determine questions relating to a contract includes the power to consider the existence of the constituent parts of the contract itself. Another interpretation of that provision would lead to a situation in which one court may be called upon to decide on a claim based on a contract which is in dispute between the parties, while another court would have to establish the existence or the inexistence of that same contract. Such an interpretation would lead to a fragmentation of proceedings in one and the same type of case. Such a result is not assumed to be in the interests of legal certainty, as the Court observed in this judgment, and therefore not in the interests of both the plaintiff and the defendant. The Court stated in this respect:

> 'It is clear from the provisions of the Convention, and in particular from the Preamble thereto, that its essential aim is to strengthen in the Community the legal protection of persons therein established. For that purpose, the Convention provides a collection of rules which are designed *inter alia* to avoid the occurrence, in civil and commercial matters, of concurrent litigation in two or more Member States and which, in the interests of legal certainty and for the benefit of the parties, confer jurisdiction upon the national court territorially best qualified to determine a dispute.
> It follows ... that, in the cases provided for in Article 5(1) of the Convention, the national court's jurisdiction to determine questions relating to a contract includes the power to consider the existence of the constituent parts of the contract itself, since that is indispensable in order to enable the national court in which proceedings are brought to examine whether it has jurisdiction under the Convention.'[141]

The decision delivered by the Court in *Benincasa v Dentalkit* can be compared with the *Effer v Kantner* case. The Court had to answer the question whether the courts of a Contracting State which have been designated in a jurisdiction clause validly concluded under the first paragraph of Article 17 also have exclusive jurisdiction where the action seeks a declaration that the contract containing that clause is void. The Court stated that the legal certainty which Article 17 seeks to secure could easily be jeopardized if one party to the contract could frustrate that rule simply by claiming that the whole of the contract was void on grounds derived from the applicable substantive law.[142] The Court referred to the principle

---

[141] 38/81 *Effer v Kantner* 6,7; compare also 73/77 *Sanders v Van der Putte* 21,22.

[142] C-269/95 *Benincasa v Dentalkit* 29. In this judgment, the Court recalled that it is for the national court to interpret the clause conferring jurisdiction invoked before it in order to determine which disputes fall within its scope. In this case, the jurisdiction clause referred to 'any dispute' relating to the interpretation, performance or 'other aspects' of the contract (point 31, re C-214/89 *Duffryn v. Petereit* 37).

that a (further) multiplication of jurisdiction must be avoided and concluded that the courts of a Contracting State which have been designated in a jurisdiction clause validly concluded under the first paragraph of Article 17, also have exclusive jurisdiction where the action seeks a declaration that the contract containing that clause is void.[143] Any other decision would have the result of various courts ruling on different aspects of one type of case.[144]

The principle of 'avoiding fragmentation of proceedings with regard to one and the same legal relationship', is all the more compelling, as the Court recently held in *Gabriel*, when that relationship involves a party deemed to be weaker due to his socio-economic position, such as a consumer.[145] An interpretation of the term 'consumer', which constitutes the substantive scope of Article 13, first paragraph, which would have the result that certain claims under a contract concluded by a consumer fall within the jurisdiction rules of Articles 13 to 15, whereas other actions that are linked so closely to that contract as to be indissociable are subject to other rules, cannot be accepted.[146] The Court referred in this judgment to the need to avoid, as far as possible, a situation in which several courts have jurisdiction in respect of one and the same contract. Other principles, such as the principle of the protection of the weaker party due to its socio-economic position and the principle of a sound administration of justice, pointed towards the same decision. The Court held:

> 'In view of the fact that a multiplicity of courts having jurisdiction risks placing at a particular disadvantage a party deemed to be weak, such as a consumer, it is in the interest of the proper administration of justice that the latter should be able to bring before one and the same court – *in casu* that of his place of domicile – all of the difficulties that are likely to arise from a contract which the consumer has been induced to conclude by reason of the professional's use of forms of wording liable to mislead the other contracting party.'[147]

The principle of 'avoiding fragmentation of proceedings' not only requires that the substantive scope of the rules of jurisdiction is to be interpreted sufficiently widely so as to prevent the fragmentation of proceedings, it could also be an interpretative guideline with regard to terms constituting the *connecting link* of rules of jurisdiction. The principle requires that interpretations of the connecting link that would lead to a fragmentation of proceedings as regards one and the same legal relationship should be avoided.

---

143 C-269/95 *Benincasa v Dentalkit* 26 (re *Effer v Kanter* 6; C-125/92 *Mulox* 11), 31 (re C-214/89 *Duffryn v Petereit* 33),32. Notice that another interpretation would not necessarily multiply the bases of jurisdiction, it may lead, however, to the fragmentation of proceedings.

144 Compare also 23/78 *Meeth v Glacetal* 8,9; and C-214/89 *Duffryn v Petereit* 20.

145 C- 96/00 *Gabriel* 56, 57 (re C-256/00 *Besix v Kretzschmar* 27).

146 C- 96/00 *Gabriel* 57 (re C-256/00 *Besix v Kretzschmar* 27).

147 See C-96/00 *Gabriel* 58.

In *Shevill v Presse Alliance*, the Court was confronted with a case in which this guideline was at stake. The Court had to answer questions on the interpretation of Article 5, point 3.[148] The case concerned international libel by a newspaper article that had been distributed in several Contracting States. The question focused on the interpretation of the connecting factor of Article 5, point 3, 'the place where the harmful event occurred'. After reiterating *Bier v Mines de potasse*, in which it was decided that this place should be considered to be both the place of the event giving rise to the damage and the place where the damage occurred, the Court decided that in cases of international libel 'the place where the damage occurred' is the place where the publication is distributed, when the victim is known in these places. Next, the Court decided that in the type of case at hand, the concept 'place where the damage occurred' should be interpreted to mean that 'the courts of each Contracting State in which the defamatory publication was distributed and in which the victim claims to have suffered injury to his reputation are territorially the best placed to assess the libel committed in that state and to determine the extent of the corresponding damage'.[149] That interpretation clearly leads to a fragmentation of proceedings. However, the Court stated that such an interpretation was justified by the requirement of a sound administration of justice.[150] The Court was aware, though, of the disadvantages of different courts having jurisdiction as regards various aspects of one and the same legal relationship. It held:

> '... there are admittedly disadvantages to having different courts ruling on various aspects of the same dispute ...'[151]

Obviously, an interpretation of the rules of jurisdiction that avoids situations in which different courts have jurisdiction in one and the same case is to the advantage of both the plaintiff and the defendant. It allows the plaintiff easily to identify the court before which he may bring an action and enables the defendant reasonably to foresee the court before which he may be sued. However, it is the defendant who benefits the most from the application of this principle.

First, consider the situation in which the Convention allows a situation of two or three alternative courts having jurisdiction as regards one and the same legal relationship. The plaintiff then has the advantage of a choice between two or three courts before which he may bring a given case. In such a situation the defendant may still be able reasonably to *foresee* before which *courts* he may be sued by the plaintiff and the plaintiff may still be able easily to identify the court before which he may bring an action.[152] More difficulties may arise, though, if a

---

[148] C-68/93 *Shevill v Presse Alliance* 31,32.
[149] C-68/93 *Shevill v Presse Alliance* 31.
[150] C-68/93 *Shevill v Presse Alliance* 31.
[151] C-68/93 *Shevill v Presse Alliance* 32.
[152] Compare section 4.1 of this chapter.

larger number of alternative courts have jurisdiction, particularly for the defendant. If a considerable number of alternative courts have jurisdiction in one and the same type of case, it is not very likely that the defendant can *predict* in *which* of these courts he will be sued by the plaintiff. Moreover, where such a multiplicity of courts having jurisdiction exists, this heightens the risk of forum shopping by the plaintiff. It enables the plaintiff to choose the court which he judges to be the most favourable to his interests. For that reason alone, a (further) multiplication of jurisdiction is already detrimental to the defendant. A multiplicity of courts may not only reduce the foreseeability and the predictability for the defendant as to the court(s) before which he will be sued by the plaintiff, there is also some unfairness for the defendant if a multiplicity of courts creates possibilities for the plaintiff of forum shopping.[153]

Secondly, as far as the disadvantages of fragmentation of proceedings are concerned, these disadvantages are also different for the plaintiff and the defendant. The plaintiff would have the choice between bringing his claims as to the various aspects of the dispute before different courts or bringing his entire claim before the courts of the defendant's domicile. The defendant never has that option, and is dependent on the choice made by the plaintiff.

On the basis of the foregoing, we assume that the defendant benefits the most from the principle that a multiplicity of courts having jurisdiction with regard to one and the same legal relationship is to be avoided.

To conclude this section, it follows from the Court's case law that the principle of 'avoiding a multiplicity of courts having jurisdiction in one and the same case', although not absolute, is an important guideline for the interpretation of the rules of jurisdiction. The following requirements flow from this principle:

- avoiding alternative courts having jurisdiction with regard to one and the same legal relationship, which requires a not too broad or multifarious interpretation of terms and concepts constituting the connecting link of rules of jurisdiction, and
- avoiding fragmentation of proceedings, which requires a not too restrictive interpretation of concepts constituting the substantive scope of these jurisdictions, and a not too broad interpretation of the connecting link of the jurisdictional rules.

[153] Compare C-256/00 *Besix v Kretzschmar* 27 (re 14/76 *De Bloos* 9; 266/85 *Shenavai* 8; C-125/92 *Mulox* 21; C-383/95 *Rutten* 18; C-420/97 *Leathertex* 31),34,35.

4.3 National courts should be able readily to decide whether they are competent to hear a case

C Art. 5(1)	R 5(1)
C Art. 17	R 23

The principle of legal certainty as to jurisdiction, also implies that the court seised should be able readily to decide whether it is competent to hear a case on the basis of the rules of jurisdiction of the Convention.[154] Both the plaintiff and the defendant benefit from the application of this principle.

As appears from *Castelletti v Trumpy*, this requirement is settled case law and entails that a court should be able to decide whether or not it has jurisdiction, without having to consider the substance of the case:

> 'As the Court has repeatedly stated, it is in keeping with the spirit of certainty, which constitutes one of the aims of the Convention, that the national court seised should be able readily to decide whether it has jurisdiction on the basis of the rules of the Convention, without having to consider the substance of the case ...'[155]

When answering the questions of the national court with regard to the interpretation of the first paragraph of Article 17, the Court held in this judgment that considerations other than those connected with the formal requirements laid down in Article 17, such as concerning the links between the court designated and the relationship at issue, concerning the validity of the clause, or concerning the substantive rules of liability which are applicable before the chosen court, should not be taken into account by the national court in order to decide whether it has jurisdiction in a case at hand.[156]

The Court followed a similar line of argument with regard to the interpretation of the terms 'matters relating to a contract' in Article 5, point 1, when it held, in *Peters v ZNAV*, that no distinction should be made between an obligation arising from the act of becoming a member of an association and an obligation that results from that act in conjunction with a decision of an organ of the association. Apart from the argument that a multiplicity of courts having jurisdiction in one and the same type of case should be avoided, the Court argued that an interpretation which would imply that the court would have to consider the substance of the case is neither in accordance with the purposes or the spirit of the Convention. It held:

---

[154] C-269/95 *Benincasa v Dentalkit* 27.

[155] C-159/97 *Castelletti v Trumpy* 48 (re 34/82 *Peters v ZNAV* 17; C-288/92 *Custom Made v Stawa* 20; C-269/95 *Benincasa v Dentalkit* 28,29).

[156] C-159/97 *Castelleti v Trumpy* 52.

> 'Moreover, respect for the purposes and spirit of the Convention requires an interpretation of Article 5 which enables the national court to rule on its own jurisdiction without being compelled to consider the substance of the case'.[157]

The Court has confirmed this viewpoint in several other judgments.[158]

5. Legal certainty as to judgments: avoiding irreconcilable decisions

C Art. 5	R 5	C Art. 17	R 23	C Art. 27(3)	R 34(3)
C Art. 6	R 6	C Art. 21 to 23	R 27 to 30		

It needs no further argument than that by virtue of the principle of legal certainty, certainty as to the recognition and enforcement of the judgment should also be ensured. In this respect, we recall here that the general aspects of legal certainty – the sub-principles 'uniformity of rights and obligations flowing from the Convention' and 'respect for the linguistic boundaries of the Convention's provisions' – contribute to 'legal certainty as to the recognition and enforcement of foreign judgments' as well, as was seen in section 1 of this chapter.

Although the Court has not expressly referred to this issue, we nevertheless assume that legal certainty as to the recognition and enforcement of judgments within the Community area also requires that irreconcilable decisions are to be avoided. In this respect, the Court, on several occasions, has emphasized the importance of an interpretation of the rules of jurisdiction, in particular Articles 5, 6, 17 and 21 to 23, that avoids a multiplicity of courts having jurisdiction in one and the same case. Such an interpretation limits the risk of irreconcilable decisions, which in turn is a ground for refusing the recognition and enforcement of judgments.[159] Where the Court considers such an interpretation to contribute to legal certainty as to jurisdiction, we assume that the Court considers an interpretation that avoids the risk of irreconcilable decisions to contribute also to legal certainty as to judgments.

The Court has expressed its concern with the issue of irreconcilable decisions, for example in *Weber v Universal Ogden*, when interpreting the concept 'place of performance' of the relevant obligation in Article 5, point 1, in cases related to contracts of employment. The Court stated:

> 'The Court has also held that, where work is performed in more than one Contracting State, it is important to avoid any multiplication of courts having jurisdiction in order

---

[157] 34/82 *Peters v ZNAV* 17, compare C-295/95 *Farrell v Long* 13,14-23.

[158] Among others C-364/93 *Marinari v Lloyd's* 19 (re 241/83 *Rösler v Rottwinkel* 23; C-26/91 *Handte v TMCS* 19); C-51/97 *Réunion européenne v Spliethoff's* 34 (re *Marinari* 19; *Handte* 19).

[159] Compare section 1 of chapter 3, text following note 39.

to preclude the risk of irreconcilable decisions and to facilitate the recognition and enforcement of judgments in States other than those in which they were delivered and that, consequently, Article 5(1) of the Brussels Convention cannot be interpreted as conferring concurrent jurisdiction on the courts of each Contracting State in whose territory the employee performs part of his work ...'.[160]

A similar line of argument is followed by the Court in *Besix v Kretzschmar* in which the Court, as was seen in section 4.2, answered questions on the interpretation of the concept 'place of performance' in Article 5, point 1, with regard to an obligation not to do something.[161] The Court stated:

> 'Second, the Court has consistently held that it is essential to avoid, so far as possible, creating a situation in which a number of courts have jurisdiction in respect of one and the same contract, in order to preclude the risk of irreconcilable decisions and to facilitate the recognition and enforcement of judgments in States other than those in which they were delivered.'[162]

The principle of legal certainty as to the recognition and enforcement of judgments also puts some constraints on the interpretation of Article 27, point 3, as the Court clarified in *Leather v Polstermöbel*.[163] It implies that if a decision is irreconcilable with a judgment given in a Contracting State, it must be clear that the court of that state in which recognition is sought lacks the (discretionary) power to authorise recognition and enforcement of the foreign judgment. The Court argued as follows:

> 'it would be contrary to the principle of legal certainty, which the Court has repeatedly held to be one of the objectives of the Brussels Convention ... to interpret Article 27(3) as conferring on the court of the State in which recognition is sought the power to authorise recognition of a foreign judgment when it is irreconcilable with a judgment given in that Contracting State.'[164]

---

[160] C-37/00 *Weber v Universal Ogden* 42 (re *Mulox* 21,23; *Rutten* 18).

[161] See section 4.2 of this chapter, text following note 135.

[162] C-256/00 *Besix v Kretzschmar* 27 (re 14/76 *De Bloos* 9; 266/85 *Shenavai* 8; C-125/92 *Mulox* 21; C-383/95 *Rutten* 18; C-420/97 *Leathertex* 31). Notice that in the *Besix v Kretzschmar* case, the question as regards the interpretation of Article 5, point 1, does not so much relate to avoiding a further multiplication of heads of jurisdiction, but avoiding the application of a rule of jurisdiction, where that would inevitably lead to the jurisdiction of a number of courts with respect to one and the same contract, for reasons that lie in the specific nature of the contract. Notice furthermore that a (further) multiplication of bases of jurisdiction, such as in *Bier v Mines de potasse* or *Besix v Kretzschmar*, does not necessarily heighten the risk of irreconcilable decisions.

[163] Compare also section 1 of chapter 3, text following note 30.

[164] C-80/00 *Leather v Polstermöbel* 51 (re 38/81 *Effer v Kantner* 6; C-440/97 *Concorde v Panjan* 23; C-256/00 *Besix v Kretzschmar* 24).

CONCLUSIONS AND SUMMARY

In this chapter we have discussed what legal certainty implies under the Convention. As was seen in this chapter, and as will also be seen in the next chapter, the Court brings the principle of legal certainty mostly into play when interpreting the rules of jurisdiction. Legal certainty is then used in order to reinforce other sub-principles or just in combination with other sub-principles; in most of these cases, arguments based on different sub-principles point in the same direction. From those cases in which legal certainty conflicts with other (sub-)principles it appears that the principle of legal certainty is not absolute, in that the requirements that flow from it are to be fulfilled at any cost. The principle of legal certainty is sometimes outweighed by one or more sub-principles flowing from the other main principles underlying the Convention. As was seen in this chapter, the principle of legal certainty embodies two general aspects and three aspects that concern specific topics. We present the following scheme of the third main principle:

(3) The Principle of Legal Certainty
implies:

(3.1) Equality and uniformity of rights and obligations arising from the Convention

(3.2) Respect for the wording (the linguistic boundaries) of the Convention's provisions

(3.3) Legal certainty with regard to the scope of the Convention

(3.4) Legal certainty with regard to the allocation of jurisdiction

(3.5) Legal certainty with regard to judgments within the Community area

Under the Convention, these distinctly different aspects of legal certainty mainly *entail the following*:

(3.1) Equality and uniformity of rights and obligations arising from the Convention, *requiring*:
(3.1.1) Autonomous interpretation of concepts used in the Convention,
if possible and appropriate, and in case the legal issue belongs to the core issues which the Convention aims to regulate (that is the determination of jurisdiction, the facilitation of the recognition and enforcement of judgments and the scope of the Convention), or the legal issue does not in itself belong to the

core issues which the Convention aims to regulate, but the answer given by the applicable national (substantive or procedural) law would undermine the objectives of the Convention.

(3.1.2) The Convention to prevail over national provisions that are incompatible with it

(3.2) Respect for the wording (the linguistic boundaries) of the Convention's provisions, which implies: 'words trump principles', in that a 'principled' interpretation must be in line, or, at least, must not be prohibited by the wording of the Convention

(3.3) Legal certainty with regard to the scope of the Convention, *requires*:

- as regards the substantive scope, the applicability of the Convention is to be determined only by reason of the subject-matter of the action or the legal relationship between the parties to the action and by a clear distinction between issues that do (jurisdiction and recognition and enforcement) and do not (substantive and procedural law, and execution) belong to the Convention's core business
- as far as the formal scope is concerned, the relevant provisions should be interpreted so as to ensure that persons domiciled in the territory of the Convention's Contracting States benefit from its protective rules

(3.4) Legal certainty with regard to the allocation of jurisdiction, *implies*:

(a) Legal certainty for the plaintiff

(b) Legal certainty for the defendant,
implying:

(3.4.1) Clarity as to the rules of jurisdiction, requiring an interpretation of the rules of jurisdiction so as to ensure a certain and reliable criterion of jurisdiction

(3.4.2) The avoidance of a multiplicity of courts having jurisdiction as regards one and the
same legal relationship, *entailing*:

(3.4.2.1) the avoidance of *alternative* courts having jurisdiction as regards one and the same legal relationship

(3.4.2.2) the avoidance of *different* courts having jurisdiction as regards various aspects of one and the same legal relationship: the avoidance of *fragmentation of proceedings*, *requiring*:

- a not too broad or multifarious interpretation of concepts constituting the connecting link of jurisdictions and a not too restrictive interpretation of concepts constituting the substantive scope of jurisdictions

(3.4.3) national courts should be able readily to decide whether they are competent to hear a case

(3.5) Legal certainty as to judgments within the Community area, *requires*:
- avoidance of irreconcilable judgments, and
- no discretion for the court of the state in which enforcement is sought in deciding whether an irreconcilable judgment may be enforced.

Chapter 6
THE FOURTH MAIN PRINCIPLE: DISPUTES SHOULD BE DECIDED BY AN APPROPRIATE COURT

INTRODUCTION

The fourth main principle underlying the Convention is the principle that disputes should be decided by an appropriate court. This principle is the most general and most important factor that determines the content of the rules contained in Title II of the Convention, regulating which court may decide a given type of dispute.

The Jenard Report states in this regard: 'the rules of jurisdiction codified in Title II determine which State's courts are most appropriate to assume jurisdiction, taking into account all relevant matters ...'[1] Just as the other main principles, this fourth main principle flows from the most general principle underlying the Convention as a whole: the principle of strengthening in the Community the legal protection of persons therein established.[2]

The Court has confirmed the existence of this fourth main principle that disputes should be decided by an appropriate court, and the relationship between that principle and the principle of strengthening the legal protection of persons established within the Community. *Handte v TMCS* is illustrative in this respect.[3] In that judgment, when replying to a question as to the interpretation of one of the rules of jurisdiction, the Court, first, recalled that expressions constituting the substantive scope of the rules of jurisdiction are to be interpreted independently.[4] The Court then held:

> 'Secondly, it should be noted that, according to the Preamble to the Convention, one of its objectives is to "strengthen in the Community the legal protection of persons therein established". In that connection, the Expert Report ... states that: "... the rules of jurisdiction codified in Title II determine which State's courts are most appropriate to assume jurisdiction, taking into account all relevant matters ...".'[5]

---

[1] Jenard Report, OJ 1979 C 59, p 1,15.

[2] See section 1 of chapter 2, text following note 8 and 10; and compare, in particular, 288/82 *Duijnstee v Goderbauer* 11,12.

[3] C-26/91 *Handte v TMCS*.

[4] C-26/91 *Handte v TMCS* 10.

[5] C-26/91 *Handte v TMCS* 11,12; see also C-129/92 *Owens v Bracco* 20,21.

After having stated that the objective of the Convention is to ensure that the rules of jurisdiction laid down in the Convention determine which State's courts are most appropriate to assume jurisdiction, the Court continued in *Handte v TMCS*:

> 'The Convention achieves that objective by laying down a number of jurisdictional rules which determine the cases, exhaustively listed in Sections 2 to 6 of Title II of the Convention, in which a defendant domiciled or established in a Contracting State may, under a rule of special jurisdiction, or must, under a rule of exclusive jurisdiction or prorogation of jurisdiction, be sued before a court of another Contracting State.'[6]

More concrete principles give further substance to the rather indeterminate notion that disputes should be decided by an appropriate court. From the Convention and the Court's case law, it follows that the jurisdictional rules of the Convention attribute jurisdiction to the national courts out of concern for 'proper protection of the weaker party' and 'proper protection of the wishes of the parties', and to ensure that, in certain well-defined situations which are exhaustively listed in the Convention, the court which 'is in the best position to hear the case' has jurisdiction.[7] We will refer to these concerns as the following three sub-principles:

(1) the principle of the protection of the weaker party
(2) the principle of party autonomy, and
(3) the principle of a sound administration of justice

Under the Convention, the division of jurisdictions is based on these sub-principles. As will become clear in this chapter, these sub-principles which all flow from the main principle that disputes should be decided by an appropriate court may pull in different directions. The significance of the main principle that disputes should be decided by an appropriate court itself lies in guaranteeing the pursuit of all of these different sub-principles together and at the same time.

Though being the most important influence, the principle that disputes should be decided by an appropriate court is not the only factor influencing the design and content of these rules of jurisdiction. As was seen before, the other main principles, 'free movement of judgments', 'protection of the rights of the defence' and 'legal certainty', and their sub-principles, also have an influence on the interpretation of the rules that confer jurisdiction on the national courts.[8] We will refer to these other (sub-)principles when we discuss the relative weight of the (sub-)principles flowing from the fourth main principle that disputes are to be

---

[6] C-26/91 *Handte v TMCS* 13.

[7] Compare, among others, C-295/95 *Farrel v Long* 19; C-96/00 *Gabriel* 39 (re *Shearson* 19,20,22,24); C-37/00 *Weber v Universal Ogden* 40 (re *Mulox* 18,19; *Rutten* 17); C-387/98 *Coreck v Handelsveem* 14 (re *Meeth v Glacetal* 5); and C-288/92 *Custom Made v Stawa* 12 (re *Tessili* 13).

[8] Compare section 1 of chapter 3, text following note 35; section 2 of chapter 4, text following note 39; and chapter 5, sections 1 to 4, in particular section 4.2, text following note 115.

decided by an appropriate court.[9] Although these other (sub-)principles have some influence on the content of the rules of jurisdiction, the principle that disputes should be decided by an appropriate court is to be considered as the main guideline for the pursuit of one of the principal objectives of the Convention, expressed in its Preamble as 'the determination of rules of jurisdiction'.

Each of the three sub-principles that further define the idea that disputes should be decided by an appropriate court ('protection of the weaker party', 'party autonomy' and 'sound administration of justice') embodies a particular notion as to which court is appropriate to decide a dispute. The answer to the question as to which court is considered appropriate under the Convention, is not only to be found in the rules of jurisdiction laid down in Title II of the Convention, but also in the three sub-principles underlying these rules of jurisdiction, in the requirements that flow from them and in the way in which those sub-principles are weighed relative to each other. The order in which these sub-principles are discussed in this chapter is not so much based on their relative weight, but rather on their increasing complexity.

1. The principle of the protection of the weaker party

Introduction

Within the specific context of the issue which we are considering, namely, which national court should be competent to hear a given dispute, the principle of the protection of the weaker party requires the following: jurisdiction should be attributed in such a way that the weaker party in a case is given jurisdictional advantage over the stronger party so as to counterbalance his relative weakness.

The Convention employs three distinctly different notions as to who is the weaker party in a dispute, which can be expressed in three different sub-principles:

(1) the principle of the protection of the party who is weaker due to his procedural position
(2) the principle of the protection of the party who is weaker due to his socio-economic position
(3) the principle of the protection of the party that might be unaware of a jurisdiction clause incorporated in a contract by the other party (the significance of this sub-principle can only be fully appreciated in the context of the principle of party autonomy, to be discussed in section 2 of this chapter)

[9] Sections 1 to 3 of this chapter.

1.1 The principle of the protection of the party who is weaker due to his procedural position

C Art. 2	R 2
C Art. 3	R 3

One of the most general presumptions underlying the rules of jurisdiction as contained in Title II of the Convention, is that the defendant is the weaker party due to his procedural position. As the Court put it in *Farrell v Long*:

> 'the defendant as the party who, being the person sued, is generally in a weaker position.'[10]

Due to the weaker position of the defendant in the proceedings, the principle that disputes should be decided by an appropriate court implies that the defendant should be given jurisdictional advantage over the plaintiff. This, in turn, implies *(a)* that jurisdiction should be attributed to the court of the defendant's domicile, as it is supposed to be easier for the defendant to defend himself before the courts of his own state, *(b)* hostility towards the *forum actoris* and *(c)* hostility towards other jurisdictional advantages for the plaintiff.

The requirement that jurisdiction should be attributed to the court of the defendant's domicile, expressed in the maxim *actor sequitur forum rei,* is laid down in the first paragraph of Article 2 of the Convention. As the Jenard Report states:

> 'The maxim "*actor sequitur forum rei*", which expresses the fact that law leans in favour of the defendant, is even more relevant in the international sphere than it is in national law. It is more difficult, generally speaking, to defend oneself in the courts of a foreign country than in those of another town in the country where one is domiciled.'[11]

The Court has confirmed this viewpoint as regards the first paragraph of Article 2, among others in *Josi Reinsurance v UGIC*, in which it held:

> 'That jurisdictional rule is a general principle ... because it makes it easier, in principle, for a defendant to defend himself.'[12]

Naturally, the principle of the protection of the defendant due to his weaker procedural position, implying that a defendant should be given jurisdictional advan-

---

[10] C-295/95 *Farrell v Long* 19.

[11] Jenard Report, OJ 1979 C 59, p. 18 (re Report by Professor Fragistas – Hague Conference on private international law – preliminary doc. No. 4, May 1964, for the tenth session).

[12] C-412/98 *Josi Reinsurance v UGIC* 35 (re C-26/91 *Handte v TMCS* 14, and Jenard Report OJ 1979 C 59, p. 18).

tage over the plaintiff, is hostile towards the attribution of jurisdiction in a manner which would be advantageous to the plaintiff. This implies, for example, that it is hostile to attributing jurisdiction to the courts of the state of the plaintiff's domicile. Article 3 expresses this hostility to the *forum actoris*, since it prohibits a plaintiff from invoking against a defendant domiciled in a Contracting State national rules of exorbitant jurisdiction which are based, in particular, on the plaintiff's domicile or residence. The Court has confirmed this hostility of the Convention on several occasions, among others in *Dumez France v Hessische Landesbank*, *Shearson v TVB* and *Josi Reinsurance v UGIC*.[13] In *Dumez France v Hessische Landesbank*, for example, the Court held:

> 'Moreover, the hostility of the Convention towards the attribution of jurisdiction to the courts of the plaintiff's domicile was demonstrated by the fact that the second paragraph of Article 3 precluded the application of national provisions attributing jurisdiction to such courts for proceedings against defendants domiciled in the territory of a Contracting State.'[14]

The principle of the protection of the party who is weaker due to his procedural position also prohibits, as it is hostile towards the attribution of jurisdiction in a manner which would be advantageous to the plaintiff, an interpretation of rules of jurisdiction that would give the plaintiff the possibility to remove the defendant from (or deprive him of) the courts of the state that would otherwise be competent, for no good reason.[15] The principle furthermore implies that an interpretation of jurisdictional rules by which the plaintiff is given the advantage of choosing the court which he judges to be most favourable to his interests, should be avoided. In particular, it rejects an interpretation that would have the result of numerous courts having jurisdiction as regards one and the same legal relationship, as such an interpretation endangers the risk of forum shopping by the plaintiff and makes the court before which the defendant can be sued unpredictable for the defendant.[16]

The requirement that a defendant should be given 'home court advantage' and the hostility of the Convention towards the *forum actoris* and other advantages for the plaintiff, do not only follow from the principle of the 'protection of the party who is weaker due to his procedural position'. Similar requirements follow from the main principles we have considered earlier: 'free movement of judg-

---

[13] C-220/88 *Dumez France v Hessische Landesbank* 16,19; C-89/91 *Shearson v TVB* 17; and, C-412/98 *Josi Reinsurance v UGIC* 50; see also C-51/97 *Réunion européenne v Spliethoff's* 34; and C-7/98 *Krombach v Bamberski* 4.

[14] C-220/88 *Dumez France v Hessische Landesbank* 16.

[15] Compare section 2 of chapter 4, text following note 44, and section 4.1 of this chapter, text following note 4.

[16] Compare section 4.2 of chapter 5, text following note 152.

ments', 'protection of the rights of the defence' (in particular, 'the right to be heard before an appropriate court') and 'legal certainty'.

As to the connection between, in particular, the jurisdictional rule contained in Article 2, by which the defendant is given 'home court advantage', and the principle 'free movement of judgments', the Court has expressed the view that Article 2 is to be considered as a counterpoise to the relative large degree of free movement of judgments that the Convention allows. As the Court put it in *Autoteile v Malhé*:

> 'According to Article 2, persons domiciled in a Contracting State are to be sued in the courts of that state. That provision is intended to protect the rights of the defendant; it serves as a counterpoise to the facilities provided by the Convention with regard to the recognition and enforcement of foreign judgments.'[17]

The Jenard Report confirms this connection between the principle of the 'free movement of judgments', and the safeguards granted to the defendant in the original proceedings, where it states that more freedom of judgments can justifiably be realized in the recognition and enforcement stage, the better the defendant has been protected in the stage of the original procedure.[18]

As to the connection between the jurisdictional rule contained in Article 2 and the hostility of the Convention towards advantages for the plaintiff, on the one hand, and the principle 'protection of the rights of the defence', on the other, that connection needs no further argument here. As was already seen in chapter 4 of this study, the Court has consistently held that all the provisions of the Convention, both those contained in Title II on jurisdiction and those contained in Title III on recognition and enforcement, express the principle that the rights of the defence should be protected.[19] The principle of the protection of the rights of the defence entails the protection of the right to be heard in an appropriate court, in particular the right to be heard in one's own state, and hostility towards the *forum actoris* and other advantages for the plaintiff.

Finally, as to the connection between the requirement that a defendant should be given 'home court advantage', the hostility towards the *forum actoris* and other advantages for the plaintiff, on the one hand, and the principle of legal certainty, on the other, we refer to what has been observed in section 4.2 of chapter 5 on legal certainty as to jurisdiction and the requirement to avoid a (further) multiplication of jurisdiction in relation to one and the same legal relationship.[20] As was seen there, a multiplicity of courts would reduce the predictability of the competent court for the defendant and would enable the plaintiff to choose the court which he judges to be most favourable to his interests.

---

[17] 220/84 *Autoteile v Malhé* 15.

[18] See Jenard Report, OJ 1979 C 59, p. 42.

[19] Compare the introduction to chapter 4, text following note 1.

[20] See section 4.2 of chapter 5, text following note 115.

As is clear from the foregoing, the principle of the protection of the party who is weaker due to his procedural position coincides with requirements flowing from the other main principles, 'free movement of judgments', 'protection of the rights of the defence' and 'legal certainty'.

The principle of the protection of the party who is weaker due to his procedural position weighed in relation to other principles

C Art. 2 to 6	R 2 to 6	C Art. 16	R 22	C Art. 26	R 33
C Art. 8	R 9	C Art. 17	R 23	C Art. 28	R 35
C Art. 14	R 16	C Art. 24	R 31	C Art. 34	R 41,45

As any typical principle underlying the Convention, the principle of the 'protection of the party who is weaker due to his procedural position' does *not* function as an *absolute* principle.

This follows, *first* of all, from Article 4 of the Convention: if the defendant is not domiciled in a Contracting State, the jurisdiction of the courts of each Contracting State is not governed by the Convention, but shall, subject to the provisions of Article 16 (and Article 17), be determined by the law of that state.[21]

Secondly, this is evident from the general scheme of the Convention, from which it follows that a violation of the principle underlying Article 2 of the Convention, although it is considered as a counterpoise to the relative large degree of free movement of judgments, is not an obstacle to the recognition and enforcement of judgments. This becomes clear from Articles 26 and 34, second paragraph, in conjunction with Article 28, first and third paragraph, of Title III of the Convention. Therefore we may presume that, at the end of the day, the principle of free movement of judgments overrides the principle of the protection of the weaker party due to his procedural position.

Furthermore, the fact that the principle 'protection of the party weaker due to his procedural position' does not function as an absolute principle also follows from the system of the rules on jurisdiction laid down in Title II of the Convention. The principle does not in all cases determine the court which is to have jurisdiction: the rules of jurisdiction under Title II of the Convention do allow courts other than that of the defendant's domicile to decide disputes in certain well-defined cases. As will be seen as we go along, other competing principles underlie these rules of jurisdiction. Those other (sub-)principles may prevail over the principle of the protection of the party who is weaker due to his procedural position and set aside the requirement that, in principle, the courts of the defendant's home state are to have jurisdiction (compare Articles 5, 6, 16 and 17). These principles can even overcome, in a limited number of cases, the hostility towards attributing jurisdiction to the plaintiff's domicile; see, for example, Article 8, first paragraph, point 2, and Article 14, first paragraph, relating to mat-

[21] C-412/98 *Josi Reinsurance v UGIC* 51; and compare C-318/93 *Brenner v Reynolds* 17,18.

ters of insurance and consumer contracts respectively.[22] In this respect, we also have to keep in mind that the prohibition in Article 3 of relying on rules of exorbitant jurisdiction in favour of the defendant does not apply to the special regime provided for by Article 24, as the Court held in *Van Uden v Deco-Line*.[23]

Despite the fact that the principle of the protection of the party who is weaker from a procedural point of view which underlies Article 2, can be overruled by other principles, Article 2 is still to be considered as the cornerstone within the overall system of the rules conferring jurisdiction on the national courts. The system of the jurisdictional rules of the Convention is, after all, such that only in a limited number of well-defined cases, which are exhaustively listed, jurisdiction has been attributed to courts other than those of the defendant's domicile (and sometimes even to courts of the plaintiff's domicile). As the Court put it in *Josi Reinsurance v UGIC*:

> 'It is only by way of derogation from that fundamental principle, that the courts of the Contracting State in which the defendant has its domicile or seat are to have jurisdiction, that the Convention provides, under the first paragraph of Article 3 thereof, for the cases, exhaustively listed in Sections 2 to 6 of Title II, in which a defendant domiciled or established in a Contracting State may, where the situation is covered by a rule of special jurisdiction, or must, where it is covered by a rule of exclusive jurisdiction or a prorogation of jurisdiction, be excluded from the jurisdiction of the courts of the State in which it is domiciled and sued in a court of another Contracting State.'[24]

The fact that Article 2 is to be considered as the cornerstone of the jurisdictional rules laid down in Title II, has the following influence on the Court's interpretation of the rules of jurisdiction: the Court has clearly and repeatedly established that the rules of jurisdiction that derogate from Article 2 should be interpreted restrictively in the sense that an interpretation of these rules which deviates from Article 2 may not go beyond the cases that are exhaustively listed in these rules and that are expressly envisaged by the Convention. As the Court put it in *Josi Reinsurance v UGIC*:

> 'it is settled case law that the rules of jurisdiction which derogate from the general principle, set out in the first paragraph of Article 2 of the Convention, that the courts of the Contracting State in which the defendant is domiciled or established are to have

---

[22] See hereafter section 1.2 to 3 of this chapter.

[23] C-391/95 *Van Uden v Deco-Line* 42. See on Article 24 also section 3.1.2 of this chapter, text following note 330.

[24] C-412/98 *Josi Reinsurance v UGIC* 36; compare 12/76 *Tessili v Dunlop* 12,13; C-365/88 *Hagen v Zeehaghe* 10; C-288/92 *Custom Made v Stawa* 12 (re *Tessili* 13); and, C-68/93 *Shevill v Presse Alliance* 18.

jurisdiction, cannot give rise to an interpretation going beyond the cases expressly envisaged by the Convention ...'[25]

At any rate, as the Court has argued in *Kalfelis v Schröder*, an exception to the principle underlying Article 2 of the Convention, as for example laid down in Article 6, point 1, 'must be treated in such a manner that there is no possibility of the very existence of that principle being called in question.'[26] On the other hand, as the Court has indicated, for example in *Effer v Kantner*, the provisions of jurisdiction that derogate from Article 2 should not be interpreted too restrictively, with the result that these provisions would be in danger of being deprived of their legal effect or would be rendered almost wholly redundant.[27] In other words, the rules of Sections 2 to 6 of Title II should be interpreted in such a way that, for the cases listed in those provisions, the principle(s) underlying them is/are actually realized. In the next sections we will see how the Court, using this general guideline, has attempted to achieve a balance between the different sub-principles flowing from the fourth main principle that disputes should be decided by an appropriate court by, on the one hand, giving due influence to the principle of protection of the party that is weaker from a procedural point of view, which underlies Article 2, and, on the other hand, giving due influence to the various other sub-principles underlying the provisions that derogate from Article 2.[28]

In this section, we have established that the sub-principle of the protection of the party who is weaker due to his procedural position clearly underlies the Convention. It underlies, in particular, the general rule of jurisdiction laid down in Article 2. The sub-principle of the protection of the party who is weaker due to his procedural position, in particular, requires:

home court advantage for the defendant, hostility towards the *forum actoris* and other advantages for the plaintiff, such as choosing the court which he judges to be most favourable to his interests. These aspects of the principle of the protection of the party who is weaker due to his procedural position in their turn require:

---

[25] C-412/98 *Josi Reinsurance v UGIC* 49 (re *Handte* 14; *Shearson v TBV* 15,16; *Benincasa v Dentalkit* 13; *Réunion européenne v Spliethoff's* 16); see also 73/77 *Sanders v Van der Putte* 17,18; 33/78 *Somafer v Saar-Ferngas* 7; C-115/88 *Reichert v Dresdner Bank I* 9; C-261/90 *Reichert v Dresdner Bank II* 25 (re *Sanders* 17,18; *Reichert* 9); C-26/91 *Handte v TMCS* 14; C-89/91 *Shearson v TVB* 15,16 (re *Bertrand* 17; *Handte* 14); C-292/93 *Lieber v Göbel* 12 (re *Reichert* 9); C-364/93 *Marinari v Lloyd's* 13; C-106/95 *Mainschiffahrts v Les Gravières* 14 (re *Salotti* 7; *Segoura* 6),29 (re *Tessili* 13); C-269/95 *Benincasa v Dentalkit* 13 (re *Shearson* 14,15,16); C-99/96 *Mietz v Intership* 27 (re *Bertrand* 17; *Shearson* 14,15,16; *Benincasa* 13,14); C-51/97 *Réunion européenne v Spliethoff's* 16 (re *Benincasa* 13).

[26] 189/87 *Kalfelis v Schröder* 8.

[27] 38/81 *Effer v Kantner* 7 (re *Sanders*); C-439/93 *Lloyd's v Campenon* 17; and 21/76 *Bier v Mines de potasse* 20.

[28] See hereafter sections 1.2 to 3.

- a restrictive interpretation of the rules of jurisdiction derogating from Article 2, or,
- at any rate, an interpretation of these rules by which the very existence of the general principle of Article 2 would not be called into question or by which the defendant would not be removed from (or deprived of) other competent courts, for no good reason
- an interpretation of these rules of jurisdiction by which a multiplication of jurisdiction is avoided

1.2 The principle of the protection of the party who is weaker due to his socio-economic position

C Art. 5(1,2nd sentence)	R 18 to 21	C Art. 7 to 15	R 7 to 17
C Art. 5(2)	R 5(2)	C Art. 17, paras. 4 and 6	R 23(5)

Apart from the party who is weaker due to his procedural position, which is supposed to be the defendant, the Convention also aims to provide protection to the party who is deemed to be weaker from a socio-economic point of view, which in the legal field entails that most often he is also less experienced in legal matters than the other party.[29] The principle is expressed in Articles 7 to 12 and 13 to 15, Article 5, point 1, second sentence, Article 5, point 2, and Article 17, paragraphs 4 and 6. From these Articles it appears that the following categories of persons (at least, as far as they are domiciled in a Contracting State) are considered to be weaker in this sense:

- insurance policyholders (as well as the insured and the beneficiary of the policy)
- consumers
- maintenance creditors, and
- employees[30]

As regards insurance policyholders (the insured and the beneficiary of the policy) and consumers, their status as persons to be considered weaker due to their socio-economic position was already taken into account at the time when the Convention was first drafted, as is also evident from the Jenard Report.[31] In its case law,

---

[29] See for example, C-89/91 *Shearson v TVB* 18.

[30] With regard to a tenant, the requirement that a tenant-defendant is to be sued in the courts of his home state is implemented in the form of Art. 16(1a), which grants exclusive jurisdiction to the courts of the state in which the immovable property is situated. It should be noted that the 'protection of the tenant', though recognized in decisions by the Court (compare 133/81 *Ivenel v Schwab* 16) as a consideration underlying Art. 16(1a) was not the principal reason for the jurisdictional rule contained in this Article: the principal reason is related to the principle 'sound administration of justice', see below, section 3.1.3 of this chapter, text following note 353.

[31] Jenard Report, OJ 1979 C 59, p. 29; and Schlosser Report, OJ 1979 C 59, p. 117.

as will be seen below, the Court has made clear that these persons are worthy of protection.

As regards jurisdiction in matters relating to *insurance*, the Court held, in *Gerling v Tesoro*, that the purpose of the provisions of Section 3, where they afford the insured a wider range of jurisdiction than that available to the insurer and exclude any possibility of a clause conferring jurisdiction for the benefit of the insurer:

> 'was to protect the insured who is most frequently faced with a predetermined contract the clauses of which are no longer negotiable and who is in a weaker economic position.'[32]

As regards jurisdiction over *consumer contracts*, the Court has held, as for example in *Benincasa v Dentalkit*, that Articles 13 and 14 of the Convention were

> 'designed to protect the consumer as the party deemed to be the weaker party economically.'[33]

The status of the *maintenance creditor*, as a party who is weaker due to his socio-economic position, was also mentioned in the Jenard Report. The Court confirmed that position of the socio-economic weaker maintenance creditor in *Farrell v Long*. In that judgment, the Court observed:

> 'Article 5(2) is intended to offer the maintenance applicant, who is regarded as the weaker party in such proceedings, an alternative basis of jurisdiction. In adopting that approach, the drafters of the Convention considered that that specific objective had to prevail over the objective of the rule contained in the first paragraph of Article 2, which is to protect the defendant as the party who, being the person sued, is generally in a weaker position.'[34]

As regards *contracts of employment*, the drafters of the Convention did not consider it appropriate to insert into the Convention a provision giving specific jurisdiction in this field.[35] A special status as a party who is weaker due to his socio-economic position was not expressly given to the employee at the time when the Convention was first drafted. Employees were first given that status by the Court in *Ivenel v Schwab* and *Six Constructions v Humbert.* When answering questions on the interpretation of Article 5 point 1, with regard to contracts of employment, it referred to the need to ensure adequate protection for the employee, who is in

---

[32] 201/82 *Gerling v Tesoro* 17.

[33] C-269/95 *Benincasa v Dentalkit* 17; compare 150/77 *Bertrand v Ott* 18; C-89/91 *Shearson v TVB* 18; C-96/00 *Gabriel* 39 (re *Shearson* 19,20,22,24).

[34] C-295/95 *Farrell v Long* 19; and compare Jenard Report, OJ 1979 C 59, p. 24 and 25, as to the ratio of Art. 5, point 2.

[35] See Jenard Report OJ 1979 C 59, p. 24.

the weaker position from the social point of view.[36] This concern to afford proper protection to the employee was confirmed by the amendments as adopted by the 1989 Accession Convention.[37] Most recently, in *Pugliese v Finmeccanica*, the Court consistently held:

> 'in matters relating to contracts of employment, interpretation of Article 5(1) ... must take account of the concern to afford proper protection to the employee as the weaker of the contracting parties from the social point of view.'[38]

Although all of these categories have been recognized as persons worthy of protection, the jurisdictional protection granted to them is not always similar.

In the context of the question of which court should be given jurisdiction, the principle that persons who are weaker from a socio-economic point of view should be protected, requires that the weaker party should be given a jurisdictional advantage. What this 'jurisdictional advantage' implies, depends, primarily, on whether the socio-economically weaker party is *(a)* the defendant or *(b)* the plaintiff or *(c)* whether there is a jurisdiction clause.

C Art. 5 (1,2nd sentence)	R 18 to 21	C Art. 11 (1st para.)	R 12(1)
C Art. 5(2)	R 5(2)	C Art. 14 (2nd para.)	R 16(2)

When the party who is weaker from a socio-economic point of view is the *defendant*, the case for attributing jurisdiction to the court of the defendant's domicile is reinforced: it follows not only from the principle of the protection of the party who is weaker due to his procedural position but also from the principle of the protection of the party who is weaker from a socio-economic point of view.

With regard to the insurance policyholder (the insured and the beneficiary of the policy), within the meaning of Section 3 of the Convention, and the consumer, within the meaning of Section 4 of the Convention, the rule that they may only be sued in courts situated in the state of their domicile is implemented in Article 11, first paragraph, and Article 14, second paragraph, respectively.[39]

---

[36] 133/81 *Ivenel v Schwab* 14 (re Experts' Report on the Convention on the law applicable to contractual obligations, OJ 1980, C 282, p. 1); and 32/88 *Six Constructions v Humbert* 13,14 (re 133/81 *Ivenel v Schwab*; 266/85 *Shenavai v Kreischer)*.

[37] Article 4 of the 1989 Accession Convention, OJ 1989 L 285; compare Almeida Cruz Report, OJ 1990 C 189, No. 23.

[38] C-437/00 *Pugliese v Finmeccanica* 18 (re *Mulox* 18,19; *Rutten* 17; *Weber* 40).

[39] Notice that Art. 11 expressly provides that without prejudice to the provisions of the third paragraph of Art. 10, an insurer may bring proceedings only in the courts of the Contracting State in which the defendant is domiciled, irrespective of whether he is the policyholder, the insured or a beneficiary. The provision reflects a strong perspective on the principle of the protection of the weaker party, whereas exceptions to Art. 2, such as contained in Art. 5 of the Convention, are not permitted. A similar provision is contained in Art. 14, expressly providing that, notwithstanding the first paragraph of Art. 14, proceedings may be brought against a consumer by the other party to the contract only in the courts of the Contracting State in which the consumer is domiciled. And, here too, the Convention does not permit exceptions.

With regard to contracts of employment, if the position of the employee is that of a defendant, Article 2 provides that the courts of the state in which the employee is domiciled have jurisdiction. However, under the Convention, as was established by the Court in *Ivenel v Schwab* and *Six Constructions v Humbert,* and confirmed by Article 5, point 1, as amended by the 1989 Accession Convention, the employer-plaintiff may, as an alternative, choose to bring proceedings regarding the employment contract before the court of 'the place where the employee habitually carries out his work' or 'discharges his obligations towards his employer'.[40] If the employee has been required to work in more than one state, it follows from *Mulox v Geels*, *Rutten v Cross Medical* and *Weber v Ogden* that the place of performance can be that 'where or from which the employee principally discharges his obligations towards his employer', or 'where he has established the centre of his working activities', or 'where or from which, taking account of all the circumstances of the case, he in fact performs the essential part of his duties *vis-à-vis* his employer', usually being the place 'where he spends most of his working time engaged on his employer's business'.[41] As was seen, though, most recently in *Pugliese v Finmeccanica,* that case law cannot always be fully transposed to the case at hand. Other relevant factors are to be taken into account in order to determine which court has jurisdiction.[42] The bottom line is, that according to the Court's case law, the criterion of jurisdiction as laid down in Article 5, point 1, second sentence – the place where the employee habitually carries out his work – is indeed (though not only) inspired by a concern to afford proper protection to the party to the contract who is the weaker from the socio-economic point of view: the place where the employee 'habitually carries out his work' is, apart from the court of his domicile, 'least expensive for the employee to ... defend himself against, court proceedings'.[43] In addition to the principle of the protection of the party who is weaker due to his socio-economic position, this jurisdic-

---

[40] Compare 133/81 *Ivenel v Schwab* 15; 32/88 *Six Constructions v Humbert* 10 (re 133/81 *Ivenel v Schwab*; 266/85 *Shenavai v Kreischer*),14 (re *Ivenel v Schwab*; *Shenavai v Kreischer*),15; C-125/92 *Mulox v Geels* 19. See Art. 4 of the 1989 Accession Convention. Compare Art. 19, point 2(a) of Regulation 44/2001, that refers to 'the place where the employee habitually carries out his work or in the courts for the last place where he did so'. As follows from *Six Constructions v Humbert* 22, Art. 5, point 1, second sentence, is not applicable to contracts of employment performed entirely outside the territory of the Contracting States, since the employee carries out all his work in non-contracting countries.

[41] C-125/92 *Mulox v Geels* 26; C-383/95 *Rutten v Cross Medical* 27; C-37/00 *Weber v Universal Ogden* 48 (re *Mulox v Geels*; *Rutten v Cross Medical*),49 (re *Rutten* 22,24),50,58; compare C-256/00 *Besix v Kretzschmar* 38 (re *Mulox* 16,20,26; *Rutten* 26); C-437/00 *Pugliese v Finmeccanica* 19 (re *Mulox* 26; *Rutten* 23; *Weber* 58). See also chapter 5, section 4.2.1, text following note 130.

[42] C-437/00 *Pugliese v Finmeccanica* 22-26.

[43] C-125/92 *Mulox v Geels* 18,19; compare 133/81 *Ivenel v Schwab* 14 (re Experts'Report, OJ 1980 C 282, p. 1); 32/88 *Six Constructions v Humbert* 13; and C-383/95 *Rutten v Cross Medical* 20 (re C-288/92 *Custom Made v Stawa* 25; *Ivenel*; *Shenavai*; Almeida Cruz Report, OJ 1990 C 189, pp. 35,44,45),22.

tional rule is also based, as appears from the Court's case law, on the principle 'avoiding multiplication of jurisdiction' and on the principle 'sound administration of justice'.[44] The latter principle will be discussed in section 3 of this chapter.[45]

In matters concerning maintenance, the person considered worthy of protection is considered to be the maintenance creditor. He (or she) will most typically need protection when he is in the procedural position of a plaintiff, that is, as the person asking for maintenance. If the maintenance creditor is the defendant, it is clear from Article 2, which confers jurisdiction on the courts of the state of the defendant's domicile, in conjunction with Article 5, point 2, which confers jurisdiction on the courts for the place where the maintenance creditor is domiciled (or habitually resident), that an exception to the jurisdiction of the courts of the maintenance creditor's domicile is only admitted if the matter is ancillary to proceedings concerning the status of a person: The court which, according to its own law, has jurisdiction to entertain those proceedings has jurisdiction as an alternative, unless that jurisdiction is based solely on the nationality of one of the parties.

C Art. 5(1,2nd sentence)	R 18 to 21	C Art. 8,1st para., 2.	R 9(1b)
C Art. 5(2)	R 5(2)	C Art. 14,1st para.	R 16(1)

When the party who is weaker from a socio-economic point of view is the *plaintiff*, the requirement that the socio-economically weaker party should have jurisdictional advantage would imply granting him the possibility to sue the defendant in his, the plaintiff's, home state (or an equivalent court) and granting him a choice between that court and the court where the defendant is domiciled or seated. Clearly, in this type of situation, the principle that the party who is weaker due to his socio-economic position should be protected comes into direct conflict with the principle that the party who is considered to be weaker due to his procedural position as the defendant should be protected. The Convention has resolved this conflict in favour of the first principle.

This is apparent, *first*, from the fact that in case the socio-economically weaker party is the plaintiff, he may sue the defendant in the court of the state where he, the plaintiff, is domiciled, thereby infringing the Convention's general hostility towards the attribution of jurisdiction to the courts of the plaintiff's domicile.[46] With regard to matters relating to insurance and consumer contracts, this is ex-

---

[44] Compare C-437/00 *Pugliese v Finmeccanica* 16 (re *Mulox* 11; *Rutten* 13), 17 (re *Mulox* 17; *Rutten* 16; *Weber* 39) and 18 (re *Mulox* 18,19; *Rutten* 17; *Weber* 40); compare section 4.2.1 of chapter 5, text following note 130 and section 3.1.1 of this chapter, text following notes 179 and 182.

[45] C-37/00 *Weber v Universal Ogden* 39 (re C-125/92 *Mulox v Geels* 17; C-383/95 *Rutten v Cross Medical* 16),40 (re *Mulox* 18,19; *Rutten* 27); compare 133/81 *Ivenel v Schwab* 15; 266/85 *Shenavai v Kreischer* 16.

[46] Compare C-89/91 *Shearson v TVB* 17 (re C-220/88 *Dumez France v Hessische Landesbank* 16,19); C-412/98 *Josi Reinsurance v UGIC* 50 (re *Dumez* 16,19 ; *Shearson* 17).

pressed in Article 8, first paragraph, point 2, and Article 14, first paragraph, respectively. With respect to matters of maintenance, this appears from Article 5, point 2, which allows the maintenance creditor to sue the maintenance debtor in the state of the creditor's domicile (or, if the matter is ancillary to proceedings concerning the status of a person, in the court which, according to its own law, has jurisdiction to entertain those proceedings, unless that jurisdiction is based on the nationality of one of the parties).[47]

With regard to matters relating to individual contracts of employment, a somewhat different version of this implication is laid down in Article 5, point 1, which provides that the employee-plaintiff may sue his employer in the courts of the place where the employee 'habitually carries out his work',[48] or, if the employee does not habitually carry out his work in any one country, in the courts of the place 'where the business which engaged the employee was or is now situated'.

The fact that the principle of the 'protection of the socio-economically weaker party' is allowed to infringe upon the principle of the 'protection of the party who is weaker due to his procedural position' is apparent, *secondly*, from the fact that, in those cases where the party who is weaker from a socio-economic point of view is the plaintiff, he is given a choice between, at least, two forums: the court of his own domicile (or an equivalent court) and the court where the defendant is domiciled or seated.[49] For the various categories of persons considered to be weaker this is laid down, as regards the insurance policyholder (the insured and the beneficiary of the policy), in Article 8, first paragraph, point 1, in conjunction with point 2 (and 3),[50] as regards the consumer, in Article 14, first paragraph, as regards employees, in Article 5, point 1, in conjunction with Article 2,[51] and, as regards maintenance creditors, Article 5, point 2, jo. Article 2.[52]

C Art. 12	R 13	C Art. 17, 4th and 6th para.	R 23(5)
C Art. 15	R 17		

When the socio-economically weaker party is a party who has *'agreed'* to a jurisdiction clause, he is granted protection as well. As the Court has pointed out,

[47] Compare C- 295/95 *Farrell v Long* 19.

[48] Compare text following note 40 of this section.

[49] Compare C-412/98 *Josi Reinsurance v UGIC* 37-40.

[50] See also Art. 9: In respect of liability insurance or insurance of immovable property, the insurer may in addition be sued in the courts of the place where the harmful event occurred.

[51] Here, the employee-plaintiff has the choice of bringing his proceedings before the courts of the State of the defendant's domicile and the courts of the place where the employee 'habitually carries out his work' or, in case the employee 'does not habitually carry out his work in any one country'(see text following note 40 of this section), the courts of the place where the business which engaged the employee was or is now situated.

[52] Clearly, the requirement of avoiding, as far as possible, a multiplicity of courts having jurisdiction as regards one and the same legal relationship or type of case, flowing from the principle 'legal certainty as to jurisdiction', has been set aside, at least to a certain extent, in the interest of the protection of the party who is weaker from a socio-economic point of view; compare section 4.2 of chapter 5.

these persons are generally less experienced in legal matters and they are most frequently faced with a predetermined contract, the clauses of which are no longer negotiable.[53] For these reasons, the Convention imposes, in order to protect the weaker party, restrictions on the possibility to choose the forum. As will be seen in the next section on the principle of party autonomy, the Convention generally recognizes the parties' freedom to agree to submit disputes to a particular forum. In order to protect the weaker party against a choice of forum agreement which might be imposed upon him by the stronger party, the Convention contains several safeguards, in particular with regard to matters of insurance, consumer contracts and contracts of employment. Thus, in Article 12 and Article 15 in conjunction with Article 17, fourth paragraph, and in Article 17, sixth paragraph, insurance policyholders (the insured and the beneficiaries), consumers and employees are protected as follows: in derogation of the general rule on choice of forum contained in Article 17, agreements concluded before a dispute arises will have no legal force, unless certain conditions (most of them exclusively) to the advantage of the weaker insurance policyholder, consumer or employee, are fulfilled. The maintenance creditor lacks this advantage.

The principle of the protection of the party who is weaker due to his socio-economic position weighed in relation to other principles

C Art. 5	R 5	C Art. 17, 4th and 6th para.	R 23(5)
C Art. 6	R 6	C Art. 28	R 35

As was seen in the foregoing paragraphs, the principle of the protection of the party who is weaker due to his socio-economic position is firmly established under the Convention. As appears from the system of rules of jurisdiction laid down in Title II of the Convention and as was seen in the foregoing paragraphs, the sub-principle of the protection of the party who is weaker due to his socio-economic position overrides the principle of the protection of the defendant, being the weaker party due to his procedural position. Whereas the latter sub-principle only requires some jurisdictional advantage for the defendant, the principle of the protection of the party who is weaker due to his socio-economic position requires somewhat more: protection of that party as a defendant *and* a plaintiff. Furthermore, as was seen before, the principle places some restraints on the principle of party autonomy (as follows from Article 17, fourth and sixth paragraphs). Also, as will be seen later, the principle may override (or coincide with) the principle of a sound administration of justice, as far as it underlies Article 5, and places restrictions on that principle, as far as it underlies Article 6.[54] Finally, according to Article 28, first paragraph, with regard to matters of insurance and consumer con-

[53] 201/82 *Gerling v Tesoro* 17.

[54] Compare sections 3.1 and 3.2.1 of this chapter.

tracts, that principle may even overrule the first main principle underlying the Convention: the principle of free movement of judgments.[55]

C Art. 2	R 2	C Art. 5(2)	R 5(2)	C Art. 13	R 15
C Art. 4	R 4	C Art. 8	R 9	C Art. 14	R 16
C Art. 5, 1,2nd sentence	R 18 to 21	C Art. 11	R 12	C Art. 16	R 22

However, under the Convention, the principle of the protection of the party who is weaker due to his socio-economic position is not absolute. This already appears from Articles 2, 4, 5, point 1 and 2, and Articles 8, 11 and 14: the socio-economically weaker party is only protected as a defendant and a plaintiff if he is domiciled in a Contracting State. Notice also, that the protection of consumers is restricted to certain types of consumer contracts, and that for consumer contracts with regard to the supply of goods or services several conditions have to be fulfilled, in order to consider these contracts as 'consumer contracts' within the meaning of Section 4 of Title II of the Convention (Article 13).[56] Finally, the principle of the protection of the party who is weaker due to his socio-economic position is set aside by the principle of sound administration of justice, as far as it underlies Article 16, or coincides with that principle.[57]

The Court's case law reveals the significance which the Court attaches to the principle of the protection of the party who is weaker due to his socio-economic position and how it guides the Court's interpretations of the provisions directly influenced by that principle.[58] Quite a number of cases placed before the Court involving the provisions of the Convention which have the objective of protecting persons deemed to be weaker socio-economically, concern the *substantive scope* of these provisions. In deciding these cases, the Court (in general) adopts the approach that is typical of the model of principles: it interprets the provision concerned in light of the principle immediately underlying it (here, the principle of the protection of the party who is weaker due to his socio-economic position), as well as in light of the principled system underlying the jurisdictional rules of Title II of the Convention, or even broader, underlying the Convention as a whole.[59] It appears from the Court's case law that the principle of the protection of the party who is weaker due to his socio-economic position is particularly

---

[55] See, however, also Art. 28, third paragraph.

[56] Compare text following note 75 of this section.

[57] Compare note 30 of this section.

[58] 150/77 *Bertrand v Ott* 17-21; C-89/91 *Shearson v TVB* 15,16 (re *Bertrand* 17, *Handte* 14), 17 (re C-220/88 *Dumez France* 16,19)-22 (re *Bertrand* 21, Expert Report, OJ 1979 C 59, p. 71)-24; C-269/95 *Benincasa v Dentalkit* 13 (re *Shearson v TVB* 14,15,16),14 (re C-220/88 *Dumez France* 16,19; *Shearson* 17); C-99/96 *Mietz v Intership* 27 (re *Bertrand* 17; *Shearson* 14,15,16; *Benincasa* 13,14),31.

[59] As was already seen in chapters 3, 4 and 5, other main principles, such as the principle 'free movement of judgments', 'protection of the rights of the defence' and 'legal certainty', have an influence on the interpretation of rules of jurisdiction.

weighed and balanced in relation to the principle of the protection of the defendant, being the weaker party due to his procedural position. This weighing of interests generally results in a *restrictive* interpretation of the substantive scope of the jurisdictional rules that protect the socio-economically weaker party.

C Art. 2	R 2
C Art. 13	R 15

Consumers as the weaker party
The Court's case law as regards consumer contracts is in particular illustrative of the Court's reasoning, when justifying its restrictive interpretation of the *substantive scope* of the rules of jurisdiction relating to consumer contracts. *Shearson v TVB* is representative for the most essential considerations in this type of case.[60] Before answering the different questions that were submitted by the national court on the interpretation of Article 13, the Court had to decide a preliminary point.[61] That preliminary point was whether the plaintiff in the case at hand could be regarded as a 'consumer' within the meaning of Section 4 of the Convention and, therefore, was to benefit from the special rules governing jurisdiction laid down by the Convention with respect to consumer contracts. The Court had to answer the question whether the term 'consumer' within the meaning of Section 4, includes the case in which an action for the recovery of debts was brought against a company, not by the private individual who was the other party to the contract, but by a company who was the assignee of the rights of that individual.

The Court's answer was in the negative, and in coming to this conclusion, it used the following line of reasoning. First, it recalled that the concept '*consumer*', within the meaning of Article 13, must be interpreted independently, by reference principally to the system and objectives of the Convention.[62] In doing so, the Court, as usual, pointed out that the most general principle of the Convention's jurisdictional rules, contained in Article 2, attributes jurisdiction to the courts of the state of the defendant's domicile. The Court then continued, by arguing that it is only by way of derogation from this principle, that the Convention provides for jurisdictions for the cases exhaustively listed in Sections 2 to 6 of Title II of the Convention, in which a defendant may or must be sued in the courts of another state. Therefore, according to the Court, the rules of jurisdiction which derogate from Article 2 should not be given an interpretation going beyond the cases envisaged by the Convention.[63] The Court pointed out that this must apply *a fortiori* with respect to a rule of jurisdiction, such as contained in

[60] C-89/91 *Shearson v TVB*.
[61] C-89/91 *Shearson v TVB* 9.
[62] C-89/91 *Shearson v TVB* 13 (re 150/77 *Bertrand v Ott* 14,16,19; C-26/91 *Handte v TMCS* 10); and compare section 1 and 1.1 of chapter 5.
[63] C-89/91 *Shearson v TVB* 14-16 (re 150/77 *Bertrand v Ott* 17; *Handte* 14); compare section 1.1 of this chapter, text following note 25.

Article 14, which allows a consumer, within the meaning of Article 13, to sue the defendant in the state of the plaintiff's domicile.[64]

Having established this, the Court then went on to determine which cases are envisaged by the Convention with the term 'consumer' in Article 13. In doing so, the Court referred to the principle that inspired the special rules of jurisdiction for consumers: the concern to protect the consumer as the party deemed to be economically weaker and less experienced in legal matters than the other party to the contract.[65] The consumer must not therefore be discouraged from suing by being compelled to bring his action before the court in the Contracting State in which the other party to the contract is domiciled. The Court then held, that the protective role of the special jurisdictional rules for the consumer implies that the application of these rules should not be extended to persons for whom that protection is not justified; it should be restricted to persons in need of protection.[66] A legal person which acts as the assignee of the rights of the individual to the original contract is not considered to be worthy of the protective rules of jurisdiction, and hence should not be considered to be a 'consumer' for the purpose of Article 13. This conclusion, which follows from the argumentation according to the model of principles is, as the Court observed, also in line with the wording of the relevant provisions (and therefore in accordance with the principle of legal certainty, which requires respect for the linguistic boundaries of the Convention).[67] Article 13, first paragraph, defines 'consumer' as a person acting 'for a purpose which can be regarded as being outside his trade or profession'. Hence, both the wording and the function of the relevant provisions support the same conclusion.[68] In *Benincasa v Dentalkit*, the Court consistently held that the specific protective rules enshrined in Article 14 in conjunction with the first paragraph of Article 13, apply only to contracts concluded outside and independently of any trade or professional activity or purpose, whether present or future.[69]

In *Konsumenteninformation v Henkel,* the Court explicitly recalled its decision in *Shearson v TVB*, that a legal person which acts as the assignee of the rights of a private final consumer, without itself being a party to a contract between a professional and a private individual, cannot be regarded as a consumer.[70] It held in that judgment that that (restrictive) interpretation of the term consumer, within the meaning of Section 4, also applies in respect of a consumer protection organisation which has brought an action as an association on behalf of consumers.[71]

---

[64] C-89/91 *Shearson v TVB* 17 (re C-220/88 *Dumez France v Hessische Landesbank* 16,19).

[65] C-89/91 *Shearson v TVB* 18.

[66] C-89/91 *Shearson v TVB* 19.

[67] Compare section 2 of chapter 5.

[68] C-89/91 *Shearson v TVB* 20-22 (re *Bertrand* 21; Expert Report OJ 1979 C 59, p. 71)-24.

[69] C-269/95 *Benincasa v Dentalkit* 18,19.

[70] C-167/00 *Konsumenteninformation v Henkel* 33 (re C-89/91 *Shearson v TVB)*.

[71] Idem. C-167/00 *Konsumenteninformation v Henkel* 33.

In *Bertrand v Ott*, the Court used a similar line of reasoning in terms of the principles underlying the different rules of jurisdiction and their relationship to other principles of the Convention, when it concluded that the term 'sale of goods on instalment credit terms' in Article 13, first paragraph, point 1, does not extend to the sale of a machine which one company agrees to manufacture for another company, on the basis of a price paid by means of bills of exchange spread over a period of time.[72] As the Court observed in that judgment:

> 'a restrictive interpretation of the second paragraph of Article 14, in conformity with the objectives pursued by Section 4, entails the restriction of the jurisdictional advantage described above to buyers who are in need of protection, their economic position being one of weakness in comparison with sellers by reason of the fact that they are private final consumers and are not engaged, when buying the product acquired on instalment credit terms, in trade or professional activities.'[73]

In *Mietz v Intership*, the Court was asked whether the concept 'sale of goods on instalment credit terms' within the meaning of Article 13, first paragraph, point 1, must be understood as extending to the following contract between a yacht building company and an individual. The contract was described by the parties as a 'contract of sale' involving the construction of a yacht conforming to a standard model type but featuring a number of alterations. One of the contracting parties, the yacht building company, undertook to manufacture the yacht and to transfer the property in it to the other contracting party, an individual, who, by way of consideration, undertook to pay the price in several instalments. The final instalment had to be paid before possession of the yacht was transferred. The Court argued that Article 13, first paragraph, point 1, is intended to protect the purchaser only where the vendor has granted him credit, that is to say, where the vendor has transferred to the purchaser possession of the goods in question before the purchaser has paid the full price. The reason why protective rules of jurisdiction apply in such a case, as the Court observed in *Mietz v Intership*, is that, on the one hand, the purchaser may, when the contract is concluded, be misled as to the real amount which he owes, and, on the other, he will bear the risk of loss of those goods while remaining obliged to pay any outstanding instalments. The Court then pointed out that these considerations did not apply to the case at hand where the price had to be paid in full before the transfer of possession took place: the special protection referred to in Article 13, first paragraph, point 1, of the Convention cannot be extended to the purchaser solely on the grounds that he has been allowed to pay the price in several instalments. When justifying its restric-

[72] 150/77 *Bertrand v Ott* 17.
[73] 150/77 *Bertrand v Ott* 21.

tive interpretation of Article 13, the Court used a principle-based reasoning, similar to that in *Shearson v TVB*.[74]

Most recently, as regards 'jurisdiction over consumer contracts', the Court had an opportunity to recall its case law on the (restrictive) interpretation of Article 13 in *Gabriel*.[75] In this case, the Court had to answer questions on the interpretation of the two conditions laid down in Article 13, first paragraph, point 3(a) and (b), with regard to contracts for the supply of goods or services. These conditions stipulate that the rules of jurisdiction contained in Section 4 only apply, when a consumer concludes a contract regarding the supply of goods or services if (a) the trader has taken steps to market his goods or services in the country where the consumer resides and (b) the consumer has taken certain steps 'necessary for the conclusion of the contract' in the state in which he is domiciled.[76] In its judgment, the Court first recalled that the concepts used in Article 13 are to be construed independently (in accordance with the principle of legal certainty, requiring 'equality and uniformity of rights and obligations'). Next, it referred to the wording and the underlying purpose of Article 13 (in accordance with the requirement of 'respect for the linguistic boundaries of the Convention' and the principle of the protection of the socio-economic weaker party). The Court then referred to the remarks in the Schlosser Report on the Second Accession Convention on these additional conditions and clarified that those concurrent conditions were designed to ensure that there are close connections between the contract at issue and the State in which the consumer is domiciled.[77] These conditions in themselves prove that the principle of the protection of the weaker party due to his socio-economic position, is not absolute. It seems that the principle 'sound administration of justice' requiring a direct, territorial link between the court and a case, also plays a role. However, if these conditions are satisfied, then the protection of the weaker party due to his socio-economic position is justified. In *Gabriel*, the Court concluded as to the conditions set out in Article 13, first paragraph, point 3(a) and (b) that: 'where a consumer has been contacted at his home by one or more letters sent by a professional vendor for the purpose of bringing about the placement of an order for goods offered under the conditions determined by that vendor, and where the consumer has in fact placed such an order in the Contracting State in which he is domiciled, the action by which such a consumer seeks through judicial proceedings brought against the vendor to obtain a

---

[74] C-99/96 *Mietz v Intership* 26 (re 150/77*Bertrand v Ott* 14,14,16,19; C-89/91 *Shearson v TVB* 13; C-269/95 *Benincasa v Dentalkit* 12), 27 (re *Shearson* 14,15,16; *Benincasa* 13,14),28 (re *Bertrand* 20)-31.

[75] C-96/00 *Gabriel* 37 (re 150/77 *Bertrand v Ott* 14,15,15; C-89/91 *Shearson v TVB* 13; C-269/95 *Benincasa v Dentalkit* 12; C-99/96 *Mietz v Intership* 26)-39 (re *Shearson v TVB* 19,20,22,24).

[76] C-96/00 *Gabriel* 41 (re Schlosser Report, OJ 1979 C 59, at p. 118), 42 (re Giuliano and Lagarde Report on the Rome Convention), 43-46.

[77] C-96/00 *Gabriel* 40,41 (re Schlosser Report, OJ 1979 C 59, at p. 118), 42 (re Giuliano and Lagarde Report on the Rome Convention).

prize which he has apparently won is an action relating to a contract concluded by a consumer within the meaning of Article 13, first paragraph, point 3, of the Brussels Convention.'[78]

C Art. 12	R 13
C Art. 17, 4th para.	R 23(5)

Insurance policyholders (the insured an the beneficiary of the policy) as the weaker party

Gerling v Tesoro and *Josi Reinsurance v UGIC* are illustrative of the Court's reasoning with regard to the *substantive scope* of jurisdictional rules regarding matters relating to insurance.[79]

In *Josi Reinsurance v UGIC*, the Court decided on a restrictive application of the provisions of Section 3 of Title II, on 'Jurisdiction in matters relating to insurance'.[80] After having recalled that these rules reflect the underlying concern to protect the insured, being the weaker party due to his socio-economic position, the Court held, though, that the rules of Section 3 laid down to that end should, in accordance with both the letter and the spirit and purpose of these provisions, not be extended to persons for whom that protection is not justified, particularly not to the relationship between a reinsured and his reinsurer in connection with a reinsurance contract.[81]

In *Gerling v Tesoro*, the Court also referred to the principle immediately underlying the provisions of Section 3. In this case the Court decided in favour of a broad interpretation of the provisions concerned. The Court had to answer the question whether Article 17, paragraph 4 in conjunction with Article 12 is to be interpreted as meaning that under a contract of insurance a person in whose favour the contract is made but who is not a party to the contract and who is separate from the insured, is entitled to rely on a clause extending jurisdiction inserted for his benefit although he has not himself signed it, albeit the insurer and insured have duly done so. The Court answered that question in the affirmative. The Court first recalled that the requirements as to form, as laid down in Article 17, are to ensure that the consent of the parties who by an agreement intend to confer jurisdiction on the court(s) of their choice is clearly and precisely demonstrated and established. However, the Court pointed out that Article 17 does not have the object of subjecting a third party benefiting from the requirements imposed on others to the same requirements.[82] It then observed:

---

[78] C-96/00 *Gabriel* 53; compare also section 4.2.2 of chapter 5, text following note 145.

[79] 201/82 *Gerling v Tesoro* 17; C-412/98 *Josi Reinsurance v UGIC* 64 (re 201/82 *Gerling v Tesoro* 17).

[80] C-412/98 *Josi Reinsurance v UGIC* 67.

[81] C-412/98 *Josi Reinsurance v UGIC* 62-64 (re 201/82 *Gerling v Tesoro* 17), 65 (re *Shearson v TVB* 19),67.

[82] 201/82 *Gerling v Tesoro* 13 (re 24/76 *Salotti*; 25/76 *Segoura*; 784/79 *Porta Leasing*)14,15. As will be seen hereafter, that interpretation is in accordance with the principle of party autonomy, underlying Article 17; compare text following note 6 of section 2.1 of this chapter.

> 'Consideration of the provisions of Section 3 of the Convention relating to jurisdiction in matters relating to insurance confirms that view. It is apparent from a consideration of the provisions of that section ... that in affording the insured a wider range of jurisdiction than that available to the insurer and in excluding any possibility of a clause conferring jurisdiction for the benefit of the insurer their purpose was to protect the insured who is most frequently faced with a predetermined contract the clauses of which are no longer negotiable and who is in a weaker economic position. Moreover, Article 12 ... allows the parties to depart from the provisions of Section 3 "by an agreement .. (2) which allows the policy-holder, the insured or a beneficiary to bring proceedings in courts other than those indicated in this section". It is thus clear that the Convention has expressly provided for the possibility of stipulating clauses conferring jurisdiction not only in favour of the policy-holder, being a party to the contract, but also in favour of the insured and the beneficiary who may not be parties to the contract...'[83]

The Court arrived at its decision by principle-based reasoning. Both the principle of party autonomy, directly underlying Article 17, and the principle of the protection of the weaker party due to his socio-economic position, directly underlying the rules of jurisdiction of Section 3 of the Convention were taken into account. Both principles pointed in the direction of a broad interpretation of Article 12.

C Art. 5 (1,2nd sentence) R 18 to 21

Employees as the weaker party
As regards contracts of employment, the Court's case law clearly shows the view of the Court that the principle 'protection of the party deemed to be economically weaker and less experienced in legal matters' applies to employees and that they should be given certain jurisdictional advantages over the other party to the contract.[84]

In most decisions in which reference was made to this principle, the focus was on the connecting link between such a contract and the competent court, as expressed in Article 5, point 1, second sentence, rather than on the substantive scope of that provision.[85] As is evident from that case law, the Court assumes that the protection of the employee is best ensured if disputes relating to a contract of employment fall within the jurisdiction of the courts of the place 'where the employee habitually carries out his work', since that is the place where it is least expensive for the employee to commence or defend court proceedings.[86]

With regard to the substantive scope of the special jurisdictional rule as regards 'contracts of employment', the Court's case law shows that it does not de-

---

[83] 201/82 *Gerling v Tesoro* 16,17.

[84] See this section, text following notes 36 and 40.

[85] See note 41 of this section; and compare text following note 130 of chapter 5, section 4.2.1.

[86] 32/88 *Six Constructions v Humbert* 13; C-125/92 *Mulox v Geels* 18,19; C-383/95 *Rutten v Cross Medical* 16,17; and, C-37/00 *Weber v Universal Ogden* 40; and compare text following note 43 of this section.

fend a broad interpretation. The Court has made it clear in *Shenavai v Kreischer* that the application of the special jurisdictional rule contained in Article 5, point 1, second sentence, is only justified by the particularities of a contract of employment.[87] When these specific features of a contract of employment do not exist, the application of the special jurisdictional rule is neither necessary nor appropriate, as the Court consistently held in *Shenavai v Kreischer, Leathertex v Bodetex* and *Concorde v Panjan*.[88]

C Art. 2	R 2
C Art. 5(2)	R 5(2)

Maintenance creditors as the weaker party
As regards matters of maintenance, in *Farrel v Long* (the only case related to these matters), the Court adopted, rather exceptionally, a broad interpretation of the substantive scope of one of the provisions derogating from Article 2, namely, Article 5, point 2, which is intended to offer the maintenance applicant an alternative basis of jurisdiction. After having recalled that concepts of the Convention must be interpreted autonomously (in accordance with the principle 'equality and uniformity of rights and obligations'), the Court referred to the principle of avoiding, as far as possible, a (further) multiplication of jurisdictions (in accordance with the principle of legal certainty as to jurisdiction) and to the principle of strengthening the protection of persons established within the Convention, which is the most general principle underlying the Convention.[89] The Court then referred to the principle directly underlying Article 5, point 2, which prevails over the principle underlying Article 2:

> 'Article 5(2) is intended to offer the maintenance applicant, who is regarded as the weaker party in such proceedings, an alternative basis of jurisdiction. In adopting that approach, the drafters of the Convention considered that that specific objective had to prevail over the objective of the rule contained in the first paragraph of Article 2, which is to protect the defendant as the party who, being the person sued, is generally in a weaker position.'[90]

The Court's answer to the question whether 'maintenance creditor' in Article 5, point 2, covers any person applying for maintenance without drawing any distinction between those already recognized and those not yet recognized as entitled to maintenance, was that such a distinction should not be drawn.[91] The vari-

---

[87] 266/85 *Shenavai v Kreischer* 16.

[88] 266/85 *Shenavai v Kreischer* 17; C-420/97 *Leathertex v Bodetex* 36 (re *Shenavai v Kreischer* 17); C-440/97 *Concorde v Panjan* 19 (re *Shenavai v Kreischer* 17); and C-256/00 *Besix v Kretzschmar* 40 (re *Shenavai v Kreischer* 17, *Concorde v Panjan* 19; *Leathertex v Bodetex* 36).

[89] C-295/95 *Farrel v Long* 12 (re C-125/92 *Mulox* 10; C-383/95 *Rutten v Cross Medical* 12),13 (re *Mulox* 11; *Rutten* 13); and compare section 1.1 and 4.2.1 of chapter 5.

[90] C-295/95 *Farrel v Long* 19.

[91] C-295/95 *Farrel v Long* 27; compare section 4.1 of chapter 5, text following note 99.

ous principles to which the Court referred in this judgment apparently all pointed in the same direction, namely that of a broad interpretation of the concept 'maintenance creditor'.

To conclude this section, the sub-principle of the protection of the party who is weaker due to his socio-economic position, though not absolute, is firmly established under the Convention. In addition, we recall here that which was discussed in section 4.2 of chapter 5: as regards the protection of the party who is weaker due to his socio-economic position, the Court has, on several occasions, observed that the avoidance of a multiplicity of courts as regards one and the same legal relationship, is a fortiori required when the protection of such a person is concerned.[92] The main requirements that flow from that principle are:

the protection of insurance policyholders (the insured and the beneficiary of the policy), consumers, employees and maintenance creditors in that they are given jurisdictional advantages, such as

- home court advantage (or the advantage of an equivalent court), as a defendant as well as a plaintiff
- a choice for the weaker party as plaintiff between at least two forums: the court of the defendant's domicile and the court of his own domicile (or an equivalent court)
- protection against a jurisdiction clause which might be imposed upon them by the stronger party

1.3 The principle of the protection of the party that might be unaware of a jurisdiction clause incorporated in a contract by the other party

C Art. 17 (1st para.) R 23(1)

A third consequence of the principle of the protection of the weaker party is connected with the requirements as to the validity of a jurisdiction clause, under the first paragraph of Article 17.[93] That provision has a manifold purpose. It is not only to ensure legal certainty, as was seen before, or to ensure that consensus between the parties is in fact established, as will be seen hereafter, it also aims to protect the weaker party to the contract by avoiding jurisdiction clauses, incorporated in a contract by one party, going unnoticed. The Court has confirmed this viewpoint on several occasions, as for example in *Castelletti v Trumpy*, in which it stated:

---

[92] Compare section 4.2.1, text following note 130 and section 4.2.2, text following note 147 of chapter 5.

[93] As amended by Art. 11 of the 1978 Accession Convention and by Art. 7 of the 1989 Accession Convention.

> 'the provision's aim was ... to protect the weaker party to the contract by avoiding jurisdiction clauses, incorporated in a contract by one party, going unnoticed.'[94]

The principle entails that a party faced with a jurisdiction clause incorporated in a contract by one person alone and which might go unread, must be protected. The protection of such a party lies in the fact that jurisdiction clauses are only valid if the formal requirements laid down in Article 17 are fulfilled.[95] Since the principle 'protection of the party that might be unaware of a jurisdiction clause incorporated in a contract by one party alone' in itself does not give specific jurisdictional advantages, and since, from another angle, that requirement also belongs to the core of the principle of party autonomy, we will elaborate on this issue in the following section, in which the latter principle will be discussed.

Conclusions and summary

As was seen in this section, the sub-principles that flow from the principle of the protection of the weaker party, in particular the principle of the protection of the defendant as the weaker party due to his procedural position and the principle of the protection of the weaker party due to his weaker socio-economic position, are firmly established under the Convention. These principles are not absolute, though, and are particularly weighed and balanced in relation to each other.

The principle of the protection of the weaker party is clearly one of the sub-principles that guides the Court's interpretation of the rules of jurisdiction, laid down in Title II of the Convention. The following scheme of the first sub-principle that flows from the fourth main principle, the principle that disputes should be decided by an appropriate court, can be presented:

(4.1) The sub-principle of the protection of the weaker party *entails*:

- (4.1.1) Protection of the party who is weaker due to his procedural position
- (4.1.2) Protection of the party who is weaker due to his socio-economic position
- (4.1.3) Protection of the party that might be unaware of a jurisdiction clause incorporated in a contract by the other party

---

[94] C-159/97 *Castelletti v Trumpy* 19 (re *Mainschiffahrts* 17); compare C-106/95 *Mainschiffahrts v Les Gravières Rhénanes* 15 (re 24/76 *Salotti* 7; 25/76 *Segoura* 6),17; and C-116/02 *Gasser v MISAT* 50.

[95] See Expert Report, OJ 1979 C 59, p. 37, and 150/80 *Elefanten Schuh v Jacqmain* 24; C-106/95 *Mainschiffahrts v Les Gravières Rhénanes* 17; C-159/97 *Castelletti v Trumpy* 19.

The more concrete sub-principles that flow from the sub-principle of the protection of the weaker party, in their turn *imply the following requirements*:

(4.1.1) Protection of the party who is weaker due to his procedural position, *requires*:
- home court advantage for the defendant, hostility towards the *forum actoris* and other advantages for the plaintiff, such as choosing the court which he judges to be most favourable to his interests. These aspects in their turn *require*:
- a restrictive interpretation of the rules of jurisdiction derogating from Article 2, or,
- at any rate, an interpretation of these rules by which the very existence of the general principle of Article 2 would not be called into question, or by which the defendant would not be removed from (or deprived of) other competent courts, for no good reason
- an interpretation of the rules of jurisdiction such that a multiplication of jurisdiction is avoided

(4.1.2) Protection of the party who is weaker due to his socio-economic position, *requires*:
the protection of insurance policyholders (the insured and the beneficiary of the policy), consumers, employees and maintenance creditors in that they are given jurisdictional advantages, such as
- home court advantage (or the advantage of an equivalent court), as a defendant and a plaintiff
- a choice for the weaker party as the plaintiff between at least two forums: the court of the defendant's domicile and the court of his own domicile (or an equivalent court)
- protection against a choice of forum agreement which might be imposed upon them by the stronger party
- an interpretation of the rules of jurisdiction such that a multiplication of jurisdiction is avoided

(4.1.3) the protection of the party that might be unaware of a jurisdiction clause incorporated in a contract by the other party (the significance of this principle can only be truly appreciated in light of the principle of party autonomy, to be discussed in the next section).

2. The principle of party autonomy

Introduction

C Art. 17	R 23
C Art. 18	R 24

A second sub-principle that gives substance to the general principle that disputes are to be decided by an appropriate court is the principle of party autonomy. In the specific context of the issue which we are considering, namely, which court is appropriate to decide a particular case, the principle of party autonomy implies the following: a forum which both parties have agreed upon under their own free will, should be competent to hear the case. This implies that the parties have the right to decide for themselves that a court or the courts of a particular Contracting State or States shall have jurisdiction.

In the Convention there are two provisions that clearly recognize the freedom of the parties to confer jurisdiction on a forum of their choice, namely Articles 17 and 18. These provisions each pertain to the choice of forum, although the will of the parties is expressed in a different form. The Court has confirmed this view in *Elefanten Schuh v Jacqmain* and *Spitzley v Sommer*: the two provisions indicate that the Convention allows the parties, so far as is possible and subject to the limits laid down in Article 17, paragraph one to six, and in the second sentence of Article 18, to choose the court to which they intend to submit the settlement of their disputes.[96] Both Articles 17 and 18 deal with the prorogation of jurisdiction; Article 17 is concerned with the prorogation of jurisdiction by (formal) agreement, while Article 18 deals with implied prorogation resulting from the defendant entering an appearance without contesting the jurisdiction of the court seised of the proceedings.

Naturally, both parties will benefit from the Convention's generosity as to the choice of forum. Within the context of prorogation by agreement, there is a risk, though, that one of the parties will be faced with a jurisdiction clause in a contract which he might not have read. Within the context of prorogation by the appearance of the defendant, both parties run a risk. The plaintiff runs the risk that the defendant appears and (successfully) contests the jurisdiction of the court, and the defendant runs the risk of being tempted by the plaintiff's choice of court, thereby submitting to a court which he would not otherwise have chosen.

2.1 Prorogation by explicit agreement

C Art. 17	R 23

Article 17 expresses the principle that the parties may confer jurisdiction on a court (or courts) of their own choice, provided that an agreement between the

[96] 150/80 *Elefanten Schuh v Jacqmain* 8-10; and, 48/84 *Spitzley v Sommer* 13-15.

parties has been concluded and that that agreement satisfies certain formal requirements. In *Anterist v Crédit Lyonnais*, the Court held:

> 'Article 17 of the Convention embodies the principle of the parties' autonomy to determine the court or courts with jurisdiction...'[97]

According to Article 17, first paragraph, the agreement between the parties by which they confer jurisdiction on a court (or courts) should be expressed in writing or evidenced in writing, or in a form which accords with practices which the parties have established between themselves, or in international trade or commerce, in a form which accords with a usage of which the parties are or ought to have been aware and which in such trade or commerce is widely known to, and regularly observed by, parties to contracts of the type involved in the particular trade or commerce concerned.

One of the purposes of the enumeration of these formal requirements in the Convention was, as was seen before, to ensure legal certainty.[98] The formal requirements are expressly prescribed in the Convention and are to be considered as limited, in order to allow the parties reasonably to foresee which court(s) will have jurisdiction. Consequently, the Court has held that the Contracting States are not free to lay down any requirements other than those contained in the Convention.[99]

The most essential purpose of these formal requirements of Article 17, first paragraph,[100] is however to ensure that the consensus between the parties is clearly and precisely demonstrated and is actually established.[101] Since consensus between the parties lies at the heart of the principle of party autonomy and therefore is equally applicable to prorogation of jurisdiction by agreement, the Convention and the Court seek appropriate guarantees that both parties really have consented to the clause waiving the normal rules of jurisdiction as laid down in Title II of the Convention.[102]

Moreover, and in order to give due influence to the principle directly underlying Article 17, being the principle of party autonomy, the Court has, when inter-

---

[97] 22/85 *Anterist v Crédit Lyonnais* 14; and compare C-387/98 *Coreck v Handelsveem* 14 (re 23/78 *Meeth v Glacetal* 5).

[98] See chapter 5, section 4.1, text following note 109: 150/80 *Elefanten Schuh v Jacqmain* 24-26; C-269/95 *Benincasa v Dentalkit* 28 (re *Mainschiffahrts* 34), 29.

[99] Idem.

[100] See also Article I of the Protocol Annexed to the 1968 Convention, OJ 1978, L 304 p. 36.

[101] 24/76 *Salotti v Rüwa* 7; 25/76 *Segoura v Bonakdarian* 6; 784/79 *Porta-Leasing v Prestige* 5 (re *Salotti; Segoura*),9; 150/80 *Elefanten Schuh v Jacqmain* 25; 201/82 *Gerling v Tesoro* 13 (re *Salotti; Segoura*); 71/83 *Tilly Russ v Nova* 14 (re *Salotti*; *Segoura*; *Porta-Leasing*); 221/84 *Berghöfer v ASA* 13 (re *Salotti*; *Segoura*; *Porta-Leasing*),16; 22/85 *Anterist v Crédit Lyonnais* 14,17; 313/85 *Iveco Fiat v Van Hool* 9 (re *Berghöfer*),10; C-106/95 *Mainschiffahrts v Les Gravières Rhénanes* 15 (re *Salotti* 7; *Segoura* 6); 159/97 *Castelletti v Trumpy* 34 (re 150/80 *Elefanten Schuh v Jacqmain* 25).

[102] Among others, 24/76 *Salotti v Rüwa* 9; and 25/76 *Segoura v Bonakdarian* 8.

preting that provision, indicated that, *(a)* the national courts have to examine whether consensus between the parties has actually been established, *(b)* the formal requirements laid down in Article 17 must be strictly construed, and *(c)* other elements of Article 17 should not be construed too narrowly. The following case law illustrates this.

The Court has expressed its concern with consensus between the parties on various occasions, for the first time in *Salotti v Rüwa*.[103] It held that Article 17, under which certain formal requirements as to the agreement between the parties are listed, imposes upon the *national courts the duty of examining* whether a clause conferring jurisdiction upon the court in question was in fact the subject of consensus.[104] The Court recalled this viewpoint, most recently, in *Coreck v Handelsveem*:

> 'The Court has held that, by making the validity of a jurisdiction clause subject to the existence of an "agreement between the parties", Article 17 of the Convention imposes on the court before which the matter is brought the duty of examining first whether the clause conferring jurisdiction upon it was in fact the subject of consensus between the parties, which must be clearly and precisely demonstrated, and that the purpose of the requirements as to form imposed by Article 17 is to ensure that consensus between the parties is in fact established ...'[105]

In quite a number of cases, the Court has argued that, in order to ensure that consensus between the parties is in fact established and appears from the agreement, the *formal requirements* as regards these 'agreements', listed in Article 17, first paragraph, must be *strictly construed*. The following quotation taken from *Berghöfer v ASA* illustrates this viewpoint:

> 'According to settled case-law ... the requirements set out in Article 17 governing the validity of jurisdiction clauses must be strictly construed since the purpose of Article 17 is to ensure that the parties have actually consented to such a clause and that their consent is clearly and precisely demonstrated.'[106]

Naturally, a strict interpretation of the formal requirements of Article 17 is in accordance with the principle of party autonomy, since it aims to ensure that the consensus between the parties is clearly and precisely demonstrated and established. As was seen before, such an interpretation is also required by the principle

---

[103] 24/76 *Salotti v Rüwa*.

[104] 24/76 *Salotti v Rüwa* 7.

[105] C-387/98 *Coreck v Handelsveem* 13 (re *Salotti v Rüwa* 7; 25/76 *Segoura v Bonakdarian* 6; C-106/95 *Mainschiffahrts v Les Gravières Rhénanes* 15); and compare 313/85 *Iveco Fiat v Van Hool* 5 (re *Salotti* and *Segoura*).

[106] 221/84 *Berghöfer v ASA* 13 (re *Salotti v Rüwa* 7; *Segoura v Bonakdarian* 6; *Porta-Leasing v Prestige* 5,9; *Tilly Russ v Nova* 14,19).

'protection of the party that might be unaware of a jurisdiction clause incorporated in a contract by one party alone'.[107] As appears from the Court's case law, a strict interpretation of the formal requirements is furthermore required by certain sub-principles which underlie other rules of jurisdiction: the principle of the protection of the party who is weaker due to his procedural position (which underlies Article 2) and the principle of sound administration of justice (as far as it underlies Articles 5 and 6).[108] The Court has consistently held that these sub-principles, which also relate to the main principle that disputes should be decided by an appropriate court, have an influence on the interpretation of the formal requirements of Article 17. The formal requirements of Article 17 must be strictly construed and applied, so as to ensure that consensus between the parties is established, since it cannot be presumed that a party would waive the advantage of the normal rules conferring jurisdiction: Articles 2, 5 and 6. As the Court already observed in *Salotti v Rüwa*, as regards the interpretation of these requirements:

> 'the way in which that provision (Article 17, *ebjp*) is to be applied must be interpreted in the light of the effect of the conferment of jurisdiction by consent, which is to exclude both the jurisdiction determined by the general principle laid down in Article 2 and the special jurisdictions provided for in Articles 5 and 6 of the Convention. In view of the consequences that such an option may have on the position of the parties to the action, the requirements set out in Article 17 governing the validity of clauses conferring jurisdiction must be strictly construed.'[109]

In order to meet the requirement of a strict interpretation of the formal requirements of Article 17, the Court indicated in *Salotti v Rüwa* that the mere fact that a clause conferring jurisdiction is printed among the general conditions of one of the parties on the reverse of a contract drawn up on the commercial paper of that party does not in itself satisfy the requirements under the first paragraph of Article 17 that a jurisdiction clause shall be in writing or evidenced in writing. In such a case, no guarantee is given that the other party has really consented to the clause waiving the normal rules of jurisdiction. The requirement of writing, under the first paragraph of Article 17, is satisfied only if the reference to these general conditions including such a clause is express and therefore can be checked by a party exercising reasonable care.[110] In *Segoura v Bonakdarian*, the Court decided that in the case of an orally concluded contract, the requirements of the first para-

---

[107] See section 1.3 of this chapter, text following note 93; compare 150/80 *Elefanten Schuh v Jacqmain* 24; C-106/95 *Mainschiffahrts v Gravières Rhénanes* 17; C-159/97 *Castelletti v Trumpy* 19 (re *Mainschiffahrts* 17).

[108] See before section 1.1 and, hereafter, section 3 of this chapter.

[109] 24/76 *Salotti v Rüwa* 7; compare 25/76 *Segoura v Bonakdarian* 6;784/79 *Porta-Leasing v Prestige* 5 (re *Salotti; Segoura*); 71/83 *Tilly Russ v Nova* 14 (re *Salotti*; *Segoura*; *Porta-Leasing*); 221/84 *Berghöfer v ASA* 13 (re *Salotti*; *Segoura*; *Porta-Leasing*; *Tilly Russ*); and C-106/95 *Mainschiffahrts v Gravières Rhénanes* 14 (re *Salotti*; *Segoura*).

[110] 24/76 *Salotti v Rüwa* 9,13.

graph of Article 17 that a jurisdiction clause shall be in writing or evidenced in writing, are satisfied only if the confirmation in writing accompanied by a notification of the general conditions of sale has been accepted in writing by the other party.[111] In addition, the Court decided in *Berghöfer v ASA* that, if jurisdiction is conferred by express oral agreement, the requirement that the jurisdiction clause shall be evidenced in writing is only satisfied in case the written confirmation of the agreement by one of the parties (not necessarily the party who is to be affected by the agreement) was received by the other party and the latter raised no objection.[112] More specifically, the Court held in *Iveco Fiat v Van Hool*, that where a written agreement containing a jurisdiction clause and stipulating that the agreement can only be renewed in writing has expired but has continued to serve as the legal basis for the contractual relations between the parties, the jurisdiction clause contained in that agreement may still satisfy the formal requirements of Article 17. However, that is only the case if, under the applicable law, the parties could validly renew their original agreement otherwise than in writing, or if, conversely, one of the parties has confirmed in writing either the jurisdiction clause or the set of terms which has been tacitly renewed and of which the jurisdiction clause forms a part, without any objection from the other party to whom such confirmation has been notified.[113]

In the context of international trade and commerce, the requirement that the parties should have explicitly consented has been progressively relaxed: in order not to impede international commerce, a jurisdiction clause may be validly concluded in a form that accords with practices which the parties have established between themselves, or in international trade and commerce, in a form which accords with a usage of which the parties are or ought to have been aware and which in such trade or commerce is widely known to, and is regularly observed by, parties to contracts of the type involved in the particular trade or commerce concerned (Article 17, first paragraph (b) and (c)). However, and despite the relaxations incorporated in Article 17 by the 1978 and 1989 Accession Conventions,[114] it is the

---

[111] 25/76 *Segoura v Bonakdarian* 12.

[112] 221/84 *Berghöfer v ASA* 14,16.

[113] 313/85 *Iveco Fiat v Van Hool* 5 (re *Salotti*; *Segourai*),9 (re *Berghöfer v ASA* 13,16),10. Notice furthermore that para. 2 of Art. I of the Protocol of the 1968 Convention imposes more special and more strict conditions which are superimposed on those in Art. 17, OJ 1978, L 304 p. 36. In *Porta-Leasing v Prestige*, the Court pointed out that these additional requirements to Art. 17, laid down in Art. I of the Protocol, must be met in a case concerned with the validity of a jurisdiction clause to be used against a person domiciled in Luxembourg. These additional requirements imply that such a clause, besides being in writing as required by Art. 17 itself, is mentioned in a provision specially and exclusively meant for this purpose and specifically signed by the party domiciled in Luxembourg. The Court held, though, that a separate document is not required; see 784/79 *Porta-Leasing v Prestige* 5 (re *Salotti*; *Segoura v Bonakdorian*)-9.

[114] Compare Art. 11 of the 1978 Accession Convention, OJ 1978 L 304, p. 1, Schlosser Report, OJ 1979 C 59, p. 124; and Art. 7 of the 1989 Accession Convention, OJ 1989, L 285, p. 1, Almeida Cruz Report, OJ 1990, C 189, No. 26.

opinion of the Court that the provision's aim is still to ensure that real consent was established, as the Court held in *Mainschiffahrts v Gravières Rhénanes* and *Castelletti v Trumpy*.[115] Following a similar line of reasoning as in *Mainschiffahrts v Gravières Rhénanes*, the Court recalled in *Castelletti v Trumpy* that:

> 'in spite of the flexibility introduced into Article 17, the provision's aim was still to ensure that there was real consent on the part of the persons concerned so as to protect the weaker party to the contract by avoiding jurisdiction clauses, incorporated in a contract by one party, going unnoticed.'[116]

Thus, we assume that even these more liberal requirements as to form are also to be construed strictly, since the purpose of Article 17 is to ensure that there is consensus between the parties. As regards these flexibilities as to form, the Court has clarified several expressions used in the second and third case (b and c) mentioned in the second sentence of the first paragraph of Article 17, such as 'usage in international trade or commerce', 'form which accords with practices', and the parties' 'awareness of the usage' of such a form, in *Mainschiffahrts v Gravières Rhénanes*, *Castelletti v Trumpy* and *Tilly Russ v Nova*.[117]

In the cases discussed in the foregoing paragraphs, the Court has justified a strict interpretation of the formal requirements of Article 17, by referring to the principle directly underlying this provision, the principle of party autonomy. When justifying a strict interpretation of the formal requirements of Article 17, the Court has also referred to the system of jurisdictional rules, implying that due influence is given to the principles underlying other rules of jurisdiction, such as 'protection of the weaker party due to his procedural position' and 'sound administration of justice'. The Court also referred to the principle that the party that might be unaware of a jurisdiction clause incorporated in a contract by the other party, is to be protected, and to the principle of legal certainty in order to justify such an interpretation.[118]

If the requirement is fulfilled that the consensus between the parties as regards the clause conferring jurisdiction has been clearly and precisely demonstrated, there seems to be no reason to apply Article 17 restrictively. Thus, except for the formal requirements laid down in Article 17, that provision should not be applied too restrictively.

---

[115] C-106/95 *Mainschiffahrts v Gravières Rhénanes* 17; C-159/97 *Castelletti v Trumpy* 19 (re *Mainschiffahrts* 17).

[116] C-159/97 *Castelletti v Trumpy* 19 (re *Mainschiffahrts v Gravières Rhénanes* 17); and C-106/95 *Mainschiffahrts v Gravières Rhénanes* 17; and compare 150/80 *Elefanten Schuh v Jacqmain* 24.

[117] C-106/95 *Mainschiffahrts v Gravières Rhénanes* 25; C-159/97 *Castelletti v Trumpy* 22-30,31-39,40-45; 71/83 *Tilly Russ v Nova* 18,19.

[118] Compare this section, text following notes 98, 106-109, 116.

A not too restrictive interpretation of Article 17 accords with the general view of the Court, that when interpreting the rules of jurisdiction laid down in Title II of the Convention, one should take care that these rules are not deprived of their legal effect, since each of them represents a distinctly different notion of the principle that disputes should be decided by an appropriate court.[119] In this respect, the Court has made a clear statement on the principle directly underlying the exclusive jurisdiction contained in Article 17, in *Coreck* v *Handelsveem*:

> 'Article 17 is based on a recognition of the independent will of the parties to a contract in deciding which courts are to have jurisdiction to settle disputes falling within the scope of the Convention ...' [120]

The viewpoint that Article 17 allows the parties to come to an agreement as to which court or courts of a Contracting State are to have jurisdiction as regards the settlement of their disputes, implies an interpretation of expressions and concepts constituting the substantive scope of Article 17, such as 'agreement conferring jurisdiction' or 'in connection with a particular legal relationship', that is not too narrow, in order to meet the principle of party autonomy which directly underlies that provision. As will be seen below, other principles also sustain a not too restrictive interpretation of these concepts of Article 17. The following case law of the Court illustrates this.

In *Duffryn v Petereit*, the Court had to answer a question on the interpretation of the concept '*agreement conferring jurisdiction*', which serves as a criterion for determining the exclusive jurisdiction laid down in Article 17.[121] When answering that question, the Court, first of all, stated that that concept should be regarded as independent (in accordance with the principle of legal certainty, requiring 'equality and uniformity of rights and obligations').[122] The Court then observed that a clause conferring jurisdiction in the statutes of a company limited by shares is an agreement which is binding on all the shareholders – whether that shareholder opposed the adoption of the clause or became a shareholder after the clause was adopted – if that jurisdiction clause is contained in the statutes of the company.[123] This (rather broad) interpretation of the concept 'agreement conferring jurisdiction' was justified by the Court by referring to the principle of legal certainty: another interpretation would lead to a multiplication of the bases of jurisdiction for disputes arising from the same legal relationship as between the

---

119 Compare section 1 of this chapter; compare 38/81 *Effer v Kantner* 7 (re *Sanders*); C-439/93 *Lloyd's v Campenon* 17.

120 C-387/98 *Coreck v Handelsveem* 14 (re 23/78 *Meeth v Glacetal* 5); compare 22/85 *Anterist v Crédit Lyonnais* 14.

121 C-214/89 *Duffryn v Petereit*.

122 C-214/89 *Duffryn v Petereit* 14 (re 34/82 *Peters v ZNAV*); C-116/02 *Gasser v MISAT* (re *Duffryn* 14)

123 C-214/89 *Duffryn v Petereit* 15 (re 34/82 *Peters v ZNAV* 13)-19.

company and its shareholders.[124] If the statutes of the company concerned are lodged in a place to which the shareholder may have access or are contained in a public register, the formal requirements of Article 17, first paragraph, must be considered to have been complied with as well. The Court considers this latter interpretation of the formal requirements to be in accordance with the purpose of these requirements, which is to ensure that the consensus between the parties is in fact established.[125]

In *Duffryn v Petereit*, the Court also gave its interpretation of the condition laid down in Article 17 that a jurisdiction clause may only refer to disputes which have arisen or which may arise '*in connection with a particular legal relationship*'. The Court pointed out that that condition is intended to limit the scope of an agreement conferring jurisdiction in order to avoid a party being taken by surprise by the assignment of jurisdiction to a given forum.[126] A clause conferring jurisdiction contained in a company's statutes satisfies that requirement, if it relates to disputes which have arisen or which may arise in connection with the relationship between the company and its shareholders as such. It is for the national court, however, to interpret such clauses in order to determine which disputes fall within their scope.[127]

In *Meeth v Glacetal*, the Court held, as regards the expression 'in connection with a particular legal relationship', that Article 17 cannot be interpreted as prohibiting the court before which a dispute has been brought in pursuance of a clause conferring jurisdiction upon it, from taking into account a set-off connected with the legal relationship in dispute. Such an interpretation would not only be in violation of the principle that underlies Article 17, the principle of party autonomy, as the Court observed, but it also conflicts with the principle to avoid 'a multiplicity of courts having jurisdiction'.[128]

In *Anterist v Crédit Lyonnais* and *Coreck v Handelsveem*, the Court clearly stated that, since Article 17 embodies the principle of party autonomy, its purpose is to protect the wishes of the parties concerned, which in turn requires that that provision is to be construed in a manner consistent with those wishes.[129] As the Court put it in *Coreck v Handelsveem*:

---

[124] C-214/89 *Duffryn v Petereit* 20; compare section 4.2.2 of chapter 5, text following note 142.

[125] C-214/89 *Duffryn v Petereit* 22-24 (re *Salotti* 7)-29

[126] C-214/89 *Duffryn v Petereit* 31. We assume that that requirement meets the principle of 'legal certainty as to jurisdiction', in particular the principle that a plaintiff should be able easily to identify the competent court and a defendant reasonably to foresee the court before which he may be sued; compare section 4 of chapter 5, text following note 95.

[127] C-214/89 *Duffryn v Petereit* 30-37; compare C-269/95 *Benincasa v Dentalkit* 31 (re *Duffryn* 37). The jurisdiction clause in the case at hand referred to 'any dispute' relating to the interpretation, performance or 'other aspects' of the contract.

[128] 23/78 *Meeth v Glacetal* 8,9; section 4.2.2 of chapter 5.

[129] 22/85 *Anterist v Crédit Lyonnais* 14; and 387/98 *Coreck v Handelsveem* 14 (re 23/78 *Meeth v Glacetal* 5).

> 'if the purpose of Article 17 of the Convention is to protect the wishes of the parties concerned, it must be construed in a manner consistent with those whishes where they are established.'[130]

In this judgment, the Court had to reply to the question of the national court as to whether the words 'have agreed' in the first paragraph of Article 17 must be interpreted as meaning that a jurisdiction clause must be formulated in such a way that it is possible to identify the court having jurisdiction on its wording alone. The Court, first, referred to the purpose underlying Article 17, which is to protect the wishes of the parties concerned, requiring that provision to be construed in a manner consistent with those whishes where they are established.[131] The Court then continued, as regards in particular the validity of a jurisdiction clause incorporated in the bill of lading,[132] which at the same time also contained an identity of carrier clause:[133]

> 'It follows that the words "have agreed" in the first sentence of the first paragraph of Article 17 of the Convention cannot be interpreted as meaning that it is necessary for a jurisdiction clause to be formulated in such a way that the competent court can be determined on its wording alone. It is sufficient that the clause states the objective factors on the basis of which the parties have agreed to choose a court or the courts to which they wish to submit disputes which have arisen or may arise between them. Those factors, which must be sufficiently precise to enable the court seised to ascertain whether it has jurisdiction, may, where appropriate, be determined by the particular circumstances of the case'.[134]

As to the question whether such a jurisdiction clause is valid as against any third party, the Court observed in that same judgment, and in accordance with settled case law:

> 'the validity of a jurisdiction clause under Article 17 of the Convention must be assessed by reference to the relationship between the parties to the original contract ... it can be pleaded against the third party holding the bill of lading so long as, under the relevant national law, the holder of the bill of lading succeeds to the shipper's rights and obligations ... If he did, there is no need to ascertain whether he accepted the jurisdiction clause in the original contract.'[135]

---

[130] 387/98 *Coreck v Handelsveem* 14 (re 23/78 *Meeth v Glacetal* 5).

[131] 387/98 *Coreck v Handelsveem* 14 (re 23/78 *Meeth v Glacetal* 5).

[132] Stipulating: 'any dispute arising under this Bill of Lading shall be decided in the country where the carrier has his principal place of business'.

[133] Stipulating: 'the Contract evidenced by this Bill of Lading is between the Merchant and the Owner of the vessel named herein (or substitute) … If, despite the foregoing, it is adjudged that any other is the Carrier and/or bailee of the goods shipped hereunder …)

[134] 387/98 *Coreck v Handelsveem* 15.

[135] 387/98 *Coreck v Handelsveem* 20 (re 71/83 *Tilly Russ v Nova* 24, C-159/97 *Castelletti v Trumpy* 41,42),23 (re 71/83 *Tilly Russ v Nova* 24; and, C-159/97 *Castelletti v Trumpy* 41)-25 (*Tilly*

The requirement not to interpret Article 17 too narrowly, in order to meet the underlying principle of party autonomy, does not only extend to expressions such as 'agreement conferring jurisdiction' or 'in connection with a particular legal relationship' within the meaning of Article 17, but, as we may conclude from the Court's case law, it also applies to other aspects of Article 17.[136]

For example, in *Meeth v Glacetal,* the Court held that the wording of Article 17 cannot be interpreted as intending to exclude the right of the parties to agree on two or more courts for the purpose of settling any disputes which may arise. In particular, it cannot be interpreted as prohibiting an agreement under which the two parties to a contract for sale, who are domiciled in different states, can be sued only in the courts of their respective states.[137] In *Anterist v Crédit Lyonnais*, the Court stated that if the parties have agreed that a court or the courts of the Contracting State in which one of the parties is domiciled are to have jurisdiction, such an agreement is not necessarily to be regarded as having been concluded for the benefit of only one of the parties, within the meaning of the third paragraph of Article 17. Another interpretation of Article 17, third paragraph, that places a restriction on the effect of such an agreement, in that the party that would benefit from that agreement shall retain the right to bring proceedings in any other court which has jurisdiction by virtue of the Convention, would not meet the principle of party autonomy embodied in that Article. If it was the common intention of the parties to confer an advantage on one of the parties, this intention must however be clear from the terms of the jurisdiction clause or from all the evidence to be found therein or from the circumstances in which the contract was concluded.[138] In *Benincasa v Dentalkit*, the Court also decided in favour of a broad interpretation of Article 17. It held that the courts of a Contracting State which have been designated in a jurisdiction clause, validly concluded under the first paragraph of Article 17, also have exclusive jurisdiction where the action seeks in particular a declaration that the contract containing that clause is void.[139] As was seen before, when justifying that decision, the Court referred to the principle of legal certainty as to jurisdiction, in particular to the requirement of 'avoiding

---

Russ 25)-27. Compare *Gerling v Tesoro*, in which the Court held, in a case concerned with a contract of insurance, that if the formal requirements are fulfilled and the consent of the parties has been clearly and precisely manifested, a clause conferring jurisdiction must be considered as being inserted also for the benefit of the insured who is not a party to the contract but a person distinct from the policyholder (201/82 *Gerling v Tesoro* 20); compare section 1.2 of this chapter, text following note 82.

[136] See, for example, 25/79 *Sanicentral v Collin* 7, in which the Court argued that a jurisdiction clause included in contracts of employment concluded prior to that date must be considered valid in judicial proceedings instituted after the entry into force of the Convention.

[137] 23/78 *Meeth v Glacetal* 5,6. The Court particularly referred to the wording of Art. 17, in accordance with the principle of legal certainty, requiring respect for the linguistic boundaries of the Convention; compare section 2 of chapter 5, text following note 72.

[138] 22/85 *Anterist v Crédit Lyonnais* 14-17.

[139] C-269/95 *Benincasa v Dentalkit* 32

multiplication of jurisdiction'.[140] Such an interpretation does not conflict with the principle directly underlying Article 17, the principle of party autonomy.

Finally, the Court has observed, on several other occasions, for example in *Zelger v Salinitri*, that Article 17, since it relates only to the will of the parties, in fact dispenses with any objective connection between the relationship in dispute and the court designated.[141]

In most of the cases discussed in the foregoing paragraphs, in which a broad interpretation of Article 17 was defended by the Court, reference was made (implicitly or expressly) to the principle directly underlying Article 17, namely the principle of party autonomy.[142] In addition, the Court resorted to the principle of legal certainty, requiring an independent interpretation, respect for the wording of the Convention and/or avoidance of a multiplicity of courts having jurisdiction.[143]

2.2 **Prorogation by appearance**

C Art. 16	R 22	C Art. 18	R 24
C Art. 17	R 23		

In case of Article 18, the consent of both parties to submit a dispute to a particular forum is presumed to appear from their conduct in the following sense: if the plaintiff submits a dispute to a court, and the defendant appears and does not contest this court's jurisdiction, both parties are presumed to have agreed to submit the dispute to this forum. As the Court put it in *Spitzley v Sommer*:

> 'Article 18 in particular is based on the idea that, by entering an appearance before the court seised of the proceedings by the plaintiff, without contesting that court's jurisdiction, the defendant is by implication signifying his consent to the hearing of the case by a court other than that designated by the other provisions of the Convention.'[144]

It is clear that Article 18 must not be interpreted too restrictively, in order not to deprive Article 18 of its legal effect or make it fully redundant. This view is confirmed by the Court's case law and can be demonstrated by *Elephanten Schuh v Jacqmain.*[145]

The question put to the Court concerned the interpretation of the second sentence of Article 18. That provision reads: 'This rule shall not apply where appear-

[140] Compare section 4.2.2 of chapter 5, text following note 144.

[141] 56/79 *Zelger v Salinitri I* 4; C-106/95 *Mainschiffahrts v Les Gravières Rhénanes* 34 (re *Zelger v Salinitri* 4); C-269/95 *Benincasa v Dentalkit* 28 (*Mainschiffahrts* 34); C-159/97 *Castelletti v Trumpy* 50 (re *Zelger v* Salinitri 4; *Mainschiffahrts* 34; *Benincasa* 35)-52; see hereafter section 2.3 of this chapter, text following note 171.

[142] See this section, text following notes 120, 123, 124, 129, 136, 139, 142.

[143] See this section, text following notes 122, 124, 128, 137, 140.

[144] 48/84 *Spitzley v Sommer* 15.

[145] 150/80 *Elefanten Schuh v Jacqmain.*

ance was entered solely to contest jurisdiction, or where another court has exclusive jurisdiction by virtue of Article 16'. The Court was asked whether, in order to exclude the jurisdiction of the court seised, a defendant must confine himself strictly to contesting that jurisdiction, or whether he was allowed to contest the jurisdiction of the court as well as the substance of the claim. Arriving at a decision, the Court considered both the wording of the provision in question (in accordance with the principle of legal certainty), as well as the right to submit a defence on the substance of the case (in accordance with the principle of the protection of the rights of the defence).[146] With regard to the text of Article 18, the Court established that there is a difference between the different language versions of this Article, which makes it unclear what, according to the wording of Article 18, is precisely meant.[147] Next, the Court used the principle 'protection of the rights of the defendant', in particular the right to submit a defence on the substance of the case, to come to a conclusion which results in an interpretation that is not too restrictive. The Court indicated that under the law of civil procedure of certain Contracting States, a defendant who raises the issue of jurisdiction and no other might be barred from making his submissions as to the substance if the court rejects his plea that it has no jurisdiction. As the Court pointed out, an interpretation of Article 18 which enables such a result to be arrived at would be contrary to the right of the defendant to defend himself in the original proceedings, which is one of the aims of the Convention; hence the alternative interpretation is more in keeping with 'the objectives and spirit of the Convention'.[148] That interpretation implies that Article 18 does apply where the defendant makes submissions as to a national court's jurisdiction as well as on the substance of the case, provided that, if the challenge to jurisdiction is not preliminary to any defence as to the substance, it does not occur after the making of the submissions which under national procedural law are considered to be the first defence addressed to the court seised. As was seen before, the decision of the Court was confirmed by *C.H.W. v G.J.H.* and *Rohr v Ossberger.*[149]

The view that Article 18 must not be interpreted too restrictively, being itself an autonomous (authentic) expression of the principle 'party autonomy', also became apparent when the Court had to decide on the relationship between the choice of forum of Articles 17 and 18. As regards this relationship, the Court established in *Elefanten Schuh v Jacqmain* that parties which have concluded an agreement conferring jurisdiction within the meaning of Article 17 are not prevented from voluntarily submitting their dispute (in the way described in Article 18) to a court other than that stipulated in the agreement. In its decision, the

---

[146] Compare section 2 of chapter 5, text following note 56; and section 5 of chapter 4, text following note 68.

[147] 150/80 *Elefanten Schuh v Jacqmain* 14.

[148] Idem: *Elefanten Schuh v Jacqmain* 14.

[149] See text following note 68 of section 5 of chapter 4.

Court took account of the wording of the provisions at issue, as well as of the principled system underlying the Convention.[150] The Court pointed out that the plain text of Article 18 provides only that the jurisdictional rule contained in this Article is not to apply where appearance was entered solely to contest jurisdiction, or where another court has jurisdiction according to Article 16. The case envisaged in Article 17 is not, according to the text of Article 18, one of the exceptions which this Article allows to the jurisdictional rule it lays down. However, this analysis of the text is not sufficient. Before coming to its final conclusion, the Court also established that 'the principle-based theory' underlying the Convention does not point in a different direction:

> 'Moreover, neither the general scheme nor the objectives of the Convention provide grounds for the view that the parties to an agreement conferring jurisdiction within the meaning of Article 17 are prevented from voluntarily submitting their dispute to a court other than that stipulated in the agreement.'[151]

Having established that the interpretation that an explicit choice of forum under Article 17 can be overruled by a later implicit choice of forum according to Article 18 is in line with the wording of these provisions and that it is not out of line with the principled system underlying the Convention, the Court decided that this interpretation is the right one.[152]

The principle of party autonomy weighed in relation to other principles

C Art. 2	R 2	C Art. 12	R 13	C Art. 18	R 24
C Art. 5	R 5	C Art. 15	R 17	C Art. 28	R 35
C Art. 6	R 6	C Art. 17	R 23		

From the foregoing, we may conclude that under the Convention the principle of party autonomy has been firmly established: the Convention allows prorogation by explicit agreement as well as by an appearance of the defendant.

As is typical of principles, the principle of the parties' autonomy is not given absolute weight: although in certain cases it outweighs other competing principles, in other cases it is outweighed by, or 'mixed' with other principles. This appears *(a)* from the system of the rules of jurisdiction and from the general scheme of the Convention, which are taken as given as far as the Court is concerned. The relative weight of the principle 'party autonomy' also appears *(b)* from the continuing process of weighing the principles, underlying the Convention, in relation to each other by the Court: the principle of party autonomy is weighed against other principles, such as 'free movement of judgments', 'legal

---

[150] 150/80 *Elefanten Schuh v Jacqmain* 9,10.

[151] 150/80 *Elefanten Schuh v Jacqmain* 10; and compare 48/84 *Spitzley v Sommer* 25 (re *Elefanten Schuh*).

[152] 150/80 *Elefanten Schuh v Jacqmain* 11.

certainty', 'protection of the rights of the defence' and other sub-principles flowing from the principle that disputes are to be decided by an appropriate court.

From the system of jurisdictional rules laid down in Title II of the Convention, it is evident that both Article 17 and 18 can set aside several of the jurisdictional rules contained in the Convention. They prevail over Article 2, which implies that the principle of party autonomy can set aside the rule which was inspired by the principle of the 'protection of the party who is weaker from a procedural point of view'.[153] Parties can also, by either an explicit or implicit choice of forum, set aside the rules contained in Article 5 and 6, which, as will be seen in the next section, are mainly an expression of the principle 'sound administration of justice'.[154]

However, as is explicitly stated in Article 17 and 18, neither an explicit nor an implicit choice of forum can set aside the rules of exclusive jurisdiction under Article 16, conferring jurisdiction on the courts of a Contracting State on the basis of the location of immovable property, the seat of a company, an entry in a public register or the place where a judgment is to be enforced. As will be seen in the next section, that provision is an expression of the principle 'sound administration of justice'.[155]

If 'party autonomy' conflicts with 'protection of the party who is weaker due to his socio-economic position', a balance is struck: neither of the two principles wins the day at the cost of the other principle; instead, both of them are realized to some degree. As we have seen in the previous section, the principle 'protection of the party who is weaker from a socio-economic point of view' has placed certain constraints on party autonomy without however completely prevailing over it. In comparison to the general rule of Article 17, these rules contain certain safeguards in order to protect the party who is weaker due to his socio-economic position (insurance policyholders, consumers and employees): an agreement concluded before the dispute has arisen has no legal effect, by virtue of Article 17, third paragraph in conjunction with Articles 12 and 15, and Article 17, sixth paragraph, unless certain conditions (to the advantage of the weaker party) are fulfilled.[156]

As regards the scheme of the Convention as a whole, it appears from Article 28, first paragraph, laid down in Title III of the Convention, that a violation of Article 17 or 18 in the state of the original proceedings does not constitute an obstacle to the free movement of judgments, unless a party who is weaker due to his socio-economic position is involved. The principle of the free movement of judgments overrides the principle of party autonomy.

---

[153] Compare section 1.1 of this chapter, text following note 10.

[154] See hereafter section 3 of this chapter.

[155] The reasons that explain why Art. 16 completely outweighs the principle of party autonomy will be discussed in section 3.1.3 of this chapter, text following note 359.

[156] Compare section 1.2 of this chapter, text following note 54.

We also refer to the wording of the first sentence of the first paragraph of Article 17. This clarifies that Article 17 only applies where the twofold condition is satisfied that 1) at least one of the parties to the contract is domiciled in a Contracting State and 2) the jurisdiction clause designates a court or the courts of a Contracting State.[157] According to the Court in *Coreck v Handelsveem*, the latter condition owes its existence to the fact that the Convention is intended to facilitate the mutual recognition and enforcement of judicial decisions, meaning: the free movement of Contracting States' judgments within the Community area.[158]

As was just seen, the relative weight of the principle of party autonomy, as expressed in Articles 17 and 18, is determined by the system of principles underlying the Convention, including the main principles 'free movement of judgments', 'protection of the rights of the defence', 'legal certainty' and 'disputes should be decided by an appropriate court' as well as the sub-principles that flow from them. The Court's case law makes it clear that the process of weighing these principles in relation to each other, which was already done by the drafters of the Convention, continues when the Court interprets the rules of jurisdiction and uses that principled system in order to arrive at its decisions. These principles may pull in different directions, though, sometimes requiring a restrictive and sometimes a broad interpretation or application of the provisions concerned.

As was seen in this section, when interpreting Articles 17 and 18, the Court has given due influence to the principle directly underlying these provisions, the principle of party autonomy. That principle, as appears from the Court's case law, requires, first of all, that national courts have the duty to examine whether the clause conferring jurisdiction upon it was in fact the subject of consensus between the parties.[159] It also requires a strict interpretation of the formal requirements, laid down in Article 17, first paragraph. As was seen before, such an interpretation is sustained by other principles: the principle of the protection of the party which is weaker due to his procedural position and the principle of a sound administration of justice, as well as the principle of the protection of the party that might be unaware of a jurisdiction clause incorporated in a contract by one party alone.[160]

On the other hand, it appeared from the foregoing that the principle of party autonomy may sometimes require a broad interpretation of Articles 17 and 18. When justifying its interpretations, the Court regularly referred to other principles as well, such as 'avoiding multiplication of jurisdiction', 'legal certainty' and 'protection of the rights of the defence'.[161]

---

[157] Contrary to Art. 17, though, under Art. 18 the domicile of the parties is not relevant; compare C-412/98 *Josi Reinsurance v UGIC* 44,45.

[158] C-387/98 *Coreck v Handelsveem* 17,18.

[159] Compare this section, text following note 104.

[160] See this section, text following note 107.

[161] Compare notes 143 and 148 of this section.

As regards the principle 'avoiding multiplication of jurisdiction' we refer here to the case law on the substantive scope of Article 17, in which a broad interpretation of concepts, such as '*agreement conferring jurisdiction*' and '*in connection with a particular relationship*' was defended.[162]

The Court resorted to the principle 'legal certainty', requiring 'equality and uniformity of rights and obligations', in that the Convention prevails over national rules that are incompatible with it, in *Elefanten Schuh v Jacqmain*. Applying that principle to Article 17 implies that the formal requirements applicable to agreements conferring jurisdiction are restricted to those expressly prescribed in that provision and that Contracting States are not free to lay down any requirements other than those contained in the Convention.[163] The Contracting States are not allowed to make further restrictions in relation to the autonomy of the parties as ensured by the Convention.

Finally, as was seen in this section, the principle 'protection of the rights of the defence' also had an influence on the interpretation of Article 18. It allows the defendant, by virtue of Article 18, not only to contest the jurisdiction but also to submit at the same time in the alternative a defence on the substance of the action without thereby losing his right to raise an objection as to lack of jurisdiction.[164]

That same principle, the principle of the protection of the rights of the defence, was taken into account by the Court in *Mietz v Intership*, in addition to the principle 'sound administration of justice', as will be seen hereafter.[165] It resulted in a restrictive interpretation of Article 18. It was held by the Court in that judgment, that the appearance of the defendant before a court dealing with interim measures cannot, by itself, suffice to confer on that court, by virtue of Article 24, unlimited jurisdiction to order any provisional or protective measure which the court might consider appropriate if it had jurisdiction under the Convention as to the substance of the matter.[166]

2.3 Jurisdiction clauses versus agreements concerning the place of performance

C Art. 5(1)	R 5(1)
C Art. 17	R 23

As was seen in the foregoing sections, Article 17 allows the parties to choose the court to which they intend to submit the settlement of their disputes by explicit

[162] Compare this section, text following note 121; compare also section 1 of chapter 3, text, following note 41; section 5 of chapter 5, text following note 159; section 4.2.2 of chapter 5, text following note 142 and this section, text following note 128; compare 23/78 *Meeth v Glacetal* 8; C-269/95 *Benincasa v Dentalkit* 26 (re *Effer v Kantner* 6; 125/92 *Mulox v Geels* 11),29; and 48/84 *Spitzley v Sommer* 21 (re *Meeth v Glacetal*),22

[163] Compare section 1.2 of chapter 5, text following note 42 and note 99 of this section.

[164] 150/80 *Elefanten Schuh v Jacqmain* 14-17; 25/81 *C.H.W. v G.J.H.* 13; and 201/82 *Gerling v Tesoro* 21; see note 168 of section 5 of chapter 4.

[165] See section 3.1.2 of this chapter.

[166] 99/96 *Mietz v Intership* 52; compare section 3.1.2 of this chapter, text following note 350.

agreement. That Article lists several formal requirements which must be fulfilled in order to establish the validity of such an agreement. If the parties have not agreed on the jurisdiction of a court, Article 5, point 1, provides that in matters relating to a contract, the court of the place of performance of the obligation in question has jurisdiction. The question has arisen whether an agreement – effective under national law – specifying the place of performance of the obligation which is at issue in the proceedings, suffices to found jurisdiction in that place under Article 5(1) or whether that agreement has to comply with the formal requirements laid down in Article 17.

When answering that question in *Zelger v Salinitri*, the Court held that the jurisdictions provided for in Article 5, point 1, and Article 17 are to be distinguished.[167] The Court referred in that judgment to the principle which directly underlies Article 5, point 1: the principle of sound administration of justice, in particular the principle that courts that have the advantage of first-hand knowledge of the facts, the ease of taking evidence and/or knowledge of the applicable law should be able to decide a case. That principle is one other sub-principle that flows from the fourth main principle that disputes should be decided by an appropriate court and will be discussed in the next section. It requires a direct link between the dispute and the court called upon to take cognizance of it.[168] The Court decided that if the parties to the contract are permitted by the law applicable to the contract to specify the place of performance of an obligation without satisfying any special condition of form, an agreement as to the place of performance of the obligation is sufficient to found jurisdiction in that place within the meaning of Article 5, point 1.[169] However, as the Court observed in *Mainschiffahrts v Les Gravières Rhénanes,* whilst the parties are free to agree on a place of performance of a contractual obligation, they are not entitled to designate, with the sole aim of specifying the court having jurisdiction, a 'place of performance' which has no real connection with the reality of the contract and at which the obligations arising under the contract could not be performed in accordance with the terms of that contract. An agreement that specifies a place of performance which has no actual connection with the real subject-matter of the contract becomes fictitious and is governed by Article 17. Such an agreement is subject to the formal requirements which that provision sets out.[170] Contrary to Article 5, point 1, Article 17 does not require any objective connection between the relationship in dispute and the court designated. It only requires that the formal requirements prescribed by that provision are fulfilled. Any further review of the validity of the

---

[167] 56/79 *Zelger v Salinitri I* 4.

[168] 56/79 *Zelger v Salinitri I* 3; C-106/95 *Mainschiffahrts v Gravières Rhénanes* 29 (re 12/76 *Tessili v Dunlop* 13);30 (re *Zelger* 5)-34 (re *Zelger* 4),35

[169] 56/79 *Zelger v Salinitri I* 4-6.

[170] C-106/95 *Mainschiffahrts v Gravières Rhénanes* 29 (re 12/76 *Tessili v Dunlop* 13);30 (re *Zelger* 5),31-34 (re *Zelger* 4),35.

jurisdiction clause and of the intentions of the party which inserted it must be excluded.[171]

Conclusions and summary

The Convention clearly recognizes the principle of party autonomy, as is confirmed by the Court's case law. As was seen in this section this second sub-principle of the fourth main principle that disputes should be decided by an appropriate court embodies two more concrete sub-principles:

(4.2) The sub-principle of party autonomy
entails:

(4.2.1) Prorogation by explicit agreement

(4.2.2) Prorogation by appearance

The sub-principles that flow from the principle of party autonomy in turn *imply the following requirements*:

(4.2.1) Prorogation by agreement *requires*:
- national courts to examine of their own motion whether consensus as to the jurisdiction clause, within the meaning of Article 17, was actually established
- formal requirements to be restricted to those laid down in Article 17, and to be construed strictly
- other elements of Article 17 not to be interpreted too narrowly

(4.2.2) Prorogation by appearance, *requires*:
- Article 18 to imply that the defendant may contest jurisdiction and at the same time make submissions as to the substance of the case, and
- Article 18 to apply, even if a clause conferring jurisdiction on another court has been validly concluded under Article 17.

---

[171] See also C-159/97 *Castelletti v Trumpy* 50 (re *Zelger v Salinitri I* 4; *Mainschiffahrts* 34; *Benincasa* 28),51; and C-106/95 *Mainschiffahrts v Gravières Rhénanes* 30 (re *Zelger* 5)-34 (re *Zelger* 4)-36.

3. The principle of a sound administration of justice

Introduction

C Art. 5	R 5	C Art. 16 (1,a)	R 22 (1,1st sentence)
C Art. 6	R 6		

The two sub-principles flowing from the main principle that disputes should be decided by an appropriate court, which were discussed in the foregoing sections of this chapter, the principle of the protection of the weaker party and the principle of party autonomy, both focus on the parties to the dispute: they allocate disputes to a national court on the basis of the fact that the weaker party needs to be protected or on the basis of the will of the parties to submit their dispute to a forum of their own choice. The third principle which gives substance to the notion that jurisdiction should be attributed to an appropriate court, the principle of a sound administration of justice, has a different focus: in allocating a case to a particular national court, the fact that that court is considered to be able to decide the case in a proper manner, with a view to the efficacious conduct of the proceedings, is considered important. As will be seen, according to the Court's case law, this principle underlies different rules of jurisdiction laid down in Title II of the Convention. The Court's observation in *Besix v Kretzschmar* with regard to Article 5, being one of the provisions based upon that principle, can be seen as an illustration of this case law. In that judgment the Court, referring back to a number of cases, argued as follows:

> 'The reason for the adoption of the jurisdictional rule ... was concern for sound administration of justice and efficacious conduct of proceedings ...'[172]

When attempting to pin down more exactly what the principle of 'a sound administration of justice' actually implies, it appears that two distinctly different notions are actually subsumed under this principle. As these notions aim to realize a different 'good', by giving a distinctly different interpretation to the general notion of 'an efficient and sound administration of justice', we will give each of them the status of a separate sub-principle.

The first sub-principle is aimed at a sound administration of justice in the following sense: it intends to promote the situation in which a given type of case is decided in an efficient way, namely on the basis of first-hand knowledge of facts, proximity of evidence and/or knowledge of the applicable law.[173] The Court re-

---

[172] C-256/00 *Besix v Kretzschmar* 31 (re 12/76 *Tessili v Dunlop* 13; 266/85 *Shenavai v Kreischer* 6; C-125/92 *Mulox v Geels* 17; C-220/88 *Dumez France v Hessische Landesbank* 17; C-68/93 *Shevill v Presse Alliance* 19; C-364/93 *Marinari v Lloyd's* 10).

[173] Compare 21/76 *Bier v Mines de potasse* 17; 73/77 *Sanders v Van der Putte* 11,13,17; 125/79 *Denilauler v Couchet Frères* 15; 38/81 *Effer v Kantner* 7; C-391/95 *Van Uden v Deco-Line* 39; 241/

ferred to that sub-principle, for example, in *Rösler v Rottwinkel*, when answering questions on the interpretation of Article 16, point 1(a), one of the provisions that is based on that sub-principle. According to the Court, that jurisdictional rule seeks:

> 'to ensure a rational allocation of jurisdiction by opting for a solution whereby the court having jurisdiction is determined on the basis of its proximity to the property since that court is in a better position to obtain first-hand knowledge of the facts ...'[174]

We will refer to this sub-principle as 'the principle that a court that has the advantage of first-hand knowledge of the facts, ease of taking evidence and/or knowledge of the law applicable should decide a case' or, in short, the principle that disputes should be decided by a court that has certain practical advantages.

The second sub-principle aims to promote 'a sound administration of justice' in a very different sense. It has the objective of ensuring that, within the Community, related cases are decided by a single court. In *Kalfelis v Schröder*, the Court had to answer a question on the interpretation of Article 6, point 1, one of the provisions based on that sub-principle. The Court observed:

> 'where the actions ... are related when the proceedings are instituted ... it is expedient to hear and determine them together...'[175]

We will refer to this sub-principle as 'the principle that an entire dispute should be decided by a single court'. That principle is based on the assumption that, if there is already a close connecting factor between a dispute and a court, it is efficient that that court decides all the different aspects of that dispute together.[176]

Apart from contributing to a sound administration of justice in the sense of an efficient organization of the proceedings, this principle also diminishes the risk of irreconcilable decisions within the Community area. This second sub-principle therefore also contributes to the principle 'free movement of judgments' and to the principle 'legal certainty as to judgments'.[177]

Although the distinction between these two sub-principles of the principle of a sound administration of justice, namely, the principle that disputes should be decided by a court that has certain practical advantages, such as proximity of evi-

---

83 *Rösler v Rottwinkel* 20; C-256/00 *Besix v Kretzschmar* 31 (re 12/76 *Tessili v Dunlop* 13; *Shenavai* 6; *Mulox* 17; C-220/88 *Dumez France v Hessische Landesbank* 17; C-68/93 *Shevill* 19; C-364/93 *Marinari* 10).

[174] 241/83 *Rösler v Rottwinkel* 20.

[175] 189/87 *Kalfelis v Schröder* 12; compare C-365/88 *Hagen v Zeehaghe* 11; C-341/93 *Danvaern v Schuhfabriken* 16.

[176] Compare C-365/88 *Hagen v Zeehaghe* 11 (re 33/78 *Somafer v Saar-Ferngas* 7).

[177] Compare 189/87 *Kalfelis v Schröder* 11; compare chapter 3, text following note 40 and section 3.2.1 of this chapter, text following note 428.

dence and/or law and the principle that an entire dispute should be decided by a single court, is not made as explicitly by the drafters of the Convention or by the Court, it closely corresponds to what they actually do.

3.1 The principle that a court that has the practical advantage of first-hand knowledge of the facts, ease of taking evidence and/or knowledge of the applicable law should decide a case

C Art. 5	R 5	C Art. 24	R 31
C Art. 16	R 22		

As was just seen, the principle of a sound administration of justice entails the principle that disputes should be allocated to the national court which can most efficiently ascertain the facts relevant to the dispute and/or apply the national law that is applicable. That principle can only be met, though, if there is a direct, *territorial* link between the facts of a case, on the one hand, and the competent court, on the other.[178] This requirement is expressed by the provisions which have been generated by this principle: Articles 5, 16 and 24. The Court's case law confirms this. Although the principle is clearly the main justifying reason behind each of these provisions, the interpretation of these provisions, as will be seen in the following paragraphs, is strongly influenced by other (sub-)principles as well. There are significant differences in this respect between the cases described in the provisions to which the principle that 'disputes should be decided by a court that has certain practical advantages', directly underlies, particularly with regard to how that principle is weighed in relation to other (sub-)principles. We will discuss these differences with regard to these provisions below, in sections 3.1.1 to 3.1.3.

3.1.1 *Special jurisdiction under Article 5*

C Art. 2	R 2	C Art. 56 (1,2nd sentence)	R 18 to 21
C Art. 5	R 5		

Most of the jurisdictional rules of Article 5 are based on the principle of a sound administration of justice, more in particular, on the principle that disputes should be decided by a court that has certain practical advantages. Clearly, the plaintiff benefits the most from this principle, as far as it underlies Article 5. It is the plaintiff that has, according to the wording of Article 5, the option of bringing his case before the court that has these practical advantages. In the alternative, if the plaintiff is not convinced of the advantages of that court for his case, he can bring his case before the court provided for in Article 2. Naturally, it is the defendant

[178] 38/81 *Effer v Kantner* 6; 34/82 *Peters v ZNAV* 11; C-365/88 *Hagen v Zeehaghe* 11; 106/95 *Mainschiffahrts v Les Gravières Rhénanes* 29.

who benefits the most from the latter jurisdiction, since that is the court of his domicile.

However, two of the provisions contained in Article 5 are not, or at least not solely, based on the principle that the court that has the advantage of first-hand knowledge of the facts, ease of taking evidence and/or knowledge of the law applicable should decide a case. As was seen before, the jurisdictional rule for contracts of employment, contained in Article 5, point 1, second sentence, and the rule for matters relating to maintenance, contained in Article 5, point 2, are based on considerations relating to the principle of the protection of the party who is weaker due to his socio-economic position.[179] However, considerations relating to the principle that disputes should be decided by a court that has certain practical advantages based on a territorial link between the dispute and the court have also played some, though maybe only a minor role. With regard to maintenance, the drafters of the Convention noted that the court of the place of the maintenance creditor's domicile is in the best position to determine the extent of his or her need for maintenance, implicitly referring to certain practical advantages which such a court may have.[180] That court is also best qualified from the perspective that the maintenance creditor is the weaker party due to his socio-economic position.[181] With regard to the jurisdictional rule for employment contracts, the Court has pointed out, for example in *Ivenel v Schwab*:

> 'that in the matter of contracts Article 5(1) of the Convention is particularly concerned to attribute jurisdiction to the court of the country which has a close connection with the case; that in the case of a contract of employment the connection lies particularly in the law applicable to the contract; and that according to the trend in the conflict rules in regard to this matter that law is determined by the obligation characterizing the contract in question and is normally the obligation to carry out work.'[182]

Such cases therefore are, as the Court held in *Shenavai v Kreischer*:

> 'linked to the place where the activities are pursued, which determines the application of mandatory rules and collective agreements.' [183]

Thus, the court best qualified to hear a case related to contracts of employment, from the perspective of a sound administration of justice, is the court of the place 'where the employee habitually carries out his work'. That court is also best

---

[179] See section 1.2 of this chapter, text following note 29.

[180] Jenard Report, OJ 1979 C 59, p 25

[181] See section 1.2 of this chapter, text following note 34.

[182] 133/81 *Ivenel v Schwab* 15; and compare 266/85 *Shenavai v Kreischer* 6,16; C-125/92 *Mulox v Geels* 17,18; C-288/92 *Custom Made v Stawa* 12,13; C-383/95 *Rutten v Cross* 16; C-440/97 *Concorde v Panjan* 29; C-37/00 *Weber v Universal Ogden* 40 (re *Mulox* 18,19; *Rutten* 17).

[183] 266/85 *Shenavai v Kreischer* 16; compare C-37/00 *Weber v Universal Ogden* 39 (re *Mulox* 17; *Rutten* 16).

qualified, as was seen before, from the perspective of the protection of the party who is weaker due to his socio-economic position.[184]

The other jurisdictions provided for by Article 5, are inspired solely by the principle that disputes should be decided by a court that has the practical advantage of first-hand knowledge of the facts, ease of taking evidence, and/or knowledge of the applicable law. As was seen before, that principle requires a direct, territorial link between the facts of a case and the court. In light of this requirement, Article 5, point 1, attributes jurisdiction, in matters relating to a contract, to the court of the place of the performance of the obligation in question; Article 5, point 3, allows a plaintiff to bring a case concerning matters relating to tort, delict or quasi-delict before the court of the place where the harmful event occurred; Article 5, point 4, allows the plaintiff to bring a civil claim concerning for damages or restitution based on an act giving rise to criminal proceedings, before the court seised of those proceedings; Article 5, point 5, allows the plaintiff to bring his dispute arising out of the operation of a branch, agency or other establishment, before the court of the place where the branch, agency or establishment is situated; Article 5, point 6, refers to the state in which a trust is domiciled, and Article 5, point 7, refers to the court under the authority of which the cargo or freight has been arrested to secure payment or could have been so arrested, but bail or other security has been given.

In all these situations it is assumed that the particular territorial link between the type of case in question (contract, tort, etc.) and the court which may be called upon to hear the case, as mentioned in these provisions, (usually) constitutes the closest connecting factor. By attributing jurisdiction to the court that is as closely connected as described in the provision concerned, it is ensured that a court that has certain practical advantages as regards a certain type of case, is able to decide such cases in accordance with the principle of a sound administration of justice and efficacious conduct of proceedings.

The Court explicitly expressed this viewpoint in *Besix v Kretzschmar* with regard to Article 5, point 1, when it held:

> 'The reason for the adoption of the jurisdictional rule in Article 5(1) of the Brussels Convention was concern for sound administration of justice and efficacious conduct of proceedings ... The court of the place where the contractual obligation giving rise to the action is to be performed will normally be the most appropriate for deciding the case, in particular on the grounds of proximity and ease of taking evidence.'[185]

As regards Article 5, point 3, the Court made a similar observation in *Konsumenteninformation v Henkel*. The Court considered:

---

[184] See section 1.2 of this chapter, text following note 40.

[185] C-256/00 *Besix v Kretzschmar* 31 (re 12/76 *Tessili v Dunlop* 13, 266/85 *Shenavai v Kreischer* 6, C-125/92 *Mulox v Geels* 17, C-220/88 *Dumez France v Hessische Landesbank* 17, C-68/93 *Shevill v Presse Alliance* 19, C-364/93 *Marinari v Lloyd's* 10).

> 'The rule of special jurisdiction laid down in Article 5(3) of the Brussels Convention is based on the existence of a particularly close connecting factor between a dispute and the courts for the place where the harmful event occurred, which justifies the attribution of jurisdiction to those courts for reasons relating to the sound administration of justice and the efficacious conduct of proceedings ... The courts for the place where the harmful event occurred are usually the most appropriate for deciding the case, in particular on the grounds of proximity and ease of taking evidence.'[186]

And, in *Somafer v Saar-Ferngas*, when answering questions on the interpretation of the words 'dispute arising out of the operations of a branch, agency or other establishment' in Article 5, point 5, the Court stated:

> 'The meaning of the words "dispute arising out of the operations of a branch, agency or other establishment", which are the basis of the jurisdiction given by Article 5(5), are different from one Contracting State to another ... Their function in the context of the Convention must be decided in relation to the general rule conferring jurisdiction contained in Article 2(1) of the Convention ... Although Article 5 makes provision in a number of cases for a special jurisdiction, which the plaintiff may choose, this is because of the existence, in certain clearly-defined situations, of a particularly close connecting factor between a dispute and the court which may be called upon to hear it, with a view to the efficacious conduct of the proceedings.'[187]

The foregoing quotations clearly show that the principle of a sound administration of justice and efficacious conduct of proceedings underlies Article 5 and that it requires a direct, territorial link between a certain type of case and a court, in order to have the practical advantages of proximity of evidence and/or law, as regards such a case.

The principle that disputes should be decided by a court that has the practical advantage of first-hand knowledge of the facts, ease of taking evidence and/or knowledge of the applicable law, as far as it underlies Article 5, weighed in relation to other (sub-)principles

C Arts. 2 to 18	R 2 to 24	C Arts. 21 to 24	R 27 to 30
C Art. 16	R 22	C Art. 28 (1st para.)	R 35(1)
C Art. 17	R 23		

As was seen before, the principle directly underlying a provision often has a considerable influence on the interpretation of the provision concerned. The exact

[186] C-167/00 *Konsumenteninformation v Henkel* 46 (re 21/76 *Bier v Mines de potasse* 11,17; C-220/88 *Dumez France v Hessische Landesbank* 17, C-68/93 *Shevill v Presse Alliance* 19, C-364/93 *Marinari v Lloyd's* 10).

[187] 33/78 *Somafer v Saar-Ferngas* 6,7; compare also 56/79 *Zelger v Salinitri I* 3;133/81 *Ivenel v Schwab* 11; 34/82 *Peters v ZNAV* 11; 218/86 *Schotte v Rothschild* 9, 16; C-439/93 *Lloyd's v Campenon* 21; C-106/95 *Mainschiffahrts v Les Gravières Rhénanes* 29, 31; C-51/97 *Réunion européenne v Spliethoff's* 27; and Jenard Report OJ 1979 C 59, p. 22.

meaning of the concepts constituting the *connecting factor* (place of performance of the obligation in question, place where the harmful event occurred, etc.) and the *substantive scope* (matters relating to a contract, tort, etc.) of the different rules of jurisdiction of Article 5 are, however, also strongly influenced by other principles which underlie the system of jurisdictional rules and the general scheme of the Convention as a whole. This implies that the Court's interpretation of these rules cannot be explained by simply referring to the principle of a sound administration of justice. That principle, at least as far as it underlies Article 5, is frequently weighed in relation to other principles.

The principle that disputes should be decided by a court that has certain practical advantages, as far as it underlies Article 5, carries relatively little weight. This is evident from the system of jurisdictional rules laid down in Title II (Articles 2 to 18), from which it appears that the principle that disputes should be decided by a court that has certain practical advantages was already weighed in relation to other principles at the time when the Convention was drafted. With regard to the principle of the 'protection of the party who is weaker from a socio-economic point of view', we recall here that that principle prevails over the principle of a sound administration of justice, as far as it underlies Article 5. The special jurisdictional rules contained in Article 5 are set aside by the Convention's protective rules for insurance policyholders (the insured and the beneficiary of the policy) and consumers (Sections 3 and 4 of Title II of the Convention), for matters concerning contracts of employment (Article 5, point 1, second sentence) and for maintenance (Article 5, point 2).[188] From the system of jurisdictional rules, it is also evident that the principle 'party autonomy' prevails over the jurisdictions provided for in Article 5, and therefore prevails over the principle 'sound administration of justice', as far as it underlies Article 5: parties are free to agree (either by an explicit or implicit choice of forum) that courts other than those under Article 5 have jurisdiction.[189]

From Article 5, it also follows that in the cases described therein, the plaintiff is given a choice between bringing the dispute either before the courts of the defendant's domicile, by virtue of Article 2, or before the courts which have jurisdiction according to Article 5. This is a clear derogation from the 'cornerstone' principle of the Convention's jurisdictional rules, that the defendant being in a weaker position due to his procedural role, is to be protected.[190]

---

[188] See section 1.2 of this chapter.

[189] See section 2 of this chapter.

[190] See section 1.1 of this chapter. With regard to the principle 'sound administration of justice' as far as it underlies other provisions of the Convention – in particular Arts. 6, 16 and 21 to 24 – that principle may prevail over the principle 'sound administration of justice' as far as it underlies Art. 5. The principle 'sound administration of justice' as far as it underlies Art. 16 overrides this same principle as far as it underlies Art. 5, and as far as the principle 'sound administration of justice' underlies Art. 5, it may be set aside by this same principle, as far as it underlies Art. 6, if the plaintiff so chooses, and by the principle as far as it underlies Arts. 21 to 24, in case these provisions apply; see below sections 3.1.2-3.2.

From the general scheme of the Convention, it furthermore appears that the principle underlying Article 5 does not constitute an obstacle to the free movement of judgments, in that judgments of other Contracting states that conflict with that principle would not be recognized and enforced in other Contracting States (Article 28, first paragraph). The principle 'free movement of judgments' prevails over the principle 'sound administration'.

As has been pointed out in the foregoing chapters, the Court usually continues the process of weighing and balancing as was done by the designers of the Convention, when it interprets the Convention's rules of jurisdiction by using principle-based reasoning. This also applies when the Court interprets Article 5. The Court weighs the principle of a sound administration of justice, as far as it underlies that provision, in relation to other principles, to the principle of a sound administration as far as it underlies other rules of jurisdiction and to the principles 'protection of the party who is weaker from a socio-economic point of view', 'party autonomy', 'protection of the party who is weaker due to his procedural position', 'legal certainty' and 'free movement of judgments'.

With regard to the principle 'sound administration of justice' as far as it underlies Articles 6, 16, 21 to 24, its influence on the interpretation of Article 5 will be discussed in sections 3.1.2 to 3.2.2.

With regard to the principle 'protection of the party who is weaker from a socio-economic point of view', we refer to the Court's general considerations as to its restrictive interpretation of the rules of jurisdiction to which that principle directly underlies as discussed in section 1.2 of this chapter.[191] With regard to the principle 'party autonomy', we refer to the Court's considerations as to its strict interpretation of the formal requirements of Article 17 as discussed in section 2 of this chapter, in that 'Article 17 ... must be interpreted in the light of the effect of the conferment of jurisdiction by consent, which is to exclude both the jurisdiction determined by the general principle laid down in Article 2 and the special jurisdictions provided for in Articles 5 and 6 ...'.[192]

As far as the principle 'protection of the party who is weaker due to his procedural position' is concerned, it was seen that the principle 'sound administration of justice' clearly comes into conflict with the principle of the protection of the defendant and even overrules that principle, if the plaintiff so chooses. The Court is well aware of these consequences of Article 5 and has repeatedly held that the plaintiff's freedom of choice under Article 5 is only given in view of the existence in certain well-defined cases of a particularly close relationship between a dispute and the court which may be called upon to hear the case.[193] In this respect, the Court has argued that an interpretation going beyond the situations en-

---

[191] See in particular text following note 59 of section 1.2 of this chapter.

[192] See in particular text following note 109 of section 2 of this chapter.

[193] Compare section 1.1 of this chapter, text following note 25.

visaged by the Convention should be avoided. Thus, the Court observed, for example in *Mainschiffahrts v Les Gravières Rhénanes*:

> 'According to the case-law of the Court, jurisdiction derogating from the general rule that the defendant's courts should have jurisdiction was introduced by Article 5(1) in view of the existence in certain well-defined cases of a particularly close relationship between a dispute and the court which may be called upon to take cognizance of the matter, with a view to the effective organization of the proceedings ...'[194]

and stated in *Josi Reinsurance v UGIC* in more general terms:

> 'it is settled case-law that the rules of jurisdiction which derogate from the general principle, set out in the first paragraph of Article 2 of the Convention, that the courts of the Contracting State in which the defendant is domiciled or established are to have jurisdiction, cannot give rise to an interpretation going beyond the cases expressly envisaged by the Convention ...'[195]

The Court has made clear, however, that an interpretation that would deprive Article 5 of its legal effect or render Article 5 almost wholly redundant, should also be avoided, since such an interpretation would ignore the underlying objective of Article 5 itself, namely 'sound administration of justice and efficacious conduct of proceedings', based on proximity of evidence and/or law.[196] Thus, a too restrictive interpretation would not be appropriate either.

As was seen in chapter 5, when interpreting the provisions of the Convention, including those conferring jurisdiction on the national courts such as Article 5, the Court has in quite a number of cases resorted to the principle of legal certainty for different reasons. The principle of legal certainty requires an autonomous interpretation of concepts used in the rules of jurisdiction, respect for the wording of the jurisdictional rules, clarity as to what these provisions imply, that a court should be able readily to decide whether it has jurisdiction and, in particular, the avoidance of a (further) multiplication of jurisdiction in relation to one and the same legal relationship.[197]

Finally, we recall here that the principle that disputes should be decided by a court that has certain practical advantages, as far as it underlies Article 5, has been weighed in relation to the main principle 'free movement of judgments'.[198]

---

194 C-106/95 *Mainschiffahrts v Les Gravières Rhénanes* 29 (re 12/76 *Tessili v Dunlop* 13).

195 C-412/98 *Josi Reinsurance v UGIC* 49 (re C-26/91 *Handte v TMCS* 14, C-89/91 *Shearson v TVB* 15,16, C-269/95 *Benincasa v Dentalkit* 13, C-51/97 *Réunion européenne v Spliethoff's* 16; compare 33/78 *Somafer v Saar-Ferngas* 7; 56/79 *Zelger v Salinitri I* 3; 189/87 *Kalfelis v Schröder* 19; C-220/88 *Dumez France v Hessische Landesbank* 17 (re *Bier v Mines de potasse* 10,11),19; C-364/93 *Marinari v Lloyd's* 13.

196 21/76 *Bier v Mines de potasse* 20; 38/81 *Effer v Kantner* 7 (re 73/77 *Sanders v Van der Putte*); and compare C-439/93 *Lloyd's v Campenon* 17.

197 See chapter 5, section 1, 2, 4 and 5.

198 See section 1 of chapter 3.

As becomes particularly clear from *Weber v Universal Ogden* and *Besix v Kretzschmar*, the principle 'free movement of judgments' also implies avoiding an interpretation of Article 5 that would lead to a (further) multiplication of jurisdiction, as such an interpretation could heighten the risk of irreconcilable decisions and therefore endanger the recognition and enforcement of judgments in states other than those in which they were delivered.[199]

C Art. 2	R 2	C Art. 5(3)	R 5(3)
C Art. 5(1)	R 5(1)		

Article 5, point 1

Below an exposition is given of the case law of the Court as regards the interpretation of *(a)* the *substantive scope* of Article 5, point 1, *(b)* the *connecting factor* mentioned in this provision, and *(c) agreements* with regard to the connecting factor 'place of performance of the obligation in question'. This case law makes it clear how the Court weighs the principle 'that disputes should be decided by a court that has certain practical advantages', as far as it underlies Article 5, point 1, against other principles and how the various principles sometimes reinforce each other.

With regard to the *substantive scope* of Article 5, point 1, the Court has used the method of principle-based reasoning, as for example appears from the Court's judgment in the *Effer v Kantner* case. As was seen before, the Court was asked whether a case in which a party contests the existence of a contract is '*a matter relating to a contract*'.[200] Using principle-based reasoning, the Court came to the conclusion that Article 5, point 1, applies to cases in which the existence of a contract is contested. As the Court stated in this judgment, respect for the aims and spirit of the Convention demands that Article 5, point 1, should be construed as meaning that the court called upon to decide a dispute arising out of a contract may examine, of its own motion, the essential preconditions for its jurisdiction, which implies that it should be allowed to consider a case in which the existence of the contract is disputed. This includes, in turn, the power to consider the existence of the constituent parts of the contract itself.[201] In arriving at this conclusion, the Court pointed out, first of all, that in the different language versions, the wording of Article 5, point 1, is not unequivocal. By this consideration, the Court made it clear that, in principle, it respects the wording of the Convention's provisions, in accordance with the principle of legal certainty.[202] Secondly, the Court referred to the most general principle underlying the Convention as a whole, namely the principle of strengthening in the Community the legal protection of persons therein established, for which purpose rules of jurisdiction were deter-

[199] See section 1.1 of chapter 3, text following note 40; and compare section 5 of chapter 5.
[200] Compare section 4.2.2 of chapter 5, text following note 141.
[201] 38/81 *Effer v Kantner* 7 (re 73/77 *Sanders v Van der Putte* 21,22),8.
[202] 38/81 *Effer v Kantner* 5; compare section 2 of chapter 5, text following note 56.

mined inter alia to avoid the occurrence of concurrent litigation, in the interests of legal certainty and for the benefit of the parties.[203] Here, as was shown before, the Court implicitly referred to other aspects of legal certainty, such as legal certainty as to jurisdiction, including the principle that a defendant should be able reasonably to foresee the court before which he may be sued, requiring the avoidance of multiplicity of jurisdiction, and legal certainty as to judgments, requiring the avoidance of irreconcilable judgments.[204] Furthermore, the Court took account of the principle directly underlying Article 5, point 1, when it held that, if 'matters relating to a contract' would not include cases in which the existence of a contract was contested, Article 5, point 1, would be in danger of being deprived of its legal effect, since it would be accepted that, in order to defeat this rule of jurisdiction, it would be sufficient for one of the parties to claim that the contract does not exist.[205] All these considerations were advanced to justify the Court's decision in this judgment.

Peters v ZNAV was also concerned with the substantive scope of Article 5, point 1. When answering questions on the interpretation of the concepts involved, the Court referred to the principle of legal certainty. It did so, in the first place, for reasons of equality and uniformity of rights and obligations arising from the Convention.[206] The Court pointed out in this respect that, since the concept 'matters relating to a contract' serves as a criterion to define the substantive scope of one of the rules of special jurisdiction, that concept must be interpreted autonomously, by reference chiefly to the system and objectives of the Convention.[207] The Court decided that claims made by an association against one of its members with regard to the payment of a sum of money and which have their basis in the relationship between the parties by virtue of membership of the association, is 'a matter relating to a contract': membership of an association creates between the members close links of the same kind as those which are created between the parties to a contract, and therefore may be regarded as contractual for the purpose of the application of Article 5, point 1.[208] The Court did not expressly justify this autonomous interpretation of the words 'matters relating to a contract' in Article 5, point 1. However, that interpretation can be considered to be in accordance with the principle of legal certainty as to jurisdiction and judgments, which requires the avoidance of a multiplicity of courts having jurisdiction as to one and the same type of case and the avoidance of irreconcilable decisions: by classifying membership of an association as contractual, it is possible for *all* the difficulties which may arise on the occasion of the performance

[203] 38/81 *Effer v Kantner* 6.

[204] See chapter 5, section 4.2.2, text following note 119 and section 5, text following note 162 and section 1.1 of chapter 3, text following note 40.

[205] See 38/81 *Effer v Kantner* 7 (re *Sanders v Van der Putte*).

[206] Compare section 1.1 of chapter 5, text following note 15.

[207] 34/82 *Peters v ZNAV* 9,10 (re 33/78 *Somafer v Saar-Ferngas*).

[208] 34/82 *Peters v ZNAV* 13.

of obligations arising from the membership of such an association, to be brought before the same court.[209] In that same judgment, the Court explicitly referred to the principle of legal certainty when it held that, in order to determine whether or not an obligation of a member towards an association falls within 'matters relating to a contract', a distinction between obligations arising simply from the act of becoming a member and those resulting from that act in conjunction with a decision made by an organ of the association should not be drawn. When justifying its decision, the Court pointed out that an interpretation of Article 5, point 1, that would lead to a (further) multiplication of jurisdiction is to be avoided, as far as possible.[210]

In *Arcado v Haviland*, the Court consistently held that, in accordance with the principle of legal certainty, the concept 'matters relating to a contract' should be regarded as an independent concept, so as to ensure, as far as possible, the equality and uniformity of the rights and obligations arising out of the Convention.[211] Deviating from what the Court usually does when attributing the required autonomous meaning to the Convention's provisions, namely making reference to the principles and the scheme of the Convention, the Court in this case referred to Council Directive 86/653. On the basis of this directive, the Court decided that proceedings relating to the wrongful repudiation of an independent commercial agency agreement and the payment of commission due under such an agreement are 'matters relating to a contract' within the meaning of Article 5, point 1, since these claims find their very basis in that agreement.[212]

Notice that in the above-mentioned cases a *broad* interpretation is given to the substantive scope of Article 5, point 1. In *Handte v TMCS,* on the other hand and as was seen before, the Court decided on a *restrictive* interpretation of the notion 'matters relating to a contract', in that it does not apply to an action between a sub-buyer of goods and the manufacturer, who is not the seller of the goods to the sub-buyer, relating to defects in those goods.[213] In such a case there is no contractual relationship between the sub-buyer and the manufacturer, because there is no obligation freely assumed by one party towards the other.[214] When justifying that decision, the Court first referred to the principle 'equality and uniformity of rights and obligations' which requires an autonomous interpretation.[215] Also, the

---

[209] 34/82 *Peters v ZNAV* 12,13,15. Compare chapter 5, section 4.2.2 and 5. See hereafter, as regards the interpretation of the connecting factor place of performance of the obligation in question, also text following note 241.

[210] 34/82 *Peters v ZNAV* 16-18; compare section 4.2.2 of chapter 5, text following note 137.

[211] 9/87 *Arcado v Haviland* 10 (re 34/82 *Peters v ZNAV*).

[212] 9/87 *Arcado v Haviland* 9, 10 (re 34/82 *Peters v ZNAV*),11-14 (re Council Directive 86/653 of 18 December 1986, OJ 1986 I, 382, p. 17)-16; compare section 1.1 of chapter 5, text following note 23.

[213] C-26/91 *Handte v TMCS* 21; compare section 4.1 of chapter 5, text following note 113.

[214] C-26/91 *Handte v TMCS* 15,16,20.

[215] C-26/91 *Handte v TMCS* 10 (re 34/83 *Peters v ZNAV* 9,10; 9/87 *Arcado v Haviland* 10, 11).

Court recalled its interpretation as to the relationship between Article 2, and the rules of jurisdiction derogating from it: in order to give due influence to the principle of the protection of the defendant, underlying Article 2, an interpretation that goes beyond the type of cases which the Convention envisages by the notion of 'matters relating to a contract', should be avoided.[216] Next, the Court referred to the most general principle underlying the Convention as a whole, the principle of strengthening in the Community the legal protection of persons therein established, which requires, amongst other things, legal certainty as to jurisdiction.[217] According to the Court, the principle of legal certainty as to jurisdiction particularly requires that the jurisdictional rules which derogate from the general principle of Article 2 should be interpreted in such a way as to enable a normally well-informed defendant to reasonably foresee before which courts, other than those of the state in which he is domiciled, he may be sued.[218] In a situation such as this, the application of the special jurisdictional rule of Article 5, point 1, to an action brought by a sub-buyer of goods against the manufacturer is not foreseeable by the latter, and is therefore incompatible with the principled system underlying the Convention.[219]

A similar line of reasoning was followed by the Court in *Réunion européenne v Spliethoff's*, in which the Court recalled that the phrase 'matters relating to a contract' is not to be understood as covering a situation in which there is no obligation freely assumed by one party towards the other. Hence, the Court decided that Article 5, point 1, also did not apply to an action by which the consignee of goods found to be damaged on completion of a transport operation by sea and then by land, or by which his insurer who has been subrogated to his rights after compensating him, seeks redress for the damage suffered, not against the person who issued that document covering the maritime transport but against the person whom the plaintiff considered to be the actual maritime carrier.[220] In addition to that line of reasoning, the Court referred to the division between the jurisdictions within Article 5, particularly between Article 5, point 1, relating to matters of contract, and Article 5, point 3, relating to torts. That division is justified by the principle of a sound administration of justice, as it attributes jurisdiction to a national court on the basis of a particular close connecting factor with respect to a particular type of case. This division of jurisdictions requires a restrictive (or not too broad) interpretation of Article 5, point 1.[221]

---

[216] C-26/91 *Handte v TMCS* 13,14; compare section 1.1 of this chapter, text following note 25; and this section, text following note 195.

[217] C-26/91 *Handte v TMCS* 11,12 (re Expert Report OJ 1979 C 59, p. 1).

[218] C-26/91 *Handte v TMCS* 18,19

[219] Compare C-26/91 *Handte v TMCS* 21.

[220] C-51/97 *Réunion européenne v Spliethoff's* 15 (re 34/82 *Peters v ZNAV* 9,10; 9/87 *Arcado v Haviland* 10,11; C-26/91 *Handte v TMCS* 10), 16 (re C-269/95 *Benincasa v Dentalkit* 13), 17 (*Handte* 15)-22 (re 189/87 *Kalfelis v Schröder* 18)-26.

[221] C-51/97 *Réunion européenne v Spliethoff's* 22 (re 189/87 *Kalfelis v Schröder* 18), 26.

In *Tacconi v Sinto Maschinenfabrik*, the Court followed the same line of argument. First, it recalled its case law as to an independent interpretation of the concepts constituting the substantive scope of rules of jurisdiction. Secondly, it recalled its case law as to the principle of legal certainty, requiring the claimant to identify easily the court in which he may sue the defendant and the defendant reasonably to foresee in which court he may be sued, as well as its case law on the division of jurisdictions following from Article 5, points 1 and 3.[222] Next, it recalled its decision in *Handte v TMCS* and *Réunion européenne v Spliethoff's*, that Article 5, point 1, does not cover a situation characterized by the absence of obligations freely assumed by one party towards another.[223] On the basis of these considerations, the Court concluded that an action, arising from a possible breach of the rule requiring the parties to act in good faith in negotiations conducted with a view to the formation of a contract, is not covered by the expression 'matters relating to a contract'. Taking account of the system of rules of jurisdiction, in particular the division between the jurisdictions of Article 5, points 1 and 3, the Court held, as it did in *Réunion européenne v Spliethoff's*, that such an action is covered by the phrase 'matters relating to tort, delict or quasi-delict' within the meaning of Article 5, point 3.[224]

Finally, we recall here the Court's case law on the substantive scope of Article 5, point 1, and the division between jurisdictions as regards contracts in general, on the one hand, and consumer contracts, insurance and contracts of employment, on the other, by which the Court normally arrives at a restrictive interpretation of the substantive scope of the specific jurisdictions which aim to protect the socio-economically weaker party.[225] As was seen in section 1.2 of this chapter, the division between jurisdictions as regards these two types of contracts emerges from the two different principles which are involved here: 'sound administration of justice' and 'protection of the social-economically weaker party'.

As regards the notion of '*place of performance of the obligation in question*', which is the *factor that connects* a dispute to a court in the cases that fall within the scope of 'matters relating to a contract', the Court has delivered a number of decisions which demonstrate that the Court uses principle-based reasoning, at least as far as possible.

First of all, the Court was asked to decide which obligation was actually meant by '*obligation*' – the term 'obligation in question' was not used in all the different language versions of the 1968 Convention – in a case concerned with a con-

---

[222] C-334/00 *Tacconi v Sinto Maschinenfabrik* 19 (re 34/82 *Peters v ZNAV* 9,10; *Reichert* 15; *Handte* 10), 20 (re C-295/95 *Farrell* 13; C-256/00 *Besix* 25,26), 21 (re *Kalfelis* 18, *Reichert* 16, C-51/97 *Réunion européenne* 22).

[223] C-334/00 *Tacconi v Sinto Maschinenfabrik* 23 (re *Handte* 15; *Réunion européenne* 17).

[224] C-334/00 *Tacconi v Sinto Maschinenfabrik* 27; see also hereafter in this section, text following note 269.

[225] Compare section 1.2 of this chapter, text following notes 63, 81, 87.

tract granting an exclusive sales concession and successive sales concluded in the performance of the said contract. In its judgment in the *De Bloos v Bouyer* case, the Court first adduced the need to avoid, as far as possible, creating a situation in which a number of courts have jurisdiction with respect to one and the same contract (in accordance with the principle 'legal certainty' and 'free movement of judgments').[226] Hence, the Court observed that therefore Article 5, point 1, cannot be interpreted as referring to any obligation whatsoever arising under the contract in question.[227] Next, the Court confirmed its respect for the wording of the different language versions of Article 5, point 1 (in accordance with the principle 'legal certainty').[228] The Court then concluded that the expression 'obligation' refers only to the contractual obligation which forms the basis of the legal proceedings, which corresponds to the contractual right on which the plaintiff's action was based.[229] That interpretation was corroborated by the 1978 Accession Convention. The Court held, more specifically, with regard to disputes in which the grantee of an exclusive sales concession charges the grantor with having infringed the exclusive concession and asserts the right to be paid damages or seeks a dissolution of the contract, 'the word "obligation" refers ... to the contractual obligation of the grantor which corresponds to the contractual right relied upon by the grantee in support of the application'.[230]

The notion '*place of performance* of the obligation in question' has, as was seen before, given rise to a more fundamental question. In its decision *Tessili v Dunlop*, the Court had to depart from the general guidelines followed in the majority of its case law, that the concepts used in the Convention should be given an autonomous interpretation.[231] The Court decided that it could not give the notion 'place of performance of the obligation' an independent interpretation. It pointed out that that notion cannot be understood otherwise than by reference to the substantive law applicable under the conflict of laws rules of the court before which the matter is brought.[232] The Court deemed it impossible to provide any more substantial guidance to the interpretation of 'place of performance' due to the differences between national laws of contract and the absence of a legal development of any unification in the substantive law applicable.[233] In other words, the principle of equality and uniformity of rights and obligations was set aside in this case, not because there is a counter-principle underlying the Convention which pulls in the opposite direction but simply because the Court felt that, for contracts

[226] 14/76 *De Bloos v Bouyer* 8,9.

[227] 14/76 *De Bloos v Bouyer* 10.

[228] 14/76 *De Bloos v Bouyer* 11,12; and compare section 2 of chapter 5.

[229] 14/76 *De Bloos v Bouyer* 13; compare C-420/97 *Leathertex v Bodetex* 31 (re *De Bloos v Bouyer*),32; and see also, *Tacconi v Sinto Maschinenfabrik* 22.

[230] 14/76 *De Bloos v Bouyer* 15.

[231] See section 1.1 of chapter 5, text following note 24; and, A-G Darmon.

[232] 12/76 *Tessili v Dunlop* 13,15.

[233] 12/76 *Tessili v Dunlop* 14.

in general, it could not establish uniform criteria since the determination of the place of performance of obligations depends on the contractual context to which these obligations belong.[234]

In *Concorde v Panjan*, the Court was asked to reconsider its decision in *Tessili v Dunlop*.[235] The Court refused, however, to overrule its earlier decision and it stuck to the argumentation employed in *Tessili v Dunlop*. The Court recalled that, where it had given the expression 'place of performance' an autonomous interpretation in the case of contracts of employment, that decision was justified by the particularities of this type of contract, and, as was seen before, by the principle of the protection of the party who is the weaker from a socio-economic point of view, namely the employee.[236] Where no such particular features exist, the Court is convinced that it is neither necessary nor possible to identify the obligation which characterizes the contract and to centralize at its place of performance jurisdiction over disputes concerning *all* the obligations under the contract.[237] Next, the Court referred to the principle of legal certainty as to jurisdiction, in particular to the principle that a normally well-informed defendant should reasonably foresee before which courts, other than those of the State in which he is domiciled, he may be sued. According to the Court, that principle justifies its decision not to refer to the nature of the legal relationship and the circumstances of the case, when determining 'the place of performance of the obligation in question'.[238] Moreover, the Court recalled that Article 5, point 1, was designed with a view to efficient organization of procedure. It pointed out that an interpretation of Article 5, point 1, for contracts other than contracts of employment, to the effect that the place of performance must be determined in accordance with the law which governs the obligation at issue, has the advantage that the competent court is the court of the place where the obligation in question is to be performed in accordance with the law which is applicable to it.[239] The Court continued by stating that the risk that the law applicable to the determination of the

---

[234] 12/76 *Tessili v Dunlop* 14; compare, C-440/97 *Concorde v Panjan* 23,24. Notice that Art. 5, point 1, of Regulation 44/2001, stipulates that for the purpose of that provision and unless otherwise agreed, the place of performance of the obligation in question shall be: in the case of the sale of goods, the place in a Member State where, under the contract, the goods were delivered or should have been delivered, and, in the case of the provision of services, the place in a Member State where, under the contract, the services were provided or should have been provided. In other situations, Art. 5, point 1, under c in conjunction with a, confers jurisdiction on the courts of the 'place of performance of the obligation in question', to be understood by reference to the substantive law applicable under the conflict of laws rules of the court before which the matter is brought.

[235] C-440/97 *Concorde v Panjan* 10.

[236] C-440/97 *Concorde v Panjan* 18 (re C-125/92 *Mulox v Geels* 15,18). Compare section 1.1 of chapter 5, text following note 28; and 1.2 of this chapter, text following notes 40, 87.

[237] C-440/97 *Concorde v Panjan* 19 (re 266/85 *Shenavai v Kreischer* 17),20.

[238] C-440/97 *Concorde v Panjan* 23 (re C-129/92 *Owens v Bracco* 32), 24 (re C-26/91 *Handte v TMCS* 18, 25.

[239] C-440/97 *Concorde v Panjan* 29 (re *Shenavai* 18; *Custom Made v Stawa* 12,13).

place of performance will vary depending on the court seised is diminished by the 1980 Rome Convention, and that it is for the national legislature to define a place of performance which takes both the interests of the sound administration of justice and the interests of adequate protection for individuals fairly into account.[240]

With regard to the place of performance of obligations arising out of the act of becoming a member of an association, the Court stated in *Peters v ZNAV*, that under national legal systems it is usually stipulated that the place in which an association is established is to be the place of performance of these obligations. The Court pointed out that the application of Article 5, point 1, in this type of case therefore has practical advantages: the court of the place in which the association has its seat is in fact the best suited to understand the documents of constitution, the rules and decisions of the association, and the circumstances out of which the dispute arose.[241] It also has the practical advantage that it is possible for all the difficulties which may arise on the occasion of the performance of obligations arising from the membership of such an association, to be brought before the same court.[242] Where the Court explicitly referred to the principle 'sound administration of justice', requiring that the courts that have the practical advantage of first-hand knowledge of the facts, proximity of evidence or law, should be competent to hear the case, it shows that it is aware of the underlying principle of Article 5, point 1.[243]

C Art. 2	R 2	C Art. 17	R 23
C Art. 5(1)	R 5(1)		

As was seen in section 2.3 of this chapter, the Court has delivered two decisions, in *Zelger v Salinitri* and *Mainschiffahrts v Les Gravières Rhénanes*, regarding the situation in which the parties to a contract have *agreed on the place where the obligation in question is to be performed.*[244] The question was asked under what conditions such an agreement is valid and therefore is allowed to determine which court, according to the jurisdictional rule contained in Article 5, point 1, has jurisdiction. More in particular, the question was raised whether such an agreement has to comply with the formal conditions stated in Article 17. When looking at the argumentation of these two decisions together, it appears that the

[240] C-440/97 *Concorde v Panjan* 30 (re 1980 Rome Convention),31.

[241] 34/82 *Peters v ZNAV* 11, 14. In this decision the Court had already decided that claims made by an association against one of its members, which have their basis in the relationship between the parties by virtue of membership of the association, is 'a matter relating to a contract'; see this section, text following note 208.

[242] 34/82 *Peters v ZNAV* 12; compare section 4.2.2 of chapter 5, text following note 137.

[243] 34/82 *Peters v ZNAV* 11.

[244] 56/79 *Zelger v Salinitri I* 3-6; and, C-106/95 *Mainschiffahrt v Les Gravières Rhénanes* 28-35. compare: C-440/97 *Concorde v Panjan* 28; compare section 2.3 of this chapter, text following note 167.

Court has taken a coherent stance from the point of view of the 'principled structure' underlying the Convention's jurisdictional provisions.

In *Zelger v Salinitri*, the Court pointed out that Article 5, point 1, creates a ground for jurisdiction which is an exception to the general rule of jurisdiction provided for in Article 2, at the option of the plaintiff. That ground for jurisdiction is justified by the existence of a direct link between the dispute and the court called upon to take cognizance of the case (in accordance with the principle that disputes should be decided by a court that has certain practical advantages).[245] In contrast, Article 17 sets aside both the rule of general jurisdiction of Article 2 as well as the rules of special jurisdiction contained in Article 5, and dispenses with any objective connection between the legal relationship and the court designated. It is because of the fact that Article 17 allows parties to agree on a forum which has no objective connection with the case, that Article 17 requires compliance with the strict rules as to form which are set out in Article 17 (in order to meet the principle of party autonomy, as was seen in section 2.1 of this chapter). Consequently, if the parties to a contract are permitted by the law applicable to the contract to specify the place of performance of an obligation without special conditions as to form, such an agreement is sufficient to ground jurisdiction in that place within the meaning of Article 5, only if there is a real connection between the agreed place and the reality of the contract (and indeed that court therefore has certain practical advantages).[246] Thus, in the case *Zelger v Salinitri*, the oral agreement between an Italian and a German merchant on the place of performance of the obligation – Munich, being the place for the repayment of the loan which had been extended by the German to the Italian merchant – was considered to be valid under Article 5, point 1, because that agreement was permitted under the applicable law and the place agreed upon did have a real connection with the contract.[247]

In *Mainschiffahrt v Les Gravières Rhénanes*, the Court came to an opposite conclusion with regard to an oral agreement as to the place of performance of a contractual obligation.[248] The Court established that the place of performance that the parties to the contract had agreed upon, had no real connection with the reality of the contract. Interpreting Article 5, point 1, in light of its underlying principle, which requires a direct link between the dispute and the court, the Court indicated that such an agreement could not vest jurisdiction in a court on the basis of Article 5, point 1. Doing so would allow the circumvention of Article 17, without there being a reason that could justify it, as there was in the *Zelger v Salinitri* case.

---

[245] 56/79 *Zelger v Salinitri I* 3.

[246] 56/79 *Zelger v Salatrini I* 4-6; and, C-106/95 *Mainschiffahrt v Les Gravières Rhénanes* 29 (re 12/76 *Tessili v Dunlop* 13), 30 (re 56/79 *Zelger v Salinitri I* 5),31.

[247] 56/79 *Zelger v Salatrini I* 6.

[248] C-106/95 *Mainschiffahrt v Les Gravières Rhénanes* 32-35.

Recently, in *Besix v Kretzschmar*, the Court had an opportunity to recall several lines of its principle-based reasoning in relation to the interpretation of the expression 'place of performance of the obligation in question' under Article 5, point 1. As was seen before, this decision particularly demonstrates the relative weight of the principle that disputes should be decided by a court that has certain practical advantages on the basis of a direct territorial link.[249] In that judgment, the Court considered in further detail the relation between Articles 2 and 5, and the relation between the principles 'legal certainty as to jurisdiction' and 'protection of the defendant', on the one hand, and 'sound administration of justice', on the other.[250] The referring national court had found that the obligation that was relevant for the purposes of the application of Article 5, point 1, was an obligation not to do something, consisting in this case of the parties' undertaking not to commit themselves to other partners in connection with a procedure for the award of a public contract. The parties to the contract had designated neither the place of performance of that contractual obligation nor the courts having jurisdiction to hear any action relating to such an obligation, or, for that matter, the law governing the contract. Furthermore, it was clear that, given all the circumstances of the case, the parties' clear intention was to have the obligation in question honoured throughout the world, with the result that the places for its performance were particularly numerous.

The Court decided that if the relevant contractual obligation has been, or is to be performed in a number of places, jurisdiction to hear and determine the case cannot be conferred on the courts within whose jurisdiction any one of those places of performance happen to be located.[251] Article 5, point 1, was not apt to be applied in the case at hand.[252] In justifying that decision, the Court first resorted to the principle of legal certainty.[253] It recalled that, as a consequence of the most general principle underlying the Convention, the principle of strengthening in the Community the legal protection of persons established therein, the Convention provides for common rules on jurisdiction in order to guarantee certainty as to the allocation of jurisdiction.[254] In particular, the Court recalled that the principle of legal certainty as to jurisdiction requires that the jurisdictional rules which derogate from the principle laid down in Article 2, conferring jurisdiction on the defendant's home court, should be interpreted in such a way as to enable a normally well-informed defendant reasonably to foresee before which

[249] Compare section 4.2.1 of chapter 5, text following note 135.

[250] C-256/00 *Besix v Kretzschmar*.

[251] C-256/00 *Besix v Kretzschmar* 28.

[252] C-256/00 *Besix v Kretzschmar* 55.

[253] C-256/00 *Besix v Kretzschmar* 24 (re 38/81 *Effer v Kantner* 6; C-26/91 *Handte v TMCS* 11,12,18,19; C-129/92 *Owens Bank v Bracco* 32; C-288/92 *Custom Made v Stawa* 18; C-440/97 *Concorde v Panjan* 23.

[254] C-256/00 *Besix v Kretzschmar* 25 (re C-288/92 *Custom Made* 15).

courts, other than those of the state in which he is domiciled, he may be sued.[255] Also the Court recalled, referring back to settled case law, that it is essential to avoid creating a situation in which a number of courts have jurisdiction in respect of one and the same contract, in order to preclude the risk of irreconcilable decisions and to facilitate the recognition and enforcement of judgments in states other than those in which they were delivered, in accordance with the principle of legal certainty as to jurisdiction and as to judgments, and the principle of free movement of judgments.[256] The Court then stated that the special rules of jurisdiction laid down in Section 2 of Title II are justified in particular by the consideration that there is a close connecting factor between the dispute and the court called upon to resolve it.[257] More in particular, the Court observed that the reason for the adoption of Article 5, point 1, was concern for sound administration of justice and the efficacious conduct of proceedings and that the court of the place where the contractual obligation giving rise to the action is to be performed will normally be the most appropriate for deciding the case, in particular on the grounds of proximity and ease of taking evidence.[258] In such a case a single place of performance for the obligation in question must be identified (here the Court referred to the wording of Article 5, point 1, in accordance with the principle of legal certainty, in that respect should be paid to the linguistic boundaries of the Convention).[259] However, applying the traditional case law established since *Tessili v Dunlop*, as the Court normally should have done, and according to which the place of performance of the obligation in question is to be determined in accordance with the law governing the obligation in question, would in the case at hand not have the result that a single place of performance would be identified.[260] On the other hand, an autonomous interpretation of the expression 'place of performance' within the meaning of Article 5, point 1, as the Court continued, could only be established by calling into question that traditional case law.[261] Neither could the place of performance be identified on the basis of factual considerations, as in the case of a contract of employment. As the Court has ruled in its case law, such considerations are only justified in case the particularities of a contract of employment are fulfilled.[262]

---

[255] C-256/00 *Besix v Kretzschmar* 26 (re C-26/91 *Handte v TMCS* 18; and, C-440/97 *Concorde v Panjan* 24) and 52 (re C-412/98 *Group Josi* 34,35), and compare section 3.2

[256] C-256/00 *Besix v Kretzschmar* 27 (re 14/76 *De Bloos v Bouyer* 9, 266/85 *Shenavai v Kreischer* 8, C-125/92 *Mulox v Geels* 21, C-383/95 *Rutten v Cross Medical* 18, and, C-420/97 *Leathertex v Bodetex* 31), 35; and compare section 1.1 and section 3.4.2.

[257] C-256/00 *Besix v Kretzschmar* 30 (re 56/79 *Zelger v Salinitri I* 3).

[258] C-256/00 *Besix v Kretzschmar* 31 (re 12/76 *Tessili v Dunlop* 13, 266/85 *Shenavai v Kreischer* 6, C-125/92 *Mulox v Geels* 17, an by way of analogy regards Art. 5(3): C-220/88 *Dumez France v Hessische Landesbank* 17, C-68/93 *Shevill v Presse Alliance* 19, C-364/93 *Marinari v Lloyd's* 10).

[259] C-256/00 *Besix v Kretzschmar* 29, and compare section 3.2.

[260] C-256/00 *Besix v Kretzschmar* 33.

[261] C-256/00 *Besix v Kretzschmar* 36.

[262] C-256/00 *Besix v Kretzschmar* 37,38 (re *Mulox* 20,26, *Rutten* 26); 39, 40 (re *Shenavai* 17; *Concorde* 19; *Leathertex* 36)-55. It was not possible, in the present case, to apply the case law of the

In view of these (and other) considerations, all pointing in the same direction, the Court decided that Article 5, point 1, was not apt to be applied in a case characterized by a multiplicity of places for its performance, as in the case at hand. In such a case it is not possible to determine the court having the closest connection with the case by making jurisdiction coincide with the actual place for the performance of the obligation in question. An obligation not to do something as in the present case must by its very nature be honored throughout the world. It is not capable of being identified with a specific place or linked to a court which would be particularly suited to hear and determine the dispute relating to that obligation. Therefore, since in a case like this the principle 'sound administration of justice' does not really apply, jurisdiction can be determined solely in accordance with the general rule, set out in the first paragraph of Article 2 of the Convention, that persons domiciled in a Contracting State are to be sued in the courts of that State. That solution is in conformity with the scheme of the Convention and the rationale of Article 5, point 1 within that scheme.[263] Article 2 also has the advantage that it provides a certain and reliable criterion.[264] And, finally, as the Court put it: another solution would undermine the principle of the protection of the rights of the defendant, since it would have the result that a claimant might be able to affect the choice of a court which is unforeseeable for a defendant domiciled in the territory of a Contracting State (and therefore come into conflict with the principle of legal certainty as to jurisdiction).[265]

C Art. 2	R 2	C Art. 5(3)	R 5(3)
C Art. 5(1)	R 5(1)		

Article 5, point 3

The Court's case law clearly shows that the approach of principle-based reasoning is also followed by the Court when it answers questions on the interpretation of *(a)* the *substantive scope* of Article 5, point 3, and *(b)* the *connecting factor* mentioned in this provision. Since most of these cases have already been discussed in this study, we will only briefly discuss that case law here.

As regards the concept '*matters relating to tort, delict or quasi-delict*', constituting the *substantive scope* of Article 5, point 3, the Court, among others in *Kalfelis v Schröder*, has consistently held that an autonomous interpretation of that con-

---

Court as regards contracts of employment by analogy. In this respect, the Court has consistently held that, where these specific features of a contract of employment are lacking, it is not appropriate to identify the obligation which characterizes the contract and to centralize at its place of performance all jurisdiction, based on place of performance over disputes concerning all the obligations under the contract.

[263] C-256/00 *Besix v Kretzschmar* 51, 52 (re C-412/98 *Josi* 34,35), 54 (re *Josi* 49,50).

[264] C-256/00 *Besix v Kretzschmar* 50 (re 32/88 *Six Constructions* 20). As was seen in section 4.1 of chapter 5, a certain and reliable criterion of jurisdiction is in accordance with the principle of legal certainty; compare text following note 102 of that chapter.

[265] C-256/00 *Besix v Kretzschmar* 33-55.

cept is required in the light of the principles and objectives and the general scheme of the Convention, in order to ensure that the Convention is given full effect and to ensure, as far as possible, the equality and uniformity of the rights and obligations (in accordance with the principle of legal certainty).[266] As the Court decided in that judgment, the concept 'matters relating to tort, delict or quasi-delict' encompasses 'all actions which seek to establish the liability of a defendant and which are not related to a "contract" within the meaning of Article 5(1).'[267] This implies that in the case of an action based concurrently on tortious or delictual liability and on breach of contract, the court having jurisdiction by virtue of Article 5, point 3, does not have jurisdiction over the action with respect to breach of contract: a court which has jurisdiction under Article 5, point 3, over an action in so far as it is based on tort or delict, does not have jurisdiction in so far as it is not so based.[268] In order to justify that interpretation the Court referred to the division of special jurisdictions provided for by Article 5, particularly between jurisdiction as regards 'matters relating to a contract' and jurisdiction as regards 'matters relating to tort' in Article 5, points 1 and 3.[269] As was seen before, that division emerges when applying the principle of sound administration.[270] Also the Court recalled that the 'special jurisdictions' enumerated in Articles 5 and 6 must be interpreted restrictively, because they constitute derogations from the principle of the protection of the defendant, as laid down in Article 2.[271]

The Court is aware of the fact that disadvantages arise from different aspects of the same dispute being adjudicated by different courts. This consequence of its interpretation of Article 5, points 1 and 3, having the result that a multiplicity of courts may have jurisdiction with regard to different aspects of the same dispute, conflicts with the principle of legal certainty as to jurisdiction and as to judgments, with the principle of free movement of judgments, and as will be seen later with the principle that an entire dispute should be decided, as far as possible, by a single court.[272] The Court indicated in this judgment, that there are mechanisms in the Convention which can obviate these disadvantages to some extent. On the one hand, in so far as a multiplicity of courts having jurisdiction would be

---

[266] 189/87 *Kalfelis v Schröder* 15 (re 34/82 *Peters v ZNAV* 9; 9/87 *Arcado v Haviland* 10), 16; see also 1.1 of chapter 5; compare: C-167/00 *Konsumenteninformation v Henkel* 35 (re 189/87 *Kalfelis v Schröder* 17, C-261/90 *Reichert v Dresdner Bank II* 16, C-51/97 *Réunion européenne v Spliethoff's* 22); C-334/00 *Tacconi v Sinto Maschinenfabrik* 20 (re 34/82 *Peters v ZNAV* 9,10, C-261/90 *Reichert v Dresdner Bank II* 15, C-26/91 *Handte v TMCS* 10).

[267] 189/87 *Kalfelis v Schröder* 17; and compare C-167/00 *Konsumenteninformation v Henkel* 36 (re 189/87 *Kalfelis v Schröder* 17, C-261/90 *Reichert v Dresdner II* 16, C-51/97 *Reunion européenne v Spliethoff's* 22, C-96/00 *Gabriel* 33).

[268] 189/87 *Kalfelis v Schröder* 17,18.

[269] 189/87 *Kalfelis v Schröder* 16-18.

[270] See above, text following note 184 of this section.

[271] 189/87 *Kalfelis v Schröder* 19.

[272] Compare section 1 of chapter 3, sections 4.2. and 5 of chapter 6, and sections 3.2 and 4 of this chapter.

problematic to the plaintiff, he can always choose to bring his action in its entirety before the courts of the domicile of the defendant. On the other hand, Article 22, as will be seen later, allows the court first seised, in certain circumstances, to hear the case in its entirety provided that there is a connection between the actions brought before the different courts.[273]

Elaborating on *Kalfelis v Schröder*, and recalling that a concept such as 'matters relating to tort, delict and quasi-delict' in Article 5, point 3, must be considered as an independent concept, the Court consistently held in *Reichert v Dresdner Bank*, that that concept covers only actions which seek to establish the liability of a defendant and which are not related to a 'contract' within the meaning of Article 5, point 1.[274] The Court stated that an action such as the action *paulienne* in French law cannot be regarded as a claim seeking to establish the liability of a defendant in the sense in which it is understood in Article 5, point 3. The purpose of such an action is not to have the debtor ordered to make good the damage he has caused to his creditor by his fraudulent conduct, but to render ineffective, as against his creditor, the disposition which the debtor has made.[275] The Court did not justify its autonomous interpretation any further, neither by principle-based reasoning nor by reference to the general principles which stem from the corpus of national legal systems. Also, the Court had apparently no reason to refer to the division of jurisdiction as laid down in Article 5, points 1 and 3. Neither did the Court resort to its well-known consideration that Article 5, point 3, derogates from the general principle of Article 2 and therefore should not be given an interpretation that goes beyond the cases envisaged by the Convention. It is clear, though, that its restrictive interpretation of Article 5, point 3, is in accordance with the requirement that flows from the principle of the protection of the defendant that derogations from the general rule that jurisdiction should be attributed to the defendant's home court are to be interpreted restrictively.

In *Réunion européenne v Spliethoff's*, the Court decided, as was seen before, that an action by which the consignee of goods found to be damaged on completion of a transport operation by sea and then by land, or by which his insurer, who has been subrogated to his rights after compensating him seeks redress for the damage suffered, relying on the bill of lading covering the maritime transport, not against the person who issued that document on his headed paper but against the person whom the plaintiff considered to be the actual maritime carrier, does not fall within the scope of 'matters relating to a contract' within the meaning of Article 5, point 1, but is a matter relating to tort within the meaning of Article 5, point 3.[276] As was seen before, the Court referred back to the same lines of argu-

[273] 189/87 *Kalfelis v Schröder* 20; see hereafter, section 3.2.2 of this chapter.

[274] C-261/90 *Reichert v Dresdner Bank II* 15 (re 189/87 *Kalfelis v Schröder* 15,16),16 (re *Kalfelis* 17); see also C-96/00 *Gabriel* 33.

[275] C-261/90 *Reichert v Dresdner Bank II* 17 (re C-115/88 *Reichert v Dresdner Bank I* 12), 20.

[276] See text following note 220 of this section; C-51/97 *Réunion européenne v Spliethoff's* 22 (re 189/87 *Kalfelis v Schröder* 18)-26. Compare also C-96/00 *Gabriel* 33 (re 189/87 *Kalfelis v Schröder* 17, C-261/90 *Reichert v Dresdner Bank II* 16, C-51/97 *Réunion européenne v Spliethoff's* 22).

ment as used in *Kalfelis v Schröder* and arrived at its decision by principle-based reasoning.[277]

In *Tacconi v Sinto Maschinenfabrik*, the Court consistently held that, in circumstances characterized by the absence of obligations freely assumed by one party towards another on the occasion of negotiations with a view to the formation of a contract and by a possible breach of the rule which requires the parties to act in good faith in such negotiations, such an action is not covered by the expression 'matters relating to a contract', but by the phrase 'matters relating to tort, delict or quasi-delict', within the meaning of Article 5, point 3.[278] As was seen in one of the foregoing paragraphs, the Court followed principle-based reasoning in this case as well.[279]

Principle-based reasoning with respect to the interpretation of the concept 'matters relating to tort, delict or quasi-delict' was also followed in *Konsumenteninformation v Henkel*, as was seen in section 1.2 of this chapter.[280] In that judgment, the Court first decided that a preventive action brought by a consumer protection organisation for the purpose of preventing a trader from using terms considered to be unfair in contracts with private individuals, cannot be considered as being brought by a consumer within the meaning of section 4 of the Convention on jurisdiction over consumer contracts.[281] Then, the Court had to decide whether such an action is a matter relating to a contract within the meaning of Article 5, point 1, or a matter relating to tort as in Article 5, point 3.[282] It did so by recalling its case law as regards an autonomous interpretation of these concepts and its case law based on the division of jurisdiction between Article 5, points 1 and 3.[283] In light of these considerations, the Court decided that such an action, though being preventive, is a matter relating to tort, delict or quasi-delict within the meaning of Article 5, point 3, of the Convention.[284]

---

[277] C-51/97 *Réunion européenne v Spliethoff's* 15 (re 34/82 *Peters v ZNAV* 9,10; 9/87 *Arcado v Haviland* 10, 11; and, C-26/91 *Handte v TMCS* 10), 16 (re C-269/95 *Benincasa v Dentalkit* 13), 17 (re *Handte* 15), 22 (re 189/87 *Kalfelis v Schröder* 18).

[278] See this section, text following note 220.

[279] Compare text following note 224 of this section: C-334/00 *Tacconi v Sinto Maschinenfabrik* 19 (re 34/82 *Peters v ZNAV* 9,10, C-261/90 *Reichert v Dresdner Bank II* 15, C-26/91 *Handte v TMCS* 10), 20 (re C-295/95 *Farrel v Long* 13; C-256/00 *Besix* 25,26), 21 (re 189/87 *Kalfelis v Schröder* 18, C-261/90 *Reichert v Dresdner Bank II* 16, C-51/97 *Réunion européenne v Spliethoff's* 22), 23 (re C-26/91 *Handte v TMCS* 15, C-51/97 *Réunion européenne v Spliethoff's* 17)-27.

[280] C-167/00 *Konsumenteninformation v Henkel;* compare section 1.2 of this chapter, text following note 70.

[281] Idem.

[282] C-167/00 *Konsumenteninformation v Henkel* 32, 33 (re C-89/91 *Shearson*).

[283] C-167/00 *Konsumenteninformation v Henkel* 35 (re 34/82 *Peters v ZNAV* 9,10, 189/87 *Kalfelis v Schröder* 15,16, C-261/90 *Reichert v Dresdner Bank II* 15), and 36 (re *Kalfelis* 17, *Reichert* 16, C-51/97 *Réunion européene v Spliethoff's* 22, C-96/00 *Gabriel* 33).

[284] C-167/00 *Konsumenteninformation v Henkel* 41,50 (see 42-49, on the issue of a preventive action).

The *factor connecting* the dispute to a court, in Article 5, point 3, the notion '*place where the harmful event occurred*', has also given rise to a number of questions, which were most often answered by the Court on the basis of principle-based argumentation. The first and most well-known case, *Bier v Mines de potasse*, was a case of cross-border pollution. As was seen before, it raised the issue of what the expression 'place where the harmful event occurred' in Article 5, point 3, exactly means in case the damage occurred in one place and the event giving rise to it in another. The Court stated that the 'place where the harmful event occurred' is to be interpreted in such a way that the plaintiff should be given the choice to either bring the case before the court of the place where the damage occurred or the court of the place where the event giving rise to it took place.[285] The Court established that each of these two connecting factors can, depending on the circumstances of the case, constitute a significant connecting factor from the viewpoint of jurisdiction and can be particularly helpful from the point of view of evidence and the efficacious conduct of the proceedings.[286]

The Court's decision in *Bier v Mines de potasse* clearly implies a multiplication of the heads of jurisdiction of Article 5. As was seen before, that interpretation conflicts with the principle of legal certainty as to jurisdiction, requiring the avoidance of a multiplicity of courts having jurisdiction as regards one and the same legal relationship, with the principle of legal certainty as to judgments and with the principle of the free movement of judgments.[287] However, in its decision in *Bier v Mines de potasse*, the Court did not refer to any of these considerations, but focused only on the specific principle underlying the jurisdictions under Article 5: the principle of an efficient and sound administration of justice.[288] As was seen above, it held that both connecting factors are helpful from the point of view of evidence and the efficacious conduct of the proceedings.[289]

---

[285] 21/76 *Bier v Mines de potasse* 19.

[286] 21/76 *Bier v Mines de potasse* 11,15,16,17. These considerations as regards the underlying principle of Art. 5, point 3, that a court that has certain practical advantages should be able to decide a case, do not only apply to cases concerned with physical or pecuniary loss or damage, as the Court made clear in *Shevill v Presse Alliance*. They equally apply, and for the same reasons, to cases concerning injury to the reputation and good name of a natural or legal person due to a defamatory publication; compare C-68/93 *Shevill v Presse Alliance* 23. And they are equally relevant, as the Court held in *Konsumenteninformation v Henkel*, to disputes concerning compensation for damage which has already occurred or to actions seeking to prevent the occurrence of damage; compare C-167/00 *Konsumenteninformation v Henkel* 42 (re 21/76 *Bier v Mines de potasse* 18) 43 (re Directive 93/13),46 (re 21/76 *Bier v Mines de potasse* 11,17, C-220/88 *Dumez France v Hessische Landesbank* 17, C-68/93 *Shevill v Presse Alliance* 19, C-364/93 *Marinari v Lloyd's* 10), 47 (re Schlosser Report, OJ 1979 C 59, pp. 71,111), 49 (re Art. 5, point 3 of Regulation No. 44/2001).

[287] See sections 4.2. and 5 of chapter 5, and section 1.1 of chapter 3; compare for example C-220/88 *Dumez France v Hessische Landesbank* 17, (re 21/76 *Bier v Mines de potasse* 10,11),18; and C-256/00 *Besix v Kretzschmar* 27 (re 14/76 *De Bloos v Bouyer* 9, etc.) 34, 35.

[288] 21/76 *Bier v Mines de potasse* 11.

[289] 21/76 *Bier v Mines de potasse* 17, 20-22; compare section 4.2.1 of chapter 5, text following note 124.

In *Shevill v Presse Alliance*, which was also discussed earlier, the Court confirmed its decision in *Bier v Mines de potasse* that the expression 'place where the harmful event occurred' covers both the place where the damage occurred and the place of the event giving rise to it.[290] The Court decided that the notion of 'place where the damage occurred' can, in its turn, be stretched so as to include two or more places as well. The case concerned an action for damages for harm caused to the victim following a distribution of a defamatory newspaper article in several Contracting States. The Court stated that, since the court of the place where the event giving rise to the damage (the place from which the libel was issued and put into circulation) can only be the court of the place where the publisher or newspaper in question is established, that forum will generally coincide with the head of jurisdiction set out in the first paragraph of Article 2. As an alternative, and following *Bier v Mines de potasse*, the Court held that the plaintiff must have the option of bringing the action before the court of the place where the damage occurred, that is, where the events giving rise to the damage produced its harmful effect on the victim, since otherwise Article 5, point 3, would be rendered meaningless.[291] In the case of international libel through the press, the injury caused to the reputation of the person occurs in the places where the publication is distributed, when the victim is known in those places. The injury may thus occur in several states. The Court contended that the courts of each Contracting State in which the defamatory publication was distributed, are territorially the best placed to assess the libel committed in that state and to determine the damage.[292] This implies that on a proper construction of the expression 'place where the harmful event occurred' in Article 5, point 3, the courts of each of these states have jurisdiction to rule on the injury to the victim's reputation in that state (in accordance with the principle that a court that has the advantage of first-hand knowledge of the facts, ease of taking evidence and/or knowledge of the applicable law, should have jurisdiction).[293]

Clearly, both decisions in *Bier v Mines de potasse* and *Shevill v Presse Alliance* constitute a further infringement of the principle that a multiplication of bases of jurisdiction should be avoided – in addition to the infringement resulting from the fact that the plaintiff already has the option to choose between the court of Article 2 and Article 5, point 3. However, in the type of cases just described, the Court apparently attributes more weight to the considerations linked to the principle that jurisdiction should be conferred upon the court that has certain practical advantages, than to the disadvantages of the multiplication of bases of

[290] Compare section 4.2.2 of chapter 5, text following note 149; and see C-68/93 *Shevill v Presse Alliance* 20 (re 21/76 *Bier v Mines de potasse* 24,25), 21 (re *Bier v Mines de potasse* 15,17).

[291] C-68/93 *Shevill v Presse Alliance* 27 (re *Bier v Mines de potasse* 15,17).

[292] C-68/93 *Shevill v Presse Alliance* 19 (re 21/76 *Bier v Mines de potasse* 11; C-220/88 *Dumex France v Hessische Landesbank* 17), 21 (re *Bier v Mines de potasse* 15,17),31.

[293] C-68/93 *Shevill v Presse Alliance* 31-33.

jurisdiction.[294] With regard to these disadvantages, the Court repeated in *Shevill v Presse Alliance* its considerations as regards the Convention's mechanisms as to avoid them: the plaintiff always has the option of bringing his entire claim before the courts either of the defendant's domicile or of the place where the publisher of the defamatory publication is established.[295]

Some other decisions show however that the Court puts limits on how far this notion of the 'place where the damage occurred' may be stretched. In *Dumez France v Hessische Landesbank*, the Court stuck to one of its by now well-known lines of reasoning, when it held that if the efficacious conduct of proceedings is not at stake, Article 5 should be interpreted restrictively in order to avoid a (further) multiplication of courts.[296] The Court recalled that the Convention has expressly demonstrated its hostility towards the attribution of jurisdiction to the courts of the plaintiff's domicile in Article 3, and that Article 5, point 3, constitutes an exception to the general principle underlying Article 2, that disputes should be decided by the court of the defendant's domicile.[297] It then held that despite the fact that the expression 'place where the harmful event occurred' may refer to 'the place where the damage occurred', the latter concept cannot be understood other than as indicating the place where the event giving rise to the damage, and entailing tortious, delictual or quasi-delictual liability, *directly* produced its harmful effects upon the person who is the immediate victim of that event.[298] The term 'place where the damage occurred' is not to include the place where the *indirect* victims of the damage ascertain the repercussions on their own assets.[299]

In *Marinari v Lloyd's*, the Court decided that the term 'place where the damage occurred' also does not refer to the place where the *direct* victim claims to have suffered financial damage which followed on from initial damage and which was suffered by him in another Contracting State.[300] The Court made it clear that it is well aware of the particular significance of Article 5, point 3, in that in light of the principle of a sound administration of justice it is appropriate to confer jurisdiction on a court which has the advantage of first-hand knowledge of the facts and the ease of taking evidence.[301] The choice of the plaintiff, provided by Article 5, point 3, cannot however be extended beyond the particular

[294] And, as we know by now, the multiplication of jurisdiction may conflict with the principle of legal certainty as to jurisdiction and judgments, with the principle of a free movement of judgments and the overall ideal that an entire dispute should be decided, as far as possible, by a single and appropriate court; compare sections 4.2 and 5 of chapter 6, and section 4 of this chapter.

[295] See text following note 151 of section 4.2.2 of chapter 5; compare section 4.2 of this chapter.

[296] C-220/88 *Dumez France v Hessische Landesbank* 18.

[297] C-220/88 *Dumez France v Hessische Landesbank* 16,17.

[298] C-220/88 *Dumez France v Hessische Landesbank* 16,17 (re *Bier v Mines de potasse* 10,11)-20 (re *Bier v Mines de potasse)*-22.

[299] C-220/88 *Dumez France v Hessische Landesbank* 22.

[300] C-364/93 *Marinari v Lloyd's*.

[301] Compare, C-364/93 *Marinari v Lloyd's* 10 (re *Bier v Mines de potasse* 11; *Dumez France* 17; C-68/93 *Shevill* 19)-12.

circumstances which justify it, in particular not if such an extension would negate the general principle of Article 2, and would lead to recognising the jurisdiction of the courts of the plaintiff's domicile (which would be a violation of the principle of the protection of the weaker party due to his procedural position).[302] The principle 'sound administration of justice', underlying Article 5, point 3, could not justify a further infringement of the principle 'avoiding a (further) multiplication of jurisdictions'. In addition, the principle underlying Article 2, pointed in the same direction.

In *Réunion européenne v Spliethoff's*, the case of an international transport operation discussed earlier in this section, the Court also had to answer questions on the interpretation of the term 'place where the harmful event occurred'.[303] The Court decided that, in the event that the place where the damage arose may be difficult or indeed impossible to determine, that place can be understood only as the place where the actual maritime carrier was to deliver the goods.[304] When justifying that decision, the Court referred to reasons of sound administration of justice and the efficacious conduct of proceedings. It held that the place where the actual maritime carrier was to deliver the goods displays a particularly close connecting factor with the dispute as in the type of case at hand.[305] It also referred to the principle of the protection of the defendant who is weaker due to his procedural position, indicating that derogations from Article 2, as in Article 5, point 3, should not be extended beyond the particular circumstances which justify it. The Court held that the term 'place where the harmful event occurred' cannot be construed so extensively as to encompass any place where the adverse consequences can be felt of an event which has already caused damage actually arising elsewhere. And it held that in most cases that would result in attributing jurisdiction to the court of the place of the plaintiff's domicile.[306] When justifying its decision as to its interpretation of the term 'place where the harmful event occurred', the Court furthermore referred to the principle of legal certainty. It held that in a case such as this, where the place where the damage arose may be difficult or indeed impossible to determine, the 'place where the harmful event occurred' could only

---

[302] C-364/93 *Marinari v Lloyd's* 13. In addition, while rejecting several considerations of the German Government, the Court observed that there is no basis for interpreting Art. 5, point 3, by reference to the applicable rules on non-contractual civil liability. Such an interpretation would be incompatible with the objective of a clear and certain attribution of jurisdiction. As was seen before, this is in accordance with the principle of legal certainty as to jurisdiction, requiring that the court should be able readily to decide whether it is competent to hear a case on the basis of the rules of jurisdiction of the Convention; C-364/93 *Marinari v Lloyd's* 19 (re 241/83 *Rösler v Rottwinkel* 23, C-26/91 *Handte v TMCS* 19); and compare section 4.3 of chapter 5, text following note 154; and compare section 1.2 of chapter 5.

[303] Compare text following note 276.

[304] C-51/97 *Réunion européenne v Spliethoff's* 27-37.

[305] C-51/97 *Réunion européenne v Spliethoff's* 27,36.

[306] C-51/97 *Réunion européenne v Spliethoff's* 29,30,34 (re C-220/88 *Dumez France v Hessische Landesbank* 16,19; C-89/91 *Shearson v TVB* 17).

be understood as the place where the actual maritime carrier was to deliver the goods. Another interpretation, by which 'place where the harmful event occurred' is understood as the place of final delivery or the place where the damage was ascertained, would make the determination of the competent court dependent on uncertain factors, and would, as the Court put it, be incompatible with the objective of the Convention to provide for a clear and certain attribution of jurisdiction (in accordance with the principle of legal certainty).[307]

C Art. 5(4) R 5(4)

Article 5, point 4
There are only a few cases in which reference is made to Article 5, point 4. That Article provides for the jurisdiction of a court, concerning a civil claim for damages or restitution which is based on an act giving rise to criminal proceedings when that particular court is seised of those criminal proceedings. None of these cases are directly involved with the interpretation of Article 5, point 4, neither with regard to its substantive scope, nor with regard to the concept containing the territorial link required.[308] Nonetheless, it must be assumed that the principle that disputes should be decided by a court that has certain practical advantages underlies Article 5, point 4. The territorial link required by this principle is the place where the court having jurisdiction to entertain the criminal proceedings, sits. In order to secure that a civil claim can always be brought before an appropriate court from the perspective of a sound administration of justice and the efficacious conduct of the proceedings, such a claim can be brought before the court of the place where the harmful event occurred, by virtue of Article 5, point 3, as well as for the criminal court having jurisdiction to entertain the criminal proceedings in which the civil claim plays a role, by virtue of Article 5, point 4.[309] We assume that if the Court would have to interpret this provision, it would normally use principle-based reasoning, in order to justify its autonomous interpretations.

C Art. 2 R 2
C Art. 5(5) R 5(5)

Article 5, point 5
Article 5, point 5 provides that in case of a dispute arising out of the operations of a branch, agency or other establishment, a person domiciled in a Contracting State may be sued in the courts of the place in which the branch, agency or other establishment is situated. The Court's case law as regards the interpretation of this provision is consistent with its method of reasoning which is characteristic of

[307] C-51/97 *Réunion européenne v Spliethoff's* 33,34 (re C-364/93 *Marinari v Lloyd's* 19),36; and compare section 4.1 and 4.3 of chapter 5.

[308] 120/79 *Cavel v Cavel II*; C-172/91 *Sonntag v Waidmann*; compare section 3 of chapter 5, in particular note 81; and 157/80 *Rinkau* and C-7/98 *Krombach v Bamberski*; in particular section 4 of chapter 4, text following note 61.

[309] Compare Jenard Report, OJ 1979 C 59/26.

the case law under Article 5 in general. The Court does not so much refer to the principle directly underlying this provision, but most often to other principles, mainly the principle of legal certainty, requiring respect for the wording of the provision, clarity as to rules of jurisdiction and the avoidance of a (further) multiplication of jurisdiction. Also, the Court refers to the principle of the protection of the party weaker due to his procedural position, which underlies Article 2, and to the division of jurisdiction, as laid down in Article 5. This becomes clear from the Court's decision in *Somafer v Saar-Ferngas.*[310]

The questions on the interpretation of Article 5, point 5, put to the Court in the *Somafer v Saar-Ferngas* case, were related to an action which was brought by a German undertaking against a French undertaking with a registered office on French territory and a place of contact in Germany described on its notepaper as 'representation for Germany'. The action was concerned with the recovery of expenses incurred by the German undertaking to protect gas mains belonging to it from any damage which might have been caused by demolition work which the French undertaking was carrying out in the vicinity of these gas mains on behalf of the Saarland. In answering the questions whether the terms constituting the *territorial link* and *substantive scope* of this special jurisdiction should have an independent interpretation and, if so, how these terms are to be understood, the Court, first of all, stated that the words 'dispute arising out of the operations of a branch, agency or other establishment' in Article 5, point 5, indeed require an independent interpretation.[311] In arriving at an autonomous interpretation, the Court used principled-based reasoning. The Court referred to the system of jurisdictional rules, in particular to the relation between Article 2 and Article 5, and held that the justification for the exceptions to Article 2 contained in Article 5, is solely in the interests of a sound administration of justice and the efficacious conduct of proceedings.[312] In addition, the Court observed that a multiplication of the bases of jurisdiction in one and the same case is not desired and that it is therefore necessary and in accordance with the principle of legal certainty and the legal protection of persons within the Community to avoid a wide and multifarious interpretation of these exceptions.[313] The Court stated that, since these exceptions to Article 2 are based on the existence of a particularly close connecting factor between a dispute and the competent court, an autonomous interpretation must show that special link.[314] Although the Court did not expressly mention it, this is also in accordance with the principle of legal certainty as to jurisdiction, in that a plaintiff should be able easily to identify the court before which he may bring an action and a defendant reasonably to foresee the court before which he may be

[310] 33/78 *Somafer v Saar-Ferngas*; compare text following note 187 in this section.

[311] 33/78 *Somafer v Saar-Ferngas* 4,5,6; compare section 1.1 of chapter 5.

[312] 33/78 *Somafer v Saar-Ferngas* 7.

[313] 33/78 *Somafer v Saar-Ferngas* 7; compare section 1 of chapter 2; section 1.1 of chapter 3; sections 4.2 and 5 of chapter 5; and section 1.1 of this chapter.

[314] 33/78 *Somafer v Saar-Ferngas* 8,11.

sued.[315] The Court then pointed out that an interpretation of the concept operations of 'a branch, agency or other establishment' that, without difficulty, shows the special link required in Article 5, point 5, must take account of the material signs enabling the existence of the branch, agency or other establishment to be easily recognized and the connection that there is between the local entity and the claim directed against the parent body established in another Contracting State.[316] An interpretation of that concept, which implies a place of business which has the appearance of permanency, can be considered to be in accordance with the objectives and principles underlying the Convention, if it covers the extension of a parent body, having a management and being materially equipped to negotiate business with third parties, so that the latter do not have to deal directly with such a parent body but may transact business at the place of business constituting the extension.[317]

In that same judgment, the Court also decided, without any further justification, that the concept 'operations' comprises 'on the one hand actions relating to rights and contractual or non-contractual obligations concerning the management properly so-called of the agency, branch or other establishment itself, such as those concerning the situation of the building where such entity is established or the local engagement of staff to work there.' It also comprises 'actions relating to undertakings which have been entered into at the place of business in the name of the parent body ... and which must be performed in the Contracting State where the place of business is established and also actions concerning non-contractual obligations arising from the activities in which the branch, agency or other establishment ... has engaged at the place in which it is established on behalf of the parent body.'[318] We assume, though, that the Court considered this interpretation to be in line with the principle of a sound administration of justice, particularly with the principle that disputes should be heard by the courts that have the advantage of first-hand knowledge of the facts, ease of taking evidence and/or knowledge of the applicable law.

Taking into account the above-mentioned considerations as regards the interpretation of the expression 'dispute arising out of the "operations" of a branch, agency or other establishment' in Article 5, point 5, the Court decided in *Lloyd's v Campenon*, despite what *Somafer v Saar-Ferngas* might have suggested, that that expression does not presuppose that the undertakings in question entered into by the branch in the name of its parent body are to be performed in the Contracting State in which the branch is established. The requirement of a close connect-

[315] Compare section 4.1 of chapter 5.

[316] 33/78 *Somafer v Saar-Ferngas* 11.

[317] 33/78 *Somafer v Saar-Ferngas* 12.

[318] 33/78 *Somafer v Saar-Ferngas* 13. Notice that a more restrictive interpretation could result in a fragmentation of proceedings, which would be in conflict with the principle of legal certainty as to jurisdiction and judgments, see sections 4.2 and 5 of chapter 5; see also section 4 of this chapter, concerning the overall ideal of hearing an entire dispute in a single (and appropriate) court.

ing factor can be considered to be fulfilled without the condition that the undertakings in question are to be performed in the Contracting State in which the branch is established.[319] As the Court stated, an interpretation of the concept 'operations' that would require that condition to be fulfilled, would not only render Article 5, point 5, almost wholly redundant, but would also duplicate Article 5, point 1, since that provision allows the plaintiff to bring an action in contract at the court of the place of performance of the obligation in question.[320] From these considerations it appears that the Court took account of the scheme of the Convention, in particular of the division of jurisdictions in Article 5, which is inspired by the principle of an efficient and sound administration of justice.

The conditions, as stipulated by the Court in *Somafer v Saar-Ferngas* with regard to the interpretation of the concept of 'branch, etc.', implying that, among other things, account has to be taken of the material signs enabling the existence of the branch, agency or other establishment to be easily recognized, may also be satisfied when the undertaking which acted as an extension of a company established in another Contracting State is not a subsidiary of that company but is an independent company or even its parent company, as the Court held in *Schotte v Rothschild*.[321] The Court justified its decision in this case by arguing that the close connection between the dispute and the court called upon to hear it must be assessed not only on the basis of the legal relations between legal entities established in different Contracting States but also by reference to the way in which these two undertakings behave in their business relations and present themselves *vis-à-vis* third parties in their commercial dealings: third parties doing business with the establishment acting as an extension of another company must be able to rely on the *appearance* thus created. They should be able to recognize that establishment as an establishment of the other company even if, from the point of view of company law, the two companies are independent of each other.[322] Notice that such an interpretation is assumed to contribute to legal certainty as to jurisdiction, in particular to the foreseeability of jurisdiction.[323]

The concepts of 'branch, agency or other establishment' should not be extended to the grantee of an exclusive concession. As the Court held in *De Bloos v Bouyer*, a grantee cannot be regarded as being at the head of a branch, agency or other establishment of the grantor, if he is 'subject neither to the control nor to the direction of the grantor'.[324] The Court referred in this case to the purpose and the wording of Article 5, point 5.[325] An independent commercial agent who is basically free to organize his own work and hours of work also does not have the

[319] C-439/93 *Lloyd's v Campenon* 22.

[320] C-439/93 *Lloyd's v Campenon* 17,18,21 (re Jenard Report, OJ 1979 C 59, p. 1), 22.

[321] 218/86 *Schotte v Rothschild* 9-11, 15-17.

[322] 218/86 *Schotte v Rothschild* 14-17.

[323] See section 4.1 of chapter 5, text following note 110.

[324] 14/76 *De Bloos v Bouyer* 20-23.

[325] 14/76 *De Bloos v Bouyer* 21.

character of a branch, agency or other establishment, as the Court stated in *Blanckaert v Trost*. Such an agent *appears* to third parties as an easily discernible extension of the parent body, as it is clear that the required dependency on the direction and control of the parent body is not established.[326] Although the Court did not make any express reference to the principles of legal certainty as to jurisdiction, its decision can be considered to be in line with the principle that a plaintiff should be able easily to identify the court before which he may bring an action and the principle that a defendant should be able reasonably to foresee the court before which he may be sued.[327]

C Art. 5 (6 and 7) R 5 (6 and 7)

Article 5, points 6 and 7
There is no case law as regards the interpretation of Article 5, points 6 and 7, that confirms that the principle that courts that have certain practical advantages should be able to decide the type of cases mentioned in these provisions, underlies these Articles.[328] We assume, however, that it does. We refer to the general observations of the Court in *Besix v Kretschmar*, *Konsumenteninformation v Henkel* and *Somafer v Saar-Ferngas* and to the wording of these provisions which express the required direct or territorial link.[329]

3.1.2 *Jurisdiction as to provisional measures under Article 24*

C Arts. 2,5 to 17(18)	R 2,5 to 23(24)
C Art. 24	R 31

The principle that courts that have the practical advantage of first-hand knowledge of the facts, ease of taking evidence and/or knowledge of the applicable law should have jurisdiction also plays a role in the interpretation of Article 24. That provision allows the courts of a Contracting State to order provisional or protective measures under the law of that state, even if, under the Convention, the courts of another Contracting State have jurisdiction as to the substance of the matter. The Court's case law as regards Article 24 clearly shows that the principle that courts that have certain practical advantages should be able to decide a case, does apply in cases in which provisional or protective measures are sought, particularly where that court has no jurisdiction by virtue of Article 2 or Articles 5 to (17)18.[330]

---

[326] 139/80 *Blanckaert v Trost* 9 (re 14/76 *De Bloos v Bouyer*), 10,11 (re 33/78 *Somafer v Saar-Ferngas*)-13.

[327] Compare text following notes 95 and 101 of chapter 5.

[328] Both provisions were added by Art. 5 of the (4) of the 1978 Accession Convention.

[329] See notes 185, 186, 187 in this section, section 3.1.1.

[330] 143/78 *Cavel v Cavel I*; 120/79 *Cavel v Cavel II*; 125/79 *Denilauler v Couchet Frères*; 25/81 *C.H.W. v G.J.H.*; C-261/90 *Reichert v Dresdner Bank II*; C-391/95 *Van Uden v Deco-Line*; C-99/96 *Mietz v Intership*.

The Court's judgment in *Denilauler v Couchet Frères* is illustrative in this respect. In that judgment the Court emphasized, with respect to the function attributed to Article 24:

> 'that the granting of provisional or protective measures requires particular care on the part of the court and detailed knowledge of the actual circumstances in which the measure is to take effect.'[331]

The Court then continued that the courts of the Contracting State where the assets subject to the measures sought are located, is best able to assess the circumstances which may lead to the grant or refusal of the measures sought or to the laying down of procedures and conditions which the plaintiff must observe in order to guarantee the provisional and protective character of the measures ordered.[332] Following a similar line of reasoning as in *Denilauler v Couchet Frères*, the Court held in *Van Uden v Deco-Line*, that:

> 'the granting of provisional or protective measures on the basis of Article 24 is conditional on, inter alia, the existence of a real connecting link between the subject-matter of the measures sought.'[333]

Notice that the jurisdiction of the court of the Contracting State before which provisional or protective measures are sought, in those cases that the court has jurisdiction as to the substance of a case in accordance with Articles 2 and 5 to 17(18), is assumed to be in accordance with one of the sub-principles flowing from the main principle that disputes should be decided by an appropriate court.[334] By contrast, in a case in which the court has jurisdiction solely by virtue of Article 24, the principle of an appropriate court is not yet met. We assume that this is the reason why the Court stipulated, in *Van Uden v Deco-Line* and *Mietz v Intership*, that the measures ordered in such cases must relate to specific assets of the defendant located or to be located within the territorial jurisdiction of the court to which application for such an order is made.[335] The jurisdiction of the court would then be justified by the principle that courts that have the practical advantage of first-hand knowledge of the facts, ease of taking evidence and/or knowledge of the applicable law should be able to decide the case.

---

[331] 125/79 *Denilauler v Couchet Frères* 15.

[332] 125/79 *Denilauler v Couchet Frères* 16.

[333] C-391/95 *Van Uden v Deco-Line* 39 (re *Denilauler v Couchet Frères* 16),40; C-99/96 *Mietz v Intership* 42.

[334] C-391/95 *Van Uden v Deco-Line* 19,20,22 39 (re *Denilauler v Couchet Frères* 16),40; C-99/96 *Mietz v Intership* 40-43.

[335] C-99/96 *Mietz v Intership* 40 (re *Van Uden* 19)-43.

The principle that courts that have the practical advantage of first-hand knowledge of the facts, ease of taking evidence and/or knowledge of the applicable law should be able to decide a case, as far as it underlies Article 24, weighed in relation to other principles

Clearly the principle of a sound administration of justice and the efficacious conduct of proceedings, requiring that courts that have certain practical advantages should be able to hear a case, as far as it underlies Article 24, cannot be considered to be absolute. This is particularly so where the court opted for by the plaintiff, has no jurisdiction as to the substance of the case in accordance with Article 2 or Articles 5 to 17(18).

This is already evident from *(a)* the wording and the scope of the Convention, which are to be respected in the light of the principle of legal certainty, from the substantive scope of Article 24, as defined by the Court's case law and from the Court's case law in which the sub-principle is weighed in relation to *(b)* other principles, particularly the principle of the 'protection of the rights of the defence'.

As regards the substantive scope of Article 24, the Court observed in *Cavel v Cavel*, that judicial decisions authorizing provisional or protective measures – such as the placing under seal or the freezing of assets of the spouses – in the course of proceedings for divorce do not fall within the *substantive scope of the Convention* as defined in Article 1 thereof.[336] Those measures concern or are closely connected with either questions of the status of the persons involved in the divorce proceedings or proprietary legal relations resulting directly from the matrimonial relationship or the dissolution thereof.[337] The inclusion of provisional or protective measures within the scope of the Convention is to be determined not by the nature of these measures but by the nature of the rights which they serve to protect. Whether the Convention applies to these rights is, as was seen before, to be determined either by reason of the legal relationship between the parties to the action or of the subject-matter of the action, in accordance with legal certainty as to the substantive scope of the Convention.[338] When justifying its decision in *Cavel v Cavel*, the Court explicitly referred to the wording of the Convention, in particular the wording of Articles 1 and 24 (in accordance with the principle of legal certainty, requiring respect for the linguistic boundaries of the Convention).[339] As regards the expression 'provisional, including protective, measures', constituting the substantive scope of Article 24, the Court has drawn the conclusion from the substantive scope of the Convention that these measures

[336] 143/78 *Cavel v Cavel I* 10.
[337] 143/78 *Cavel v Cavel I* 7.
[338] Compare section 3 of chapter 5, text following note 75.
[339] 143/78 *Cavel v Cavel I* 6,9.

may serve to safeguard a variety of rights as long as they concern "civil and commercial matters".[340]

In *Reichert v Dresdner Bank II*, the Court confirmed this line of reasoning from *Cavel v Cavel* in that provisional or protective measures may serve to safeguard a variety of rights.[341] It also recalled its reasoning in *Denilauler v Couchet Frères* as regards the function of Article 24, in that the granting of this type of measure requires particular care on the part of the court and detailed knowledge of the actual circumstances in which the measure is to take effect, by which the Court implicitly took account of the principle that courts that have certain practical advantages should be able to decide on a case.[342] However, as regards an action such as the *action paulienne*, the Court stated that it could not be described as a provisional or protective measure within the meaning of Article 24, since it does not seek to preserve a factual or legal situation pending a decision of the court having jurisdiction as to the substance of the matter.[343] In *Van Uden v Deco-Line*, the Court again referred to the line of argument in *Cavel v Cavel*, that as follows from the rather broad (substantive) scope of the Convention, provisional or protective measures that fall within that scope may serve to safeguard a variety of rights.[344] However, Article 24 cannot be relied on to bring within the scope of the Convention measures relating to matters which are excluded from it.[345] The Court pointed out, though, that despite the fact that arbitration is clearly excluded from the scope of the Convention, provisional measures ordered in parallel with arbitration proceedings which are not concerned with arbitration itself but with the protection of rights that are covered by the Convention's scope, can be considered as provisional measures within the meaning of Article 24.[346]

As regards the *substantive scope of Article 24*, 'provisional or protective measures', the Court stated in *Reichert v Dresdner Bank II*, that provisional or protective measures are intended to preserve a factual or legal situation so as to safeguard rights, pending a decision of the court having jurisdiction as to the substance of the matter.[347] The Court did not justify its autonomous interpretation, neither by principle-based reasoning nor by reference to the general principles which stem from the corpus of national legal systems as a whole. In *Van Uden v Deco-Line*, the Court held that it is not possible to rule out in advance that the interim payment of a contractual consideration, even in an amount corresponding

[340] 143/78 *Cavel v Cavel I* 8; C-261/90 *Reichert v Dresdner Bank II* 32 (re *Cavel v Cavel*),34;C-391/95 *Van Uden v Deco-Line* 37; compare C-99/96 *Mietz v Intership* 34-36.

[341] C-261/90 *Reichert v Dresdner Bank II* 32 (re 143/78 *Cavel v Cavel I* 8).

[342] C-261/90 *Reichert v Dresdner Bank II* 33 (re *Denilauler* 15,16).

[343] C-261/90 *Reichert v Dresdner Bank II* 35.

[344] C-391/95 *Van Uden v Deco-Line* 33 (re *Reichert v Dresdner Bank II* 32).

[345] C-391/95 *Van Uden v Deco-Line* 30 (re 143/78 *Cavel v Cavel I* 9).

[346] C-391/95 *Van Uden v Deco-Line* 31 (re C-190/89 *Rich v Impianti* 18), 32 (re Expert Report OJ 1979 C 59, pp. 92-93), 33 (re C-261/90 *Reichert v Dresdner Bank II* 32),34.

[347] C-261/90 *Reichert v Dresdner Bank II* 34.

to that sought as the principal relief, may be necessary in order to ensure the practical effect of the decision on the substance of the case. It could fall within the provision's scope: 'provisional or protective measures'. However, if the plaintiff is entitled to secure interim payment before the courts of the plaintiff's domicile, by virtue of Article 24 only, the provisional or protective character of such a measure is to be safeguarded, in that repayment to the defendant of the sum awarded must be guaranteed in these cases.[348] Although the Court did not expressly refer to the principle of the protection of the rights of the defence, we may consider this requirement to be a consequence of that principle.[349]

The principle of the protection of the rights of the defence was clearly also at stake in *Mietz v Intership*, although the Court did not expressly refer to that right. The Court found it necessary to stress that the jurisdiction laid down in Article 24 is limited and may not result in the circumvention of the rules on jurisdiction as to the substance set out in Articles 2 and 5 to 18. The Court held:

> 'the fact that the defendant appears before the court dealing with interim measures in the context of fast procedures intended to grant provisional or protective measures in case of urgency and which do not prejudice the examination of the substance cannot, by itself, suffice to confer on that court, by virtue of Article 18 of the Convention, unlimited jurisdiction to order any provisional or protective measure which the court might consider appropriate if it had jurisdiction under the Convention as to the substance of the matter.'[350]

In light of the system of jurisdictional rules, the general scheme and the principles underlying the Convention, such a court cannot be considered as an appropriate court. Under these circumstances, it cannot be assumed that the appearance of the defendant is based on his own free will. In such a situation, the principle of the protection of the defence overrides the principle of party autonomy underlying Article 18, particularly where it is not evident that the principle of a sound administration of justice is met and certain conditions meant to safeguard the provisional or protective character of such measures are fulfilled.

Finally, the principle of the protection of the rights of the defence was expressly referred to in relation to the interpretation of Article 24 in the *Denilauler v Couchet Frères* case.[351] The Court, as was seen before, decided that as regards the recognition and enforcement of provisional or protective measures, these measures must have been ordered in the state of origin pursuant to adversary proceedings, in order to fulfil the conditions imposed by title III of the Convention on the recognition and the enforcement of judicial decisions.[352]

---

[348] C-391/95 *Van Uden v Deco-Line* 45 (re C-393/96 *Antonissen v Council and Commission* 37)-48; C-99/96 *Mietz v Intership* 42.

[349] Compare chapter 4.

[350] C-99/96 *Mietz v Intership* 52.

[351] 125/79 *Denilauler v Couchet Frères* 13,17.

[352] 125/79 *Denilauler v Couchet Frères* 13-18; see section 3 of chapter 4, text following note 48.

3.1.3 *Exclusive jurisdiction under Article 16*

C Art. 2	R 2	C Art. 6	R 6	C Art. 17	R 23
C Art. 5	R 5	C Art. 16	R 22	C Art. 18	R 24

The principle of a 'sound administration of justice' in that courts that have the practical advantage of first-hand knowledge of the facts, ease of taking evidence and/or knowledge of the applicable law should hear the case, also underlies Article 16. That provision makes a number of exceptions to the general rule under Article 2, by granting exclusive jurisdiction to the courts in certain well-defined situations, regardless of the domicile of the defendant or the plaintiff. It does so on the basis of the location of immovable property, the seat of a company (or legal person or association), an entry in a public register, or the place where a judgment has been or is to be enforced.[353]

The ratio of these exclusive jurisdictions was stressed by the Jenard Report. In that Report it was stated, in particular with regard to Article 16, point 1, that conferring exclusive jurisdiction on the court of the place where the immovable property is situated is considered to be in the interest of a sound administration of justice.[354] The Jenard Report states in this respect:

> 'this type of dispute often entails checks, enquiries and expert examinations which have to be made on the spot. Moreover, the matter is often governed in part by customary practices which are not generally known except in the courts of the place, or possibly of the country, where the immovable property is situated. Finally, the system adopted also takes into account the need to make entries in land registers located where the property is situated.'[355]

It is evident from the Court's case law that the Court also considers the assignment of exclusive jurisdiction to a national court, by virtue of Article 16, to be in the interests of a sound administration of justice.[356] The Court has consistently held that the courts which are given such an exclusive jurisdiction are those which are the best placed to deal with the disputes in question. As the Court put it in *Sanders v Van der Putte*:

> 'As regards the matters listed under subparagraphs (2), (3), (4) and (5) of that Article (Article 16, *ebjp*) it is clear that the courts which are given exclusive jurisdiction are those which are the best placed to deal with the disputes in question.'[357]

---

[353] Compare, for example, 220/84 *Autoteile v Malhé* 16; C-261/90 *Reichert v Dresdner Bank II* 24 (re *Autoteile* 16).

[354] Art. 16, point 1, has been amended by Art. 6 of the 1989 Accession Convention, compare Almeida Cruz Report, OJ 1990 C 189, No. 25; Jenard/Möller Report, No. 49.

[355] See Jenard Report OJ 1979 C 59 p. 35.

[356] 73/77 *Sanders v Van der Putte* 17; and, C-280/90 *Hacker v Euro-Relais* 12 (re *Sanders v Van der Putte* 17,18).

[357] Compare, 73/77 *Sanders v Van der Putte* 11; and C-280/90 *Hacker v Euro-Relais* 12.

The Court then continued, referring to Article 16, point 1:

> 'The same applies to the assignment of exclusive jurisdiction to the courts of the Contracting State in which the property is situated in matters relating to rights in rem in, or tenancies of, immovable property. In fact, actions concerning rights in rem in immovable property are to be judged according to the rules of the state in which the immovable property is situated since the disputes which arise result frequently in checks, inquiries and expert assessments which must be carried out on the spot, with the result that the assignment of exclusive jurisdiction satisfies the need for the proper administration of justice.'[358]

As is clear from the scheme of the Convention, Article 16, just as Articles 5 and 6, constitutes an exception to the general principle laid down in Article 2 of the Convention, conferring jurisdiction upon the defendant's home court. Contrary to Articles 5 and 6, though, the exceptions laid down in Article 16 are provided by means of exclusive jurisdictions, which are not at the option of the plaintiff and can neither be overruled by an agreement of the parties conferring jurisdiction to a forum of their choice, by virtue of Article 17, nor by entering an appearance, by virtue of Article 18.

When comparing the exclusive jurisdictions of Article 16 with Articles 5 and 6, it seems that Article 16 cannot be explained merely by reasons related to the sound administration of justice. We assume that the public interests of Contracting States are an important explanatory factor. The Jenard Report and the Court's case law seem to confirm this.[359] Occasionally, the Court has also referred to the protection of the weaker party from a socio-economic point of view, in particular in relation to tenancies.[360] Nonetheless, when answering questions on the interpretation of Article 16, it primarily focuses on what it considers the essential reason for the rules of exclusive jurisdiction laid down in that provision: the practical advantages of first-hand knowledge of the facts, ease of taking evidence, and/or knowledge of the applicable law pertaining to a court that has a particularly close connection with the dispute.[361]

The majority of the decisions of the Court, in which reference is made to the essential reason for conferring exclusive jurisdiction on the courts of the Contracting States, concern proceedings which have as their object 'tenancies of immovable property', as for example in *Rösler v Rottwinkel*. The Court considered that:

---

[358] 73/77 *Sanders v Van der Putte* 12,13; compare C-294/92 *Webb v Webb* 17 (re *Sanders* 13).

[359] Compare Jenard Report, p. 35; and see 73/77 *Sanders v Van der Putte* 14; 133/81 *Ivenel v Schwab* 16; 241/83 *Rösler v Rottwinkel* 10,12; 266/85 *Shenavai v Kreischer* 10; C-292/93 *Lieber v Göbel* 20. At least on several occasions, the substantive issues involved in the exclusive jurisdictions of Art. 16, were considered to be of social importance to the Contracting States and were assumed to be related to questions of national sovereignty.

[360] Compare 133/81 *Ivenel v Schwab* 16; see also 241/83 *Rösler v Rottwinkel* 12.

[361] 220/84 *Autoteile v Malhé* 16; C-412/98 *Josi Reinsurance v UGIC* 46.

'The raison d'être of the exclusive jurisdiction conferred by Article 16(1) ... is the fact that tenancies are closely bound up with the law of immovable property and with the provisions, generally of a mandatory character, governing its use, such as legislation controlling the level of rents and protecting the rights of tenants, including tenant farmers. Article 16(1) seeks to ensure a rational allocation of jurisdiction by opting for a solution whereby the court having jurisdiction is determined on the basis of its proximity to the property since that court is in a better position to obtain first-hand knowledge of the facts relating to the creation of tenancies and to the performance of the terms thereof.' [362]

In the rare case in which, as in *Scherrens v Maenhout*, the immovable property is situated in two Contracting States, the Court decided that exclusive jurisdiction over the immovable property situated in each of these Contracting States is held by the courts of both states.[363] Notice that this decision clearly results in an infringement of the principle that a (further) multiplication of jurisdiction should be avoided. Such an infringement may not only come into conflict with the principle of the foreseeability of jurisdiction, but might also raise the risk of irreconcilable decisions and may therefore come into conflict with the principle of free movement of judgments.[364]

The principle that disputes should be decided by a court that has the advantage of first-hand knowledge of the facts, ease of taking evidence and/or knowledge of the applicable law, as far as it underlies Article 16, weighed in relation to other principles

C Art. 2	R 2	C Art. 25	R 32
C Art. 16	R 22	C Art. 28	R 35

The principle that disputes should be attributed to a court that has certain practical advantages, as far as it underlies Article 16, is well-established under the Convention and has been confirmed by the Court's case law. This clearly follows from the system of jurisdictional rules, in that Article 16 overrides all the other sub-principles that flow from the fourth main principle that disputes should be decided by an appropriate court. An infringement of these exclusive jurisdictions of the court of the state of the original proceedings can also be a threshold to the recognition and enforcement of the judgment given in that state in other Contracting States. As appears from Article 28, first paragraph, the principle that disputes should be attributed to a court that has certain practical advantages, as far as

362 241/83 *Rösler v Rottwinkel* 19,20; 158/87 *Scherrens v Maenhout* 10; C-115/88 *Reichert v Dresdner Bank I* 10; C-280/90 *Hacker v Euro-Relais* 8, 9; C-294/92 *Webb v Webb* 16,17; C-8/98 *Dansommer v Götz* 27 (re Jenard Report OJ 1979 C 59 p. 35; *Sanders* 13; *Reichert v Dresdner Bank I* 10).

363 158/87 *Scherrens v Maenhout* 9-16.

364 Compare section 1.1 of chapter 3, and sections 4.2 and 5 of chapter 5.

it underlies Article 16, even overrides the principle of free movement of judgments.

However, there are limits as to the type of cases to which Article 16 applies. When interpreting terms and concepts of Article 16, the Court follows the following lines of reasoning, which in most cases result in a restrictive interpretation of these terms and concepts. First, as is typical for the Court's interpretation of the Convention's concepts, except for its decision in the *Tessili v Dunlop* case, the Court has consistently held with regard to the concepts used in Article 16 that, in order to ensure that the rights and obligations arising out of the Convention are as equal and as uniform as possible, an independent definition of these concepts must be given.[365] As we know by now, such an interpretation meets the principle of legal certainty underlying the Convention as a whole, and is usually determined by means of principle-based reasoning.

Next, we recall here that, as already appears from the scheme of the Convention, exceptions to the general rule of Article 2 are allowed but that, according to the Court, these exceptions are only admitted in certain well-defined cases and are to be construed restrictively.[366] Consequently, the principle underlying Article 16 is weighed in relation to the principle underlying Article 2. The following quotation, taken from *Autoteile v Malhé*, is illustrative in this respect:

> 'In order to resolve that question it is necessary to have regard to the general scheme of the Convention, paying particular attention to the relationship between Article 2 and Article 16. According to Article 2, persons domiciled in a Contracting State are to be sued in the courts of that state. That provision is intended to protect the rights of the defendant; it serves as a counterpoise to the facilities provided by the Convention with regard to the recognition and enforcement of foreign judgments ... Article 16 of the Convention makes a number of exceptions to that general rule by granting exclusive jurisdiction to the courts of a Contracting State other than that specified under Article 2 in proceedings which have a particular connection with that other state, on the basis of the location of immovable property, the seat of a company, an entry in a public register or, in the case of paragraph (5), the place where a judgment is to be enforced. It follows from the specificity of the connection required by Article 16 that a party cannot make use of the jurisdiction conferred by Article 16(5) on the courts of the place of enforcement in order to bring before those courts a dispute which falls within the jurisdiction of the courts of another Contracting State under Article 2. The use for such a purpose of the application to oppose enforcement is contrary to the division of jurisdiction which the Convention intended to establish between the Court of the defendant's domicile and the court of the place of enforcement.'[367]

The Court then decided that to plead a set-off between the right whose enforcement is being sought and a claim over which the courts of that state would have

---

[365] Compare 288/82 *Duijnstee v Goderbauer* 19; C-115/88 *Reichert v Dresdner Bank I* 8 (re 73/77 *Sanders v Van der Putte*; 288/82 *Duijnstee v Goderbauer*).

[366] 220/84 *Autoteile v Malhé* 15, 16; C-412/98 *Josi Reinsurance v UGIC* 35, 36.

[367] 220/84 *Autoteile v Malhé* 14-17; compare, C-261/90 *Reichert v Dresdner Bank II* 24.

no jurisdiction if it were raised independently, is not made possible by Article 16, point 5.[368]

The Court also referred to other principles underlying other rules of jurisdiction, when it argued, in more general terms, that a restrictive interpretation of Article 16 accords with the division of jurisdiction as made by the Convention. We recall here that this division of jurisdiction is based on the main principle that disputes should be decided by an appropriate court and the weighing and balancing of all the sub-principles that flow from that main principle against each other. For that reason, too, Article 16 must not be given a wider interpretation than is required by its underlying principle. As the Court put it in *Sanders v Van der Putte*:

> 'the assignment, in the interests of the proper administration of justice, of exclusive jurisdiction to the courts of one Contracting State in accordance with Article 16 of the Convention results in depriving the parties of the choice of the forum which would otherwise be theirs and, in certain cases, results in their being brought before a court which is not that of the domicile of any of them.'[369]

Taking account of the above-mentioned considerations with regard to the interpretation of Article 16, it is clear from the Court's case law that as regards *the substantive scope* of these exclusive jurisdictions, there are limits: Article 16 must not be given a broader interpretation than is required by its objective, but an interpretation that would deprive Article 16 of its effect cannot be accepted either.[370] This principle-based reasoning can be recognized in the following cases.

In *Sanders v Van der Putte*, the Court decided that the concept '*matters relating to tenancies of immovable property*', constituting the substantive scope of Article 16, point 1, must not be interpreted as including an agreement to rent, under a usufructuary lease, a retail business carried on in immovable property rented from a third person by the lessor.[371] The Court thereby first referred to the system of jurisdictional rules, which implies that Article 16 is an exception to the general principle laid down in Article 2, and to the exclusive nature of the jurisdiction laid down in that provision.[372] Next, the Court referred to the underlying principle of Article 16 itself, the principle of a sound administration of justice, as well as to the effect of applying that principle with a view to the exclusive nature of the jurisdictions provided in that provision. The assignment of exclusive jurisdiction to the courts of the Contracting States, by virtue of Article 16, results in depriving the parties of the choice of the forum which would otherwise be theirs

[368] 220/84 *Autoteile v Malhé* 19.

[369] 73/77 *Sanders v Van der Putte* 17; compare C-8/98 *Dansommer v Götz* 21 (re *Sanders v Van der Putte*17,18, C-115/88 *Reichert v Dresdner Bank I* 9, C-292/93 *Lieber v Göbel* 12).

[370] 73/77 *Sanders v Van der Putte* 18; compare 288/82 *Duijnstee v Goderbauer* 23; C-115/88 *Reichert v Dresdner Bank I* 9; C-280/90 *Hacker v Euro-Relais* 12.

[371] 73/77 *Sanders v Van der Putte* 19.

[372] 73/77 *Sanders v Van der Putte* 8,9,10.

and, in certain cases, results in their being brought before a court which is not that of the domicile of any of them.[373] For all these reasons, Article 16 must not be given a wider interpretation than is required by their objective.[374] In *Hacker v Euro-Relais*, the Court decided that Article 16 does not apply to a contract concluded between a travel agency and a customer in the place where they are both domiciled, and providing a service concerning a short-term holiday accommodation, but also including a range of other services.[375] After having recalled the *raison d' être* of the exclusive jurisdiction conferred by Article 16, point 1, and the effect of applying that principle, the Court consistently held that Article 16 must not be given a wider interpretation than is required by its objective.[376]

With regard to the concept '*proceedings which have as their object rights in rem in immovable property*' under Article 16, point 1, also constituting the substantive scope of Article 16, point 1, the Court follows a similar line of reasoning. Illustrative in this respect is the Court's judgment in the *Reichert v Dresdner* case.[377] In that judgment the Court decided that Article 16, point 1, does not encompass the *action paulienne*, since such an action is based on the creditor's personal claim against the debtor and seeks to protect whatever security he may have over the debtor's estate: an action whereby a creditor seeks to have a disposition of a right *in rem* in immovable property rendered ineffective as against himself on the ground that it was fraudulently made by his debtor does not fall within the scope of Article 16, point 1.[378] When justifying that decision, the Court recalled that an independent definition must be given to the Convention's concepts, that Article 16 must not be given a wider interpretation than is required by its objective, in order not to deprive the parties of the choice of forum which would otherwise be theirs, and that the exclusive jurisdictions of this provision were provided, mainly, for reasons of first-hand knowledge of the facts, proximity of evidence and/or law.[379] Since the hearing of an *action paulienne* does not involve the assessment of facts or the application of rules and practices of the *locus rei sitae* in such a way as to justify conferring jurisdiction on a court of the state in which the property is situated, Article 16 cannot be interpreted as encompassing that action.[380] It only covers actions which fall within the scope of the Convention, as laid down in Article 1, and seek to determine the extent, content, owner-

[373] 73/77 *Sanders v Van der Putte* 11,12,13,17.

[374] 73/77 *Sanders v Van der Putte* 18.

[375] C-280/90 *Hacker v Euro-Relais* 14,16.

[376] C-280/90 *Hacker v Euro-Relais* 8 (re 241/83 *Rösler v Rottwinkel* 19),9 (re *Rösler* 20),10 (re *Rösler* 24),11 (re 73/77 *Sanders v Van der Putte* 15,16),12 (re *Sanders* 18).

[377] C-115/88 *Reichert v Dresdner Bank I.*

[378] C-115/88 *Reichert v Dresdner Bank I* 12,15.

[379] C-115/88 *Reichert v Dresdner Bank I* 8 (re 73/77 *Sanders v Van der Putte,* 288/82 *Duijnstee v Goderbauer*),9 (re *Sanders v Van der Putte*),10 (re *Sanders*, 241/83 *Rösler v Rottwinkel).*

[380] C-115/88 *Reichert v Dresdner Bank I* 12.

ship or possession of immovable property or the existence of other rights *in rem* therein.[381]

Consistent with this line of reasoning is the Court's decision in *Webb v Webb* on the interpretation of the concept 'rights *in rem* in immovable property', that an action for a declaration that a person holds immovable property as a trustee and for an order requiring that person to execute such documents as should be required to vest legal ownership in the plaintiff, does not constitute an action in rem within the meaning of Article 16, point 1.[382]

In *Lieber v Göbel*, the Court decided that a claim for compensation for the use of a dwelling after the annulment of a transfer of ownership is not included in the matters governed by Article 16, point 1, related to *rights in rem in and tenancies of immovable property*.[383] When justifying that decision the Court recalled its case law on the interpretation of these concepts, and its argument that Article 16 must not be given a wider interpretation than is required by its underlying principle, since it results in depriving the parties of the choice of forum which would otherwise be theirs. Where that principle is not involved and where there is no interest of the state in which the property is situated, Article 16 should not be applied.[384]

The case law of the Court also implies that Article 16, particularly Article 16, point 1, must not be interpreted too narrowly. As is well-known by now, it was introduced for reasons of first-hand knowledge of the facts, proximity of evidence and law (and in the interest of the State concerned).[385] The interpretation given to Article 16 must not render that rule ineffective, in the sense that its underlying principle is negated.

As was already seen, in *Rösler v Rottwinkel*, and with reference to *Sanders v Van der Putte*, the Court established that the expression 'proceedings which have as their object ... tenancies of immovable property', within the meaning of Article 16, point 1, covers a wide range of disputes between landlords and tenants, irrespective of whether the action is based on a right *in rem* or on a right in personam, as long as these actions are directly related to the use of the property.[386]

The Court confirmed this viewpoint as to the interpretation of Article 16, point 1, in *Dansommer v Götz*. The case was concerned with proceedings brought before a national court after a partial failure to perform a tenancy agreement, based on the tenant's obligation to maintain the property let in a proper condition and to

---

[381] C-115/88 *Reichert v Dresdner Bank I* 11.

[382] C-294/92 *Webb v Webb* 19, compare 14 (re C-115/88 *Reichert v Dresdner Bank I*)-16,17 (re 73/77 *Sanders v Van der Putte* 13).

[383] C-292/93 *Lieber v Göbel* 22

[384] C-292/93 *Lieber v Göbel* 10 (re 241/83 *Rösler v Rottwinkel* 24,25), 12 (re C-115/88 *Reichert* 9),13 (re C-294/92 *Webb* 14),14 (re Schlosser Report OJ 1979 C 59, p. 71, No. 166),15,20.

[385] Compare text following note 354 of this section.

[386] 241/83 *Rösler v Rottwinkel* 24,26 (re 73/77 *Sanders v Van der Putte* 15).

repair any damage to it which he had caused. The dispute was not directly between the owner and the tenant of the immovable property, but based on a leasing contract. Since the subject-matter was thus directly linked to a leasing contract concerning immovable property and consequently to a tenancy of immovable property within the meaning of Article 16, point 1(a), the Court decided that these proceedings fall within the exclusive jurisdiction rule laid down in that provision.[387] The Court extensively justified its decision, referring back to former decisions on the interpretation of Article 16, which by then had become settled case law. It referred to the scheme of rules of jurisdiction, particularly the relation between Article 16 and Article 2, requiring a restrictive interpretation of Article 16, and to the principle underlying Article 16, point 1(a), itself. The Court held, however, that its not too narrow interpretation of that provision in the case at hand, was borne out by its underlying purpose that a court that has the practical advantage of first-hand knowledge of the facts, proximity of evidence and/or law, should be able to decide a case.[388]

As regards the concept '*concerned with the registration or validity of patents*' within the meaning of Article 16, point 4, the Court has also held that Article 16 must not be given a broader interpretation than is required by its objective. For example, in *Duijnstee v Goderbauer*, the Court stated that only proceedings relating to the validity, existence or lapse of a patent or an alleged right of priority by reason of an earlier deposit, fall within the scope of that concept.[389] If, however, the dispute does not itself concern the validity of the patent or the existence of the deposit or registration, there is no special reason to confer exclusive jurisdiction on the court of the Contracting State in which the patent was applied for or granted. Consequently, a dispute between an employee for whose invention a patent has been applied for or obtained and his employer, where the dispute relates to their respective rights in that patent arising out of the contract of employment, is not covered by Article 16, point 4.[390] When the Court justified its decision, it recalled its case law as regards an independent interpretation of the Convention's concepts and it referred to the principle underlying Article 16.[391]

---

[387] C-8/98 *Dansommer v Götz* 38.

[388] C-8/98 *Dansommer v Götz* 21 (re 73/77 *Sander v Van der Putte* 17,18, C-115/88 *Reichert v Dresdner Bank I* 9, C-292/93 *Lieber v Göbel* 12), 22 (re C-294/92 *Webb v Webb* 14, *Lieber v Göbel* 13), 23 (re *Lieber v Göbel* 10,13,20), 24-27 (re Jenard Report OJ 1979 C 59 p. 35, *Sanders v Van der Putte* 13, *Reichert v Dresdner Bank I* 10), 28 (re Jenard Report, p. 34, 35) 31 (re C-280/90 *Hacker v Euro-Relais* 14), 36,38: ancillary clauses relating to insurance in the event of cancellation, etc., do not affect the nature of the tenancy as a tenancy of immovable property within the meaning of Art. 16, point 1(a).

[389] 288/82 *Duijnstee v Goderbauer* 24.

[390] 288/82 *Duijnstee v Goderbauer* 28; part of the Court's reasoning in this judgment has been discussed in section 1 of chapter 2, text following notes 8 and 12.

[391] 288/82 *Duijnstee v Goderbauer* 17 (re 133/78 *Gourdain v Nadler*, 150/77 *Bertrand v Ott*, 34/82 *Peters v ZNAV*), 22,23 (re Jenard Report OJ 1979, C 59, p. 30).

In *Autoteile v Malhé*, when answering questions on the concept '*proceedings concerned with the enforcement of judgments*', within the meaning of Article 16, point 5, the Court resorted to the relation between Article 2 and Article 16, and to their underlying principles, being respectively, 'protection of the weaker party due to its procedural position' and 'efficient and sound administration', in order to justify a restrictive interpretation of Article 16, point 5.[392] Thus, as was discussed before, the Court held in that judgment, that Article 16, point 5, does not make it possible, in an application to oppose enforcement made to the courts of the Contracting State in which enforcement is to take place, to plead a set-off between the right whose enforcement is being sought and a claim over which the courts of that state would have no jurisdiction if it were raised independently.[393] Another interpretation would be contrary to the division of jurisdiction which the Convention intended to establish between the court of the defendant's domicile and the court of the place of enforcement (in accordance with the main principle that disputes should be decided by an appropriate court).

In *Reichert v Dresdner Bank II*, the Court also decided on a restrictive interpretation of the concept 'proceedings concerned with the enforcement of judgments' in Article 16, point 5, when it held that an action such as the *action paulienne* under French law, did not fall within the scope of Article 16, point 5.[394] In justifying that decision, the Court referred to its decision in *Autoteile v Malhé*, and consistently repeated its viewpoint that Article 16 must not be given a wider interpretation than is required by its objective, since it results in depriving the parties of the choice of forum which would otherwise be theirs.[395] Finally, in *Owens v Bracco*, the Court recalled that line of reasoning, when it held that Article 16, point 5, which must be read in conjunction with Article 25, only applies to judgments delivered by a court or tribunal of a Contracting State.[396]

As regards Article 16, point 2, the Court has not yet had an opportunity to interpret the substantive scope of that provision. We assume, though, that the Court will follow similar lines of argument.

3.2 The principle that an entire dispute should be decided by a single court

In the introduction to this section, we discussed the fact that the principle of a sound administration of justice contains two sub-principles: the principle that courts that have the practical advantage of first-hand knowledge of the facts, ease of taking evidence, and/or knowledge of the applicable law should be able to de-

---

[392] 220/84 *Autoteile v Malhé* 14-17.

[393] 220/84 *Autoteile v Malhé* 19.

[394] C-261/90 *Reichert v Dresdner Bank II* 28; see also text following note 377 of this section.

[395] C-261/90 *Reichert v Dresdner Bank II* 24 (re 220/84 *Autoteile v Malhé* 16),25 (re 73/77 *Sanders v Van der Putte* 17,18, C-115/88 *Reichert*)-27 (re Jenard Report, OJ 1979 C 59, p. 36).

[396] C-129/92 *Owens v Bracco* 22,24.

cide a case and the principle that an entire dispute should be decided by a single court. The latter principle was introduced not only with a view to a sound administration of justice, but, also with a view to the free movement of judgments.[397]

Both sub-principles are based on the idea that a national court that has a particularly close relationship with a case should decide that case. The first sub-principle is based on the assumption that where a direct, territorial link exists between certain facts of a case and a court, that court is the best qualified to hear the case for reasons of first-hand knowledge of the facts, ease of taking evidence and/or knowledge of the applicable law. The second sub-principle expresses the idea that if a dispute is already linked to a court because this court has jurisdiction with regard to a case that is part of that dispute, that court may be the best qualified to hear *all* the different aspects of the dispute because of the disadvantages of separate proceedings. Contrary to the first sub-principle, the second sub-principle focuses not on the territorial link between the facts of the case and a court, but on the relationship between the dispute and a court that is already competent as to certain aspects of that dispute: in order to meet the principle of a sound administration of justice, it is efficient that an entire dispute will be decided by a single court. And, where both sub-principles seek to ensure an efficient exercise of judicial functions within the Community, the first sub-principle focuses on efficiently ascertaining the facts relevant to the case and/or efficiently applying the applicable law, while the second sub-principle focuses on a harmonious administration of justice, particularly on precluding conflicting and irreconcilable decisions.

We assume that both parties, the plaintiff and the defendant, benefit from a principle that enables a court to hear different aspects of an entire dispute together. However, the plaintiff who commenced the original proceedings will benefit even more, if he had an option to choose the court that suited him best. Since the principle that an entire dispute should be decided by a single court may also have the advantage of precluding irreconcilable decisions, it is the judgment-creditor who, at the end of the day, benefits the most.

With respect to the sub-principle that an entire dispute should be decided before a single court, a distinction can be made between the principle that cases related to the same dispute should be brought before a single court and the principle that actions related to the same dispute that have already been brought before different courts should be heard together by a single court.[398]

---

[397] See introduction to section 3, text following notes 175 and 177, and this section, text following note 400.

[398] See note 115, of section 4.2 of chapter 5, where we made a distinction between 'cases' and 'disputes'.

3.2.1 *The principle that related cases should be brought before a single court*

C Art. 6	R 6	C Art. 11 (2nd para.)	R 12(2)
C Art. 10 (1st and 3rd para.)	R 11(1 and 3)	C Art. 14 (3rd para.)	R 16(3)

The principle that cases related to the same dispute should be heard by a single court (or at least can be brought before a single court), underlies several provisions of the Convention, namely Article 6, Article 10, first and third paragraph, Article 11, second paragraph, and Article 14, third paragraph.

Article 6 provides that persons domiciled in a Contracting State may also be sued, as one of a number of defendants, in the courts of the place where one of them is domiciled; as a third party in an action on a warranty or guarantee or in any other third party proceedings, in the court seised of the original proceedings; in a counterclaim arising from the same contract or facts on which the original claim was based, in the court in which the original claim is pending; and, in matters relating to a contract, if the action may be combined with an action against the same defendant in matters relating to rights in rem in immovable property, in the court of the Contracting State in which the property is situated. Article 6 thus contains several 'special jurisdictions' which the plaintiff may choose because of the existence in well-defined situations of a particularly close connecting factor between a dispute and the court which may be called upon to hear it. As the Court put it in *Hagen v Zeehaghe*, when answering questions on the interpretation of Article 6, point 2:

> 'Article 6(2) makes provision for a special jurisdiction, which the plaintiff may choose because of the existence, in clearly defined situations, of a particularly close connecting factor between a dispute and the court which may be called upon to hear it, with a view to the efficacious conduct of the proceedings ... The Convention thus enables the entire dispute to be heard by a single court.'[399]

The provisions of Article 6 also have the advantage of diminishing the risk of conflicts between judgments that may constitute an obstacle as to the recognition or enforcement of judgments. They therefore contribute to the principle 'free movement of judgments'. As the Court put it in *Kalfelis v Schröder*, when answering questions of the national court on the interpretation of Article 6, point 1:

> 'In that regard, it must be noted that the abovementioned report prepared by the committee of experts referred expressly, in its explanation of Article 6 (1), to the concern to avoid the risk in the Contracting States of judgments which are incompatible with each other.'[400]

---

[399] Compare C-365/88 *Hagen v Zeehaghe* 11 (re 33/78 *Somafer v Saar-Ferngas* 7).

[400] 189/87 *Kalfelis v Schröder* 11 (re Jenard Report OJ 1979 C 59, p. 27).

If the dispute involving related cases is concerned with matters of insurance or consumer contracts the principle that related cases should be brought before a single court also applies, in the specific situations where the socio-economically weaker party has been granted certain jurisdictional advantages. As regards a counterclaim, the Convention contains two specific provisions concerning cases that involve a socio-economically weaker party. In matters relating to insurance, Article 11, second paragraph, provides that the provisions of Section 3 do not affect the right to bring a counterclaim at the court in which, in accordance with that Section, the original claim is pending. A similar provision is laid down in Article 14, third paragraph, with regard to matters related to consumer contracts. As regards actions on a warranty or guarantee, Article 10, first paragraph, provides in respect of liability insurance, that the insurer may, if the law of the court thus permits, be joined in proceedings which the injured party had brought against the insured. If actions based on liability insurance are brought by the injured party directly against the insurer, and if the law governing such direct actions provides that the policyholder or the insured may be joined as a party to the action, the courts provided for in Articles 7, 8 and 9, have jurisdiction thereover by virtue of Article 10, third paragraph.

The principle that related cases should be brought before a single court, as far as it underlies Article 6, weighed in relation to other principles

C Art. 2	R 2	C Art. 16	R 22	C Art. 27(3)	R 34(3)
C Art. 5	R 5	C Art. 17	R 23	C Art. 28	R 35
C Art. 6	R 6	C Art. 18	R 24		

As was seen above, the principle that related cases should be brought before a single court (or at least can be brought before a single court) is firmly established under the Convention. However, as is typical for the principles underlying the Convention, this principle is not absolute. The relative weight of the principle is determined by the following factors.

From the general design of the Convention, it already appears that the principle 'free movement of judgments' overrides the principle that related cases should be brought before a single court, as far as it underlies Article 6. The fact that judgments regarding related cases have been delivered by different courts does not constitute an obstacle to the recognition and enforcement of these judgments within the Community (Article 28, first and third paragraphs), unless the decisions given are irreconcilable. Also, as was seen above, the principle that related cases should be brought before a single court does not fully apply to matters related to insurance and consumer contracts. This principle does not set aside the specific rules of jurisdiction of Sections 3 and 4, which favour the protection of the socio-economically weaker party. From the system of the rules of jurisdiction, it furthermore follows that the principle underlying Article 6 does not prevail over the exclusive jurisdictions required by the principle of party autonomy, underlying Articles 17 and 18, and the principle of a sound administration, as far as it underlies Article 16 (compare also Article 6, point 3). On the other hand, the principle that related cases should be brought before a single court, as far as it underlies Article 6, clearly constitutes a derogation from the general principle laid down in Article 2, first paragraph, that jurisdiction should be vested in the courts of the defendant's home state. The principle underlying Article 6 prevails over the principle of the protection of the party who is weaker due to his procedural position, if the plaintiff so chooses. The principle may even prevail over the principle that courts that have the practical advantage of first-hand knowledge of the facts, proximity of evidence and/or the applicable law, should be able to hear a case, since the Convention makes it possible in Article 6, points 1 to 4, to attribute jurisdiction to a court irrespective of the head of jurisdiction of the court that would otherwise be competent (Articles 2 or 5), and as far as Article 6, points 2 and 3 is concerned, also irrespective of the head of jurisdiction in the original proceedings (Article 2 or 5).

From the Court's case law it is evident that the process of weighing and balancing which was carried out by the designers of the Convention, is to be continued. For example, the Court has consistently held that the special jurisdictions of Article 6, as much as those of Article 5, are to be interpreted restrictively, or at any rate, cannot give rise to an interpretation going beyond the cases envisaged by the Convention, since these jurisdictions constitute derogations from the general principle that jurisdiction is vested in the courts of the defendant's home state, as laid down in Article 2.[401] Therefore, although the principle that related cases are to be decided together prevails over the principle of the protection of the weaker party due to his procedural position, the latter principle clearly has an influence on the relative weight of the former. The Court expressed that view for example in *Kalfelis v Schröder* as regards Article 6, point 1, by stating that where this provision is an exception to the general principle laid down in Article 2, that exception must be treated in such a manner that there is no possibility of the very existence of that general principle being called into question.[402]

As follows from the Court's case law and, in particular, from the wording of Article 6, point 2, the principle is restricted in yet another way: the special jurisdictions provided for in Article 6 may not be used by the plaintiff with the sole object of ousting the jurisdiction of the courts of the State where one of the defendants is domiciled or removing the third party from the jurisdiction of the court which would otherwise be competent.[403] As will be discussed in section 4

[401] 189/87 *Kalfelis v Schröder* 8,19; 32/88 *Six Constructions v Humbert* 18 (re 189/87 *Kalfelis v Schröder)*; 365/88 *Hagen v Zeehaghe* 10; C-51/97 *Réunion européenne v Spliethoff's* 16 (re C-269/95 *Benincasa v Dentalkit* 13),47; C-412/98 *Josi Reinsurance v UGIC* 49, (re *Handte* 14, C-89/91 *Shearson v TVB* 15,16, C-51/97 *Réunion européenne v Spliethoff's* 16); see section 3.1 of this chapter, text following note 195.

[402] 189/87 *Kalfelis v Schröder* 8; and C-51/97 *Réunion européenne v Spliethoff's* 47 (re *Kalfelis* 8,9).

[403] 189/87 *Kalfelis v Schröder* 9 (re Jenard Report 1979 OJ 1979 C 59, p. 26); C-365/88 *Hagen v Zeehaghe* 13; C-51/97 *Réunion européenne v Spliethoff's* 47 (re *Kalfelis* 8,9).

of this chapter, these considerations are related to the overall ideal of hearing an entire dispute, as far as possible, before a single *and* appropriate court and require (among other things) respect for the proper division of jurisdictions under the Convention.

The above-mentioned considerations of the Court advocate a *restrictive* interpretation of Article 6. On the other hand, as is also typical of the Court's principle-based reasoning in general, the principle underlying the provision concerned must also be taken into account, in order to ensure, as far as possible, that this provision is fully effective. Since Article 6 has a purpose of its own, namely to ensure that an entire dispute should be decided by a single court, it must be assumed that an interpretation that would make Article 6 fully redundant cannot be accepted.[404] This consideration favours a *broad* interpretation or at least an interpretation that is not too restrictive.

Naturally, the most persuasive argument for a broad interpretation of Article 6 lies in the fact that, as the Court pointed out in *Kalfelis v Schröder* and as was stated in the Jenard Report, Article 6 aims to avoid the risk of conflicts between judgments within the Community. Article 6 has a twofold purpose. It was not only introduced in order to provide for an appropriate court, as was seen before, it was also introduced out of concern for the risk of irreconcilable judgments resulting from separate proceedings.[405] Since irreconcilable judgments are an obstacle to the recognition and enforcement of judgments (Article 27, point 3), that purpose contributes to the achievement of free movement of judgments. Article 6 cannot therefore be interpreted too restrictively.

Finally, notice that reference to the principle of legal certainty, implying respect for the linguistic boundaries of the Convention, naturally also has an influence on the relative weight of the principle that related cases should be decided together, as is shown for example, from the Court's judgment in *Réunion européenne v Spliethoff's*, as will be seen below.[406] As was seen before, an interpretation suggested by the principle directly underlying a provision must be supported by the words of the relevant rule, or at least not be prohibited by them.

To conclude, as was seen in the foregoing paragraphs, the principle that related cases should be brought before a single court is weighed in relation to the principles 'protection of the weaker party due to his procedural or socio-economic position', 'party autonomy', 'sound administration of justice', as far as it underlies in particular Articles 5 and 16, 'legal certainty' and 'free movement of judgments'. When interpreting concepts of Article 6, considerations based on these principles may point in the direction of a restrictive or a broad interpretation of

---

[404] See text following note 27, section 1.1 of this chapter

[405] 189/87 *Kalfelis v Schröder* 11; see also, Jenard Report, OJ C 59 p. 27; compare C-51/97 *Réunion européenne v Spliethoff's* 48.

[406] C-51/97 *Réunion européenne v Spliethoff's* 44,46.

Article 6. The following case law illustrates the Court's principle-based reasoning with regard to Article 6.

A *restrictive interpretation* of Article 6, based on considerations related to principles which favour such an interpretation, such as the 'protection of the weaker party due to his procedural position', followed from *Kalfelis v Schröder* and *Réunion européenne v Spliethoff's*.[407] In both judgments, the Court had to answer questions on the interpretation of Article 6. The Court first recalled that Article 6, point 1, is an exception to the general principle of Article 2, protecting the defendant for reasons of his weaker procedural position, and that the existence of that general principle must not be called into question.[408] After having stated that the principle 'legal certainty', implying equality and uniformity of rights and obligations, requires an independent interpretation of the terms of Article 6, the Court decided in *Kalfelis v Schröder* and recalled in *Réunion européenne v Spliethoff's*, that Article 6, point 1, only applies where there exists a 'connection between the various actions brought by the same plaintiff against the different defendants' at the time of the institution of the proceedings.[409] Moreover, that connection must be of such a kind that 'it is expedient to hear and determine them together in order to avoid the risk of irreconcilable judgments resulting from separate proceedings'.[410] Although in both judgments the Court referred to the principle 'free movement of judgments', requiring the avoidance of the risk of irreconcilable judgments, *prima facie* suggesting a broad interpretation of Article 6, it decided in favour of a restrictive interpretation of that provision.[411]

In *Kalfelis v Schröder*, the Court held that a court which has jurisdiction under Article 5, point 3, over an action in so far as it is based on tort or delict does not have jurisdiction over that action in so far as it is not so based. From this it follows, as the Court held in *Réunion européenne v Spliethoff's*, that two claims in one action for compensation, directed against different defendants and based in one instance on contractual liability and in the other on liability in tort or delict cannot be regarded as being connected.[412] The idea that related cases are to be decided together, as far as possible, applies only to disputes as regards one and the same legal relationship.

Furthermore, the Court observed in *Réunion européenne v Spliethoff's*, referring to the very wording of Article 6, point 1, in accordance with the principle of

---

[407] 189/87 *Kalfelis v Schröder* 8,9; C-51/97 *Reunion européenne v Spliethoff's* 47 (re *Kalfelis* 8,9).

[408] 189/87 *Kalfelis v Schröder* 8.

[409] 189/87 *Kalfelis v Schröder* 10,12; C-51/97 *Réunion européenne v Spliethoff's* 48 (re *Kalfelis*).

[410] 189/87 *Kalfelis v Schröder* 13; C-51/97 *Réunion européenne v Spliethoff's* 48 (re *Kalfelis*).

[411] 189/87 *Kalfelis v Schröder* 11; C-51/97 *Réunion européenne v Spliethoff's* 48 (re *Kalfelis*).

[412] C-51/97 *Réunion européenne v Spliethoff's* 22 (re *Kalfelis*),49 (re *Kalfelis*),50; and see 189/87 *Kalfelis v Schröder* 21.

legal certainty implying 'respect for the linguistic boundaries of the Convention', that this provision only applies if the proceedings in question are brought before the courts of a Contracting State of the place where one of the defendants is domiciled.[413] Hence, the Court argued, that 'a defendant domiciled in a Contracting State cannot be sued in another Contracting State before a court seised of an action against a co-defendant not domiciled in a Contracting State'.[414]

A strict application of Article 6, point 3, follows from *Danvaern v Schuhfabriken*. In that decision, the Court held that Article 6, point 3, by which a person domiciled in a Contracting State may be sued in a counterclaim arising from the same contract or facts on which the original claim was based, in the court in which the original claim is pending, 'applies only to claims by defendants which seek the pronouncement of a separate judgment or decree'. It does not apply to the situation where a defendant raises, as a pure defence, a claim which he allegedly has against the plaintiff'.[415] In this case, the Court did not resort to its familiar principle-based reasoning. It was sufficient for the Court to refer to the national laws of the Contracting States and the various language versions of the Convention, in accordance with the principle of legal certainty, requiring 'equality and uniformity of rights and obligations' and 'respect for the linguistic boundaries of the Convention'.[416]

The view that Article 6 should *not be interpreted too restrictively* because it has a purpose of its own, played a role in *Hagen v Zeehaghe*. In that judgment the Court referred to the principle underlying Article 6 that with a view to the efficacious conduct of proceedings, an entire dispute should be heard, as far as possible, by a single court.[417] The Court had to answer a question on the interpretation of Article 6, point 2, which enables a person domiciled in a Contracting State to be sued as a third party in third party proceedings, in the court seised of the original proceedings. The Court held in that judgment that the related nature of the main action and the action on a warranty or guarantee suffices to found jurisdiction on the part of the court in which the action on a warranty or guarantee has been brought, 'irrespective of the basis on which it has jurisdiction in the original proceedings' and that 'in this respect, the jurisdiction provided for in Article 2 and that provided for in Article 5 are equivalent'.[418] The Court did not explicitly refer to the wording of Article 6, but it is clear that the general terms in which Article 6, point 2, is couched, does not deter such an interpretation.[419]

---

[413] C-51/97 *Réunion européenne v Spliethoff's* 44-46.

[414] C-51/97 *Réunion européenne v Spliethoff's* 44,45,52; see previously, text following note 86, in section 3 of chapter 5.

[415] C-341/93 *Danvaern v Schuhfabriken*18.

[416] C-341/93 *Danvaern v Schuhfabriken* 12,17; compare sections 1.1 and 2 of chapter 5.

[417] C-365/88 *Hagen v Zeehaghe* 11 (re 33/78 *Somafer v Saar-Ferngas*).

[418] C-365/88 *Hagen v Zeehaghe* 11 (re 33/78 *Somafer v Saar-Ferngas*).

[419] Compare C-365/88 *Hagen v Zeehaghe* 9.

In *Hagen v Zeehaghe*, the Court also had to answer the question whether Article 6, point 2 requires the court to grant leave to bring an action on a warranty or guarantee, or whether the court may asses the admissibility of the application for leave in the light of the rules of the national procedural law. The Court held that Article 6, point 2, merely determines which court has jurisdiction and is not concerned with conditions for admissibility. After having referred to the purpose of the Convention, which is not to unify procedural rules but to determine which court has jurisdiction in disputes relating to civil and commercial matters and to facilitate the enforcement of judgments, the Court stated that, as regards procedural rules, reference must be made to the national rules applicable by the national court.[420] However, the application of national procedural rules may, in accordance with the principle of legal certainty, not have the effect of restricting the application of the rules of jurisdiction laid down in the Convention.[421] The Court then decided that a request for leave to bring the action on the warranty or guarantee cannot be refused on the basis of the national procedural law on the ground that the third party resides or is domiciled in a Contracting State other than that of the court seised of the original proceedings.[422]

The Court has not yet been called upon to decide questions relating to Article 6, point 4, which provides that a person domiciled in a Contracting State may also be sued, in matters relating to a contract, if the action may be combined with an action against the same defendant in matters relating to rights *in rem* in immovable property, in the court of the Contracting State in which the property is situated. In light of the Court's case law as discussed above, we may expect that this provision must be construed on the basis of considerations similar to those invoked when the Court interpreted Article 6, points 1 to 3. The same must be assumed when questions of interpretation arise with respect to Article 6a, providing that a court, having jurisdiction by virtue of the Convention in actions relating to liability from the use or operation of a ship, shall also have jurisdiction over claims for the limitation of such liability.

3.2.2 *The principle that related actions already brought before different courts should be decided by a single court*

C Arts. 21 to 23 R 27 to 30

With respect to the principle that an entire dispute should be decided by a single court, the Convention not only provides that related cases should be brought be-

---

[420] C-365/88 *Hagen v Zeehaghe* 17-19 (re 129/83 *Zelger v Salinitri II*; 148/84 *Deutsche Genossenschaftsbank v Brasserie du Pêcheur*; 145/86 *Hoffmann v Krieg*); compare section 3 of chapter 5.

[421] C-365/88 *Hagen v Zeehaghe* 13,19 (re 129/83 *Zelger v Salinitri II;* 148/84 *Deutsche Genossenschaftsbank v Brasserie du Pêcheur;* 145/86 *Hoffmann v Krieg*),20 (re 288/82 *Duijnstee v Goderbauer*); compare section 1.2 of chapter 5.

[422] C-365/88 *Hagen v Zeehaghe* 22.

fore a single court (or at least can be brought before a single court). It also aims to realise this principle by providing that related actions already brought before the courts of different Contracting States should be decided by a single court.

The principle of a sound administration of justice, implying that related actions which have been brought before the courts of different Contracting States can be decided by a single court, clearly underlies Articles 21 to 23 on *lis pendens* and related actions. Article 21 implies that where proceedings have the same cause of action and are between the same parties, it should be possible to decide them together. Article 22 requires that where related actions are brought in the court of different Contracting States, it should be possible to decide them together. Article 23 provides that where actions are brought within the exclusive jurisdiction of several courts, these actions should be decided together by the court first seised. The Court has made it clear that these provisions do not attribute jurisdiction to a court of a Contracting State to try an action which is related to another action of which that court is seised pursuant to the rules of the Convention. Instead, these provisions are intended to establish how related actions which have been brought before courts of different Contracting States, are to be dealt with in order to improve co-ordination of the exercise of judicial functions within the Community.[423]

The Court's case law confirms that it follows from the principle of a sound administration of justice that, in order to avoid parallel proceedings, related actions which have already been brought before the courts of different Contracting States, should be decided together.[424] The following quotation, taken from *Gübisch v Palumbo*, is illustrative in this respect. The Court stated in that judgment:

> 'Article 21, together with Article 22 on related actions, is contained in Section 8 of Title II of the Convention; that section is intended, in the interests of the proper administration of justice within the Community, to prevent parallel proceedings before the courts of different Contracting States ...'[425]

Apart from the aims of proper administration of justice, particularly the aim of improving the co-ordination of the exercise of judicial functions within the Community, Articles 21 to 23 have another purpose, namely to avoid conflicting and contradictory, in particular irreconcilable decisions.[426] As the Court observed in *Gubisch v Palumbo*:

---

[423] 150/80 *Elefanten Schuh v Pierre Jacqmain* 19; and C-406/92 *Tatry v Maciej Rataj* 54.

[424] 144/86 *Gubisch v Palumbo* 8; C-406/92 *Tatry v Maciej Rataj* 54.

[425] 144/86 *Gubisch v Palumbo* 8; compare C-351/89 *OUI v NHIC* 15,16; C-406/92 *Tatry v Maciej Rataj* 31,51,54; C-163/95 *Von Horn v Cinnamond* 13, and, compare 17; C-351/96 *Drouot v CMI* 17; see also 42/76 *De Wolf v Cox* 10/11,12.

[426] Compare C-406/92 *Tatry v Maciej Rataj* 54.

'Those rules are therefore designed to preclude, in so far as is possible and from the outset, the possibility of a situation arising such as that referred to in Article 27(3), that is to say the non-recognition of a judgment on account of its irreconcilability with a judgment given in a dispute between the same parties in the State in which recognition is sought.[427]

The requirement of avoiding irreconcilable judgments flows from the principle of legal certainty with regard to judgments and from the principle of free movement of judgments, as was seen earlier.[428]

The principle that related actions already brought before different courts should be decided by a single court, as far as it underlies Articles 21 to 23, weighed in relation to other principles

C Art. 16(5)	R 22(5)	C Art. 28 (1st and 3rd para.)	R 35 (1 and 3)
C Arts. 21 to 23	R 27 to 30	C Art. 57	R 71
C Art. 27(3)	R 34(3)		

As is clear from the Convention and the Court's case law, the principle underlying Articles 21 to 23 is firmly established under the Convention. However, as is typical of principles, this principle is not absolute. The relative weight of the principle is influenced by the following.

From the general scheme of the Convention it follows that the principle 'free movement of judgments' overrides the principle that related actions already brought before different courts should be decided by a single court. The fact that related cases have been decided by different courts does not constitute an obstacle to the recognition and enforcement of judgments within the Community (Article 28, first and third paragraphs), unless these judgments are irreconcilable.

From the Court's case law it is evident that the process of weighing and balancing the principles that underlie the Convention against each other is to be continued, particularly where the concepts and terms of Articles 21 to 23 must be given an autonomous interpretation.[429] For example, it appears from that case law that the principle of legal certainty has an influence on the interpretation of Articles 21 to 23. As will be seen below, applying that principle may result in a broad or restrictive interpretation of Articles 21 to 23. Also, the Court takes ac-

---

[427] 144/86 *Gubisch v Palumbo* 8, compare 42/76 *De Wolf v Cox* 11,12.

[428] See section 1 of chapter 3, text following note 35 and section 5 of chapter 5, text following note 159.

[429] 144/86 *Gubisch v Palumbo* 11; C-406/92 *Tatry v Maciej Rataj* 46 (re *Gubisch v Palumbo* 11). As was seen in the *Zelger v Salinitri* case, an independent interpretation is not always appropriate, especially where procedural formalities are involved and any indication as to the meaning of the expression concerned, in this case the expression 'first seised' in Art. 21, is absent. The Court recalled in that judgment, that the unification of procedural formalities has never been the objective of the Convention and that reference must be made to the national applicable law. Compare section 1.1 of chapter 5, text following note 35. Notice, though, that Art. 30 of Section 9 of Regulation 44/2001 determines in detail when a court shall be deemed to be seised, for the purposes of that Regulation.

count of the principles which directly underlie these provisions, namely the principle that related actions should be decided, as far as possible, by a single court and the principle of the free movement of judgments. In light of these underlying principles, the Court has strong reasons to defend a broad interpretation of these provisions.[430] In addition, since Articles 21 to 23 do not *confer* jurisdiction on the national courts, a broad interpretation of these provisions will not constitute (further) derogations from the general principle laid down in Article 2, or heighten the risk of a (further) multiplication of jurisdiction. This is another argument lending support to an interpretation of Articles 21 to 23 that is not too narrow.[431]

The following case law is illustrative of this principle-based reasoning of the Court. That reasoning will more often result in a broad, rather than in a restrictive interpretation.

From the Court's case law it is evident that the Court favours an interpretation of Articles 21 to 23 that is *not too restrictive. Gubisch v Palumbo* is illustrative in this respect. When answering questions submitted by the national court on the interpretation of terms used in Article 21, the Court took account of several of the considerations that support an interpretation that is not too narrow. The question put to the Court was whether Article 21 applies in a situation in which one of the parties has brought an action before a court for the enforcement of an obligation stipulated in an international contract of sale and another action is subsequently brought against him by the other party in another Contracting State for the rescission or discharge of the same contract. After having recalled that the terms used in Article 21 are in principle to be construed independently and with a view to the underlying principles, and after having explained what these underlying principles are, namely the sound administration of justice and the free movement of judgments, the Court referred to the wording of Article 21.[432] The Court then decided that the concept of *lis pendens* pursuant to Article 21, cannot be restricted so as to mean two claims which are entirely identical: Article 21 applies where two actions are between the same parties and involve the same cause of action and the same subject-matter; it does not lay down any further conditions. Therefore, as the Court observed, it must be held that Article 21 covers a case where a party brings an action before a court in a Contracting State for the rescission or discharge of an international sales contract whilst an action by the other party to enforce the same contract is pending before a court in another Contracting

---

[430] Compare 144/86 *Gubisch v Palumbo* 14,15; and see C-351/89 *OUI v NHIC* 16 (re *Gubisch v Palumbo*); and C-406/92 *Tatry v Maciej Rataj* 52.

[431] Compare 32/88 *Six Constructions v Humbert* 18 (re *Kalfelis v Schröder*); see also 189/87 *Kalfelis v Schröder* 8,19; 365/88 *Hagen v Zeehaghe* 10; C-51/97 *Réunion européenne v Spliethoff's* 47 (re *Kalfellis* 8,9); and C-420/97 *Leathertex v Bodetex* 38 (re 150/80 *Elefanten Schuh v Jacqmain* 19; *Réunion européenne v Spliethoff's* 39).

[432] 144/86 *Gubisch v Palumbo* 6,8,14; compare also note 427 of this paragraph.

State.[433] The Court argued that another interpretation 'would run counter to the objectives of the Convention', which is intended to strengthen legal protection throughout the territory of the Community, to prevent parallel proceedings before the courts of different Contracting States, to avoid conflicts between decisions which might result therefrom and to facilitate recognition in each Contracting State of judgments given in any other Contracting State.[434]

In *OUI v NHIC*, the Court followed a similar line of reasoning, when answering the question whether Article 21 applies irrespective of the domicile of the parties to the two sets of proceedings. First, the Court referred to the wording of Article 21. Next, it referred to 'free movement of judgments' and to the principles directly underlying Article 21, the principle of a sound administration of justice, which is intended to prevent parallel proceedings, and the principle of legal certainty as to judgments which requires the avoidance of conflicts between decisions which might result therefrom (in accordance with 'free movement of judgments'). From these considerations it follows, as the Court then argued, that Article 21 must be interpreted broadly.[435] Hence, the Court stated that Article 21 must be applied both where the jurisdiction of the court is determined by the Convention itself and where it is derived from the legislation of a Contracting State in accordance with Article 4 of the Convention. Article 21 covers all situations of *lis pendens* before courts in Contracting States, irrespective of the domicile of the parties to the two sets of proceedings.[436] In *OUI v NHIC*, the Court also had to answer the question whether Article 21 must be interpreted as meaning that, if it does not decline jurisdiction, the court second seised may only stay its proceedings, or whether Article 21 permits or requires it to examine whether the court first seised has jurisdiction and, if so, to what extent. When answering that question, the Court took account of the wording of Article 2, the scheme of the Convention and the principle underlying Article 21 itself.[437] It then held that the only other possibility available, as an alternative solution, to the court second seised, which should normally decline jurisdiction, is to stay the proceedings if the jurisdiction of the court first seised is contested, but that it cannot itself examine the jurisdiction of the court first seised.[438]

In *Tatry v Maciej Rataj*, the Court had to answer several questions from the national court on the applicability and the interpretation of Articles 21 and 22. One of these questions was concerned with the interpretation of Article 57 of the Convention. That Article provides that the Convention shall not affect any spe-

---

[433] 144/86 *Gubisch v Palumbo* 14-17,19.

[434] 144/86 *Gubisch v Palumbo* 8,18.

[435] C-351/89 *OUI v NHIC* 13-15 (re C-220/88 *Dumez France v Hessische Landesbank*),16 (re 144/86 *Gubisch v Palumbo*); C-116/02 *Gasser v MISAT* 41 (re *OUI v NHIC* 16).

[436] C-351/89 *OUI v NHIC* 18.

[437] C-351/89 *OUI v NHIC* 20-22 (re Jenard Report, OJ 1979 C 59, p. 1)-25.

[438] C-351/89 *OUI v NHIC* 26. Notice that Art. 21 was adapted to this decision, by virtue of Art. 8 of the 1989 Accession Convention.

cialized convention to which the Contracting States are or will be parties and which, in relation to particular matters, govern jurisdiction or the recognition or enforcement of judgments. The question put to the Court was whether Article 57 implies that a specialized convention always precludes the application of the provisions of the Brussels Convention (here, Articles 21 and 22), or only as far as the legal issue is regulated by that specialized convention. When answering that question, the Court referred to the principles or objectives of the Convention, in particular to the principle of strengthening the legal protection of persons within the Community and the principle of free movement of judgments. It then held that, subject to a proper construction of Article 57, the specialized convention precludes the application of the provisions of the Convention only when the specialized convention regulates the legal issue involved.[439] Consequently, Articles 21 and 22 apply when such a specialized convention contains certain rules of jurisdiction but no provisions as to *lis pendens* or related actions.

Next, the Court answered one of the questions with regard to the term 'between the same parties' in Article 21. After having recalled that the terms used in Article 21 must be regarded as independent and after having referred to the principles underlying this provision and to the wording of Article 21, the Court pointed out that the 'same parties' in Article 21 in fact implies that the parties to the two actions are identical, but that their procedural position in the proceedings is not relevant.[440]

In *Tatry v Maciej Rataj* the Court also interpreted the concept 'same cause of action' in Article 21. The Court held that 'cause of action' comprises the facts and the rule of law relied upon as the basis of the action. Therefore, an action seeking to have the defendant held liable for causing loss and ordered to pay damages, has the same cause of action and the same object as earlier proceedings brought by that defendant seeking a declaration that he is not liable for that loss. These actions have the same object, since the issue of liability is central to both actions.[441] When justifying that interpretation of Article 21, the Court particularly relied on the wording of the majority of the language versions.[442]

Furthermore, the Court held in its judgment in *Tatry v Maciej Rataj* that the terms 'same cause of action' and 'between the same parties', within the meaning of Article 21, cover a situation in which the previous action, brought by the owner of a ship before a court of a Contracting State, is an action *in personam* for a declaration that that owner is not liable for alleged damage to the cargo transported by his ship, whereas the subsequent action was brought by the owner of the cargo before a court of another Contracting State by way of an action *in rem*

---

[439] C-406/92 *Tatry v Maciej Rataj* 24,27.

[440] C-406/92 *Tatry v Maciej Rataj* 29 (re 144/86 *Gubisch v Palumbo* 8-11),30-35; see also section 2 of chapter 5.

[441] C-406/92 *Tatry v Maciej Rataj* 38-44.

[442] C-406/92 *Tatry v Maciej Rataj* 37.

concerning an arrested ship, and subsequently continued both *in rem* and *in personam*, or solely *in personam*, according to the distinctions drawn by the national law of that other Contracting State.[443] The Court justified that decision by stating that the terms 'same cause of action' and 'between the same parties' have an independent meaning, and that therefore the distinction drawn by the law of a Contracting State between an action *in personam* and an action *in rem* is not material for the interpretation of Article 21.[444]

Tatry v Maciej Rataj was also concerned with the interpretation of the term 'related actions' used in the third paragraph of Article 22. The 'related actions' were, as was seen above, one action brought by one group of cargo owners against a shipowner seeking damages for harm caused to part of the cargo carried in bulk under separate but identical contracts, and the other action in damages was brought in another Contracting State against the same shipowner by the owners of another part of the cargo shipped under the same conditions and under contracts which were separate from but identical to those between the first group and the shipowner. The Court decided that, on a proper construction of Article 22, it is sufficient, in order to establish the necessary relationship between these actions, that separate trial and judgment would involve the risk of conflicting decisions, without necessarily involving the risk of giving rise to mutually exclusive legal consequences (meaning: irreconcilable decisions).[445] When justifying this (rather) broad interpretation of Article 22, the Court took account of the wording of the different language versions, the scheme of the Convention and implicitly referred to the principle directly underlying that provision, the principle that an entire dispute should be decided by a single court and which requires the avoidance of conflicting and contradictory decisions, even where the separate judgments are not 'irreconcilable'. As the Court observed here, 'sound administration of justice' which, among other things, requires the avoidance of conflicting and contradictory decisions, should be distinguished from the principle of free movement of judgments, which particularly requires the avoidance of irreconcilable decisions in Article 27, point 3.[446]

Most recently, in *Gantner v Basch*, the Court recalled its case law that Article 21 applies when two actions between the same parties involve the same subject-matter and that the subject-matter of the dispute refers to the end intended by the action.[447] In that same judgment the Court established that Article 21 must be construed as meaning that, in order to determine whether two claims brought between the same parties before the courts of different Contracting States have the same subject-matter, account should only be taken of the claims of the respective

---

443 C-406/92 *Tatry v Maciej Rataj* 45,47.

444 C-406/92 *Tatry v Maciej Rataj* 46 (re *Gubisch v Palumbo* 11).

445 C-406/92 *Tatry v Maciej Rataj* 52,57.

446 C-406/92 *Tatry v Maciej Rataj* 51 (re Jenard Report, OJ 1979 C 59, p. 41,42),52,53 (re 145/86 *Hoffmann v Krieg* 22),54-57.

447 C-111/01 *Gantner v Basch* 25 (re *Gubisch* 14; *Tatry* 41).

applicants, and not of the grounds of defence necessarily submitted at a later date by a defendant. When justifying its interpretation, the Court referred to the wording of Article 21 (in accordance with the principle of legal certainty), to the principle that directly underlies that provision (the principle of a sound administration of justice, requiring an efficient exercise of judicial functions within the Community) and to Article 30 of Council Regulation 44/2001.[448] And, in *Gasser v MISAT*, the Court decided that a national court second seised whose jurisdiction has been claimed under an agreement conferring jurisdiction may not, by way of derogation from Article 21, give judgment in the case without waiting for a declaration from the court first seised that it has no jurisdiction.[449] The Court referred to the principles underlying that provision, namely 'sound administration of justice', 'legal certainty as to judgments' and 'free movement of judgments'.[450] In that same judgment, the Court held furthermore that Article 21 cannot be derogated from where, in general, the duration of proceedings before the courts of the Contracting State in which the court first seised is established is excessively long.[451] At this point, the Court recalled that the Convention is based on the trust which the Contracting States accord to each other's legal systems and judicial institutions and it referred to the principle of legal certainty, requiring individuals to foresee with sufficient certainty which court will have jurisdiction.[452]

Of course, there is a limit to the extent to which Articles 21 to 23 apply. For example, the principle of legal certainty requires that the Court takes account of the scope and the wording of the Convention which may result in a *restrictive* interpretation. The application of provisions of the Convention to proceedings that by virtue of their subject-matter do not fall within the scope of the Convention, cannot be accepted, and an interpretation against the very wording of the provisions of the Convention, is rarely given by the Court.[453] Other considerations may also point towards a restrictive interpretation of Articles 21 to 23. In particular, we refer here to the argument that a person should not be (deprived of or) removed from (the choice of) the courts that would otherwise be theirs, for no good reason. The latter argument will be discussed in more detail in the next section.[454] As regards a restrictive interpretation of Articles 21 to 23, the following decisions are illustrative.

In *Owens v Bracco*, the Court held that Articles 21, 22 and 23 do not apply to proceedings, or issues arising in proceedings in Contracting States concerning the recognition and enforcement of judgments given in civil and commercial matters

---

[448] C-111/01 *Gantner v Basch* 4,26,27 (re OJ 2001 L 12, p. 1)-32.
[449] C-116/02 *Gasser v MISAT* 54.
[450] C-116/02 *Gasser v MISAT* 41 (re *Gubisch* 8; *OUI* 16).
[451] C-116/02 *Gasser v MISAT* 73.
[452] C-116/02 *Gasser v MISAT* 72; compare also note 3 of chapter 3.
[453] Compare section 2 of chapter 5.
[454] Compare section 4.1 of this chapter.

in non-Contracting States, where Article 16, point 5, applies only to 'judgments given in a Contracting State'.[455] The Court thereby referred to the scope, the scheme and the wording of the Convention.[456] It also referred to the principles underlying the Convention, in particular the principle 'free movement of judgments', 'strenghtening the legal protection of persons established within the Community', and the principle 'legal certainty as to jurisdiction'.[457] And, it recalled that the principle of the protection of the defendant, being the weaker party due to his procedural position, requires a restrictive interpretation of the rules of jurisdiction derogating from it, including Article 16, point 5.[458] In light of all these considerations requiring a not too broad application of Articles 21, 22 and 23, the Court could justify its negative answer to the question of the national court. These provisions do not apply if the court first seised is a court where enforcement of a judgment of a non-Contracting State is sought.

Tatry v Maciej Rataj, as was seen before, also illustrates that there is a limit to the extent to which Article 21 applies.[459] The Court held in that decision that 'same parties' in Article 21 in fact implies that the parties to the two actions are identical, in accordance with the wording of that provision, although their procedural position may not necessarily be the same.[460] Naturally, that decision has the disadvantage of different courts deciding on different aspects of the same dispute.[461]

In *Drouot v CMI*, the Court had to answer the question whether Article 21 is applicable in the case of two actions for contribution to the general average. One action was brought by the insurer of the hull of a vessel against the owner and the insurer of the cargo which the vessel was carrying when it sank. The other was brought by the latter two parties against the owner and the charterer of the vessel. When answering that question, the Court recalled that the terms used in Article 21 must, in principle, be regarded as independent, and referred to the principles underlying Articles 21 to 23. The Court then took account of the wording of Article 21, and consistently held that this Article must be understood as requiring, as a condition of the obligation of the second court seised to decline jurisdiction, that the parties to the two actions are identical.[462] That condition is to be applied even in a case where there may be such a degree of identity between the interests

---

455 C-129/92 *Owens v Bracco* 37.

456 C-129/92 *Owens v Bracco* 17,18,34 (re C-190/89 *Rich* 26).

457 C-129/92 *Owens v Bracco* 19-21 (re Jenard Report, OJ 1979 C 59, p. 15),32 (re 38/81 *Effer* 6).

458 C-129/92 *Owens v Bracco* 22-26, 29-32 (re 38/81 *Effer* 6)-34 (re C-190/89 *Rich* 26), 36 (re *OUI*).

459 See text following note 440, in this section.

460 C-406/92 *Tatry v Maciej Rataj* 32.

461 See hereafter section 4.2 of this chapter.

462 C-351/96 *Drouot v CMI* 15,16 (re C-406/92 *Tatry* 30),17 (re C-406/92 *Tatry* 32),18 (re C-406/92 *Tatry* 33)-24.

of an insurer and those of its insured, that a judgment delivered against one of them would have the force of *res judicata* as against the other. Such a degree of identity would be the case, *inter alia*, where an insurer, by virtue of its right of subrogation, brings or defends an action in the name of its insured without the latter being in a position to influence the proceedings. However, the application of Article 21 cannot have the effect of precluding the insurer and its insured, where their interests diverge, from asserting their respective interests before the courts as against the other parties concerned. It is for the national court, though, to ascertain whether this is in fact the case.[463] Although the Court did not mention this issue, it is clear that a strict application of the condition that the two actions have to be identical has the disadvantage of different courts deciding on different aspects of the same dispute. It is compatible, though, with the ideal that a person should not be deprived of or removed from (the choice of) the court that would otherwise be competent, for no good reason, to be discussed hereafter.[464]

Finally, a restrictive application of Article 21, was argued by the Court in *Von Horn v Cinnamond*, in a case involving the temporal application of Article 21 with regard to proceedings of which one had been brought before the date of entry into force of the Convention between those States and the second after that date.[465] The Court typically took account of the scheme of the Convention, the wording of the different language versions of Article 21, and several of the principles underlying the Convention as a whole, such as the principle 'free movement of judgment' and 'strengthening the protection of legal persons in the Community' and the principle 'sound administration of justice'.[466] The Court decided that where proceedings involving the same cause of action and between the same parties are pending in two different States, the first proceedings having been brought before the date of entry into force of the Convention between those States and the second proceedings after that date, the court second seised must apply Article 21 if the court first seised has assumed jurisdiction on the basis of a rule which accords with the provisions of the Convention or with the provision of a convention which was in force between the two States concerned when the proceedings were instituted, and must do so provisionally if the court first seised has not yet ruled on whether it has jurisdiction. On the other hand, the court second seised must not apply Article 21 if the court first seised has assumed jurisdiction on the basis of a rule which does not accord with the provisions of the Convention or with the provisions of a convention which was in force between those two States when proceedings were instituted. Although the Court referred to several

---

463 C-351/96 *Drouot v CMI* 25.

464 See hereafter section 4.1 of this chapter.

465 C-163/95 *Von Horn v Cinnamond* 27.

466 C-163/95 *Von Horn v Cinnamond* 12,13 (re 144/86 *Gubisch v Palumbo* 8; C-351/89 *OUI v NHIC* 16),17 (re C-220/88 *Dumez France v Hessische Landesbank* 18; *OUI* 15),23 (re *OUI* 24).

principles that would favour a broad interpretation, it was not however clear how these principles relate to the decision given.

CONCLUSIONS AND SUMMARY

In this section it has been seen that the principle of a sound administration of justice and efficacious conduct of proceedings is firmly established under the Convention. The principle is not absolute, though. The relative weight of that principle appears from the system of jurisdictional rules, the general scheme of the Convention and from the Court's case law on the interpretation of the specific provisions to which that principle directly underlies.

As regards the sub-principle that courts that have the practical advantage of first-hand knowledge of the facts, proximity of evidence or law should be able to decide the dispute, the relative weight of this principle is evident from the Court's reasoning as to a restrictive interpretation of the rules of jurisdiction, to which that principle underlies. In this respect, most of the Court's arguments are based on the division of jurisdiction in Title II of the Convention, resulting from the distinctly different sub-principles that flow from the main principle that disputes are to be decided by an appropriate court. The main requirements that flow from the principle that courts that have certain practical advantages should be able to decide a case, is that there is a direct or territorial link between the facts of the case and the court that is competent to hear the case and that account is taken of the division of jurisdiction, implied by that principle. As regards the principle that an entire dispute should be decided before a single court, its relative weight is particularly determined by the principles, 'free movement of justice' and 'legal certainty' which have a strong influence on the interpretation of the provisions to which that principle directly underlies. In order for the principle to apply, it is required that there is a close connecting factor between the dispute and the competent court, meaning that the cases involved are related. To conclude this section, we present the following scheme of the sub-principle of a sound administration of justice:

(4.3) The sub-principle of sound administration of justice *entails*:

- (4.3.1) A court that has the practical advantage of first-hand knowledge of the facts, ease of taking evidence and/or knowledge of the applicable law should be able to decide a case

- (4.3.2) An entire dispute should be decided before a single court

The *main requirements* that flow from these two sub-principles are:

(4.3.1) The sub-principle that a court that has the practical advantage of first-hand knowledge of the facts, ease of taking evidence and/or knowledge of the applicable law should be able to decide the case, *requires*:
- a direct, territorial link between the facts of the case and the court seised
- that account is taken of the division of jurisdiction, implied by this principle

(4.3.2) The sub-principle that an entire dispute should be decided before a single court, *requires*:
(4.3.2.1) Related cases to be brought before a single court
(4.3.2.2) Related actions already brought before different courts, to be decided together

4. The overall ideal that an entire dispute should be heard by a single and appropriate court

Introduction

From the foregoing sections in this chapter, it appears that the rules of jurisdiction contained in Title II of the Convention are applied in the light of their underlying principles, as well as in the light of the principles underlying the Convention as a whole. We have seen that the system of principles underlying the Convention as a whole has a major influence on the relative weight of the principles directly underlying the specific provisions as to the jurisdiction of the national courts. In the foregoing sections we have discussed the approach of the Court in this respect, as it appears from the Court's case law.

However, the analysis of the Court's principle-based reasoning with regard to the Convention's rules of jurisdiction would not be complete, if no attention were to be paid to the role of certain subordinate considerations which are used by the Court when it justifies its interpretations of the rules of jurisdiction. These considerations, when taken together, clarify that, after all, the Convention, with its rules of jurisdiction, aims at one overall, though not always attainable ideal: the ideal of an entire dispute, as far as possible, being heard by a single *and* appropriate court. This overall ideal consists of two parts.

One part of this overall ideal is the part that relates to '*disputes before an appropriate court*'. This part can be pursued by several of the sub-principles discussed earlier: the principle of the 'protection of a weaker party (due to his procedural or socio-economic position)', the principle of 'party autonomy' (by agreement or appearance)' and the principle that 'a court that has the practical advantage of first-hand knowledge of the facts, proximity of evidence and/or law, should be able to hear the case'.[467] As was seen in the foregoing sections, these distinctive principles cannot be fully applied at the same time and are weighed in relation to each other. For this purpose the Court has used distinctive lines of reasoning. In particular, the Court has held that the rules of jurisdiction derogating from the general principle laid down in Article 2 must be interpreted in such a manner that there is no possibility of the very existence of that general principle being called into question, that these provisions derogating from Article 2 must only be applied in the situations envisaged by the Convention, but that an interpretation of the derogations that would render them (and their underlying principles) completely redundant, cannot be accepted. When using these (and other) lines of argument, the Court respects the division of jurisdictions as provided for in the rules contained in Title II of the Convention, interpreted in the light of the principles underlying them and underlying the Convention as a whole.

The second part of the overall ideal that an entire dispute should, as far as possible, be heard by a single and appropriate court, is the part that relates to '*an entire dispute before one single court*'. This can be pursued by the sub-principles 'related cases to be brought before a single court' and 'related actions already brought before different courts to be decided by a single court', so as to avoid the disadvantages of separate (or parallel) proceedings.[468] This part of the overall ideal is supported by 'legal certainty as to jurisdiction', particularly by the sub-principle that 'fragmentation of proceedings' should be avoided', and 'legal certainty as to judgments' which requires avoiding the risk of irreconcilable decisions (both in turn also contributing to the principle of 'free movement of judgments').[469]

It is obvious that the overall ideal that an entire dispute should be heard by a single and appropriate court cannot always be attained, simply because the principle that disputes should be decided by an appropriate court and the principle that an entire dispute should be heard by a single court, may point in different directions. When interpreting the rules of jurisdiction, these distinctive aspects of the overall ideal may come into conflict with each other. This is particularly evident, when we consider the sub-principles that flow from the principle of a sound administration of justice. Some of them are intended to promote the ideal of an entire dispute being decided by a single court, others are meant to promote the ideal of disputes being decided by an appropriate court, being a court that has a direct, territorial link with the case.

These conflicting aspects have to be balanced. In order to balance these conflicting aspects of the overall ideal that a dispute should be heard by a single and appropriate court, several subordinate considerations have been introduced by the

[467] Compare sections 1 to 3.1 of this chapter. See Arts. 2 and 5, Arts. 7 to 18, and Art. 24.

[468] Compare section 3.2 of this chapter, and see Art. 6, Art. 10, paragraph 1, Art. 11, paragraph 2, Art. 14, paragraph 3, and Arts. 21 to 23.

[469] See sections 4.2 and 5 of chapter 5.

Court, as is shown by the Court's case law. A distinction can be made between the following considerations: (1) a party must not be deprived of or removed from the courts that would otherwise be competent, for no good reason; this consideration favours the ideal of an appropriate court; (2) the disadvantages of a fragmentation of proceedings can be mitigated; this consideration favours the ideal of a single court hearing the entire dispute; and, although playing only a very modest role, (3) the maxim *accessorium sequitur principale*, which also favours the ideal of a single court hearing the entire dispute. Two of these considerations take care that the aspect of 'an entire dispute before a single court' is ensured. These considerations clearly aim to minimize the irreconcilability of judgments, or at least to make clear that irreconcilability can be avoided. They are therefore not only an important indicator of this overall ideal of hearing an entire dispute by a single and appropriate court, but also sustain one of the main principles of the Convention, namely 'free movement of judgments.' The other consideration primarily takes care that the aspect 'disputes before an appropriate court' is not undermined and that the division of jurisdictions as intended by the Convention is indeed respected.

At first sight, these subordinate considerations may not seem to play a pivotal role, but taken together they function as lubricating oil when pursuing this overall ideal that an entire dispute should be decided by a single and appropriate court. They will be discussed in further detail in the following sub-sections (4.1 to 4.3).

4.1 A party must not be deprived of or removed from the courts that would otherwise be competent, for no good reason

C Art. 5	R 5	C Art. 17	R 23	C Art. 28	R 35
C Art. 6	R 6	C Art. 21	R 27		
C Art. 16	R 22	C Art. 24	R 31		

The consideration that a party must not be deprived of or removed from the jurisdiction of the court which would otherwise be competent in his case, for no good reason, relates to the overall ideal that disputes are to be decided, as far as possible, by a single and appropriate court. It relates to the part 'disputes before an appropriate court.' In fact, it requires that the division of jurisdiction which the Convention intended to establish and considers appropriate from the perspective of the procedural and socio-economic position of the parties, the autonomy of the parties and the practical advantages of certain courts, is respected.[470]

This consideration clearly plays a role under the Convention. It is directly expressed by the very wording of Article 6, point 2, which provides that a person may also be sued as a third party in an action on a warranty or guarantee or in any other third party proceedings, in the court seised of the original proceedings, 'unless these were instituted solely with the object of removing him from the ju-

[470] Compare 220/84 *Autoteile v Malhé* 17; C-51/97 *Réunion européenne v Spliethoff's* 46-50.

risdiction of the court which would be competent in his case.'[471] The role of that consideration also becomes evident from the Court's case law, since the Court has resorted to it on other occasions where Article 6, point 2, does not apply.

For example, the Court has argued, with reference to the Jenard Report, that Article 6, point 1, cannot be interpreted in such a manner that it would give a plaintiff the liberty to make a claim against a number of defendants with the sole object of ousting the jurisdiction of the courts of the State where one of the defendants is domiciled.[472] The defendant must not be deprived of the benefit of the protective rules laid down by the Convention, for no good reason.[473]

The Court's case law with regard to the exclusive jurisdictions, laid down in Articles 16 and 17, is also illustrative in this respect. On several occasions the Court has used the argument that the parties should not be deprived of the choice of forum which would otherwise be theirs, for no good reason, as is particularly illustrated by the Court's case law on the interpretation of Article 16.[474]

As regards Article 16, it is settled case law that Article 16 must not be given a wider interpretation than is required by its objective. Such an interpretation is contrary to the division of jurisdiction which the Convention intended to establish, and results in depriving the parties of the choice of forum which would otherwise be theirs, and, in certain cases, results in their being brought before a court which is not that of any of them.[475] As the Court put it in *Sanders v Van der Putte*:

> 'the assignment, in the interests of the proper administration of justice, of exclusive jurisdiction to the courts of one Contracting State in accordance with Article 16 of the Convention results in depriving the parties of the choice of the forum which would otherwise be theirs and, in certain cases, results in their being brought before a court which is not that of the domicile of any of them. Having regard to that consideration the provisions of Article 16 must not be given a wider interpretation than is required by their objective.'[476]

As regards Article 17, we recall the Court's case law concerning the interpretation of the formal requirements of Article 17, in which the Court sought appropriate guarantees that the parties really had consented to the clause waiving the normal rules of jurisdiction. The Court has held on several occasions, that it cannot

---

[471] C-365/88 *Hagen v Zeehaghe* 13; 56/79 *Zelger v Salinitri I* 3,4.

[472] Jenard Report, OJ 1979 C 59, 5.3; 189/87 *Kalfelis v Schröder* 8,9; C-51/97 *Réunion européenne v Spliethoff's* 47 (re *Kalfelis v Schröder* 8,9).

[473] C-51/97 *Réunion européenne v Spliethoff's* 46.

[474] See before section 3.1.3 of this chapter ; text following note 369.

[475] 73/77 *Sanders v Van der Putte* 17,18; C-115/88 *Reichert v Dresdner Bank I* 9 (re *Sanders v Van der Putte*); 220/84 *Autoteile v Malhé* 17; C-280/90 *Hacker v Euro-Relais* 12; C-292/93 *Lieber v Göbel* 12 (re 115/88 *Reichert v Dresdner Bank I* 9); 8/98 *Dansommer v Götz* 21 (re *Sanders v Van der Putte* 17,18, C-115/88 *Reichert v Dresdner Bank I* 9, C-292/93 *Lieber v Göbel* 12).

[476] 73/77 *Sanders v Van der Putte* 17.

be presumed that one of the parties waives the advantage of the normal rules conferring jurisdiction.[477] Another interpretation of the formal requirements of Article 17 would have the result that (one of) the parties would be deprived of the Court that would otherwise be competent.

With regard to respect for the division of (appropriate) jurisdictions as expressed by the scheme of rules of jurisdictions in Title II, we also refer to the Court's case law on the division of jurisdictions as follows from Article 5, points 1 and 3, in particular to *Kalfelis v Schröder* and *Réunion européenne v Spliethoff's*. In these judgments, the Court made it clear that a court which has jurisdiction under Article 5, point 3 over an action in so far as it is based on tort or delict does not have jurisdiction over that action in so far as it is not so based.[478] Notice that another interpretation of the jurisdictions concerned could have the result that the defendant would be deprived of the court that would otherwise be competent.

Furthermore, we refer to the Court's decisions on the interpretation of Article 24. As was seen before, the Court has consistently held that the fact that the defendant appears before the court dealing with interim measures in the context of expeditious procedures intended to grant provisional or protective measures cannot, by itself, suffice to confer on that court, by virtue of Article 18 of the Convention, unlimited jurisdiction to order any provisional or protective measures which the court might consider appropriate if it had jurisdiction under the Convention as to the substance of the case. The rules on jurisdiction as to the substance set out in Articles 2 and 5 to 17(18) of the Convention, cannot be circumvented in this way.[479]

Finally, we recall here the Court's decisions as regards the application of Article 21. The Court has argued that the application of Article 21 cannot have the effect of precluding a party from asserting its interests before the court that would otherwise be competent.[480]

All the above-mentioned considerations reinforce the principle that disputes should be decided before an appropriate court. The argument that a party must not be deprived of or removed from the court(s) which would otherwise be competent in his case, for no good reason, sustains the respect to be paid to the distinctive, general, special and exclusive jurisdictions that are considered to be appropriate in the cases envisaged by the Convention.[481]

---

[477] 25/76 *Segoura v Bonakdarian* 8; compare 24/76 *Salotti v Rüwa* 9; C-106/95 *Mainschiffahrts v Les Gravières Rhénanes* 14 (re *Salotti v Rüwa* 7; *Segoura* 6),15 (re *Salotti* 7; *Segoura* 6).

[478] 189/87 *Kalfelis v Schröder* 19; C-51/97 *Réunion européenne v Spliethoff's* 49 (re *Kalfelis*).

[479] C-99/96 *Mietz v Intership* 47 (re *Van Uden*),52; and C-391/95 *Van Uden v Deco-Line* 46.

[480] C-351/96 *Drouot v CMI* 20; and compare C-406/92 *Tatry v Maciej Rataj* 33.

[481] C-106/95 *Mainschiffahrts v Les Gravières Rhénanes* 14 (re 24/76 *Salotti* 7; 25/76 *Segoura* 6), 73/77 *Sanders v Van der Putte* 17.

The argument that a party must not be deprived of or removed from the jurisdiction of the court(s) which would otherwise be competent in his case, for no good reason, generally requires a restrictive interpretation of the rules of jurisdiction. It is in particular used to secure the division of jurisdictions that are considered appropriate within the European Community. It may conflict though with the second part of the overall ideal that disputes are to be decided by a single and appropriate court: 'an entire dispute before a single court'. The lines of argument which are discussed in the following section clarify how the disadvantages of applying the principle 'disputes before an appropriate court' can be mitigated.

4.2 Mitigating the disadvantages of having different courts ruling on different aspects of the same dispute

C Art. 2	R 2	C Art. 21	R 27
C Art. 5(3)	R 5(3)	C Art. 22	R 28

The application of the principle that disputes should be heard by an appropriate court may have the effect of fragmenting the proceedings, as the Court observed, among others, in *Effer v Kantner*, *Gabriel* and in particular in *Shevill v Presse Alliance*.[482] Here we should recall that in *Shevill v Presse Alliance*, the Court held that, on a proper construction of the expression 'place where the harmful event occurred' in Article 5, point 3, of the Convention, the victim of a libel by a newspaper article distributed in several Contracting States may bring an action for damages against the publisher before the courts of each of the Contracting States in which the publication was distributed and where the victim claims to have suffered injury to his reputation, although these courts have jurisdiction to rule solely on the damage caused in the State of the court seised.[483] The Court recognised in that decision that there are admittedly disadvantages in having different courts ruling on various aspects of the same dispute, but pointed out that, in this case, the Convention provides in Article 2 and Article 5, point 3, for possibilities to mitigate these disadvantages. The Court considered as follows:

> 'Although there are admittedly disadvantages to having different courts ruling on various aspects of the same dispute, the plaintiff always has the option of bringing his entire claim before the courts either of the defendant's domicile or of the place where the publisher of the defamatory publication is established.'[484]

The same argument was used in *Kalfelis v Schröder*.[485] As was seen before, the Court held in this case that a court which has jurisdiction under Article 5, point 3,

[482] 38/81 *Effer v Kantner* 6,7 (re 73/77 *Sanders v Van der Putte*); C-96/00 *Gabriel* 56,57 (re C-256/00 *Besix v Kretzschmar* 27); and C-68/93 *Shevill v Presse Alliance* 31,32.

[483] C-68/93 *Shevill v Presse Alliance* 33.

[484] C-68/93 *Shevill v Presse Alliance* 32.

[485] 189/87 *Kalfelis v Schröder* 19,20,21.

over an action in so far as it is based on tort or delict does not have jurisdiction over that action in so far as it is not so based. Hence, the Court admitted that such an interpretation may result in the fragmentation of proceedings. It pointed out, however, that the Convention provides for several solutions that may mitigate these disadvantages. In this case, the Court pointed to Article 2 as well as to Article 22. The Court considered as follows:

> 'Whilst it is true that disadvantages arise from different aspects of the same dispute being adjudicated upon by different courts, it must be pointed out, on the one hand, that a plaintiff is always entitled to bring his action in its entirety before the courts for the domicile of the defendant and, on the other, that Article 22 of the Convention allows the first court seised, in certain circumstances, to hear the case in its entirety provided that there is a connection between the actions brought before the different courts.'[486]

A similar line of reasoning was followed by the Court in *Réunion européenne v Spliethoff's* and in *Leathertex v Bodetex.* [487]

Tatry v Maciej Rataj is also illustrative of the Court's concern for the effect of the fragmentation of proceedings when interpreting the rules of jurisdiction.[488] In that decision the Court held that a restrictive application of Article 21 may involve a fragmentation of the proceedings. It continued, however, that this disadvantage may be mitigated by Article 22. The Court argued:

> 'Article 21 requires the second court seised to decline jurisdiction only to the extent to which the parties to the proceedings pending before it are also parties to the action previously started before the court of another Contracting State. It does not prevent the proceedings from continuing between the other parties. Admittedly, that interpretation of Article 21 involves fragmenting the proceedings. However, Article 22 mitigates that disadvantage. That Article allows the second court seised to stay proceedings or to decline jurisdiction on the ground that the actions are related, if the conditions there set out are satisfied.'[489]

From these decisions, it becomes evident that, under the Convention and in addition to the principles directly underlying the rules of jurisdiction, the overall ideal that disputes should be decided as far as possible by a single and appropriate court, is indeed aimed at.

4.3 The maxim *accessorium sequitur principale*

The overall ideal that an entire dispute should be heard by a single and appropriate court, particularly the part 'entire dispute before a single court', is also ex-

---

[486] 189/87 *Kalfelis v Schröder* 20.
[487] C-51/97 *Réunion européenne v Spliethoff's* 51; and C-420/97 *Leathertex v Bodetex* 38,41,42.
[488] See text following note 461, of section 3.2.2 of this chapter.
[489] C-406/92 *Tatry v Maciej Rataj* 33,34.

pressed by the maxim *accessorium sequitur principale*. The maxim appears from the Court's case law, but has only been applied with regard to contracts of employment. That maxim implies that where various obligations are at issue, it will be the principal (characteristic) obligation which will determine the national court's jurisdiction.

Shenavai v Kreischer is illustrative in this respect.[490] In that judgment, as was seen before, the Court recalled its case law, in which it was decided that in the particular case of a dispute concerned with a number of obligations arising under the same contract and forming the basis of the proceedings commenced by the plaintiff, the court before which the matter is brought will, when determining whether it has jurisdiction, be guided by the maxim *accessorium sequitur principale*, meaning that: where various obligations are at issue, it will be the principal (characteristic) obligation which will determine its jurisdiction.[491] However, *Leathertex v Bodetex* makes it clear that, normally, the maxim is to be applied only to contracts of employment.[492] In that judgment, the Court had to reply to the question whether under Article 5, point 1, the same court has jurisdiction to hear the whole of an action founded on two obligations of equal rank, namely the obligation to pay compensation in lieu of notice and the obligation to pay commission, arising from the same contract.[493] According to the conflict rules of the Contracting State of the court seised, one of these obligations was to be performed in the forum state and the other in another Contracting State.[494] The Court recalled that the place of performance of the obligation in question is to be determined by the law governing that obligation according to the conflict rules of the court seised.[495] The Court then held that when the specific features of a contract of employment do not exist, it is neither necessary nor appropriate to identify the obligation which characterizes the contract.[496] In this respect, the Court argued:

> 'when a dispute relates to a number of obligations of equal rank arising from the same contract, the court before which the matter is brought cannot, when determining whether it has jurisdiction, be guided by the maxim accessorium sequitur principale referred to by the Court in ... the judgment in Shenavai ...'[497]

In addition, the Court considered, as is typical in this type of case:

---

[490] 266/85 *Shenavai v Kreischer*.

[491] 266/85 *Shenavai v Kreischer* 11 (re 133/81 *Ivenel v Schwab*),19; compare section 1.2 of this chapter, text following notes 40 and 87.

[492] C-420/97 *Leathertex v Bodetex*.

[493] C-420/97 *Leathertex v Bodetex* 19.

[494] C-420/97 *Leathertex v Bodetex* 34.

[495] C-420/97 *Leathertex v Bodetex* 33 (re 12/76 *Tessili v Dunlop* 13; C-288/92 *Custom Made v Stawa* 25; and, C-440/97 *Concorde v Panjan*),36; and, see, 14/76 *De Bloos v Bouyer* 8,9,10.

[496] C-420/97 *Leathertex v Bodetex* 36 (re *Shenavai v Kreischer* 17).

[497] C-420/97 *Leathertex v Bodetex* 39.

> 'It should be remembered that, while there are disadvantages in having different courts ruling on different aspects of the same dispute, the plaintiff always has the option, under Article 2 of the Convention, of bringing his entire claim before the courts for the place where the defendant is domiciled.'[498]

Although the maxim accessorium sequitur principale has only been applied with regard to contracts of employment, it shows however, that the overall ideal of an entire dispute being heard, as far as possible, by a single and appropriate court, is pursued under the Convention.

Conclusions

The overall ideal that an entire dispute should be heard by a single and appropriate court, is recognized by the Court, as becomes clear from its case law. It contains two aspects, namely 'disputes before an appropriate court' and 'an entire dispute before a single court'. These two aspects of the overall ideal are reinforced by several subordinate considerations which were discussed in this section, in particular, the considerations that 'a party must not be deprived of or removed from the courts that would otherwise be competent, for no good reason', and that 'disadvantages of several courts having jurisdiction as regards different aspects of a dispute can be mitigated under the Convention'. These subordinate arguments are used to strike a balance between the conflicting aspects of the overall ideal of an entire dispute being heard by a single and appropriate court. In short, this overall ideal particularly requires, in addition to the principles flowing from the main principle that disputes should be decided by an appropriate court, that:

(4.1) A party should not be deprived of or removed from the courts that would otherwise be competent, for no good reason
(4.2) The disadvantages of having different courts ruling on different aspects of the same dispute can be circumvented under the Convention

Conclusions and summary

To conclude this chapter on the fourth main principle, we represent the following scheme of the principle that disputes should be decided by an appropriate court, including the overall ideal of having an entire dispute decided by a single and appropriate court:

---

498 C-420/97 *Leathertex v Bodetex* 41.

(4) The Principle that Disputes should be Decided by an Appropriate Court *implies*:

(4.1) Protection of the weaker party
entailing:
(4.1.1) Protection of the party who is weaker due to his procedural position
(4.1.2) Protection of the party who is weaker due to his socio-economic position
(4.1.3) Protection of the party that might be unaware of a jurisdiction clause incorporated in a contract by the other party

(4.2) The sub-principle of party autonomy
entailing:
(4.2.1) Prorogation by agreement
(4.2.2) Prorogation by appearance

(4.3) Sound administration of justice with a view to the efficacious conduct of the proceedings
entailing:
(4.3.1) A court that has the practical advantage of first-hand knowledge of the facts, ease of taking evidence and/or knowledge of the law applicable should be able to decide a case
(4.3.2) An entire dispute should be decided by a single court
requiring that:
(4.3.2.1) Related cases should be brought before a single court
(4.3.2.2) Related actions already brought before different courts should be decided together

(4.4) The overall ideal of an entire dispute being heard by a single and appropriate court *implies*, in addition to the sub-principles that already flow from this fourth main principle, that:
(4.4.1) A party should not be deprived of or removed from the courts that would otherwise be competent, for no good reason, and that
(4.4.2) The disadvantages of several courts having jurisdiction as regards different aspects of a dispute can be mitigated.

FINAL CONCLUSIONS

In the foregoing chapters we have described how the Court has justified its interpretations of the provisions of the 1968 Brussels Convention. It appeared that in most cases the Court established that the Convention's terms and concepts should be interpreted autonomously, independent from the meaning which they have in the national law of the states that happen to be involved in the particular case. In these cases, the Court has used principle-based reasoning to decide on the (autonomous) meaning to be given to the Convention's provisions: when interpreting the Convention, the Court has referred to the system of principles underlying the Convention. It should be noted that in some instances the Court has not (only) taken account of the system of principles underlying the Convention itself, but (also) of the general principles that stem from the corpus of the national legal systems of the Contracting States or of the meaning which a concept has in Community law. However, overall it can be concluded that principle-based reasoning has been the main method of interpretation used by the Court. Dworkin's legal theory, described in chapter 1, which contends that the law does not only consist of a legal order's explicit legal provisions but also of the principles that are presupposed by them, clearly applies to the Brussels Convention. As the Court's case law makes clear, the Convention's provisions cannot be properly understood without taking into account the system of principles lying beyond these provisions.

In this study we have attempted to uncover the content of the system of principles that the Court has used to interpret the Convention's provisions. Two dimensions to this system of principles can be distinguished: a vertical and a horizontal dimension. The vertical dimension refers to the relation between more general and more concrete principles, while the horizontal dimension concerns the way in which principles are weighed in relation to each other in case they conflict.

The vertical dimension of the system of principles employed by the Court has not been too difficult to uncover. We have identified one overarching general principle ('legal protection of persons established in the Community'), four main principles ('free movement of judgments', 'protection of the rights of the defence', 'legal certainty' and 'disputes to be decided by an appropriate court') and a set of more concrete sub-principles that flow from each of these four main principles. Appendix 1 contains a scheme of these principles and sub-principles. It seems that over the years, the Court has developed a better sense of the set of principles that in its view underlies the Convention's provisions. In its later decisions, the Court is more complete in enumerating the principles that apply to the case to be decided.

As was seen, quite a number of cases that have been presented to the Court concern cases in which conflicting principles pertain. This implies that the horizontal dimension of the system of principles, which shows the way the Court has weighed conflicting principles, is of importance. This dimension is far more difficult to capture: the weighing of conflicting principles appears to be a complex process that cannot be reduced to a number of hard-and-fast rules. When we evaluate the way the Court has resolved the conflict between the Convention's principles in terms of the three standards of rationality, described in chapter 1, the following conclusions can be drawn.[1] The requirement of consistency demands that the conflict between principles should be resolved in a consistent manner throughout a legal order. We conclude that the Court tries to act consistently in the way it weighs the various principles. This is apparent from the fact that in coming to its decisions, the Court often explicitly takes into account the way the designers of the Convention have weighed conflicting principles and also the way the Court itself has done in its previous decisions. We have not investigated whether, in the cases decided by the Court, this requirement of consistency pointed to a single decision. However, our impression is that it is quite possible that in a number of cases, several possible decisions could have been selected, each of them not being inconsistent with the way in which conflicting principles have been previously weighed. In the decisions taken by the Court under the Brussels Convention, the second standard of rationality in the implementation of conflicting principles, the optimisation requirement, does not appear. This by no means implies that the Court does not consider this requirement to be relevant when dealing with opposing principles, it merely means, in our view, that it stays implicit. We assume that the Court uses the third standard, the prohibition of disproportionality, whenever it rejects certain interpretations, representing a particular way of weighing conflicting principles, because they would lead 'to the very existence of one of the principles being called into question'.[2]

All in all, this study's investigation has made clear which principles and subprinciples the Court has used in interpreting the Convention. With these principles, we have identified an important part of the catalogue of reasons that the Court uses to argue for or against a particular interpretation. We have concluded that the way the Court has weighed principles in case they conflict cannot always be grasped in all of its details. This does not mean, however, that principles are not of any use in these cases: they at least make clear, on a more fundamental level, what is at stake, thus leading to a more conscious decision.

---

[1] See chapter 1, section 3, text following note 19.

[2] See for example 189/87 *Kalfelis v Schröder* 8; 24/76 *Salotti v Rüwa* 7; C-68/93 *Shevill v Presse Alliance* 27 (re 21/76 *Bier v Mines de potasse*15,17; C-439/93 *Lloyd's v Campenon* 17,18,21,22; 73/77 *Sanders v Van der Putte* 18.

With the introduction of Regulation No. 44/2001, which has essentially replaced the Brussels Convention, the Convention's system of principles remains very relevant. Important indications for this view can be found in the Initial Proposal of the Regulation itself. This expressly states that the Regulation closely corresponds to the Brussels Convention, that the Regulation has the same essential structure and basic principles, and tries to realise the same objectives. In addition, it is evident from the preliminary considerations of the Regulation that most of the principles that play a pivotal role in the Court's case law under the Convention are also of importance for the Regulation. These considerations refer to the principle of the free movement of judgments, the principle of legal certainty, the principle of the protection of the rights of the defence and the sub-principles that flow from the principle of 'an appropriate court', namely, 'protection of the weaker party', 'party autonomy' and 'a sound and harmonious administration of justice'.[3] Moreover, continuity in the results achieved under the Convention has been a general consideration.[4]

The most general principle mentioned in the Preamble of the Convention, implying that the overall purpose of the Convention was the strengthening of the legal protection of persons established in the Community, is not mentioned in these considerations accompanying the Regulation. We assume, though, that this principle also plays a role under the Regulation. We find evidence for this assumption in the Action Plan of the Council and the Commission on how best to implement the provisions of the Treaty of Amsterdam on an area of freedom, security and justice. These provisions were introduced in the EC Treaty, in the Articles 61(c) and 65, on which the Regulation was founded. The Action Plan stated that the provisions adopted in Amsterdam have the objective of maintaining and developing the European Union as an area of freedom, security and justice, by creating a secure environment, with the full backing of a system of justice, in which all Union citizens and residents can have confidence. Thus the Action Plan reinforces the principle of strengthening within the Community, the legal protection of persons established therein.[5]

On some points, innovations have been introduced in Regulation No. 44/2001. The chief innovations are the following. The Regulation provides for an autonomous definition of the seat of a legal person instead of the determination of this seat by reference to the rules of private international law of the State in which jurisdiction is exercised (compare Article 60 of the Regulation to Article 53 of the Convention); as well as an autonomous definition of 'place of performance' for two types of contracts (compare Article 5, point 1, sub. b, of the Regulation to

---

[3] OJ L 12/1, 16.1.2001, p. 1 ff, considerations 6,11,12,13,14,15,18.

[4] See considerations 5,19. On the other hand, since both legal instruments are closely related to each other, the Regulation in its turn will have an influence on the interpretation of the Convention; see for example C-111/01 *Gantner v Basch* 28 (re Regulation 44/2001).

[5] OJ C 19/1, 23.1.1999, p. 286 ff.

Article 5, point 1 of the Convention). In addition, under the Regulation, the substantive scope of the provisions governing consumer contracts is extended, so as to offer consumers better protection, notably in the field of electronic commerce (compare Article 15 of the Regulation to Article 13 of the Convention). Furthermore, it contains a separate section on jurisdiction over individual contracts of employment (compare Articles 18 to 21). And, it contains an autonomous definition of the date on which a case is pending in order to make the *lis pendens* rules more effective (compare Articles 27 to 29 in conjunction with Article 30 of the Regulation to Articles 21 and 23 of the Convention). Finally, several changes with regard to the procedure for recognition and enforcement have been implemented (compare Articles 38 to 56 of the Regulation to Articles 31 to 49 of the Convention). In particular, in the first phase of the enforcement proceedings, a declaration of enforceability cannot be refused on the grounds laid down in Articles 34 and 35 of the Regulation (Articles 27 and 28 of the Convention), whereas this was possible under the Convention (compare Article 41 of the Regulation to Article 34 of the Convention). Although the changes with regard to the procedure for the recognition and enforcement of judgments seem to imply that the rights of the defence are restricted to some extent, generally these innovations do not lead to any fundamental changes in the system of principles we have identified.

It should be pointed out that it is not unlikely, now that the rules on jurisdiction and recognition and enforcement of judgments have become a truly integral part of European Community law, that the Court will take into account some of the general EC principles when interpreting the Regulation. Examples of such principles are the principles of subsidiarity and proportionality, to be found in Article 5 of the EC Treaty, and the principles of equality, certainty and the protection of legitimate expectations.[6] However, we do think that the system of principles as described in this study will continue to provide the main reasons which motivate the Court to adopt or reject certain interpretations of the Regulation's provisions.

As we have argued, the system of principles underlying the Brussels Convention is similar to the system of principles that has inspired the Regulation's provisions and that the European Court of Justice will use to interpret the EC Regulation. This Regulation applies to all present EC Member States (except for Denmark) and will apply to all future EC Member States. In this sense, this system of principles can be said to represent the European system of principles that has inspired the European rules on jurisdiction and the recognition and enforcement of judgments in civil and commercial matters and that will have a major influence on the way the Court will interpret these rules in the future.

[6] Compare also note 19 in section 2 of chapter 2.

APPENDICES

APPENDIX 1

System of Principles underlying the 1968 Brussels Convention

The Most General Principle
Legal Protection of Persons established in the Community

The Four Main Principles

Sub-Principles

1 Free Movement of Judgments

(1) Full respect for another Contracting State's judgments
(2) Swift and simple procedure for recogniton and enforcement

2 Rights of the Defence

(1) Right to a proper service of the document instituting the proceedings
(2) Right to be heard in an appropriate court
(3) Right to an inter partes hearing
(4) Right to be defended by a lawyer
(5) Right to submit a defence on the substance of the case
(6) Protection of the interest of the defendant in staying execution proceedings in case of an appeal in the state of origin
(7) Right to be properly served with the decision delivered

3 Legal Certainty

(1) Equality and uniformity of rights and obligations
(2) Respect for the Convention's wording
(3) Legal certainty as to the scope of the Convention
(4) Legal certainty as to jurisdiction:
  (a) Legal certainty for the plaintiff
  (b) Legal certainty for the defendant
    (1) Clarity as to rules of jurisdiction
    (2) Avoiding further multiplication of jurisdiction as regards one and the same legal relationship
      (1) Avoiding alternative courts
      (2) Avoiding fragmentation of proceedings
    (3) National courts should be able readily to decide on their competence
(5) Legal certainty as to judgments: Avoiding irreconcilable decisions

4 Disputes in an Appropriate Court

(1) Protection of the weaker party
  (1) Protection of the procedurally weaker party
  (2) Protection of the socio-economically weaker party
(2) Party autonomy
  (1) Prorogation by explicit agreement
  (2) Prorogation by appearance
(3) Sound administration of justice
  (1) Courts that have the practical advantage of first-hand knowledge of the facts, ease of taking evidence and/or knowledge of the applicable law, should be competent
  (2) Entire disputes to be decided by a single Court
    (1) Related cases to be brought before a single court
    (2) Related cases brought before different courts, to be decided together
(4) The overall ideal of having an entire dispute decided by a single *and* appropriate court
  (1) A party must not be deprived of or removed from courts which are otherwise competent, for no good reason
  (2) Disadvantages of fragmentation of proceedings can be circumvented

APPENDIX 2

1968 Brussels Convention on jurisdiction and the enforcement of judgments in civil and commercial matters (consolidated version)

PREAMBLE

THE HIGH CONTRACTING PARTIES TO THE TREATY ESTABLISHING THE EUROPEAN ECONOMIC COMMUNITY,

DESIRING to implement the provisions of Article 220 of that Treaty by virtue of which they undertook to secure the simplification of formalities governing the reciprocal recognition and enforcement of judgments of courts or tribunals,

ANXIOUS to strengthen in the Community the legal protection of persons therein established,

CONSIDERING that it is necessary for this purpose to determine the international jurisdiction of their courts, to facilitate recognition and to introduce an expeditious procedure for securing the enforcement of judgments, authentic instruments and court settlements,

HAVE DECIDED to conclude this Convention ...'

Council Regulation (EC) No 44/2001 on jurisdiction and the recognition and enforcement of judgments in civil and commercial matters

THE COUNCIL OF THE EUROPEAN UNION,

HAVING REGARD to the Treaty establishing the European Community, and in particular Article 61(c) and Article 67(1) thereof,

HAVING REGARD to the proposal from the Commission(1),

HAVING REGARD to the opinion of the European Parliament(2),

HAVING REGARD to the opinion of the Economic and Social Committee(3),

WHEREAS:
(1) The Community has set itself the objective of maintaining and developing an area of freedom, security and justice, in which the free movement of persons is ensured. In order to establish progressively such an area, the Community should adopt, amongst other things, the measures relating to judicial cooperation in civil matters which are necessary for the sound operation of the internal market.
(2) Certain differences between national rules governing jurisdiction and recognition of judgments hamper the sound operation of the internal market. Provisions to unify the rules of conflict of jurisdiction in civil and commercial matters and to simplify the formalities with a view to rapid and simple recognition and enforcement of judgments from Member States bound by this Regulation are essential.
(3) This area is within the field of judicial cooperation in civil matters within the meaning of Article 65 of the Treaty.
(4) In accordance with the principles of subsidiarity and proportionality as set out in Article 5 of the Treaty, the objectives of this Regulation cannot be sufficiently achieved by the Member States and can therefore be better achieved by the Community. This Regulation confines itself to the minimum required in order to achieve those objectives and does not go beyond what is necessary for that purpose.
(5) On 27 September 1968 the Member States, acting under Article 293, fourth indent, of the Treaty, concluded the Brussels Convention on Jurisdiction and the Enforcement of Judgments in Civil and Commercial Matters, as amended by Conventions on the Accession of the New Member States to that Convention (hereinafter referred to as the 'Brussels Convention')(4). On 16 September 1988 Member States and EFTA States concluded the Lugano Convention

on Jurisdiction and the Enforcement of Judgments in Civil and Commercial Matters, which is a parallel Convention to the 1968 Brussels Convention. Work has been undertaken for the revision of those Conventions, and the Council has approved the content of the revised texts. Continuity in the results achieved in that revision should be ensured.

(6) In order to attain the objective of free movement of judgments in civil and commercial matters, it is necessary and appropriate that the rules governing jurisdiction and the recognition and enforcement of judgments be governed by a Community legal instrument which is binding and directly applicable.

(7) The scope of this Regulation must cover all the main civil and commercial matters apart from certain well-defined matters.

(8) There must be a link between proceedings to which this Regulation applies and the territory of the Member States bound by this Regulation. Accordingly common rules on jurisdiction should, in principle, apply when the defendant is domiciled in one of those Member States.

(9) A defendant not domiciled in a Member State is in general subject to national rules of jurisdiction applicable in the territory of the Member State of the court seised, and a defendant domiciled in a Member State not bound by this Regulation must remain subject to the Brussels Convention.

(10) For the purposes of the free movement of judgments, judgments given in a Member State bound by this Regulation should be recognised and enforced in another Member State bound by this Regulation, even if the judgment debtor is domiciled in a third State.

(11) The rules of jurisdiction must be highly predictable and founded on the principle that jurisdiction is generally based on the defendant's domicile and jurisdiction must always be available on this ground save in a few well-defined situations in which the subject-matter of the litigation or the autonomy of the parties warrants a different linking factor. The domicile of a legal person must be defined autonomously so as to make the common rules more transparent and avoid conflicts of jurisdiction.

(12) In addition to the defendant's domicile, there should be alternative grounds of jurisdiction based on a close link between the court and the action or in order to facilitate the sound administration of justice.

(13) In relation to insurance, consumer contracts and employment, the weaker party should be protected by rules of jurisdiction more favourable to his interests than the general rules provide for.

(14) The autonomy of the parties to a contract, other than an insurance, consumer or employment contract, where only limited autonomy to determine the courts having jurisdiction is allowed, must be respected subject to the exclusive grounds of jurisdiction laid down in this Regulation.

(15) In the interests of the harmonious administration of justice it is necessary to minimise the possibility of concurrent proceedings and to ensure that irreconcilable judgments will not be given in two Member States. There must be a clear and effective mechanism for resolving cases of lis pendens and related actions and for obviating problems flowing from national differences as to the determination of

the time when a case is regarded as pending. For the purposes of this Regulation that time should be defined autonomously.

(16) Mutual trust in the administration of justice in the Community justifies judgments given in a Member State being recognised automatically without the need for any procedure except in cases of dispute.

(17) By virtue of the same principle of mutual trust, the procedure for making enforceable in one Member State a judgment given in another must be efficient and rapid. To that end, the declaration that a judgment is enforceable should be issued virtually automatically after purely formal checks of the documents supplied, without there being any possibility for the court to raise of its own motion any of the grounds for non-enforcement provided for by this Regulation.

(18) However, respect for the rights of the defence means that the defendant should be able to appeal in an adversarial procedure, against the declaration of enforceability, if he considers one of the grounds for non-enforcement to be present. Redress procedures should also be available to the claimant where his application for a declaration of enforceability has been rejected.

(19) Continuity between the Brussels Convention and this Regulation should be ensured, and transitional provisions should be laid down to that end. The same need for continuity applies as regards the interpretation of the Brussels Convention by the Court of Justice of the European Communities and the 1971 Protocol(5) should remain applicable also to cases already pending when this Regulation enters into force.

(20) The United Kingdom and Ireland, in accordance with Article 3 of the Protocol on the position of the United Kingdom and Ireland annexed to the Treaty on European Union and to the Treaty establishing the European Community, have given notice of their wish to take part in the adoption and application of this Regulation.

(21) Denmark, in accordance with Articles 1 and 2 of the Protocol on the position of Denmark annexed to the Treaty on European Union and to the Treaty establishing the European Community, is not participating in the adoption of this Regulation, and is therefore not bound by it nor subject to its application.

(22) Since the Brussels Convention remains in force in relations between Denmark and the Member States that are bound by this Regulation, both the Convention and the 1971 Protocol continue to apply between Denmark and the Member States bound by this Regulation.

(23) The Brussels Convention also continues to apply to the territories of the Member States which fall within the territorial scope of that Convention and which are excluded from this Regulation pursuant to Article 299 of the Treaty.

(24) Likewise for the sake of consistency, this Regulation should not affect rules governing jurisdiction and the recognition of judgments contained in specific Community instruments.

(25) Respect for international commitments entered into by the Member States means that this Regulation should not affect conventions relating to specific matters to which the Member States are parties.

(26) The necessary flexibility should be provided for in the basic rules of this Regulation in order to take account of the specific procedural rules of certain Member States. Certain provisions of the Protocol annexed to the Brussels Convention should accordingly be incorporated in this Regulation.
(27) In order to allow a harmonious transition in certain areas which were the subject of special provisions in the Protocol annexed to the Brussels Convention, this Regulation lays down, for a transitional period, provisions taking into consideration the specific situation in certain Member States.
(28) No later than five years after entry into force of this Regulation the Commission will present a report on its application and, if need be, submit proposals for adaptations.
(29) The Commission will have to adjust Annexes I to IV on the rules of national jurisdiction, the courts or competent authorities and redress procedures available on the basis of the amendments forwarded by the Member State concerned; amendments made to Annexes V and VI should be adopted in accordance with Council Decision 1999/468/EC of 28 June 1999 laying down the procedures for the exercise of implementing powers conferred on the Commission(6),

HAS ADOPTED THIS REGULATION:

TITLE I SCOPE

Article 1

This Convention shall apply in civil and commercial matters whatever the nature of the court or tribunal. It shall not extend, in particular, to revenue, customs or administrative matters.

The Convention shall not apply to:

1. the status or legal capacity of natural persons, rights in property arising out of a matrimonial relationship, wills and succession
2. bankruptcy, proceedings relating to the winding-up of insolvent companies or other legal persons, judicial arrangements, compositions and analogous proceedings
3. social security
4. arbitration.

CHAPTER I SCOPE

Article 1

1. This Regulation shall apply in civil and commercial matters whatever the nature of the court or tribunal. It shall not extend, in particular, to revenue, customs or administrative matters.

2. The Regulation shall not apply to:

(a) the status or legal capacity of natural persons, rights in property arising out of a matrimonial relationship, wills and succession;
(b) bankruptcy, proceedings relating to the winding-up of insolvent companies or other legal persons, judicial arrangements, compositions and analogous proceedings;
(c) social security;
(d) arbitration.

3. In this Regulation, the term 'Member State' shall mean Member States with the exception of Denmark.

TITLE II JURISDICTION

Section 1 General provisions

Article 2

Subject to the provisions of this Convention, persons domiciled in a Contracting State shall, whatever their nationality, be sued in the courts of that State.

CHAPTER II JURISDICTION

Section 1 General provisions

Article 2

1. Subject to this Regulation, persons domiciled in a Member State shall, whatever their nationality, be sued in the courts of that Member State.

Persons who are not nationals of the State in which they are domiciled shall be governed by the rules of jurisdiction applicable to nationals of that State.

Article 3

Persons domiciled in a Contracting State may be sued in the courts of another Contracting State only by virtue of the rules set out in Sections 2 to 6 of this Title.

In particular the following provisions shall not be applicable as against them:

(...)

Article 4

If the defendant is not domiciled in a Contracting State, the jurisdiction of the courts of each Contracting State shall, subject to the provisions of Article 16, be determined by the law of that State.

As against such a defendant, any person domiciled in a Contracting State may, whatever his nationality, avail himself in that State of the rules of jurisdiction there in force, and in particular those specified in the second paragraph of Article 3, in the same way as the nationals of that State.

Section 2 Special jurisdiction

Article 5

A person domiciled in a Contracting State may, in another Contracting State, be sued:

1. in matters relating to a contract, in the courts for the place of performance of the obligation in question in matters relating to individual contracts of employment, this place is that where the employee habitually carries out his work, or if the employee does not habitually carry out his work in any one country, the employer may also be sued in the courts for the place where the business which engaged the employee was or is now situated;

2. in matters relating to maintenance, in the courts for the place where the maintenance creditor is domiciled or habitually resident or, if the matter is ancillary to proceedings concerning the status of a person, in the court which, according to its own law, has jurisdiction to entertain those proceedings, unless that jurisdiction is based solely on the nationality of one of the parties;

3. in matters relating to tort, delict or quasi-delict, in

2. Persons who are not nationals of the Member State in which they are domiciled shall be governed by the rules of jurisdiction applicable to nationals of that State.

Article 3

1. Persons domiciled in a Member State may be sued in the courts of another Member State only by virtue of the rules set out in Sections 2 to 7 of this Chapter.

2. In particular the rules of national jurisdiction set out in Annex I shall not be applicable as against them.

Article 4

1. If the defendant is not domiciled in a Member State, the jurisdiction of the courts of each Member State shall, subject to Articles 22 and 23, be determined by the law of that Member State.

2. As against such a defendant, any person domiciled in a Member State may, whatever his nationality, avail himself in that State of the rules of jurisdiction there in force, and in particular those specified in Annex I, in the same way as the nationals of that State.

Section 2 Special jurisdiction

Article 5

A person domiciled in a Member State may, in another Member State, be sued:

1. (a) in matters relating to a contract, in the courts for the place of performance of the obligation in question;
(b) for the purpose of this provision and unless otherwise agreed, the place of performance of the obligation in question shall be:
- in the case of the sale of goods, the place in a Member State where, under the contract, the goods were delivered or should have been delivered,
- in the case of the provision of services, the place in a Member State where, under the contract, the services were provided or should have been provided,
(c) if subparagraph (b) does not apply then subparagraph (a) applies;

2. in matters relating to maintenance, in the courts for the place where the maintenance creditor is domiciled or habitually resident or, if the matter is ancillary to proceedings concerning the status of a person, in the court which, according to its own law, has jurisdiction to entertain those proceedings, unless that jurisdiction is based solely on the nationality of one of the parties;

3. in matters relating to tort, delict or quasi-delict, in

the courts for the place where the harmful event occurred;

4. as regards a civil claim for damages or restitution which is based on an act giving rise to criminal proceedings, in the court seised of those proceedings, to the extent that that court has jurisdiction under its own law to entertain civil proceedings;

5. as regards a dispute arising out of the operations of a branch, agency or other establishment, in the courts for the place in which the branch, agency or other establishment is situated;

6. as settlor, trustee or beneficiary of a trust created by the operation of a statute, or by a written instrument, or created orally and evidenced in writing, in the courts of the Contracting State in which the trust is domiciled;

7. as regards a dispute concerning the payment of remuneration claimed in respect of the salvage of a cargo or freight, in the court under the authority of which the cargo or freight in question:

(a) has been arrested to secure such payment, or
(b) could have been so arrested, but bail or other security has been given

provided that this provision shall apply only if it is claimed that the defendant has an interest in the cargo or freight or had such an interest at the time of salvage.

Article 6

A person domiciled in a Contracting State may also be sued:

1. where he is one of a number of defendants, in the courts for the place where any one of them is domiciled;

2. as a third party in an action on a warranty or guarantee or in any other third party proceedings, in the court seised of the original proceedings, unless these were instituted solely with the object of removing him from the jurisdiction of the court which would be competent in his case;

3. on a counter-claim arising from the same contract or facts on which the original claim was based, in the court in which the original claim is pending;

4. in matters relating to a contract, if the action may be combined with an action against the same defendant in matters relating to rights in rem in immovable property, in the court of the Contracting State in which the property is situated.

the courts for the place where the harmful event occurred or may occur;

4. as regards a civil claim for damages or restitution which is based on an act giving rise to criminal proceedings, in the court seised of those proceedings, to the extent that that court has jurisdiction under its own law to entertain civil proceedings;

5. as regards a dispute arising out of the operations of a branch, agency or other establishment, in the courts for the place in which the branch, agency or other establishment is situated;

6. as settlor, trustee or beneficiary of a trust created by the operation of a statute, or by a written instrument, or created orally and evidenced in writing, in the courts of the Member State in which the trust is domiciled;

7. as regards a dispute concerning the payment of remuneration claimed in respect of the salvage of a cargo or freight, in the court under the authority of which the cargo or freight in question:

(a) has been arrested to secure such payment, or
(b) could have been so arrested, but bail or other security has been given;

provided that this provision shall apply only if it is claimed that the defendant has an interest in the cargo or freight or had such an interest at the time of salvage.

Article 6

A person domiciled in a Member State may also be sued:

1. where he is one of a number of defendants, in the courts for the place where any one of them is domiciled, provided the claims are so closely connected that it is expedient to hear and determine them together to avoid the risk of irreconcilable judgments resulting from separate proceedings;

2. as a third party in an action on a warranty or guarantee or in any other third party proceedings, in the court seised of the original proceedings, unless these were instituted solely with the object of removing him from the jurisdiction of the court which would be competent in his case;

3. on a counter-claim arising from the same contract or facts on which the original claim was based, in the court in which the original claim is pending;

4. in matters relating to a contract, if the action may be combined with an action against the same defendant in matters relating to rights in rem in immovable property, in the court of the Member State in which the property is situated.

Article 6a

Where by virtue of this Convention a court of a Contracting State has jurisdiction in actions relating to liability from the use or operation of a ship, that court, or any other court substituted for this purpose by the internal law of that State, shall also have jurisdiction over claims for limitation of such liability.

Article 7

Where by virtue of this Regulation a court of a Member State has jurisdiction in actions relating to liability from the use or operation of a ship, that court, or any other court substituted for this purpose by the internal law of that Member State, shall also have jurisdiction over claims for limitation of such liability.

Section 3 Jurisdiction in matters relating to insurance

Article 7

In matters relating to insurance, jurisdiction shall be determined by this Section, without prejudice to the provisions of Articles 4 and 5 point 5.

Article 8

An insurer domiciled in a Contracting State may be sued:

1.in the courts of the State where he is domiciled, or

2. in another Contracting State, in the courts for the place where the policy-holder is domiciled, or

3. if he is a co-insurer, in the courts of a Contracting State in which proceedings are brought against the leading insurer.

An insurer who is not domiciled in a Contracting State but has a branch, agency or other establishment in one of the Contracting States shall, in disputes arising out of the operations of the branch, agency or establishment, be deemed to be domiciled in that State.

Article 9

In respect of liability insurance or insurance of immovable property, the insurer may in addition be sued in the courts for the place where the harmful event occurred. The same applies if movable and immovable property are covered by the same insurance policy and both are adversely affected by the same contingency.

Article 10

In respect of liability insurance, the insurer may also, if the law of the court permits it, be joined in proceedings which the injured party had brought against the insured.

The provisions of Articles 7, 8 and 9 shall apply to actions brought by the injured party directly against the insurer, where such direct actions are permitted.

If the law governing such direct actions provides that

Section 3 Jurisdiction in matters relating to insurance

Article 8

In matters relating to insurance, jurisdiction shall be determined by this Section, without prejudice to Article 4 and point 5 of Article 5.

Article 9

1. An insurer domiciled in a Member State may be sued:

(a) in the courts of the Member State where he is domiciled, or

(b) in another Member State, in the case of actions brought by the policyholder, the insured or a beneficiary, in the courts for the place where the plaintiff is domiciled,

(c) if he is a co-insurer, in the courts of a Member State in which proceedings are brought against the leading insurer.

2. An insurer who is not domiciled in a Member State but has a branch, agency or other establishment in one of the Member States shall, in disputes arising out of the operations of the branch, agency or establishment, be deemed to be domiciled in that Member State.

Article 10

In respect of liability insurance or insurance of immovable property, the insurer may in addition be sued in the courts for the place where the harmful event occurred. The same applies if movable and immovable property are covered by the same insurance policy and both are adversely affected by the same contingency.

Article 11

1. In respect of liability insurance, the insurer may also, if the law of the court permits it, be joined in proceedings which the injured party has brought against the insured.

2. Articles 8, 9 and 10 shall apply to actions brought by the injured party directly against the insurer, where such direct actions are permitted.

3. If the law governing such direct actions provides

the policy-holder or the insured may be joined as a party to the action, the same court shall have jurisdiction over them.

Article 11

Without prejudice to the provisions of the third paragraph of Article 10, an insurer may bring proceedings only in the courts of the Contracting State in which the defendant is domiciled, irrespective of whether he is the policy-holder, the insured or a beneficiary.

The provisions of this Section shall not affect the right to bring a counterclaim in the court in which, in accordance with this Section, the original claim is pending.

Article 12

The provisions of this Section may be departed from only by an agreement on jurisdiction:

1. which is entered into after the dispute has arisen, or

2. which allows the policy-holder, the insured or a beneficiary to bring proceedings in courts other than those indicated in this Section, or

3. which is concluded between a policy-holder and an insurer, both of whom are domiciled in the same Contracting State, and which has the effect of conferring jurisdiction on the courts of that State even if the harmful event were to occur abroad, provided that such an agreement is not contrary to the law of that State, or

4.which is concluded with a policy-holder who is not domiciled in a Contracting State, except in so far as the insurance is compulsory or relates to immovable property in a Contracting State, or

5.which relates to a contract of insurance in so far as it covers one or more of the risks set out in Article 12a.

Article 12a

The following are the risks referred to in point 5 of Article 12:

1. any loss of or damage to:

(a) sea-going ships, installations situated offshore or on the high seas, or aircraft, arising from perils which relate to their use for commercial purposes;

(b) goods in transit other than passengers' baggage where the transit consists of or includes carriage by such ships or aircraft;

2. any liability, other than for bodily injury to pas-

that the policyholder or the insured may be joined as a party to the action, the same court shall have jurisdiction over them.

Article 12

1. Without prejudice to Article 11(3), an insurer may bring proceedings only in the courts of the Member State in which the defendant is domiciled, irrespective of whether he is the policyholder, the insured or a beneficiary.

2. The provisions of this Section shall not affect the right to bring a counter-claim in the court in which, in accordance with this Section, the original claim is pending.

Article 13

The provisions of this Section may be departed from only by an agreement:

1. which is entered into after the dispute has arisen, or

2. which allows the policyholder, the insured or a beneficiary to bring proceedings in courts other than those indicated in this Section, or

3. which is concluded between a policyholder and an insurer, both of whom are at the time of conclusion of the contract domiciled or habitually resident in the same Member State, and which has the effect of conferring jurisdiction on the courts of that State even if the harmful event were to occur abroad, provided that such an agreement is not contrary to the law of that State, or

4. which is concluded with a policyholder who is not domiciled in a Member State, except in so far as the insurance is compulsory or relates to immovable property in a Member State, or

5. which relates to a contract of insurance in so far as it covers one or more of the risks set out in Article 14.

Article 14

The following are the risks referred to in Article 13(5):

1. any loss of or damage to:

(a) seagoing ships, installations situated offshore or on the high seas, or aircraft, arising from perils which relate to their use for commercial purposes;

(b) goods in transit other than passengers' baggage where the transit consists of or includes carriage by such ships or aircraft;

2. any liability, other than for bodily injury to

sengers or loss of or damage to their baggage:

(a) arising out of the use or operation of ships, installations or aircraft as referred to in point 1 (a) above in so far as the law of the Contracting State in which such aircraft are registered does not prohibit agreements on jurisdiction regarding insurance of such risks;

(b) for loss or damage caused by goods in transit as described in point 1 (b) above;

3. any financial loss connected with the use or operation of ships, installations or aircraft as referred to in point 1 (a) above, in particular loss of freight or charter-hire

4. any risk or interest connected with any of those referred to in points 1 to 3 above.

Section 4 Jurisdiction over consumer contracts

Article 13

In proceedings concerning a contract concluded by a person for a purpose which can be regarded as being outside his trade or profession, hereinafter called 'the consumer', jurisdiction shall be determined by this Section, without prejudice to the provisions of point 5 of Articles 4 and 5, if it is:

1. a contract for the sale of goods on instalment credit terms or

2. a contract for a loan repayable by instalments, or for any other form of credit, made to finance the sale of goods or

3. any other contract for the supply of goods or a contract for the supply of services, and

(a) in the State of the consumer's domicile the conclusion of the contract was preceded by a specific invitation addressed to him or by advertising and

(b) the consumer took in that State the steps necessary for the conclusion of the contract.

Where a consumer enters into a contract with a party who is not domiciled in a Contracting State but has a branch, agency or other establishment in one of the Contracting States, that party shall, in disputes arising out of the operations of the branch, agency or establishment, be deemed to be domiciled in that State.

This Section shall not apply to contracts of transport.

passengers or loss of or damage to their baggage:

(a) arising out of the use or operation of ships, installations or aircraft as referred to in point 1(a) in so far as, in respect of the latter, the law of the Member State in which such aircraft are registered does not prohibit agreements on jurisdiction regarding insurance of such risks;

(b) for loss or damage caused by goods in transit as described in point 1(b);

3. any financial loss connected with the use or operation of ships, installations or aircraft as referred to in point 1(a), in particular loss of freight or charter-hire;

4. any risk or interest connected with any of those referred to in points 1 to 3;

5. notwithstanding points 1 to 4, all 'large risks' as defined in Council Directive 73/239/EEC(7), as amended by Council Directives 88/357/EEC(8) and 90/618/EEC(9), as they may be amended.

Section 4 Jurisdiction over consumer contracts

Article 15

1. In matters relating to a contract concluded by a person, the consumer, for a purpose which can be regarded as being outside his trade or profession, jurisdiction shall be determined by this Section, without prejudice to Article 4 and point 5 of Article 5, if:

(a) it is a contract for the sale of goods on instalment credit terms; or

(b) it is a contract for a loan repayable by instalments, or for any other form of credit, made to finance the sale of goods; or

(c) in all other cases, the contract has been concluded with a person who pursues commercial or professional activities in the Member State of the consumer's domicile or, by any means, directs such activities to that Member State or to several States including that Member State, and the contract falls within the scope of such activities.

2. Where a consumer enters into a contract with a party who is not domiciled in the Member State but has a branch, agency or other establishment in one of the Member States, that party shall, in disputes arising out of the operations of the branch, agency or establishment, be deemed to be domiciled in that State.

3. This Section shall not apply to a contract of transport other than a contract which, for an inclusive

Article 14

A consumer may bring proceedings against the other party to a contract either in the courts of the Contracting State in which that party is domiciled or in the courts of the Contracting State in which he is himself domiciled.
Proceedings may be brought against a consumer by the other party to the contract only in the courts of the Contracting State inwhich the consumer is domiciled.

These provisions shall not affect the right to bring a counter-claim in the court in which, in accordance with this Section, the original claim is pending.

Article 15

The provisions of this Section may be departed from only by an agreement:

1. which is entered into after the dispute has arisen or

2. which allows the consumer to bring proceedings in courts other than those indicated in this Section or

3. which is entered into by the consumer and the other party to the contract, both of whom are at the time of conclusion of the contract domiciled or habitually resident in the same Contracting State, and which confers jurisdiction on the courts of that State, provided that such an agreement is not contrary to the law of that State.

price, provides for a combination of travel and accommodation.

Article 16

1. A consumer may bring proceedings against the other party to a contract either in the courts of the Member State in which that party is domiciled or in the courts for the place where the consumer is domiciled.

2. Proceedings may be brought against a consumer by the other party to the contract only in the courts of the Member State in which the consumer is domiciled.

3. This Article shall not affect the right to bring a counter-claim in the court in which, in accordance with this Section, the original claim is pending.

Article 17

The provisions of this Section may be departed from only by an agreement:

1. which is entered into after the dispute has arisen; or

2. which allows the consumer to bring proceedings in courts other than those indicated in this Section; or

3. which is entered into by the consumer and the other party to the contract, both of whom are at the time of conclusion of the contract domiciled or habitually resident in the same Member State, and which confers jurisdiction on the courts of that Member State, provided that such an agreement is not contrary to the law of that Member State.

Section 5 Jurisdiction over individual contracts of employment

Article 18

1. In matters relating to individual contracts of employment, jurisdiction shall be determined by this Section, without prejudice to Article 4 and point 5 of Article 5.

2. Where an employee enters into an individual contract of employment with an employer who is not domiciled in a Member State but has a branch, agency or other establishment in one of the Member States, the employer shall, in disputes arising out of the operations of the branch, agency or establishment, be deemed to be domiciled in that Member State.

Article 19

An employer domiciled in a Member State may be sued:

1. in the courts of the Member State where he is domiciled; or

2. in another Member State:
(a) in the courts for the place where the employee habitually carries out his work or in the courts for the last place where he did so, or
(b) if the employee does not or did not habitually carry out his work in any one country, in the courts for the place where the business which engaged the employee is or was situated.

Article 20

1. An employer may bring proceedings only in the courts of the Member State in which the employee is domiciled.

2. The provisions of this Section shall not affect the right to bring a counter-claim in the court in which, in accordance with this Section, the original claim is pending.

Article 21

The provisions of this Section may be departed from only by an agreement on jurisdiction:
1. which is entered into after the dispute has arisen; or
2. which allows the employee to bring proceedings in courts other than those indicated in this Section.

Section 5 Exclusive jurisdiction

Article 16

The following courts shall have exclusive jurisdiction, regardless of domicile:

1 (a) in proceedings which have as their object rights in rem in immovable property or tenancies of immovable property, the courts of the Contracting State in which the property is situated
(b) however, in proceedings which have as their object tenancies of immovable property concluded for temporary private use for a maximum period of six consecutive months, the courts of the Contracting State in which the defendant is domiciled shall also have jurisdiction, provided that the landlord and the tenant are natural persons and are domiciled in the same Contracting State;

2. in proceedings which have as their object the validity of the constitution, the nullity or the dissolution of companies or other legal persons or associations of natural or legal persons, or the decisions of their organs, the courts of the Contracting State in which the company, legal person or association has its seat

3. in proceedings which have as their object the validity of entries in public registers, the courts of the Contracting State in which the register is kept

4. in proceedings concerned with the registration or

Section 6 Exclusive jurisdiction

Article 22

The following courts shall have exclusive jurisdiction, regardless of domicile:

1. in proceedings which have as their object rights in rem in immovable property or tenancies of immovable property, the courts of the Member State in which the property is situated.
However, in proceedings which have as their object tenancies of immovable property concluded for temporary private use for a maximum period of six consecutive months, the courts of the Member State in which the defendant is domiciled shall also have jurisdiction, provided that the tenant is a natural person and that the landlord and the tenant are domiciled in the same Member State;

2. in proceedings which have as their object the validity of the constitution, the nullity or the dissolution of companies or other legal persons or associations of natural or legal persons, or of the validity of the decisions of their organs, the courts of the Member State in which the company, legal person or association has its seat. In order to determine that seat, the court shall apply its rules of private international law;

3. in proceedings which have as their object the validity of entries in public registers, the courts of the Member State in which the register is kept;

4. in proceedings concerned with the registration or

validity of patents, trade marks, designs, or other similar rights required to be deposited or registered, the courts of the Contracting State in which the deposit or registration has been applied for, has taken place or is under the terms of an international convention deemed to have taken place

5. in proceedings concerned with the enforcement of judgments, the courts of the Contracting State in which the judgment has been or is to be enforced

Section 6 Prorogation of jurisdiction

Article 17

If the parties, one or more of whom is domiciled in a Contracting State, have agreed that a court or the courts of a Contracting State are to have jurisdiction to settle any disputes which have arisen or which may arise in connection with a particular legal relationship, that court or those courts shall have exclusive jurisdiction. Such an agreement conferring jurisdiction shall be either:

(a) in writing or evidenced in writing or

(b) in a form which accords with practices which the parties have established between themselves or

(c) in international trade or commerce, in a form which accords with a usage of which the parties are or ought to have been aware and which in such trade or commerce is widely known to, and regularly observed by, parties to contracts of the type involved in the particular trade or commerce concerned.

Where such an agreement is concluded by parties, none of whom is domiciled in a Contracting State, the courts of other Contracting States shall have no jurisdiction over their disputes unless the court or courts chosen have declined jurisdiction.

The court or courts of a Contracting State on which a trust instrument has conferred jurisdiction shall have exclusive jurisdiction in any proceedings brought against a settler, trustee or beneficiary, if relations between these persons or their rights or obligations under the trust are involved.

Agreements or provisions of a trust instrument con-

validity of patents, trade marks, designs, or other similar rights required to be deposited or registered, the courts of the Member State in which the deposit or registration has been applied for, has taken place or is under the terms of a Community instrument or an international convention deemed to have taken place.
Without prejudice to the jurisdiction of the European Patent Office under the Convention on the Grant of European Patents, signed at Munich on 5 October 1973, the courts of each Member State shall have exclusive jurisdiction, regardless of domicile, in proceedings concerned with the registration or validity of any European patent granted for that State;

5. in proceedings concerned with the enforcement of judgments, the courts of the Member State in which the judgment has been or is to be enforced.

Section 7 Prorogation of jurisdiction

Article 23

1. If the parties, one or more of whom is domiciled in a Member State, have agreed that a court or the courts of a Member State are to have jurisdiction to settle any disputes which have arisen or which may arise in connection with a particular legal relationship, that court or those courts shall have jurisdiction. Such jurisdiction shall be exclusive unless the parties have agreed otherwise. Such an agreement conferring jurisdiction shall be either:

(a) in writing or evidenced in writing; or

(b) in a form which accords with practices which the parties have established between themselves; or

(c) in international trade or commerce, in a form which accords with a usage of which the parties are or ought to have been aware and which in such trade or commerce is widely known to, and regularly observed by, parties to contracts of the type involved in the particular trade or commerce concerned.

2. Any communication by electronic means which provides a durable record of the agreement shall be equivalent to 'writing'.

3. Where such an agreement is concluded by parties, none of whom is domiciled in a Member State, the courts of other Member States shall have no jurisdiction over their disputes unless the court or courts chosen have declined jurisdiction.

4. The court or courts of a Member State on which a trust instrument has conferred jurisdiction shall have exclusive jurisdiction in any proceedings brought against a settlor, trustee or beneficiary, if relations between these persons or their rights or obligations under the trust are involved.

5. Agreements or provisions of a trust instrument

ferring jurisdiction shall have no legal force if they are contrary to the provisions of Articles 12 or 15, or if the courts whose jurisdiction they purport to exclude have exclusive jurisdiction by virtue of Article 16.

If an agreement conferring jurisdiction was concluded for the benefit of only one of the parties, that party shall retain the right to bring proceedings in any other court which has jurisdiction by virtue of this Convention.

In matters relating to individual contracts of employment an agreement conferring jurisdiction shall have legal force only if it is entered into after the dispute has arisen or if the employee invokes it to seise courts other than those for the defendant's domicile or those specified in Article 5 (1).

conferring jurisdiction shall have no legal force if they are contrary to Articles 13, 17 or 21, or if the courts whose jurisdiction they purport to exclude have exclusive jurisdiction by virtue of Article 22.

Article 18

Apart from jurisdiction derived from other provisions of this Convention, a court of a Contracting State before whom a defendant enters an appearance shall have jurisdiction. This rule shall not apply where appearance was entered solely to contest the jurisdiction, or where another court has exclusive jurisdiction by virtue of Article 16.

Article 24

Apart from jurisdiction derived from other provisions of this Regulation, a court of a Member State before which a defendant enters an appearance shall have jurisdiction. This rule shall not apply where appearance was entered to contest the jurisdiction, or where another court has exclusive jurisdiction by virtue of Article 22.

Section 7 Examination as to jurisdiction and admissibility

Article 19

Where a court of a Contracting State is seised of a claim which is principally concerned with a matter over which the courts of another Contracting State have exclusive jurisdiction by virtue of Article 16, it shall declare of its own motion that it has no jurisdiction.

Article 20

Where a defendant domiciled in one Contracting State is sued in a court of another Contracting State and does not enter an appearance, the court shall declare of its own motion that it has no jurisdiction unless its jurisdiction is derived from the provisions of the Convention.

The court shall stay the proceedings so long as it is not shown that the defendant has been able to receive the document instituting the proceedings or an equivalent document in sufficient time to enable him to arrange for his defence, or that all necessary steps have been taken to this end.

Section 8 Examination as to jurisdiction and admissibility

Article 25

Where a court of a Member State is seised of a claim which is principally concerned with a matter over which the courts of another Member State have exclusive jurisdiction by virtue of Article 22, it shall declare of its own motion that it has no jurisdiction.

Article 26

1. Where a defendant domiciled in one Member State is sued in a court of another Member State and does not enter an appearance, the court shall declare of its own motion that it has no jurisdiction unless its jurisdiction is derived from the provisions of this Regulation.

2. The court shall stay the proceedings so long as it is not shown that the defendant has been able to receive the document instituting the proceedings or an equivalent document in sufficient time to enable him to arrange for his defence, or that all necessary steps have been taken to this end.

3. Article 19 of Council Regulation (EC) No 1348/2000 of 29 May 2000 on the service in the Member States of judicial and extrajudicial documents in civil or commercial matters(10) shall apply instead of the provisions of paragraph 2 if the document instituting the proceedings or an equivalent document had to be transmitted from one Member State to another pursuant to this Regulation.

The provisions of the foregoing paragraph shall be replaced by those of Article 15 of the Hague Convention of 15 November 1965 on the service abroad of judicial and extrajudicial documents in civil or commercial matters, if the document instituting the proceedings or notice thereof had to be transmitted abroad in accordance with that Convention.

4. Where the provisions of Regulation (EC) No 348/2000 are not applicable, Article 15 of the Hague Convention of 15 November 1965 on the Service Abroad of Judicial and Extrajudicial Documents in Civil or Commercial Matters shall apply if the document instituting the proceedings or an equivalent document had to be transmitted pursuant to that Convention.

Section 8 Lis pendens - related actions

Article 21

Where proceedings involving the same cause of action and between the same parties are brought in the courts of different Contracting States, any court other than the court first seised shall of its own motion stay its proceedings until such time as the jurisdiction of the court first seised is established.

Where the jurisdiction of the court first seised is established, any court other than the court first seised shall decline jurisdiction in favour of that court.

Article 22

Where related actions are brought in the courts of different Contracting States, any court other than the court first seised may, while the actions are pending at first instance, stay its proceedings.

A court other than the court first seised may also, on the application of one of the parties, decline jurisdiction if the law of that court permits the consolidation of related actions and the court first seised has jurisdiction over both actions.

For the purposes of this Article, actions are deemed to be related where they are so closely connected that it is expedient to hear and determine them together to avoid the risk of irreconcilable judgments resulting from separate proceedings.

Article 23

Where actions come within the exclusive jurisdiction of several courts, any court other than the court first seised shall decline jurisdiction in favour of that court.

Section 9 Lis pendens - related actions

Article 27

1. Where proceedings involving the same cause of action and between the same parties are brought in the courts of different Member States, any court other than the court first seised shall of its own motion stay its proceedings until such time as the jurisdiction of the court first seised is established.

2. Where the jurisdiction of the court first seised is established, any court other than the court first seised shall decline jurisdiction in favour of that court.

Article 28

1. Where related actions are pending in the courts of different Member States, any court other than the court first seised may stay its proceedings.

2. Where these actions are pending at first instance, any court other than the court first seised may also, on the application of one of the parties, decline jurisdiction if the court first seised has jurisdiction over the actions in question and its law permits the consolidation thereof.

3. For the purposes of this Article, actions are deemed to be related where they are so closely connected that it is expedient to hear and determine them together to avoid the risk of irreconcilable judgments resulting from separate proceedings.

Article 29

Where actions come within the exclusive jurisdiction of several courts, any court other than the court first seised shall decline jurisdiction in favour of that court.

Article 30

For the purposes of this Section, a court shall be deemed to be seised:

1. at the time when the document instituting the proceedings or an equivalent document is lodged with the court, provided that the plaintiff has not subsequently failed to take the steps he was required to take to have service effected on the defendant, or

2. if the document has to be served before being

lodged with the court, at the time when it is received by the authority responsible for service, provided that the plaintiff has not subsequently failed to take the steps he was required to take to have the document lodged with the court.

Section 9 Provisional, including protective, measures

Article 24

Application may be made to the courts of a Contracting State for such provisional, including protective, measures as may be available under the law of that State, even if, under this Convention, the courts of another Contracting State have jurisdiction as to the substance of the matter.

Section 10 Provisional, including protective, measures

Article 31

Application may be made to the courts of a Member State for such provisional, including protective, measures as may be available under the law of that State, even if, under this Regulation, the courts of another Member State have jurisdiction as to the substance of the matter.

TITLE III

RECOGNITION AND ENFORCEMENT

Article 25

For the purposes of this Convention, 'judgment' means any judgment given by a court or tribunal of a Contracting State, whatever the judgment may be called, including a decree, order, decision or writ of execution, as well as the determination of costs or expenses by an officer of the court.

CHAPTER III

RECOGNITION AND ENFORCEMENT

Article 32

For the purposes of this Regulation, 'judgment' means any judgment given by a court or tribunal of a Member State, whatever the judgment may be called, including a decree, order, decision or writ of execution, as well as the determination of costs or expenses by an officer of the court.

Section 1 Recognition

Article 26

A judgment given in a Contracting State shall be recognized in the other Contracting States without any special procedure being required.

Any interested party who raises the recognition of a judgment as the principal issue in a dispute may, in accordance with the procedures provided for in Sections 2 and 3 of this Title, apply for a decision that the judgment be recognized.

If the outcome of proceedings in a court of a contracting State depends on the determination of an incidental question of recognition that court shall have jurisdiction over that question.

Article 27

A judgment shall not be recognized:

1. if such recognition is contrary to public policy in the State in which recognition is sought;

2. where it was given in default of appearance, if the defendant was not duly served with the document which instituted the proceedings or with an equivalent document in sufficient time to enable him to arrange for his defence;

Section 1 Recognition

Article 33

1. A judgment given in a Member State shall be recognised in the other Member States without any special procedure being required.

2. Any interested party who raises the recognition of a judgment as the principal issue in a dispute may, in accordance with the procedures provided for in Sections 2 and 3 of this Chapter, apply for a decision that the judgment be recognised.

3. If the outcome of proceedings in a court of a Member State depends on the determination of an incidental question of recognition that court shall have jurisdiction over that question.

Article 34

A judgment shall not be recognised:

1. if such recognition is manifestly contrary to public policy in the Member State in which recognition is sought;

2. where it was given in default of appearance, if the defendant was not served with the document which instituted the proceedings or with an equivalent document in sufficient time and in such a way as to enable him to arrange for his defence, unless the

defendant failed to commence proceedings to challenge the judgment when it was possible for him to do so;

3. if the judgment is irreconcilable with a judgment given in a dispute between the same parties in the State in which recognition is sought;

3. if it is irreconcilable with a judgment given in a dispute between the same parties in the Member State in which recognition is sought;

4. if the court of the State of origin, in order to arrive at its judgment, has decided a preliminary question concerning the status or legal capacity of natural persons, rights in property arising out of a matrimonial relationship, wills or succession in a way that conflicts with a rule of the private international law of the State in which the recognition is sought, unless the same result would have been reached by the application of the rules of private international law of that State;

5. if the judgment is irreconcilable with an earlier judgment given in a non-contracting State involving the same cause of action and between the same parties, provided that this latter judgment fulfils the conditions necessary for its recognition in the State addressed .

4. if it is irreconcilable with an earlier judgment given in another Member State or in a third State involving the same cause of action and between the same parties, provided that the earlier judgment fulfils the conditions necessary for its recognition in the Member State addressed.

Article 28

Moreover, a judgment shall not be recognized if it conflicts with the provisions of Sections 3, 4 or 5 of Title II, or in a case provided for in Article 59.

In its examination of the grounds of jurisdiction referred to in the foregoing paragraph, the court or authority applied to shall be bound by the findings of fact on which the court of the State of origin based its jurisdiction.

Subject to the provisions of the first paragraph, the jurisdiction of the court of the State of origin may not be reviewed the test of public policy referred to in point 1 of Article 27 may not be applied to the rules relating to jurisdiction.

Article 35

1. Moreover, a judgment shall not be recognised if it conflicts with Sections 3, 4 or 6 of Chapter II, or in a case provided for in Article 72.

2. In its examination of the grounds of jurisdiction referred to in the foregoing paragraph, the court or authority applied to shall be bound by the findings of fact on which the court of the Member State of origin based its jurisdiction.

3. Subject to the paragraph 1, the jurisdiction of the court of the Member State of origin may not be reviewed. The test of public policy referred to in point 1 of Article 34 may not be applied to the rules relating to jurisdiction.

Article 29

Under no circumstances may a foreign judgment be reviewed as to its substance.

Article 36

Under no circumstances may a foreign judgment be reviewed as to its substance.

Article 30

A court of a Contracting State in which recognition is sought of a judgment given in another Contracting State may stay the proceedings if an ordinary appeal against the judgment has been lodged.

A court of a Contracting State in which recognition is sought of a judgment given in Ireland or the United Kingdom may stay the proceedings if enforcement is suspended in the State of origin, by reason of an appeal.

Article 37

1. A court of a Member State in which recognition is sought of a judgment given in another Member State may stay the proceedings if an ordinary appeal against the judgment has been lodged.

2. A court of a Member State in which recognition is sought of a judgment given in Ireland or the United Kingdom may stay the proceedings if enforcement is suspended in the State of origin, by reason of an appeal.

Section 2 Enforcement

Article 31

A judgment given in a Contracting State and enforceable in that State shall be enforced in another Contracting State when, on the application of any interested party, it has been declared enforceable there.

However, in the United Kingdom, such a judgment shall be enforced in England and Wales, in Scotland, or in Northern Ireland when, on the application of any interested party, it has been registered for enforcement in that part of the United Kingdom.

Article 32

1. The application shall be submitted:

(...)

2. The jurisdiction of local courts shall be determined by reference to the place of domicile of the party against whom enforcement is sought. If he is not domiciled in the State in which enforcement is sought, it shall be determined by reference to the place of enforcement.

Article 33

The procedure for making the application shall be governed by the law of the State in which enforcement is sought.

The applicant must give an address for service of process within the area of jurisdiction of the court applied to. However, if the law of the State in which enforcement is sought does not provide for the furnishing of such an address, the applicant shall appoint a representative ad litem.

The documents referred to in Articles 46 and 47 shall be attached to the application.

Article 34

The court applied to shall give its decision without delay. The party against whom enforcement is sought shall not at this stage of the proceedings be entitled to make any submissions on the application.

The application may be refused only for one of the reasons specified in Articles 27 and 28.

Under no circumstances may the foreign judgment be reviewed as to its substance.

Article 35

The appropriate officer of the court shall without delay bring the decision given on the application to the notice of the applicant in accordance with the proce-

Section 2 Enforcement

Article 38

1. A judgment given in a Member State and enforceable in that State shall be enforced in another Member State when, on the application of any interested party, it has been declared enforceable there.

2. However, in the United Kingdom, such a judgment shall be enforced in England and Wales, in Scotland, or in Northern Ireland when, on the application of any interested party, it has been registered for enforcement in that part of the United Kingdom.

Article 39

1. The application shall be submitted to the court or competent authority indicated in the list in Annex II.

2. The local jurisdiction shall be determined by reference to the place of domicile of the party against whom enforcement is sought, or to the place of enforcement.

Article 40

1. The procedure for making the application shall be governed by the law of the Member State in which enforcement is sought.

2. The applicant must give an address for service of process within the area of jurisdiction of the court applied to. However, if the law of the Member State in which enforcement is sought does not provide for the furnishing of such an address, the applicant shall appoint a representative ad litem.

3. The documents referred to in Article 53 shall be attached to the application.

Article 41

The judgment shall be declared enforceable immediately on completion of the formalities in Article 53 without any review under Articles 34 and 35. The party against whom enforcement is sought shall not at this stage of the proceedings be entitled to make any submissions on the application.

Article 42

1. The decision on the application for a declaration of enforceability shall forthwith be brought to the notice of the applicant in accordance with the

dure laid down by the law of the State in which enforcement is sought.

procedure laid down by the law of the Member State in which enforcement is sought.

2. The declaration of enforceability shall be served on the party against whom enforcement is sought, accompanied by the judgment, if not already served on that party.

Article 43

1. The decision on the application for a declaration of enforceability may be appealed against by either party.

2. The appeal is to be lodged with the court indicated in the list in Annex III.

3. The appeal shall be dealt with in accordance with the rules governing procedure in contradictory matters.

4. If the party against whom enforcement is sought fails to appear before the appellate court in proceedings concerning an appeal brought by the applicant, Article 26(2) to (4) shall apply even where the party against whom enforcement is sought is not domiciled in any of the Member States.

Article 36

If enforcement is authorized, the party against whom enforcement is sought may appeal against the decision within one month of service thereof.
If that party is domiciled in a Contracting State other than that in which the decision authorizing enforcement was given, the time for appealing shall be two months and shall run from the date of service, either on him in person or at his residence. No extension of time may be granted on account of distance.

5. An appeal against the declaration of enforceability is to be lodged within one month of service thereof. If the party against whom enforcement is sought is domiciled in a Member State other than that in which the declaration of enforceability was given, the time for appealing shall be two months and shall run from the date of service, either on him in person or at his residence. No extension of time may be granted on account of distance.

Article 37

1. An appeal against the decision authorizing enforcement shall be lodged in accordance with the rules governing procedure in contentious matters:

(...)

2. The judgment given on the appeal may be contested only:

(...)

Article 44

The judgment given on the appeal may be contested only by the appeal referred to in Annex IV.

Article 45

1. The court with which an appeal is lodged under Article 43 or Article 44 shall refuse or revoke a declaration of enforceability only on one of the grounds specified in Articles 34 and 35. It shall give its decision without delay.

2. Under no circumstances may the foreign judgment be reviewed as to its substance.

Article 38

The court with which the appeal under Article 37(1) is lodged may, on the application of the appellant, stay the proceedings if an ordinary appeal has been lodged against the judgment in the State of origin or if the time for such an appeal has not yet expired in the latter case, the court may specify the time within which such an appeal is to be lodged .

Where the judgment was given in Ireland or the United Kingdom, any form of appeal available in the State of origin shall be treated as an ordinary appeal for the purposes of the first paragraph.

The court may also make enforcement conditional on the provision of such security as it shall determine.

Article 39

During the time specified for an appeal pursuant to Article 36 and until any such appeal has been determined, no measures of enforcement may be taken other than protective measures taken against the property of the party against whom enforcement is sought.

The decision authorizing enforcement shall carry with it the power to proceed to any such protective measures.

Article 40

If the application for enforcement is refused, the applicant may appeal:

(...)

2. The party against whom enforcement is sought shall be summoned to appear before the appellate court. If he fails to appear, the provisions of the second and third paragraphs of Article 20 shall apply even where he is not domiciled in any of the Contracting States.

Article 41

A judgment given on an appeal provided for in Article 40 may be contested only:

(...)

Article 42

Where a foreign judgment has been given in respect of several matters and enforcement cannot be authorized for all of them, the court shall authorize enforce-

Article 46

1. The court with which an appeal is lodged under Article 43 or Article 44 may, on the application of the party against whom enforcement is sought, stay the proceedings if an ordinary appeal has been lodged against the judgment in the Member State of origin or if the time for such an appeal has not yet expired; in the latter case, the court may specify the time within which such an appeal is to be lodged.

2. Where the judgment was given in Ireland or the United Kingdom, any form of appeal available in the Member State of origin shall be treated as an ordinary appeal for the purposes of paragraph 1.

3. The court may also make enforcement conditional on the provision of such security as it shall determine.

Article 47

1. When a judgment must be recognised in accordance with this Regulation, nothing shall prevent the applicant from availing himself of provisional, including protective, measures in accordance with the law of the Member State requested without a declaration of enforceability under Article 41 being required.

2. The declaration of enforceability shall carry with it the power to proceed to any protective measures.

3. During the time specified for an appeal pursuant to Article 43(5) against the declaration of enforceability and until any such appeal has been determined, no measures of enforcement may be taken other than protective measures against the property of the party against whom enforcement is sought.

Article 48

1. Where a foreign judgment has been given in respect of several matters and the declaration of enforceability cannot be given for all of them, the court or competent

ment for one or more of them.

An applicant may request partial enforcement of a judgment.

Article 43

A foreign judgment which orders a periodic payment by way of a penalty shall be enforceable in the State in which enforcement is sought only if the amount of the payment has been finally determined by the courts of the State of origin .

Article 44

An applicant who, in the State of origin has benefited from complete or partial legal aid or exemption from costs or expenses, shall be entitled, in the procedures provided for in Articles 32 to 35, to benefit from the most favourable legal aid or the most extensive exemption from costs or expenses provided for by the law of the State addressed.

However, an applicant who requests the enforcement of a decision given by an administrative authority in Denmark in respect of a maintenance order may, in the State addressed, claim the benefits referred to in the first paragraph if he presents a statement from the Danish Ministry of Justice to the effect that he fulfils the economic requirements to qualify for the grant of complete or partial legal aid or exemption from costs or expenses.

Article 45

No security, bond or deposit, however described, shall be required of a party who in one Contracting State applies for enforcement of a judgment given in another Contracting State on the ground that he is a foreign national or that he is not domiciled or resident in the State in which enforcement is sought.

Section 3 Common provisions

Article 46

A party seeking recognition or applying for enforcement of a judgment shall produce:
1. a copy of the judgment which satisfies the conditions necessary to establish its authenticity;

2. in the case of a judgment given in default, the original or a certified true copy of the document which establishes that the party in default was served with

authority shall give it for one or more of them.

2. An applicant may request a declaration of enforceability limited to parts of a judgment.

Article 49

A foreign judgment which orders a periodic payment by way of a penalty shall be enforceable in the Member State in which enforcement is sought only if the amount of the payment has been finally determined by the courts of the Member State of origin.

Article 50

An applicant who, in the Member State of origin has benefited from complete or partial legal aid or exemption from costs or expenses, shall be entitled, in the procedure provided for in this Section, to benefit from the most favourable legal aid or the most extensive exemption from costs or expenses provided for by the law of the Member State addressed.

Article 51

No security, bond or deposit, however described, shall be required of a party who in one Member State applies for enforcement of a judgment given in another Member State on the ground that he is a foreign national or that he is not domiciled or resident in the State in which enforcement is sought.

Article 52

In proceedings for the issue of a declaration of enforceability, no charge, duty or fee calculated by reference to the value of the matter at issue may be levied in the Member State in which enforcement is sought.

Section 3 Common provisions

Article 53

1. A party seeking recognition or applying for a declaration of enforceability shall produce a copy of the judgment which satisfies the conditions necessary to establish its authenticity.

the document instituting the proceedings or with an equivalent document.

Article 47

A party applying for enforcement shall also produce:

1. documents which establish that, according to the law of the State of origin the judgment is enforceable and has been served;

2. where appropriate, a document showing that the applicant is in receipt of legal aid in the State of origin.

2. A party applying for a declaration of enforceability shall also produce the certificate referred to in Article 54, without prejudice to Article 55.

Article 54

The court or competent authority of a Member State where a judgment was given shall issue, at the request of any interested party, a certificate using the standard form in Annex V to this Regulation.

Article 48

If the documents specified in point 2 of Articles 46 and 47 are not produced, the court may specify a time for their production, accept equivalent documents or, if it considers that it has sufficient information before it, dispense with their production.

If the court so requires, a translation of the documents shall be produced the translation shall be certified by a person qualified to do so in one of the Contracting States.

Article 55

1. If the certificate referred to in Article 54 is not produced, the court or competent authority may specify a time for its production or accept an equivalent document or, if it considers that it has sufficient information before it, dispense with its production.

2. If the court or competent authority so requires, a translation of the documents shall be produced. The translation shall be certified by a person qualified to Do so in one of the Member States.

Article 49

No legalization or other similar formality shall be required in respect of the documents referred to in Articles 46 or 47 or the second paragraph of Article 48, or in respect of a document appointing a representative ad litem.

Article 56

No legalisation or other similar formality shall be required in respect of the documents referred to in Article 53 or Article 55(2), or in respect of a document appointing a representative ad litem.

TITLE IV: AUTHENTIC INSTRUMENTS AND COURT SETTLEMENTS

Article 50

A document which has been formally drawn up or registered as an authentic instrument and is enforceable in one Contracting State shall, in another Contracting State, be declared enforceable there, on application made in accordance with the procedures provided for in Article 31 et seq. The application may be refused only if enforcement of the instrument is contrary to public policy in the State addressed .

CHAPTER IV: AUTHENTIC INSTRUMENTS AND COURT SETTLEMENTS

Article 57

1. A document which has been formally drawn up or registered as an authentic instrument and is enforceable in one Member State shall, in another Member State, be declared enforceable there, on application made in accordance with the procedures provided for in Articles 38, et seq. The court with which an appeal is lodged under Article 43 or Article 44 shall refuse or revoke a declaration of enforceability only if enforcement of the instrument is manifestly contrary to public policy in the Member State addressed.

2. Arrangements relating to maintenance obligations concluded with administrative authorities or authenticated by them shall also be regarded as authentic instruments within the meaning of paragraph 1.

The instrument produced must satisfy the conditions necessary to establish its authenticity in the State of origin.

3. The instrument produced must satisfy the conditions necessary to establish its authenticity in the Member State of origin.

The provisions of Section 3 of Title III shall apply as appropriate.

4. Section 3 of Chapter III shall apply as appropriate. The competent authority of a Member State where an authentic instrument was drawn up or registered shall issue, at the request of any interested party, a certificate using the standard form in Annex VI to this Regulation.

Article 51

A settlement which has been approved by a court in the course of proceedings and is enforceable in the State in which it was concluded shall be enforceable in the State addressed under the same conditions as authentic instruments.

Article 58

A settlement which has been approved by a court in the course of proceedings and is enforceable in the Member State in which it was concluded shall be enforceable in the State addressed under the same conditions as authentic instruments. The court or competent authority of a Member State where a court settlement was approved shall issue, at the request of any interested party, a certificate using the standard form in Annex V to this Regulation.

TITLE V GENERAL PROVISIONS

Article 52

In order to determine whether a party is domiciled in the Contracting State whose courts are seised of a matter, the Court shall apply its internal law.

If a party is not domiciled in the State whose courts are seised of the matter, then, in order to determine whether the party is domiciled in another Contracting State, the court shall apply the law of that State.

CHAPTER V GENERAL PROVISIONS

Article 59

1. In order to determine whether a party is domiciled in the Member State whose courts are seised of a matter, the court shall apply its internal law.

2. If a party is not domiciled in the Member State whose courts are seised of the matter, then, in order to determine whether the party is domiciled in another Member State, the court shall apply the law of that Member State.

Article 53

For the purposes of this Convention, the seat of a company or other legal person or association of natural or legal persons shall be treated as its domicile. However, in order to determine that seat, the court shall apply its rules of private international law.

In order to determine whether a trust is domiciled in the Contracting State whose courts are seised of the matter, the court shall apply its rules of private international law.

Article 60

1. For the purposes of this Regulation, a company or other legal person or association of natural or legal persons is domiciled at the place where it has its:
(a) statutory seat, or
(b) central administration, or
(c) principal place of business.

2. For the purposes of the United Kingdom and Ireland 'statutory seat' means the registered office or, where there is no such office anywhere, the place of incorporation or, where there is no such place anywhere, the place under the law of which the formation took place.

3. In order to determine whether a trust is domiciled in the Member State whose courts are seised of the matter, the court shall apply its rules of private international law.

Article 61

Without prejudice to any more favourable provisions of national laws, persons domiciled in a Member State who are being prosecuted in the criminal courts of another Member State of which they are not nationals for an offence which was not intentionally committed may be defended by persons qualified to do so, even if they do not appear in person.

However, the court seised of the matter may order appearance in person; in the case of failure to appear, a judgment given in the civil action without the person concerned having had the opportunity to arrange for his defence need not be recognised or enforced in the other Member States.

Article 62

In Sweden, in summary proceedings concerning orders to pay (betalningsföreläggande) and assistance (handräckning), the expression 'court' includes the 'Swedish enforcement service' (kronofogdemyndighet).

Article 63

1. A person domiciled in the territory of the Grand Duchy of Luxembourg and sued in the court of another Member State pursuant to Article 5(1) may refuse to submit to the jurisdiction of that court if the final place of delivery of the goods or provision of the services is in Luxembourg.

2. Where, under paragraph 1, the final place of delivery of the goods or provision of the services is in Luxembourg, any agreement conferring jurisdiction must, in order to be valid, be accepted in writing or evidenced in writing within the meaning of Article 23(1)(a).

3. The provisions of this Article shall not apply to contracts for the provision of financial services.

4. The provisions of this Article shall apply for a period of six years from entry into force of this Regulation.

Article 64

1. In proceedings involving a dispute between the master and a member of the crew of a seagoing ship registered in Greece or in Portugal, concerning remuneration or other conditions of service, a court in a Member State shall establish whether the diplomatic or consular officer responsible for the ship has been notified of the dispute. It may act as soon as that officer has been notified.

2. The provisions of this Article shall apply for a period of six years from entry into force of this Regulation.

Article 65

1. The jurisdiction specified in Article 6(2), and Article 11 in actions on a warranty of guarantee or in any other third party proceedings may not be resorted to in Germany and Austria. Any person domiciled in another Member State may be sued in the courts:

(a) of Germany, pursuant to Articles 68 and 72 to 74 of the Code of Civil Procedure (Zivilprozessordnung) concerning third-party notices,

(b) of Austria, pursuant to Article 21 of the Code of Civil Procedure (Zivilprozessordnung) concerning third-party notices.

2. Judgments given in other Member States by virtue of Article 6(2), or Article 11 shall be recognised and enforced in Germany and Austria in accordance with Chapter III. Any effects which judgments given in these States may have on third parties by application of the provisions in paragraph 1 shall also be recognised in the other Member States.

TITLE VI TRANSITIONAL PROVISIONS

(...)

TITLE VII RELATIONSHIP TO OTHER CONVENTIONS

(...)

Article 57

1. This Convention shall not affect any conventions to which the Contracting States are or will be parties and which in relation to particular matters, govern jurisdiction or the recognition or enforcement of judgments.

(...)

CHAPTER VI TRANSITIONAL PROVISIONS

(...)

CHAPTER VII RELATIONS WITH OTHER INSTRUMENTS

(...)

Article 71

1. This Regulation shall not affect any conventions to which Member States are parties and which in relation to particular matters, govern jurisdiction or the recognition or enforcement of judgments.

(...)

APPENDIX 3

Case	Date	Parties	ECR	Page
12/76	10.06.1976	*Tessili v Dunlop*	1976	1473
14/76	10.06.1976	*De Bloos v Bouyer*	1976	1497
21/76	11.30.1976	*Bier v Mines de potasse*	1976	1735
24/76	12.14.1976	*Salotti v Rüwa*	1976	1831
25/76	12.14.1976	*Segoura v Bonakdarian*	1976	1851
29/76	10.14.1976	*LTU v Eurocontrol*	1976	1541
42/76	11.30.1976	*De Wolf v Cox*	1976	1759
9,10/77	07.14.1977	*Bavaria v Eurocontrol*	1977	1517
43/77	11.22.1977	*Diamond v Riva*	1977	2175
73/77	12.14.1977	*Sanders v Van der Putte*	1977	2383
150/77	06.21.1978	*Bertrand v Ott*	1978	1431
23/78	11.09.1978	*Meeth v Glacetal*	1978	2133
33/78	11.22.1978	*Somafer v Saar-Ferngas*	1978	2183
133/78	02.22.1979	*Gourdain v Nadler*	1979	733
143/78	03.27.1979	*Cavel v Cavel I*	1979	1055
25/79	11.13.1979	*Sanicentral v Collin*	1979	3423
56/79	01.17.1980	*Zelger v Salinitri I*	1980	89
120/79	03.06.1980	*Cavel v CavelII*	1980	731
125/79	05.21.1980	*Denilauler v Couchet Frères*	1980	1553
784/79	05.06.1980	*Porta-Leasing v Prestige*	1980	1517
814/79	12.16.1980	*Netherlands State v Rüffer*	1980	3807
139/80	03.18.1981	*Blanckaert v Trost*	1981	819
150/80	06.24.1981	*Elefanten Schuh v Jacqmain*	1981	1671
157/80	05.26.1981	*Rinkau*	1981	1391
166/80	06.16.1981	*Klomps v Michel*	1981	1593
25/81	03.31.1982	*C.H.W. v G.J.H.*	1982	1189
27/81	10.22.1981	*Rohr v Ossberger*	1981	2431
38/81	03.04.1982	*Effer v Kantner*	1982	825
133/81	05.26.1982	*Ivenel v Schwab*	1982	1891
228/81	07.15.1982	*Pendy v Pluspunkt*	1982	2723
34/82	03.22.1983	*Peters v ZNAV*	1983	987
201/82	07.14.1983	*Gerling v Tesoro*	1983	2503
288/82	11.15.1983	*Duijnstee v Goderbauer*	1983	3663
71/83	06.19.1984	*Tilly Russ v Nova*	1984	2417
129/83	06.07.1984	*Zelger v SalinitriI I*	1984	2397
178/83	07.12.1984	*P v K*	1984	3033
241/83	01.15.1985	*Rösler v Rottwinkel*	1985	99
258/83	11.27.1984	*Brennero v Wendel*	1984	3971
48/84	03.07.1985	*Spitzley v Sommer*	1985	787
49/84	06.11.1985	*Debaecker v Bouwman*	1985	1779
56/84	03.28.1984	*Gallera v Maître*	1984	1769
119/84	10.03.1985	*Capelloni v Pelkmans*	1985	3147
148/84	07.02.1985	*Deutsche Genossenschaftsbank v Brasserie du Pêcheur*	1985	1981
220/84	07.04.1985	*Autoteile v Malhé*	1985	2267
221/84	07.11.1985	*Berghöfer v ASA*	1985	2699
22/85	06.24.1986	*Anterist v Crédit Lyonnais*	1986	1951

198/85	07.10.1986	*Carron v Fed Republic of Germany*	1986	2437
266/85	01.15.1987	*Shenavai v Kreischer*	1987	239
313/85	11.11.1986	*Iveco Fiat v Van Hool*	1986	3337
144/86	12.08.1987	*Gubisch v Palumbo*	1987	4861
145/86	02.04.1988	*Hoffmann v Krieg*	1988	645
218/86	12.09.1987	*Schotte v Rothschild*	1987	4905
9/87	03.08.1988	*Arcado v Haviland*	1988	1539
158/87	07.06.1988	*Scherrens v Maenhout*	1988	3791
189/87	09.27.1988	*Kalfelis v Schröder*	1988	5565
32/88	02.15.1989	*Six Constructions v Humbert*	1989	341
C-115/88	01.10.1990	*Reichert v Dresdner Bank I*	1990	I-38
C-220/88	01.11.1990	*Dumez France v Hessische Landesbank*	1990	I-74
C-305/88	07.03.1990	*Lancray v Peters*	1990	I-2742
C-365/88	05.15.1990	*Hagen v Zeehaghe*	1990	I-1860
C-190/89	07.25.1991	*Rich v Impianti*	1991	I-3855
C-214/89	03.10.1992	*Duffryn v Petereit*	1992	I-1745
C-351/89	06.27.1991	*OUI v NHIC*	1991	I-3317
C-183/90	10.04.1991	*Dalfsen v VanLoon*	1990	I-4743
C-261/90	03.26.1992	*Reichert v Dresdner Bank II*	1992	I-2149
C-280/90	02.26.1992	*Hacker v Euro-Relais*	1992	I-1111
C- 26/91	06.17.1992	*Handte v TMCS*	1992	I-3967
C- 89/91	01.19.1993	*Shearson v TVB*	1993	I-139
C-123/91	11.12.1992	*Minalmet v Brandeis*	1992	I-5661
C-172/91	04.21.1993	*Sonntag v Waidmann*	1993	I-1963
C-125/92	07.13.1993	*Mulox v Geels*	1993	I-4075
C-129/92	01.20.1994	*Owens Bank v Bracco*	1994	I-117
C-288/92	06.29.1994	*Custom Made v Stawa Metallbau*	1994	I-2913
C-294/92	05.17.1994	*Webb v Webb*	1994	I-1717
C-398/92	02.10.1994	*Mund & Fester v Hatrex*	1994	I-467
C-406/92	12.06.1994	*Tatry v Maciej Rataj*	1994	I-5439
C-414/92	06.02.1994	*Solo Kleinmotoren v Boch*	1994	I-2237
C- 68/93	03.07.1995	*Shevill v Presse Alliance*	1995	I-415
C-292/93	06.09.1994	*Lieber v Göbel*	1994	I-2535
C-318/93	09.15.1994	*Brenner v Reynolds*	1994	I-4275
C-341/93	07.13.1995	*Danvaern v Schuhfabriken*	1995	I-2053
C-364/93	09.19.1995	*Marinari v Lloyd's Bank*	1995	I-2719
C-432/93	08.11.1995	*SISRO v Ampersand*	1995	I-2269
C-439/93	04.06.1995	*Lloyd's v Campenon*	1995	I-961
C-474/93	07.13.1995	*Hengst Import v Campese*	1995	I-2113
C-275/94	03.14.1996	*Van der Linden v Berufsgenossenschaft*	1996	I-1393
C- 78/95	10.10.1996	*Hendrikman v Magenta*	1996	I-4943
C-106/95	02.20.1997	*Mainschiffahrts v Les Gravières Rhénanes*	1997	I-911
C-163/95	10.09.1997	*Von Horn v Cinnamond*	1997	I-5451
C-220/95	02.27.1997	*Boogaard v Laumen*	1997	I-1147
C-269/95	07.03.1997	*Benincasa v Dentalkit*	1997	I-3767
C-295/95	03.20.1997	*Farrell v Long*	1997	I-1683
C-383/95	01.09.1997	*Rutten v Cross Medical*	1997	I-57
C-391/95	11.17.1998	*Van Uden v Deco-Line*	1998	I-7091
C- 99/96	04.27.1999	*Mietz v Intership*	1999	I-2277
C-351/96	05.19.1998	*Drouot v CMI*	1998	I-3075
C- 51/97	10.27.1998	*Réunion européenne v Spliethoff's*	1998	I-6511
C-159/97	03.16.1999	*Castelletti v Trumpy*	1999	I-1597
C-260/97	06.17.1999	*Unibank v Christensen*	1999	I-3715
C-267/97	04.29.1999	*Coursier v FortisBank*	1999	I-2543

C-420/97	10.05.1999	*Leathertex v Bodetex*	1999	I-6747
C-440/97	09.28.1999	*Concorde v Panjan*	1999	I-6307
C- 7/98	03.28.2000	*Krombach v Bamberski*	2000	I-1935
C- 8/98	01.27.2000	*Dansommer v Götz*	2000	I-0393
C- 38/98	05.11.2000	*Maxicar v Renault II*	2000	I-2973
C-387/98	11.09.2000	*Coreck v Handelsveem*	2000	I-9337
C-412/98	07.13.2000	*Josi Reinsurance v UGIC*	2000	I-5925
C- 37/00	02.27.2002	*Weber v Universal Ogden*	2002	I-2013
C- 80/00	06.06.2002	*Leather v Polstermöbel*	2002	I-4995
C- 96/00	07.11.2002	*Gabriel*	2002	I-6367
C-167/00	10.01.2002	*Konsumenteninformation v Henkel*	2002	I-8111
C-256/00	02.19.2002	*Besix v Kretzschmar*	2002	I-1699
C-271/00	11.14.2002	*Gem. Steenbergen v Luc Baten*	2002	I-10489
C-334/00	09.17.2002	*Tacconi v Sinto Maschinenfabrik*	2002	I-7357
C-437/00	04.10.2003	*Pugliese v Finmeccanica*	2003	n.y.p.
C-111/01	05.08.2003	*Gantner v Basch*	2003	n.y.p.
C-266/01	05.15.2003	*TIARD v Staat der Nederlanden*	2003	n.y.p.
C-116/02	12.09.2003	*Gasser v MISAT*	2003	n.y.p.

MIX
Papier aus verantwortungsvollen Quellen
Paper from responsible sources
FSC® C105338

If you have any concerns about our products,
you can contact us on
ProductSafety@springernature.com

In case Publisher is established outside the EU,
the EU authorized representative is:
Springer Nature Customer Service Center GmbH
Europaplatz 3, 69115 Heidelberg, Germany

Printed by Libri Plureos GmbH
in Hamburg, Germany